Emanuel King Love

History of the first African Baptist Church

Emanuel King Love

History of the first African Baptist Church

ISBN/EAN: 9783337120504

Printed in Europe, USA, Canada, Australia, Japan

Cover: Foto ©Lupo / pixelio.de

More available books at **www.hansebooks.com**

HISTORY

OF THE

First African Baptist Church,

FROM

ITS ORGANIZATION,

JANUARY 20TH, 1788, TO JULY 1ST, 1888.

INCLUDING THE

CENTENNIAL CELEBRATION, ADDRESSES, SERMONS, ETC.

BY REV. E. K. LOVE, D. D.

SAVANNAH, GA.:
THE MORNING NEWS PRINT.
1888.

TO THE OFFICERS AND MEMBERS

OF THE

FIRST AFRICAN BAPTIST CHURCH,

FRANKLIN SQUARE, SAVANNAH, GEORGIA,

This work is affectionately dedicated by your affectionate Pastor, as a slight token of his appreciation of the uniform kindness, tender sympathy and profound consideration he has received at their hands during a delightful pastorate of three years.

INTRODUCTION.

I have been asked to introduce this work to the public. In Georgia and Alabama, where the author is known both as a speaker and writer, nothing from his versatile pen needs introduction. An hundred years have passed—most of these years were spent in hardships and sore tribulations to our poor, ignorant, down-trodden race. Our race has acted nobly and done many things that were highly commendable of the race, but no record was kept of them and hence it went without saying that the race had done something worthy of praise. This is still true. We have many grand men, eloquent and learned men, in our pulpits that nothing is known of them except in their immediate communities. This will always be so until we have a well conducted press of our own and bring out our own men, or do as Dr. Love has done—write their history.

The white press was never intended to praise and elevate the negro. They do not spend their money for that purpose. The white press, if it means no ill will to the negro, it means elevation to the white, and to support the long believed theory that the negro is inferior to the white man. A press that believes this can not elevate both races. With such prejudice the negro has been contending and struggling to rise, under adverse circumstances through the vicissitudinous cycles of an hundred years. Our race fought with unseen weapons, but multipotent. They were guided by an unseen hand, but that hand was the hand of the mighty God of Jacob. There is no other cogent reason that can be given for success or even our existence under so unfavorable circumstances. We have come thus far guided by nothing we knew of the past, with no adequate conception of the present, and no training which would enable us to compare the past and present to form anything like an intelligent idea of what the future would reveal. Our race during the hundred years that have passed was profited very little by the history of their noble men, for it was not written. If it had been written, however meagre, it would have inspired others to like and even nobler deeds. Hence, we should welcome this work into our homes and give it a careful perusal. It is well calculated to edify and delight every careful reader. The men who are referred to in this work, many of them, lie

Introduction.

in unknown graves. To the world many of their great deeds are unknown. Their eventful and eminently useful lives are not written by the historian, but, blessed consolation, they are known of Him who hath said: "I know thy works, and thy labor, and thy patience, and how thou canst not bear them which are evil: and thou hast tried them which say they are apostles, and are not, and hast found them liars. And hast borne, and hast patience, and for my name's sake hast labored, and not fainted." Rev. ii, 2–3.

He keeps the record of His saints. Although no marble shaft nor towering monument mark the place where many negro heroes lie, yet—

"God, their Redeemer, lives,
And often from the skies,
Looks down and watches all their dust
Till He shall bid it rise."

They have scattered seeds of kindness in tears, and sweat, and blood, and God has taken cognizance of all. Our blessed Jesus has said: "I know thy work: behold, I have set before thee an open door, and no man can shut it: for thou hast a little strength, and hast kept my word and hast not denied my name."—Rev., iii, 8. There is an open door of usefulness of abundant entrance into the inviting fields of christian activity, intelligent christian work and devout consecration to the service of God in lifting up fallen mankind to heaven and God. What our fathers accomplished under adverse circumstances is but thunder-peals to us to do infinitely more under so favored opportunities. Though Dr. Love complains that this work does not satisfy his own ambition of what he feels ought to be written of the Baptist church which is the mother church of all the churches in this country, this work will be very highly appreciated and will be read with profit and interest. It will be admitted that he has performed his task well, and we will not despise the day of small things. This book justly claims to be the history of the oldest church in the country. That the First African Baptist Church is the original first church organized at Brampton's barn, January 20th, 1788, the reader will decide irrefutably true when he has read the book.

S. A. McNEAL,
*Corresponding Secretary of the State S. S. Convention,
and S. S. Missionary of the State of Georgia.*

The author requested Revs. C. T. Walker, S. A. McNeal, and Prof. R. R. Wright to write the introduction of his work. He thinks best to put each of their signatures after their production. He is placed under lasting obligations to them.

It is evident that the First African Baptist Church in Savannah is the oldest colored Baptist church in America, and certainly the oldest in Georgia. We live in an age when such erroneous doctrines are sapping the foundation of revealed truth are being propagated, and many are being proselyted from the true way for want of light. It is highly expedient that a history of this grand old church (the mother of the colored Baptist churches of America) be written. Planted a century ago, on the fertile seaboard, in tears and blood, under adverse circumstances, tribulations and sore afflictions, yet she has been led to a glorious success. This laudable undertaking of the author to chronicle the deeds of the noble pioneers, and the successes attained by the church, should meet with the most hearty approbation from every lover of truth as it is in Jesus.

The sufferings of Revs. Bryan, Marshall and Campbell alone would fill a volume much larger than this one, in which the author has condensed a few facts bearing upon the general history of the church, but for the hurried manner in which he was obliged to write this work and the limited means at his command. Many of the deacons deserve much more said about them than was, but which was abridged for the same reason as that of the pastors.

The centennial sermons and papers delivered and read in Savannah by the brethren celebrating the grandest event in the history of the colored Baptists of this country will doubtless be read with interest and profit. The sermons delivered by Rev. Dr. Love, which appear in this work, are printed because they created such a wide-spread interest among the people, touched on such important subjects, and were delivered immediately after his great work as pastor begun.

The report of the committee appointed by the Baptist Convention of Georgia, at its session in 1888, to investigate the claim of the First African Baptist Church and the First Bryan Baptist Church, in Yamacraw, as to priority, will impress the readers of this book as being a very interesting document. The declaration of the Baptist Convention of Georgia that the First African Baptist Church is the banner church of the State, and the awarding of the banner to the church, is but justice, and should meet the fullest approbation of every fair-minded, intelligent reader.

This work is an important factor in the history of the negroes, and especially the Baptist. Dr. Love has done a praiseworthy act in getting the history of the negro Baptists in this State, and it is believed that this is but the beginning of a more careful, elaborate and accurate account of the negroes' doings in church and state in Georgia. The author has dealt with his subject with fidelity and ability. The photographs are arranged in admirable style.

The reader will be impressed with the wise division of this sage church into societies, mission stations, as well as dividing the city of Savannah into wards, and appointing a deacon over each ward to look after the members in said wards. By this means the church manages to keep up with its large membership.

Searchers after truth will be impressed with the fairness and impartiality of the author. He has not shunned to tell the truth, and endeavored to put the blame (where there was any) where it belonged. This book deserves a high place among the histories of the world and the author a prominent place in the front ranks of honest historians. A history that does not tell the truth will mislead for countless ages countless numbers. It seems to be the order of Divine Providence that men and nations should carve their own destiny and by their own energy and efforts rise in the scale of usefulness and prominence.

The time has come when the negro must make his own history, shape his own destiny, solve his own problem, act well his part in church and state and occupy a prominent place on the stage of progress.

This volume is submitted to the candid perusal of an intelligent public. As the author has striven with meekness, gravity and impartiality to give his people a true history, it will doubtless be deservedly esteemed by all who peruse it, and serve to stimulate and inspire unborn generations to greater usefulness and purer lives of self-denial.

The author of this work has been appointed to write the history of the negro Baptists of Georgia. While this work is not intended to be that book, it may very well be taken as the antitype, and will serve as an earnest of that book. The brethren have no fears of a biased history from Rev. Dr. Love. They know him too well for that. May God bless this work to all who may read it.

C. T. WALKER,
Pastor Tabernacle Baptist Church,
Chairman Executive Board State Baptist Sunday School Convention
and Secretary State Sunday School Convention, Augusta, Ga.

The negro occupies a peculiar place in the drama of historical life. For the past three centuries his story has been a record of trials, tribulations and disappointments, only flecked here and there by a few deeds of individual daring and heroism. Whether in the domain of story or song; whether in the arena of battle or on the forum of eloquence, the writers of the past have not accorded to their black brother the dignity of an historical character. All the literature of the past has been constructed upon the basis and assumption that the negro was not only inferior to the white man but the white man's convenience and tool. Hence, almost every reference to the negro race found in text or reference book bears the ear-marks and unmistakable stamp of race prejudice.

The histories of churches are not exempt from the influence and bias of this hydra-headed monster, race prejudice. There is, however, a growing desire not only among the colored people themselves but among the general public for any accurate, unbiased historical information with reference to the colored people. The world wants the truth.

The history of the past makes it reasonable to conclude that whether in general or special history an impartial record of the life and achievement of the negro will not be written until it is written by men of his own race.

It must be gratifying to all lovers of the race to know that there are springing up in various sections of the Union some very capable colored historians. Indeed, their works are not only respectable in number but highly creditable in the ability displayed and in the facts presented. While it would be hardly safe to say that the history of the negroes' deeds and doings has been fully written, yet it is extremely pleasant to feel that each year adds to the many worthy and valuable attempts that will before long make up a complete history of our race.

When that history is complete there will be in black and white ample vindication of the dignity and usefulness of a race which has done more and suffered more for mankind than has yet been accredited to them in the histories of the past.

No doubt the author of this book had in mind some such thoughts as are written above in presenting to the public this history of the First African Baptist Church. The author has certainly yielded to and satisfied a long-felt necessity for a full and accurate history of what is now very generally acknowledged to be the oldest colored Baptist church in this country.

The marked ability and wide and accurate learning of Dr. Love are an earnest of the fact that the book is a valuable addition to the literature of the race.

R. R. WRIGHT.
Principal Ware High School and
Editor Weekly Sentinel, Augusta Ga.

THE FIRST AFRICAN BAPTIST CHURCH.
Side View, on St. Julian Street.

CONTENTS.

CHAPTER I.

The Baptism of Rev. Andrew Bryan, his Wife, Hagar and Kate—The Organization of the Church—The Persecution of Mr. Bryan—He Purchased his Liberty—The Purchase of a Church Site in Yamacraw—The Organization of the Second African and Ogeechee Baptist Churches—The Deed of First African Baptist Church made to a Board of Trustees—A Copy of the Deed.. 1

CHAPTER II.

The Church from 1818 to 1832—Not much is known of the Church from 1788 to 1818—The Great Trouble of 1832—Mr. Marshall Influenced by the Preaching of Alexander Campbell—The Church is Expelled from the Sunsbury Association—The Split of the Church... 7

CHAPTER III.

The Continuation of the Trouble—The Third African Baptist Church enters the Association in 1833 with 155 Members—The First African Baptist Church Retains her Identity—The First African Baptist Church Endeavors to come under the Supervision of the White Baptist Church, but is Refused—The Compromise and Settlement of the Trouble—The Organization of the Third African Baptist Church—The Purchase of the Site at Franklin Square—Mr. Marshall's Deposition from the Pastorate—His Restoration........ 10

CHAPTER IV.

Continuation of the Trouble—The Split and how it was Conducted—The Numbers each Party had—The 155 Received Letters of Dismission and Organized the Third African Baptist Church—The Third African Baptist Church Changed its Name to First Bryan Baptist Church—Various Committees from the White Baptist Church Labored with the Two Contending Parties—Appeals to the Trustees, the Mayor, and other Strategies Resorted to... 18

CHAPTER V.

Rev. Mr. Marshall Re-instated—His Church back under the Supervision of the White Baptist Church—The Committee from the White Baptist Church Insisted upon it that Rev. Marshall should not be Pastor—They are Out-generaled by him—Disaffection in the Third African Church................. 25

Contents.

CHAPTER VI.

The First African Baptist Church Trying to Re-enter the Association—She Finally Enters—Her Identity Traced from 1788 to 1838, a Period of Fifty Years—She was Expelled as First African Baptist Church, 1832, and Restored as First African Baptist Church, 1837.. 28

CHAPTER VII.

The New Site at Franklin Square—The Purchase—New Building—More about Rev. Marshall—His Efforts to get Money to Build the Church Edifice—His Trip North—His Death at Richmond, Va.—Rev. Campbell takes up the Work—He Appoints a Building Committee and Completes the Church Edifice 31

CHAPTER VIII.

Rev. George Leile—His Work in Savannah and Departure for Jamaica—His Work in Jamaica—His Letters to Dr. Rippons. 34

CHAPTER IX.

Rev. Andrew Bryan—His Baptism—His Troubles—His Pastorate—His Ministry and Death.. 38

CHAPTER X.

Rev. Andrew C. Marshall—His Conversion and Baptism—Contradiction in his History—His Troubles—His Celebrity—His Great Influence—His Long Pastorate, and Death......... 41

CHAPTER XI.

Rev. William J. Campbell—His Long and Useful Life—A King among his People—His Ministry—Great Trouble—His Baptism—Called to the Pastorate—His Troubles—The Commencement of the Trouble of 1877...................................... 57

CHAPTER XII.

The Trouble of 1877—The Cause—Its Fierceness—The Split—The Call of Rev. Gibbons—The Death of Rev. Campbell, and the Final Settlement—Something Concerning Mr. Campbell's Early Troubles.. 60

CHAPTER XIII.

Rev. George Gibbons—His Call, Pastorate and Death................ 82

CHAPTER XIV.

Rev. E. K. Love—His Call—Installation—Pastorate—His Sermons—The Improvements of the Church under his Administration 85

Contents.

CHAPTER XV.   PAGE

Dr. Love's Administration—The Enlargement of the Church Edifice—The Manner of Work—The Centennial Clubs and Civic Societies—What they did—The Return of the Gibbons' Place Society—The Children's Church—Rev. Campbell's Monument.. 141

CHAPTER XVI.

The Societies of the Church—Their Membership—The Value of their Property and Condition... 149
Rev. C. H. Lyons' Sermon and the Presentation of the Banner to the Church... 152

CHAPTER XVII.

Something about the Deacons 161
Deacon Adam Johnson—His Eventful Life......................... 163
Deacons Adam Sheftall, Jack Simpson and Robert McNish. 164
Deacons W. J. Campbell and J. M. Simms 165
Deacons Murry Monroe and Patrick A. Glenn..................... 167
Deacons James Richard, Friday Gibbons and George Gibbons 168
Deacon C. L. DeLamotta.. 169
Deacon David McIntosh.. 171
Deacon F. M. Williams... 172
Deacons Richard Baker and John Nesbit 173
Deacon Robert P. Young.. 174
Deacon Pompey H. Butler... 175
Deacon Peter Williams.. 176
Deacon March Haynes 177
Deacon James H. Hooker.. 178
Deacon L. J. Pettigrew... 179
Deacon Joseph H. Williams.. 180
Deacon John H. Brown 181
Deacon Willis Harris... 182
Deacons John C. Habersham and Peter Houston................. 183
Deacon Moses L. Jackson... 185
Deacons Alexander Rannair and R. H. Johnson.................. 186
Deacon E. C. Johnson... 187
Deacon F. J. Wright.. 188
Rev. James I. Sevorres.. 189
Mr. W. G. Clark.. 190
Brethren John E. Grant and C. H. Ebbs............................... 191
Mrs. M. M. Monroe... 192

CHAPTER XVIII.

The Centennial Celebration of the Church—The Sermons, Papers, etc... 193
Report of Special Committee on the Priority of the Church....... 198
The Welcome Address, by Dr. Love...................................... 202
The Introductory Sermon, by Rev. C. T. Walker................. 206
A Centennarian at the Celebration—Mrs. Mary Jackson............ 217
Baptist Doctrine, by Rev. S. A. McNeal.... 219

Contents.

CHAPTER XVIII.—Concluded. PAGE

History of the Colored Baptists of Georgia, by Rev. G.H. Dwelle. 226
Baptist Church History, by Rev. W. H. Tillman, Sr.................. 231
The History of the Baptists, by Rev. Levi Thornton................ 236
The Wants of the Colored Ministry, by Rev. Dr. W. H. McIntosh.. 239
The Wants of the Colored Ministry, by Rev. Alexander Ellis... 245
The Wants of the Colored Ministry, by Rev. W. G. Johnson...... 249
The Relation of the White and Colored Baptists, by Rev. T. J. Hornsby.. 253
The Relation of the White and Colored Baptists, by Rev. G. S. Johnson.. 257
The American Baptist Publication Society and its Work for the Colored People, by Rev. E. K. Love, D. D............................ 261
The American Baptist Sub-Society and its Work for the Colored People, by Rev. N. W. Waterman.. 264
The Bible as Believed by Baptists, by Rev. J. C. Bryan............. 267
The Bible as Believed by Baptists, by Rev. G. M. Spratling...... 269
The Qualification and Dignity of the Ministry, by Rev. Charles H. Brightharp.. 272
The Duty of Baptists to Home Missions, by Rev. E. J. Fisher... 276
The Evils of Intemperance, by Rev. S. D. Rosier...................... 277
Are we Advancing as a Denomination? by Prof. M. P. McCrary. 280
The Duty of the Pastor to the Church, by Rev. J. W. Dunjee.... 284
The Duty of the Church to the Pastor, by Prof. Isaiah Blocker..... 287
The Duty of the Church to the Pastor, by Deacon R. H. Thomas... 292
What is our Duty to the Institutions of the Country? by Prof. H. L. Walker... 295
The Importance of Pure Baptist Literature, by Rev. E. P. Johnson.. 301
The Work and Purity of the Church, by Rev. Henry Jackson... 303
Money as a Factor in Christianizing the World, by Rev. W. R. Pettiford... 306
Baptist Church Government, by Rev. J. L. Dart...................... 310
A Letter from Dr. Tucker... 321
The Act of Baptism, by Rev. J. H. Kilpatrick, D. D.................. 327
No Royal Road to Church Prosperity, by Rev. J. H. Kilpatrick, D. D.. 341
The Duty of Parents to Sunday Schools, by Prof. James Ross... 356
Conclusion, by the Author... 358

→PREFACE←

The many clouds that have been thrown around the history of the First African Baptist Church of Savannah by designing men to rob this time-hallowed church of her pristine honor and present glory, makes it necessary to set in order the facts connected with the history of the several negro Baptist churches in Savannah, that the unfairness of the First Bryan Baptist Church, formerly the "Third African Church," in contending that she is indeed the original First African Baptist Church, may be seen. These facts will be set forth so plainly that it will not require a philosopher to understand the truth in the case. The fact that the First Bryan Baptist Church, organized some time in the last of 1832 or first of 1833, as "The Third African Church," has had on the 20th of January, of the present year, a so-called centennial celebration, and gave it to the world that they were the "First African Baptist Church" of Savannah, and that all other churches sprang forth from them, makes it proper that this work should go forth burdened with irrefutable proof in vindication of the truth of history. While the author shall state facts, and simply facts, which will show that their claim is false, and that they know it better than they appear to know their names, he shall do so in the most possible friendly spirit, with the hope of reclaiming his erring brethren.

The First African Baptist Church has had a most eventful and checkered career. She has endured indescribable suffering and has been wonderfully blessed and preserved by a hand divine. The first pastor, Rev. Andrew Bryan, was whipped until his blood dripped freely upon the ground, for no other crime than that he preached Jesus and him crucified to the poor negroes; but he continued to preach Jesus, and God continued to bless his humble preaching to Africa's sable sons and daughters. The more this church was persecuted the more she grew and thrived. From four converts (Rev. Andrew Bryan, Hannah Bryan, his wife, Kate and Hagar,) the First African Baptist Church begun its eventful career. This church was organized with 67 members by Rev. Abraham Marshall (white), on the 20th day of January, 1788, at Brampton's barn, three miles southwest of Savannah. This work contains the cuts of Rev. Andrew

Bryan, Rev. Andrew C. Marshall, Rev. W. J. Campbell, Rev. George Gibbons, and Rev. E. K. Love, present pastor; also, some of the deacons of the church. The author acknowledges the incalculable service Benedict's History of the Baptists in America has rendered him; Holcombe's Repository, furnished by Dr. Tucker; The Minutes of the Sunsbury Baptist Association, furnished by Rev. L. C. Tebeau, and the Minute Books of the Savannah Baptist Church (white), furnished by Rev. J. E. L. Holmes, D. D. The author would acknowledge with unfeigned pleasure the priceless help that Rev. Alexander Harris has given him. The First African Baptist Church is placed under lasting obligation to Rev. Harris for guiding the author in his pursuit after the truth of history in the labyrinthal mazes of the long ago. But for him the author would not have known where to have searched for the facts pertaining to this church. In the Providence of God we have, as nearly as possible, a connected history of our church, with but two broken links, through Rev. Alexander Harris, from its organization. Rev. Marshall and Deacon Adam Johnson lived in the days of Rev. Andrew Bryan, from whom they gathered all the facts, and Rev. Harris lived in the days of Rev. Marshall and Deacon Johnson, from whom he gathered all of the facts, and your humble servant, the author, lives in the days of Rev. Harris, from whom he has gathered the facts, and now writes the truth of history as it has come down from the beginning, thus bringing to us the truth of history pretty much as we receive the truth of Divine Revelation. Rev. A. Harris is a wonderful man, with a memory simply astonishing. It seems that God has spared him for just this purpose. No living man is as well prepared to give the truth of the doings of the Baptists in these parts as Rev. Harris, and a more candid, conscientious, truthful man never lived. We are indebted to Rev. Harris for a copy of the deed and much documentary proof, which we herein present. It will hardly be questioned that Benedict's History nor Dr. Holcombe's Repository contains all the facts of the history of this church. Neither can we expect to learn all from the Minute Books of the Savannah Baptist Church (white), nor the minutes of the Sunsbury Association. We must learn some from those who lived in that day. This is just the way all other histories are gotten up. The verbal statements which we have gathered from the old members who lived in those days can no more be ruled out than our recollection of things which transpired under our observation long ago. There is no more reason to suppose their memory at fault than ours. Hence we have taken pains to draw from our old brethren and sisters such information as they had in their possession, and their knowledge of men and things about whom and which we have undertaken to write. We shall feel confident that our mistakes will be viewed with a charitable eye, and our imperfection graciously passed by. The public is asked to consider our laborious task before criticising us harshly. This work is sent forth to the public with the humble prayer of the author that it may do great good, and may set in order the facts for more skilled pens than ours to give to the Baptists of Georgia a more interesting and accurate history of themselves. The author takes pleasure in the fact that those who may subsequently undertake this task will not be put to it as he has been for information.

Praying the blessings of Almighty God upon this humble effort, I am,

Yours in Gospel bonds.

EMANUEL KING LOVE.

HISTORY

OF THE

FIRST AFRICAN BAPTIST CHURCH.

CHAPTER 1.

The First African Baptist Church was organized on the 20th day of January. 1788, at Brampton's barn, three miles west of Savannah, by Rev. Abraham Marshall (white) and Jesse Peter (colored). The first fruit of this beginning was Andrew Bryan, Hannah Bryan (his wife), Hagar and Kate. These four Christians formed a nucleus around which the Baptist denomination twined in Savannah and in Georgia.

Just here we insert an extract, as taken from Dr. Henry Holcombe's Analytical Repository, published in Savannah, Ga., in 1802:

"The first ordained minister of color who came among these people was George Leile, who was liberated by Mr. Henry Sharp, of Burke county, and is now the pastor of a large church in Kingston, Jamaica. During the short time he was in this city he baptized Cate, an African woman, the property of Mrs. Eunice Hogg, Andrew, his wife Hannah, and Hagar, belonging to the venerable Mr. Jonathan Bryan. The three former have honorably obtained their freedom, and live comfortably; in fact, Andrew's estate is worth upward of five thousand dollars. Hagar is yet alive. By the *joint* and zealous efforts of these poor, illiterate slaves, it is rationally hoped, a concern was awakened for the salvation of precious souls which has produced many happy effects; and of what extent or continuance the salutary fruits of their feeble exertions may eventually be is beyond the power of calculation.

"Like a city that is set on a hill and cannot be hid, soon after they began to call on the name of the Lord Jesus and stir one another up to love and to good works, they attracted the attention of the community, and Andrew, commonly called

Andrew Bryan, with numbers of his followers, was whipped and imprisoned as means of putting a stop to their proceedings. But they found advocates and patrons among very respectable and influential characters, and, by well-doing, at length disarmed and silenced their bitterest persecutors.

"At this period Andrew began to learn to read, and obtained leave of his worthy master to occupy his barn as a place of worship, at Brampton, about three miles from Savannah. Here he publicly and to great numbers endeavored to preach; and for two years, with very little interruption, had an opportunity of showing that 'Godliness is profitable unto all things.'

"By this time their affairs were known to religious individuals at a considerable distance; and, as destitute of any one authorized to administer the sacred ordinances, they were visited by the late Rev. Thomas Burton, who, on a creditable profession of their faith, baptized eighteen of Andrew's hearers. They expressed much gratitude to Mr. Burton for his instruction and other assistance, went on their way rejoicing, and showed increased solicitude to be still more perfectly instructed in the things of God.

"The next visit they had by an ordained minister was from the Rev. Abraham Marshall, who, accompanied by a young preacher of color, Jesse Peter, not only baptized forty more of Andrew's congregation: but, on the 20th of January, 1788, constituted *them* a church and ordained *him* to both preach the gospel and administer its sacred ordinances to their proper subjects.

"Soon after being thus systematized on the gospel plan, they were permitted to build a large house of worship on the suburbs of Savannah and to serve God as they pleased on the Lord's day, from sun to sun. In this situation their number as a church rapidly increased, and all suspicions of their being influenced by unworthy motives have long given place to an esteem of their humble virtues. They have several gifted men among them, and the mother church has enlarged her boundaries by the constitution of two sable daughters—one consisting of *two hundred members*, on the 26th of December, 1802, under the denomination of the SECOND COLORED BAPTIST CHURCH IN SAVANNAH; the other, comprehending *two hundred and fifty*, on the 2d of January 1803, called the Ogeechee Colored Baptist Church; the former to be supplied by Henry Cunningham, who was ordained to the work of the ministry on January 1st, 1803; the latter by Henry Frances. Diminished by these constitutions, the First Colored Baptist Church in this city, still under the pastoral care of the aged and pious Andrew Bryan, consists of but *four hundred members.* They have divine services three times every Sunday, and the Lord's Supper quarterly. On each of these occasions, for the three last years, they have received by baptism from ten to sixty-four souls."

Great was the suffering of the pioneers of our denomination in this city. But under this terrible persecution this church thrived and was greatly blessed of God.

The Second African Baptist Church is her first offspring, which is now a flourishing church with nearly two thousand members. There has nearly always existed between these two churches the most friendly feelings. Many families of worth and intelligence are equally divided between the First African and Second African churches. To-day the wives of three of the Deacons of the First Church belong to the Second Church. In very many cases the wife and some of the children belong to one church, and the father and some of the children belong to the other. This interchange of families in the two churches form almost a demand for the pastors of the two churches to be on friendly terms. The First Church has had untold suffering. At times she has been compelled to suspend service. Her doors were more than once closed by the civil authorities. God always brought them out by raising up some white man as an instrument.

The church bought the present site on which the First Bryan Baptist Church building now stands the 3d of July, 1797. The property was sold by Rev. Andrew Bryan to a board of trustees for the First African Baptist Church, of which he was pastor, and had been for nine years and six months. He sold the land to white trustees, because it was not lawful for negroes to hold such property. We present here a copy of the deed, which we are sure will be interesting to our readers.

GEORGIA.

This Indenture, made the third......day of July, in the year of our Lord one thousand seven hundred and ninety-seven, and of the independence of the United States of America the twenty-first, between Andrew Bryan, a free black man and a preacher of the gospel by lawful authority ordained, of Savannah, in the State aforesaid, of the one part, and Thomas Polhill, William Mathews, David Fox and Josiah Fox............

....

That the said Andrew Bryan, for and in consideration of the sum of thirty pounds sterling money..
to him in hand, well, and truly, paid by the said Thomas Polhill, William Mathews, David Fox and Josiah Fox, at or be-

fore the sealing and delivering of these presents, the receipt whereof is hereby acknowledged, he, the said Andrew Bryan, *Hath* granted, bargained, sold, aliened, conveyed and confirmed, and by these presents *Doth* grant, bargain, sell, alien, convey and confirm to the said Thomas Polhill, William Mathews, David Fox and Josiah Fox, and the survivor and survivors of them, and to such successor and successors as may be appointed ....
....
..............;..\.........................
....
to and for the use of the Baptist Church of blacks at Savannah, in.....................over which the said Andrew Bryan now does and for some time past has presided as pastor and minister, one equal moiety being the half of all that lot of land (most part of the said lot) situate, lying and being at Yamacraw, above the city of Savannah aforesaid, known by the number seven (7) in the village of St. Gall, fronting Bryan or Ordingsells street, containing ninety-five feet in front and one hundred and thirty-two feet and one-half in depth, bounded west and south by land of the late Dr. Zubly, deceased, East on a lot late Richard Williams, deceased, and North on the main street leading...............Yamacraw to.................brick meetinghouse..............with the meeting-house thereon erected and standing on all and..............other the houses, out............... premises and appurtenances whatsoever to the same belonging or in anywise appertaining, which said lot was bought by William Bryan and James Whitefield, as trustees to and for the use of the said Andrew Bryan, from one Mathew Motts and Catharine, his wife, by deed of bargain and sale bearing date the fourth day of September, in the year one thousand seven hundred and ninety-three, and purchased by the said Mathew Motts of and from one Thomas Norton and Tamar, his wife, in and by a certain deed of bargain and sale to him duly executed, bearing date the twenty-first day of June, in the year one thousand seven hundred and ninety-two, all of which by the said several deeds, reference being thereunto had, will more fully and at large appear, together with the meetinghouse or building for public worship thereon erected, and being and all and singular the heredita......, rights, members and appurtenances whatsoever to the same belonging, or in anywise appertaining, and the reversion and reversions, remainder and remainders, rent, issues and profits thereof, and of every part and parts..the estate, title, interest, claim and.......................................of him, the

said Andrew, of, in and to the..............................or half part of the lot above described, and the premises hereinbefore mentioned and intended to be hereby bargained and sold unto the said Thomas Polhill, William Mathews, David Fox and Josiah Fox, and every part and parcel thereof, and on the death or decease of any or either of the said Thomas Polhill, William Mathews, David Fox or Josiah Fox, to which successor or successors, as they or a majority of the survivors shall appoint. In trust, nevertheless, to and for the only proper use, benefit and behalf of the said Baptist congregation of blacks at Savannah, now and for some time past under the direction and care of the said Andrew Bryan, forever. And it is hereby understood and declared to be the intention of the parties to these presents that the said lot and building.............................. invested in the said Thomas Polhill, William Mathews, David Fox and Josiah Fox, and the successors as aforesaid, for the sole use and purpose of the public worship of God by the society of blacks, of the Baptist persuasion, and for no other use or purpose whatsoever; that on the death or decease of any or either of the above-named—Thomas Polhill, William Mathews, David Fox or Josiah Fox—the survivor or survivors may and shall within one year thereafter nominate and appoint a successor or successors in the room of such deceased trustee, which successor or successors so appointed as aforesaid shall be considered as a party to these presents for the uses and purposes hereby mentioned and intended. And the said Andrew Bryan and his heirs, the said half lot of land and premises, and every part and parcel thereof, unto the said Thomas Polhill, William Mathews, David Fox and Josiah Fox, and their successors to be appointed as hereinbefore directed, for the uses and purposes as hereinabove set forth against him the said Andrew Bryan and his heirs, and against all and every person or persons whatsoever shall and will *Warrant* and forever defend by these presents.

In Witness whereof the said parties to these presents have hereunto set their hands and affixed their seals the day and year first above written.

                                              his
[L. S.]   ANDREW + BRYAN.
                                              mark.

Signed, sealed and delivered in the presence of

(NOTE.)—The word (five) immediately after the word (ninety) in the first page between the sixteenth lines, and also the word (half) immediately after the words (the said) in the second page between the eighteenth and nineteenth lines, were both interlined previous to the execution hereof. In the presence of us.

—— HARRISON,
ELIAS ROBERTS.

CITY OF SAVANNAH.
That the within deed was signed, sealed and delivered by Andrew Bryan for the use therein is attested on both by
ELIAS ROBERTS.

Sworn to before me on the 30th August, 1797.
HENRY PUTNAM.

Received the day and year first within written the sum of thirty pounds sterling money, being the consideration money as is within specified to be paid to me.
I say Received.

                                    his
                        ANDREW+BRYAN.
Witness: mark.
—— HARRISON,
ELIAS ROBERTS.
Dated the 3d day of July, 1797.

ANDREW BRYAN,
To
THOMAS POLHILL,
WILLIAM MATHEWS,
DAVID FOX, and
JOSIAH FOX.

Bargain and Sale
of Lot No. 7 in
Yamacraw, Village
of St. Gall.
Consideration, £30.

MOSES CLELAND,
EDWARD COPPEE,
JOSIAH PENFIELD.

The blanks in the above deed are caused by the worn condition and pieces of paper broken out in the creases. The deed is very old.

CHAPTER II.

The Church from 1818 to 1832.

Not much is known of the church from 1788 to 1818, embracing a period of thirty years that comparatively nothing is known of this grand body. The Savannah Baptist Church nor the Sunsbury Association seem to have been careful about preserving records. We are indebted to Holcombe's Repository for facts preceding 1818. He informs us that the Second African Baptist Church was organized the 26th of December, 1802, with 200 members, and that it went out from the First African Baptist Church. The Ogeechee African Baptist Church was organized also from this church January 2d, 1803, with 250 members. Rev. Henry Cunningham, who was ordained January 1st, 1803, was called to the pastorate of the Second African Baptist Church, and Rev. Henry Frances was called to the pastorate of the Ogeechee African Baptist Church. The First African Baptist Church was represented in the Sunsbury Association (white) in November, 1818, by Adam Johnson and Josiah Lloyd. The total membership was 1712. At this time there were only two colored churches in the city, viz., First African and Second African. At the session held at Hines' meeting-house, Effingham county, in November, 1819, no delegates from the church appear, nor is the church mentioned. At the session held with the Savannah Baptist Church, November, 1820, the First African Baptist Church was represented by Adam Johnson and Adam Shuftall. The total membership was 1836. At the session held November, 1821, at the Baptist meeting-house, Upper Black Creek, Effingham county, the First African Baptist Church was represented by Evans Great. The total membership was 1916. At the meeting of the association, November, 1822, at New Port, Liberty county, Ga., the First African Baptist Church was represented by Adam Shuftall and Evans Great. The total membership does not appear. At the meeting of the association held at Powers' Church, Effingham county, November, 1823, the First African Church was represented by A. Shuftall and Jack Simpson. Total membership was 1888. At the session held at Sunsbury, Liberty county, November, 1824, the First African Baptist Church was represented by A. Shuftall and A. Johnson. The total membership was 1912. At the session held at New Providence meeting-house, Effingham county, November, 1825, the First Church was represented by A. C. Marshall, A. Johnson, A. Shuftall and Jack Simpson. The total membership was 1886. At the session held at Salem meeting-house, Chatham county, November, 1826, the delegates were A. C. Marshall, A. Johnson, A. Shuftall and Jack Simpson. At the session held at New Hope meeting-house, November, 1827, the First African Baptist Church was represented by A. C. Marshall, A. Johnson and Jack Simpson. The total membership was 2,275. At the session held at the Litlle Canoochie Church, Liberty county, November, 1828, the delegates were A. C. Marshall, J. Clay and C. Ross. The total membership was 2,311. The session held at Newington Baptist Church, Screven county, November, 1829, the First African Church was represented by A. C. Marshall, J. Clay and C. Ross. Total membership, 2,357.

At Power's meeting-house, Effingham county, November, 1830, the First African Baptist Church was represented by A. C. Marshall, J. Clay and Jack Simpson. The total membership was 2,417. At the session held with the Savannah Baptist Church, November, 1831, the First Church was represented by A. C. Marshall, A. Johnson, Jack Simpson and S. Whitfield. The total membership was 2,795.

During 1832 a terrible confusion broke out in this grand old body. Rev. Andrew C. Marshall led a part of the church his way, and Deacon Adam Johnson led the other part his way. The trouble started because Rev. Marshall seems to have been influenced by one Rev. Alexander Campbell's preaching, who visited Savannah about this time. Deacon Adam Johnson opened war on Rev. Andrew C. Marshall. Deacon Adam Johnson and Rev. Marshall had been life-long friends, living together as twin lambs. They were both influential and great. When these two men met as opponents the result was fearful. Two lambs had turned upon each other with all the strength and fury of lions, and the cause of Christ suffered greatly by this unfortunate affair. Because of this trouble the church sent no delegates to the association in 1832. The Second African Baptist Church is the only colored church that was represented from Savannah at that session. If it is claimed that the First Bryan Baptist Church is the oldest church in this city, we ask where was she then?

We have no disposition to justify Rev. A. C. Marshall for adhering to the doctrines preached by Alexander Campbell, nor to deny that he did do so, but our inquiry is after the original church organized in 1788. We have traced it up to 1832 as the First African Baptist Church, under the leadership of Rev. Andrew C. Marshall. Our object will be to ascertain if it continued to exist, and in what manner and under what name.

At the session of the association held at Walthourville, November 9th and 10th, 1832, a resolution was adopted appointing "Brethren Jones, Southwell, J. S. Law, Harmon and Furman to investigate a difficulty existing in the *First African Church* of Savannah." Notwithstanding she was in trouble she was known as "the *First African Church* of Savannah." These were dark and stormy days for this old ship on the high seas. Her existence was threatened, but she was sustained by an unseen hand, and that hand was divine. The Almighty God plead her cause, and she sailed majestically once more upon a placid sea, with her snowy sails unfurled, kissing the pleasing breezes, bidding defiance to her enemies, and in their hearing, with humble joy, sung triumphantly "Deliverance will come."

The committee appointed to investigate the difficulty existing in the First African Baptist Church of Savannah reported:

"Your committee, after a serious consideration of the painful and difficult task assigned them, would present your body the following resolutions as the result of their consideration:

"*Resolved*, That we approve highly of the recommendation of the Council of Ministers that was called, viz., that A. C. Marshall be silenced, and we concur in the opinion that he be silenced indefinitely.

"*Resolved*, That the First African Church, as a member of this association, on account of its currupt state, be considered as dissolved, and that measures be adopted to constitute a new church as a branch of the white Baptist Church.*

"*Resolved*, That we advise our colored brethren in the country, now members of the First African Baptist Church in Savannah, to take letters of dismission, and either unite themselves with neighboring churches of our faith and order, or to be constituted into seperate churches."†

In the same resolutions the Second African Church of Savannah was complimented for its Christian deportment, and a copy of the resolutions ordered transmitted to the Mayor of Savannah.

At this session, therefore, it will be seen that the association

---

*When the First Bryan Baptist Church, then the Third African Church, entered the association in 1833, it did so as "Third African Church," and not as "First African." Whence this claim?

†This new church was the Third African Baptist Church, now the First Bryan Baptist Church. It is strange that it does not claim even the name, but now, as always, they themselves have recognized the First African Baptist, at Franklin Square, as First African Baptist Church.

adopted resolutions *considering* the First African Church as *dissolved*. Let us see, as we go along, if it was dissolved. Even in those terrible days of slavery everything our white brethren considered as being so, was not necessarily so; note, they did not dissolve the church, but *considered* it as dissolved. It appears that they did not attach much importance to this *consideration*, for in the same resolutions they advised that members of the First African Church should take letters of dismission and either join other Baptist churches or form other Baptist churches. If the First African Church was dissolved because of its *currupt state*, how could it give letters of dismission? It requires no difficulty to see that this bears inconsistency on its face. We do not find at this session any other church taking the place of the First African Baptist Church. We have her up to her expulsion from the Sunsbury Association as the First African Baptist Church of Savannah.

CHAPTER III.

The First African Church of Savannah in War with Herself, with the Savannah Baptist Church (White), and with the Sunsbury Association.

We have already referred to Rev. Alexander Campbell, who visited Savannah about this time, whose eloquent and profound sermons had telling effect upon the mind of Rev. Andrew C. Marshall, who partially, if not very largely, accepted the doctrine of Mr. Campbell and proclaimed his views. Deacon Adam Johnson, who was a very close thinker and well versed in the scriptures, took exception to this new departure from the old land-marks. This kindled a fire that was not soon nor easily put out, but which burned with a furious destruction for five weary years.

The "Third African Church" entered the association for the first time in the session of November, 1833, at Cowpen Branch Baptist Church, Effingham county. It was represented by T. Anderson, A. Johnson and Jack Simpson, with a membership of 155. This was the time and place that "The Third African Church" joined the association. In the minutes of the association for 1833 we read, "Application was made by the Third African Church to become a member of this association. Granted by a unanimous vote." In the minutes of the same session a resolution was adopted as follows:

"*Resolved,* That this association approves of the conduct of S. Whitfield, Joe Clay and others who separated from the First African Church, and recommend them to the fellowship of all the churches."

Notwithstanding the First African Church was expelled and declared corrupt and considered as dissolved, she still existed and was styled and called the First African Church by even those who expelled her and considered her as dissolved. Truly, what God has blessed no man can curse.

Notwithstanding the Sunsbury Association, by the recommendation of the Savannah Baptist Church (white), passed resolutions condemning the First African Baptist Church as being *corrupt,* and *considered* it as dissolved; they sold to the First African Baptist Church their house of worship as First African Baptist Church after this, and received $1,500 in payment from the First African Baptist Church, and acknowledged payment accordingly.

In the conference of the Savannah Baptist Church, November 18, 1832, is the following resolution:

"*Resolved,* That a committee be appointed to suggest the best mode to this church of taking under their care the First African Church, and to report at the next discipline meeting."

Though the First African Church is considered as dissolved, a committee is appointed to consider the best way of taking her under the supervision of the white Baptist Church. This is an acknowledgment that the church did exist. This committee reported December 24, 1832, as follows:

"The committee appointed to devise plans for the reception of the First African Church as a branch of this, reported that they could not recommend any.

"*Resolved,* That they be dismissed.

"A petition of from three to four hundred members of the First African Church was offered, in which they requested to become a branch of this church. After considerable discussion it was resolved not to receive them on the conditions they proposed, but such alterations were made in their application as the church thought advisable, and it was agreed that if they would offer to place themselves under the supervision of a committee whom they would choose out of this church, then such a measure would be agreed to by this body."

Those who are now claiming to be the original First African Baptist Church were then called the minority of the First African Church, for we find in the minutes of the Conference of Savannah Baptist Church (white), December 24, 1832, the following:

"An application was made that the minority of the First African Church be received as a branch of this church, when it was decided that it was proper that they first be formed into a church, and afterward could come under the supervision of a committee, as also the Second African, should they wish to do so."

January 4th, 1833, the First African Baptist Church addressed the following letter to the Savannah Baptist Church (white):

"We, the subscribers of the First African Church, do solicit the aid and protection of our brethren, the Baptist Church of Savannah. We propose to come under the supervision of a committee of your body, provided you will receive us on the terms and conditions following:

"1st. That we be independent in our meetings; that is, that we receive and dismiss our own members, and elect and dismiss our own officers, and, finally, manage our own concerns independently; however, with this restriction—in case any measure is taken by us which shall seem to militate against our good standing as a church of Christ we shall submit it to a committee of five members, whom we shall choose out of the Baptist Church in Savannah, whose counsel we bind ourselves to follow, provided it be not contrary to the precepts of the Gospel.

"2d. We agree to hold no meetings for discipline or other purposes until we have duly notified, by writing, one member of the Baptist Church, selected by said church. to be present, and agreeing not to pursue any measure such delegated member shall deem improper until we shall have had council of the above-named committee.

"3d. We agree to relinquish to the minority of this body all our right and title to the old church so soon as they shall agree to give up and do relinquish to us all right and title to the newly-purchased one, and when we are put in full and free possession of it, and our trustees, viz., William H. Stiles, Peter Mitchell and John Williamson, shall satisfy us that they have good and sufficient titles.

"4th. We agree to dismiss all members and such as have been members of our church, that they may either join another or form a new Baptist Church, and as soon as such church shall be satisfied with and receive them then they shall be dismissed from us.

"5th. And we oblige and bind ourselves by these presents that whenever we break any covenant above named, then, on proof thereof, we herein empower our trustees to shut up our church and cause us to desist from public worship until we fully submit to the advice of our committee."

This petition was received with "a small alteration in the second article, and was accepted as the kind of connection which might exist between this church and the First African Church." Here, it will be observed, that the Third African Baptist Church is not yet organized. In the minutes of the Conference of the Savannah Baptist Church (white), January 28, 1833, is the following:

"*Resolved*, That inasmuch as the minority of the First African (now the Third) Church have conformed to the requirements of this church in constituting themselves into a church, be received under the supervision of this body upon the same terms as the First African Church."

It will be seen that the Third African Church was organized between December 24th, 1832, and January 28th, 1833.* For in the conference of December 24th, 1832, the Third African Church was then called the minority of the First African Church, and was refused admittance into the Savannah Baptist Church (white) until they should be formed into a church. And in the conference of January 28th, 1833, they were received as Third African Baptist Church. This being the only condition (that they would form themselves into a church) upon which they would be received by said church as required by the conference of December 24th, 1832. In 1833 delegates were appointed by the Savannah Baptist Church to visit the First African Church. Notwithstanding the First African Baptist Church was received under the supervision of the Savannah Baptist Church, trouble kept brewing in its midst like a smoldering volcano; and July 22d, 1833, the Savannah Baptist Church decided that "It was thought advisable in consequence of the disorderly conduct of the First African Church not to appoint delegates to visit them this month."

Rev. Andrew C. Marshall was well acquainted with Baptist church government, and though he was a negro and had to succumb to his white brethrens' wish in everything else, he stubbornly and manfully refused to yield the freedom and independence of a Baptist church. And his people stood by him, and God raised up friends for him. The Second Baptist Church had more of the fear of the white man and perhaps more of the fear of God. The following communication will bear out that fact:

---

* It is quite clear that the "Third African Church" was organized in January, 1833, and is therefore only 55 years old.

"THE SECOND AFRICAN CHURCH TO THE SAVANNAH BAPTIST.

"DEAR BRETHREN—We have witnessed with sincere regret the many serious difficulties which have for many months existed among some of our colored churches, and which have tended to destroy our harmony and remove from us the religious privilege which we now so richly enjoy. And we have regarded with approbation the efforts our white brethren have made to secure to us the permanent possession of our present enjoyment. We are decidedly of the opinion that great advantage will arise to the colored churches by their being under the protection and supervision of the white church. We do, therefore, respectfully request that the Second African Church may be taken under the care of your body in such manner as shall by you be considered expedient.
"Very sincerely yours in the Gospel,
"[Signed]   HENRY CUNNINGHAM.
"SAVANNAH, 23d June, 1833.

"Isaac Mooter,   William Furguson,
    "Licensed Preacher,   William Rose,
"Hannibal Briton,   John Cox,
"John Deveaux,   Isaac Robert,
        "Edenborough Fleming."

The Second Church made no conditions upon which they would be accepted. They left everything with their white brethren. They were received most unanimously, of course. Rev. Andrew C. Marshall insisted upon the right of a church; that if it had the right to be a church it should be governed by the New Testament and acknowledge no master but Christ the Lord; that if the church could not be a New Testament church it should not be at all. Having right on his side it is not a wonder that he conquered and made ardent admirers of his bitterest enemies.

The First African Baptist Church at this time is again walking alone. The white Baptist Church has again refused to recognize her, but she marches right along, winning souls for heaven and God.

January 25th, 1833, the officers of the First African Church met a committee of the Savannah Baptist Church (white) and asked the following questions:

1. What duties are proper that A. Marshall shall perform in the church at this time?

2. Has any thing been done since they have occupied the

new building and come under your supervision which the committee think improper?

3. Would the committee recommend that the First African Church call Jack McQueen (who is licensed by the city authorities) to become its preacher?

To the first the committee advise that Andrew Marshall should not go into the pulpit and preach, nor administer the ordinance of baptism, nor the Lord's supper, but that there is no objection to his leading in prayer and exhortation in any meeting when such measure is consented to by the delegated brother. That there is no objection to his making pastoral visits, marrying, attending funerals and extending the right hand of fellowship, when requested to do so by the church.

To the second question the committee reply that they are gratified in receiving so good a report from the delegated brethren, and find no charge of impropriety against them.

To the third question they answer, they do not think it their business to say who should preach for the church, but they can see no impropriety in any regularly licensed brother preaching, provided he has liberty granted by the city authorities. The committee advise that neither the church nor any part of it do hold any meetings except regularly notified ones in the church.

Signed: Henry O. Wyer, Thos. Clark, W. W. Wash, Holmes Tupper and D. Votee.

It is very remarkable that these poor slaves had such indefatigable Christian manhood. Their whole deportment seemed to have said to their white brethren: "Whether it be right in the sight of God to hearken unto you more than unto God, judge ye." And when the command was made more emphatic, they seemed to have answered more emphatically: "We ought to obey God rather than men." In temporal things they hesitated not to obey those who had rule over them. In spiritual things they didn't feel it their duty to obey magistrates, but insisted upon worshipping God according to the dictates of their conscience. They were more consistent than their advisers. They had been advised by their white brethren that Rev. Andrew C. Marshall might *lead in prayer, give the right hand of fellowship, exhort, preach funerals, marry* and *visit the sick*. Is not it quite natural that they would have thought that if he was competent to do all this that there was no good reason why he should not be their pastor? And what is more praiseworthy, they had the courage of their conviction. They acted out what they believed.

Hence, on the 6th of March, 1833, we find the following in the minutes of the Savannah Baptist Church (white):

"The officers of the First African Church stated that it had called Andrew C. Marshall to be its pastor, and that they had thought it best for him to resume his pastoral duties, and wishes to know the opinion of the committee in relation to the matter. After mature deliberation, the committee can see no good reason for changing the advice given on a former occasion, and refer the church to their opinion given on the 25th of January."

But the church had arisen in the majesty of her might and acted for herself. This was as right as it was fearless and bold. It showed that she had a leader that was worthy of the consideration and respect of all men. It must be said in praise of the white people, that while it was in their power to use harsh means, and thus force their wish, they did not do so. They exhibited great patience, and used only persuasive means. Rev. Andrew C. Marshall was the bone of contention. The white Baptists were opposed to his being the pastor, because he had entertained and expressed the views of Alexander Campbell. They were zealous about "the faith once delivered to the saints." But for this great protest of the Baptists, white and black. it is quite likely that Rev. Marshall would have led thousands off after Mr. Alexander Campbell, and Savannah now, with her ten thousand negro Baptists, would have been a Campbellite city. so that even out of this great confusion good has come. The officers of the First African Church were advised at one meeting of the committee not to call Rev. A. C. Marshall as pastor, and reported at the next that they had called him as their pastor, giving as their reason that they thought it best that he should resume his pastoral duties. This was true manhood; they thought it best. They must be praised for contending for the independence of the Baptist Church in those dark days. At this meeting the committee (white) agreed upon and reported to the church (white) the following (March 22, 1833):

"The committee, after due deliberation, unwilling to take upon themselves the responsibility to advise that Andrew C. Marshall should resume his pastoral office in the First African Church. refer the matter to the trustees of said church and the city authorities. (Signed)   "H. O. WYER,
"W. W. WASH,
"THOS. CLARK,
"H. TUPPER,
"D. VOTEE,
  "*Committee.*"

It appears that Rev. Marshall had friends even among the white people. He was a wise, careful and most wonderful planner. The carefulness of his plans is seen in his success, even when the odds were against him. The learned whites seem to have been baffled by his adroitness and surpassing executive ability. He influences H. Tupper to give him a note expressive of his consent for him to enter upon his work once more which he so much loved. H. Tupper showed the committee the following note he had given to the pastor of the First African Church, which was not agreed to by the balance of the committee:

"I am satisfied there is no good reason that Andrew C. Marshall should be withheld from the pastoral office of the First African Church, and I believe that there is no objection on the part of the other members of the committee charged with its supervision except that which arises from the public prejudice against him. If, therefore, this can be removed, or it does not exist in such a degree as supposed by the committee, I think he ought to be restored as soon as the church gets permission from its trustees and the city authorities for him to be restored. But I am constrained to add that I verily fear the public is not in favor of such a measure.

"SAVANNAH, March 21st, 1833.
"(Signed) "H. TUPPER."

After getting this note, Rev. Marshall went to the trustees (who were already his friends) and obtained the following permission to begin his work of giving the bread of life to his people:

"*Permission of Trustees.*
"SAVANNAH, April 2, 1833.

"We, the trustees of the First African Church of Savannah, knowing of no reason why Andrew C. Marshall, the pastor, or other deacons or officers of the said church, should be inhibited or interrupted in the exercise of all or any of the rites, ceremonies or duties which to them or any of the congregation of said church, as disciples or seekers of Jesus Christ, belong, we do hereby give to them, to the extent of our power, every privilege which as Christians they can require.

"(Signed) "PETER MITCHELL,
"WM. H. STILES,
"*Trustees.*

This gave the suffering pastor the right to enter the church once more as its leader. But the trouble was not over.

CHAPTER IV.

The Continuation of the Trouble—More about the Split—The Restoration of Rev. Marshall.

We have said that the split occurred in 1832, and either the last of December, 1832, or the 1st of January, 1833, the final separation occurred. The trouble had been going on many months. The people carried clubs, brickbats and other such implements of war to the church with them. There was danger of a fight in the church at any time. On one occasion they had a terrible row in the church, and Mayor Warring went there with a lot of brickbats in his buggy and threw them in the church and succeeded in running the last one of them out of the church.

The time had come when a split was inevitable: it had to come. After many councils and much deliberation the time was set when all of the members must be present and this trouble settled in an unmistakable manner. The time came when the members (most of them) met. Rev. Andrew C. Marshall went on one side of the building, and Deacon Adam Johnson on the other. Then it was said: "All who agree with Rev. Andrew C. Marshall go on that side with him, and all who agree with Deacon Adam Johnson go on that side with him." About one-eighteenth of the members went with Deacon Johnson, and seventeen-eighteenths went with Rev. Marshall, for the church then numbered 2,795 members. Out of this number 155 members agreed with Deacon Adam Johnson, and the remaining 2,640 members agreed with Rev. Andrew C. Marshall. The question came up that night as to which one should take the old name of the church. Deacon Johnson, the leader of the 155, said that "There has been so much disgrace connected with the First African Church that we don't want it. Let them have it."

Subsequent to this Rev. Marshall and the church agreed to give these dissenters honorable letters of dismission if they would organize a church or join other Baptist churches. These brethren were soon organized as the Third African Baptist Church of Savannah.

The Third Church continued by this name until 1866, when Rev. Alex. Harris (then a deacon of the Third African Baptist Church) offered a motion to change its name from Third African Baptist to the First Bryan Baptist Church, which was agreed to. For thirty-three years she remained under the name of the Third African Baptist Church. During all these years she did not increase very much, owing, perhaps, to the prejudice of the negro population because they accused her of being the cause of all this trouble by fighting the pastor. Even to-day she has not as many members as the Rev. Marshall had fifty-five years ago when he left the old spot. This trouble, perhaps, more than anything else, caused a careful study of God's Word and Baptist church usage.

After this settlement, the bad feeling was kept up between the two churches in first one way and then another. Members would pass backward and forward; when they would fall out with the Third Church they would join the First Church, and when they would get dissatisfied with the First Church they would join the Third Church ; and so for years the trouble was kept up.

We have referred to the action of the officers of the First African Baptist Church reporting to the committee of the white Baptist Church that they had called Rev. Andrew C. Marshall to be their pastor. The following is the report of said committee to the Savannah Baptist Church, July 14th, 1833:

"The committee of the First African Church finding that they can no longer be of use to said church, feel disposed to withdraw from it, unless it takes up the charges which we now make, and act upon them with promptness and decision.

"1st. The compact or agreement entered into between this church and ours has been violated in several instances by holding frequent meetings without the presence of a brother delegated by our church.

"2d. This church has disregarded the advice of their committee in electing Andrew C. Marshall to the pastoral charge of the church, permitting his continuance in office without the sanction of the civil authorities.

"3d. The prevarication and evasion of Andrew C. Marshall respecting his faith and doctrine having been made manifest, the committee have lost all confidence in his character.

"4th. The opposition of A. C. Marshall to be a member of the association, thereby virtually renouncing the government of the Baptist denomination, is esteemed by the committee a position extremely dangerous to the vital interest of the colored people.

"5th. Satisfactory evidence that Andrew C. Marshall has fully, and now unequivocally, adopted the views and doctrine of Alexander Campbell, which the committee considers destructive to vital religion, and consequently ruinous to any people, and which our church has denounced as heresy.

"6th. We now call upon all disciples of our Lord and Saviour Jesus Christ, of the Baptist faith and order, in this church to come forward and have their names recorded that the committee may use their influence to restore them again to the association, but it is hoped and expected that all those of a different faith and order will peaceably withdraw from the church, or that the church, upon reorganization, will proceed immediately to purge itself of every disaffected member.

"(Signed)   "W. W. WASH,
                                      "O. M. LILLIBRIDGE,
                                      "T. VIRSTILL,
                                      "T. DOWELL."

Here was the combined wisdom and influence of the master against the servant's, learning against ignorance, and yet that grand old man, Rev. Andrew C. Marshall, out-generaled them all and held his people as by magic. The preceding document combined adroitness and learning, but the old man was equal to the task. In it the church is charged with restoring Andrew C. Marshall to the pastorate without consulting the civil authorities. What had the civil authorities to do with a Gospel church calling a Gospel minister to be their pastor? These men ought to have known that the church was established contrary to the wish of the civil authorities. They had Rev. H. O. Wyer as their pastor without consulting the civil authorities. Was their church any more of a church than the First African Baptist Church? It is surprising how far wrong men can go. They took this document to the First African Church and read it to the people and made an appeal to them, with the hope of winning them from Rev. Andrew C. Marshall, and finding themselves foiled in this cunningly devised plan, they addressed the following letter to the trustees of the First African Church:

"SAVANNAH, July 22, 1833.
"*John P. Williams, Esq.:*

"DEAR SIR—We are constrained by a sense of duty to request that you will, for a time, have the First African Church shut up until the charges against Andrew C. Marshall for preaching false doctrine shall be cleared up to all concerned. You were present when the charges were made: you heard the defense set up by Mr. Dunning, and must admit that our charge was fully sustained or different religious denominations would have been called in to judge of the correctness of our views. A thousand souls are at stake and, we think it a matter of too much importance to be neglected, and as the power is vested in us to make this demand we do so in deference to you, sir, but we cannot recognize the authority of Mr. Dunning, or any other self-made Trustee, to interfere in this matter. We believe in a few weeks, by shutting up the church now. that matters can be satisfactorily settled by all parties. We appeal to you not only as a Christian but as a large property holder to aid us in checking false doctrine among our slaves. We are, sir, with great esteem,

"Your obedient servants,
"(Signed)   "W. W. WASH,
          "THOS. DOWELL,
          "O. M. LILLIBRIDGE,
            "*Committee.*"

Things were now getting serious. The committee having failed in their carefully devised plans to break Rev. Marshall's hold upon the hearts of his people, now appeal to the Trustees of the church with whom the power of closing the church rested. But God prevented this consummation and used Mr. Williams as his instrument to defend his cause and to protect this old Zion. His answer was wise and manly. God used the man as an instrument to protect His church. The man was not himself aware of the great good he was doing for the church of Christ and his enslaved servants. God has always reserved servants for special work. This man by nature was no more of a friend to this church than those who urged that it be closed, but God had him in hand.

The following is his able and remarkable reply. This was wonderfully strange to the committee of the church under the circumstances:

          "SAVANNAH, July 26th, 1833.
"*To Messrs. W. W. Wash, Thomas Dowell and Oliver M. Lillibridge:*

"SIRS—I yesterday received your communication of the 22d instant, at which I acknowledge my surprise as well from the singular and extraordinary request you make to shut up the First African Church, as also from the fact that you gave the Trustees to understand (on the Sunday they saw you at the church) your duty as a committee had been discharged, and therefore you had nothing further to engage your attention respecting the situation of the First African Church. Thus much for my surprise at the contents of your letter.

"I must now be allowed to say that I am far from acknowledging your charge against Andrew C. Marshall for preaching false doctrine was established or supported in the least particular, unless your simple assertion is to be received as proof, for it was manifest to all present that you did not produce one testimony from the Scriptures or otherwise to support your views, and how you can with a due regard to propriety, state that 'our charge was fully sustained,' I have yet to learn, and so far foreign from my construction of duty as a Trustee, and of the plainest principle of the Gospel, is your request to 'shut up the First African Church' that I consider it incumbent on me, in connection with the other Trustees, to *see the church kept open* in order to afford Andrew C. Marshall, and the church of which he is pastor, the privilege of worshipping God to the best of their knowledge; and it is the deliberate intention of the Trustees to maintain them in the full enjoyment of all the rights and religious privileges which the laws of our country entitle them to receive.

"I am aware that comparisons are sometimes odious, yet circumstances sanction their use, for it is proper to inform you that the remark you made of Mr. Dunning's being a *self-constituted Trustee* is incorrect, and I must be allowed to inquire by what authority you exercise the office of a committee of the Baptist Church. You need not be informed that you have no authority from the African Church to act in that capacity. It is an assumption, therefore, by you, as I think your own words will prove, and I must further be allowed to repeat my former verbal remark that there is an absence of all right on your part to interfere with the peaceful demeanor and worship of 'One Thousand Souls,' even if you were a regularly constituted committee, and, believe me, I shall not stop to inquire whether you acknowledge Mr. Dunning as a Trustee or not, it will be my pleasure to act with him in that capacity, together with Mr. Delyon, who is appointed by Mr. Stiles to represent him by a *regular power of attorney*, and I am authorized by them to inform you of our united determination to prevent the *unauthorized attempts of others* from depriving a large number of our fellow beings of their religious privileges which are guaranteed to them by the laws of our State, by the word of God, and by every principle of kindness which ought to be a prominent feature in the behavior of all those who profess the Gospel.

"I am, respectfully yours, &c., &c.,
"(Signed) "JOHN P. WILLIAMSON."

This communication sounds as though this man was moved by a higher power and that his heart was inditing a good matter. He intimates that Rev. Marshall had carried his point, and so mighty was he in the Scriptures that he was an overmatch for this committee. This, gentlemen, gave the committee an unwelcome, cut respecting the independence of a church which Baptists, more than anybody else, love to parade. He very timely calls into question their right to interfere with a church worshipping God as they understand him. This would seem enough to put them to everlasting shame and eternal silence; but they were bent on ousting Rev. Marshall, and hence addressed the following letter to the Mayor of the city:

"SAVANNAH, 13th August, 1833.
"*To His Honor William T. Williams:*

"SIR—We deem it our duty to address you on the subject of the First African Church—a subject in which our community is more or less interested. This church in a former difficulty, fearing that the public authorities would interfere with their privilege as a Christian society, applied to the Baptist Church in Savannah to be taken under their care, guidance and direction. Accordingly articles of agreement were entered into between the two churches and they were permitted to choose from our body five members as their Advisory Committee, which was accordingly done. The commitee was to have all matters of controversy and difficulties arising in the church referred to them for settlement. With this arrangement our community appeared satisfied, but the time has arrived when we cannot be identified with them in any of their actions or doings. We have been compelled, though reluctantly, to give them up. This course has been deliberately and calmly considered, and our reasons for adopting it are: That Andrew C. Marshall has been preaching doctrines which our church cannot countenance. We have found by our proceedings with him that we can place no confidence in him—he deviates from the truth, and this, too, under the garb of his profession. We believe him to be a designing man, seeking only his own aggrandisement and the love of power, even at the expense of the peace and happiness of his own people. Our advice has been uniformly disregarded, and, though frequently asked, has on no occasion been followed. We should be doing violence to our own feelings by continuing longer with them. The majority of the church appear determined to go with Marshall at all hazards, and he has them so completely under his control that they are ready on all occasions to sanction his mandates, whether right or wrong. We are indeed satisfied that they are following the man, and not the Gospel of our Lord Jesus Christ. We have for some time left them to themselves, in fact, our right to interfere with them at all has been denied by some men of high standing in this community, who seem disposed to support Andrew under any circumstances. We have felt great interest in the people under his charge, and have used all the peaceful means in our power to rescue them from their blind devotion to the man, but it is in vain. Under all these circumstances we give them up, and give notice to you as the head of our community that our church will not hold itself responsible for any act of which they may be guilty in future.

"The individuals composing the First African Church are in part the property of our citizens, and it is for them, if they feel any interest in their everlasting or temporal welfare, to interpose and save them from the baneful influence of a designing man. We beg leave to refer you for details to Thomas Dowell, T. Virstill and O. M. Lillibridge, who will give your honor any information that may be in the possession of the committee not specially alluded to in this communication.

"We are, respectfully, your obedient servants,
"(Signed)   "W. W. WASH,
       "THOS. DOWELL,
       "OLIVER M. LILLIBRIDGE,
       "T. VIRSTILL,
       "S. A. PATOT,
          "*Committee.*"

And still God was with the suffering church, and this attempt proved futile. There is no record that the Mayor answered this communication. If so, it could not have been favorable to the assailants, for the church kept on in its good work. Doubtless the Mayor answered in the same spirit which the trustees did, if he answered at all. We have from the committee's own mouth: "The majority of the church appear determined to go with Andrew C. Marshall at all hazard, and he has them so completely under his control that they are ready on all occasions to sanction his mandates, whether right or wrong. We are indeed satisfied that they are following the man, and not the Gospel of our Lord Jesus Christ." A man, to carry his people contrary to the express wish of the white people in that day, and whom the people were determined to follow "*at all hazards,*" must have been indeed a very wonderfully great man. There were members of the church who would have sacrificed their lives for Rev. Marshall.

CHAPTER V.

Rev. Marshall Reinstated—The Troubles Continue—His Church Back under the Supervision of the White Baptist Church.

There can be no doubt but that the committee was mistaken in saying that the First African Church had renounced the government of the Baptist denomination. Rev. Marshall was a veritable Baptist. But he was just such a Baptist as his white brethren. He believed that the same spirit of freedom and independence that was in the white church ought to be in the colored church, and for this he contended just as an intelligent Baptist should have done. In this he was right, and God crowned his labors with the most signal success. That he had no disposition to isolate himself and church from the association of Baptists is clearly seen in the following petition, which was read before the Savannah Baptist Church (white), October 27th, 1834:

"The First African Church of Savannah reposing confidence in their brethren, the Savannah Baptist Church, and believing that they are willing to impart Christian advice to them in the circumstances under which they are placed, now throw themselves upon the friendly and Christian aid of their brethren for this purpose. Believing what they will advise will be consistent with the spirit and dictates of the Gospel, they will cheerfully comply with the advice which may be thus given. That good may result from this measure is the humble hope and prayer of, in behalf of the church.

"(Signed) "ADAM W. DOLLY,
"Clerk."

The Savannah Baptist Church sent the First African Baptist Church the following reply:

"OCTOBER 26th, 1834.

"The Savannah Baptist Church has been applied to by the First African Baptist Church for its advice in relation to its present situation and future conduct, with the spirit, they hope, with which the Christian should be actuated; and with the best wishes for the temporal and spiritual prosperity of the members of this community, submit the following as their advice:

"The course which they recommend to be pursued, they look upon as the only one that can be adopted with the well grounded hope of their being reinstated in the full enjoyment of their privileges and the Christian fellowship of their brethren. It is not to be understood that the Savannah Baptist Church, in giving the advice which is asked, take upon themselves the right to dictate what course shall be adopted. They would only be understood as advising as Christian brethren who are influenced by a lively interest of the First African Church. Our advice will seem to bear heavily upon an individual, but in advising the course herein stated, that individual's best interests are contemplated. It is considered as unquestionable that most if not all of the difficulties of this church have chiefly arisen from the imputation of their holding sentiments which are believed adverse to the fundamental truths of the Gospel; and the conduct which has grown out of an adherence to these sentiments is due to the individual who has propagated them. And here, it would be remarked, that this statement is not made with the view of criminating, but simply to express the cause of the existing difficulties. Andrew C. Marshall, who has filled the office of pastor of this church, and who has always exercised a controlling influence over it, is considered the organ through which these sentiments have been propagated. Besides preaching objectionable doctrine, which it is believed he has done, his conduct in other respects has been such as to have excited against himself strong prejudices at least, which still continue, and which it will require a long and continued series of entire propriety of conduct so far, indeed, as it is compatible with the frailties of human nature to maintain, in order to have them removed. Under these circumstances, therefore, we would advise the withdrawal of Andrew C. Marshall from the pastoral office as the first step which we think necessary to bring about a settlement of difficulties and a restoration to fellowship.

"In the next place, the disavowal of the doctrine imputed to the church should be unhesitatingly and fully made.

"Thirdly, and lastly, we would advise as an indispensable step to the settlement of the difficulties and differences between this and the other colored churches in this city in which is involved the removal of all the obstacles which interpose to prevent the attainment of this end—and here let it be remembered that we are bound to make mutual confession and concession which do not call for the relinquishment of principle in order to bring about a good understanding and state of things among Christians—to forget the past and exercise forbearance for the future. If this course be pursued, there can be very little doubt but that all is desirable will be effected. And how delightful it is to see brethren dwelling together in unity; should Andrew C. Marshall feel himself aggrieved by the advice herein given, which indeed is made necessary from the circumstances under which he has brought himself, or by the opinions and feelings entertained towards him, not only by a large portion of the religious community, but by others also, he can appeal to the association which it is believed will readily appoint a committee of investigation in relation to his case, and which will unquestionably act towards him as the circumstances which may be developed will justify and demand. In conclusion, it will be remarked that if a course of conciliation is not pursued the prejudice already created will be so riveted as not to be easily, if at all, removed, and it therefore behooves the church to act advisably and with caution. This is suggested in relation to its temporal condition and prospects, but surely its spiritual interests should be the object of paramount solicitude. If any other advice should be desired the church will readily and cheerfully afford it so far as it lies within their power to give.

"(Signed)   "J. S. LAW,
                            "A. HARMON,
                            "H. H. FURMAN,
                            "W. W. WASH,
                            "T. VIRSTILL,
                                "Committee."

Rev. A. C. Marshall was again in his church but it seemed that the trouble continued—these (white) brethren were still of the decided opinion that he ought not to be pastor, and as often as they were appealed to, they gave the same advice that Rev. Marshall should not be pastor. But in spite of them Rev. Marshall was reinstated pastor of the First African Baptist Church. In every advice asked by the First African Baptist Church, they always reserved the right to do as they thought best. They insisted upon the right of the church to refuse whatever they considered not to be after the dictates of the gospel. This teaching the committee (white) knew to have come from Rev. Marshall. Hence they always advised to get him out of the way. They feared that such independence as the gospel taught was "extremely dangerous" for the negroes to take in, being slaves. The First African Baptist Church soon after this came under the supervision of the Savannah Baptist Church. Peace did not long continue in the Third African Baptist Church. In the Conference of the Savannah Baptist Church (white), held August 24, 1835, a committee was "appointed to examine into the difficulties existing in the Third

African Church." This trouble grew out of the fact that John Simpson and family, William Munger and family, and Arthur Stevens had become dissatisfied with the inability of the pulpit to edify them and wished to leave the church, but were refused letters of dismission. They applied to the white church for admission but were rejected. Doubtless, they now regret that they had left Rev. Marshall, an able preacher of the New Testament, Surely, if the shepherd is smitten the sheep will be scattered.

CHAPTER VI.

The First African Baptist Church Trying to Re-enter the Association—She Finally Enters—Her Identity Traced from 1788 to 1838, a Period of Fifty Years. In all these Years She is First African Baptist Church.

In 1832 the First African Baptist Church was expelled. In 1835 she applied for restoration. She was refused. The trouble was not settled to the satisfaction of the association, and hence they had to wait. A committee was appointed to investigate the case and report at the next session. This year was also full of trouble and characterized by committee meetings and such like. The church, however, was not content to remain out of the association. Rev. Marshall, its pastor, had a large heart and was ready to forgive and forget the past, and march on, unitedly, to a glorious victory.

The church felt it very keenly that they were out of the association, and great was the anxiety of the church to return to the association and the communion of the saints. Hence the disappointment of the church when the delegates returned and told them that they would have to wait another year before their anticipated joy of being united with the saints could be realized. Certain terms were proposed for reconciliation. The terms must have appeared stringent to the church and aggrieved pastor. They were called upon to deny any adherence to the doctrine of Alexander Campbell, and the pastor, Rev. A. C. Marshall, was called upon to disavow any belief in the doctrine of Mr. Campbell, which he had all along denied, and the contrary of which they had on every occasion failed to prove, even if Rev. Mr. Marshall entertained such views. The committee of the church (white) interposed and prevented the First African Church from joining the association. In 1836 the First African Baptist Church sent a petition again to rejoin the association, but was again denied upon the ground that they had not complied with the terms proposed by the association through its committee. This petition was accompanied by a letter from the trustees (white), the spirit of which the association said it admired. But the church had still to wait another year, as the committee recommended that the church be refused admittance until they had complied with the terms which had been proposed as the only ground upon which reconciliation could be effected. Though this pained the heart of the church she bore it Christ-like, and still endeavored to gain the fellowship of the saints and to be one again in the household of faith.

In 1837, the First African Baptist Church appears as fair as the moon emerged from a dreadful cloud. For five years she had been in trouble and out of the association. During these five years her faith had been put to the severest test. Her enemies were strong, influential and many; they were determined, untiring, and many of them learned. With these odds the church had to contend. The church was determined, meek, humble, and, for that day, remarkably intelligent. She had a strong pastor, of iron will, many true and lasting friends. Being united among themselves, they proved to be an army too invincible for the mightiest foe. As of Rev. Andrew Bryan and this same church, their bitterest enemies were turned to most ardent admirers. During all this time the church increased in power, intellectually, spiritually, solidity and piety. Her troubles tended to develop her unknown strength and greatness which otherwise might have lain dormant. But for this trouble she might not have been the great church she is to-day. When she was yet young, she learned self-reliance and to trust in God and go ahead.

The church was restored to the association in 1837 with a membership of 1,810. She was represented in this session by A. C. Marshall and R. McNish (the latter is still alive). She was expelled in 1832 with a membership of 2,795. At that session she was represented by A. C. Marshall, A. Johnson, J. Simpson and S. Whitfield. In 1837 when the First African Baptist Church returned to the association, the Third African Church, now the First Bryan Church, was represented by S. McQueen, with a membership of 189. At this session we have the First African Baptist Church with a membership of 1,810, a Second African Church with a membership of 1,263, and a Third African Church with a membership of 189. When Rev.

Marshall went off from the old spot he carried with him 2,640 members, leaving with Deacon Adam Johnson 155 members. They returned as above stated. This was 830 members less than he left with. Where are these 830 members? They did not go very largely to the Second African Church, for their number was diminished. For at the session of 1832, at which the First African Church was expelled, the Second African Church represented 1,310 members, and at the session of 1837, when it returned, the Second Church had a membership of 1,263, 47 members less. They did not go very largely to the Third African Church, for in 1833, when it first joined the association, it represented 155 members. In 1837, four years afterward, when the First African Church was readmitted, the Third Church represented 189 members—just 34 more—only an average of 8½ members a year. During the five years' trouble of the church many of the country members had been encouraged to leave the church by the white people. Many became indifferent; many had been taken out of the city on farms, and many had been hired out or sold out of the city. This accounts for the missing 830 members. It must be noticed that the church was expelled in 1832 from the association as First African Church, with Rev. A. C. Marshall, pastor and delegate, and returned as First African Church, in 1837, with Rev. A. C. Marshall as pastor and delegate. She was dealt with all between as First African Baptist Church. Thus through the terrible troubles through which the church passed she never lost her identity. The terrible missles of the enemies fell harmlessly at her feet. Through Christ she conquered and her fame became world wide, and Rev. Marshall acknowledged as one of the ablest men of the age. Strangers visiting Savannah would not consider their visit complete if they did not visit the First African Church. After this trouble, Rev. Marshall's greatness just begun to be acknowledged throughout the country. Settled down quietly to his work, the church under his leadership increased rapidly in membership and soon ran up to several thousands. Indeed, she did come forth, as fair as the moon, as bright as the sun, and as terrible as an army with banners. The First African Baptist Church was always liberal in its contributions to missions and to the cause of Christ generally. It has left its impress upon the hearts of many ministers and others whom she has helped in times of need. Notwithstanding her troubles she bought her house of worship, for which she paid $1,500, and supported her pastor at the same time. She never refused a call for missions.

CHAPTER VII.

Th₃ New Site at Franklin Ward, or Square—The Purchase—
New Building, and more about Rev. Marshall's Efforts
to Get Money to Build the Church and to Bring
it to a Higher Plane of Usefulness and
Intelligence, and his Death.

It appears that before the split of 1832 that money had been raised to purchase the old site of the Savannah Baptist Church at Franklin Square, and before the contract had been closed the trouble commenced. When the trouble was settled the First African Baptist Church agreed to relinquish its claims to the old church property to the minority so soon as they would relinquish their claims to the new. Hence it must be that they had helped to raise some of the money before the split with which to buy the new church property.

The First African Baptist Church bought this property for $1,500. They were required to pay this amount from April 28th, 1832, by November 1st, 1832. The terms were rigid, considering those days. The bargain was authorized to be made in the Conference of the Savannah Baptist Church (white) April 28, 1832, and in the Conference of the same, May the 10th, 1832, the First African Baptist Church is credited with $1,000. The poor slaves had paid in less than thirty days this amount of money. They worked all day for the white people and paid them whatever money they made at night or between times. The church (white) ordered their Trustees to give the First African Baptist Church possession of the building as soon as they had paid the balance due. From this statement we learn that they were not to have possession until they paid all. If it be asked, Was this right and just? we answer, yes and no. Yes, because if that was the contract it was right for them to comply with the contract before they could expect possession. If they were men capable of making a contract they ought to have been compelled to keep it. No, because they were slaves, and all they had and were belonged to the white people. They owned them as slaves and ordinarily they were not allowed to make a contract. It was the duty of the white people to look out for the religious welfare of the negroes, build their churches and pay their preachers. How could the white people have expected these slaves to have money? They worked them all day and hired patrols and police nights and Sundays to see that they did not go out, except to church. Still they exacted of them $1,500 just as rigidly as if they were free men. This thought is enough to chill the blood of a liberty-loving people. The First African Baptist Church is almost the price of blood. Just how the money was raised to buy this property we can not see. God helped His people, and to Him be all the glory. We may stand on the Mount of Liberty to-day and very well exclaim, "The Lord has done great things for us, whereof we are glad!" Perhaps the church will never be called upon to suffer what she has suffered, and perhaps will never produce a set of members more earnest, more determined and more liberal.

These hardships developed wonderful characters. Whatever the negroes have learned they have paid for it dearly. About November 1st, 1832, the First African Baptist Church took charge of the building at Franklin Square. This was very providential that they should have obtained a site in so prominent a part of the city. From this place her glory commenced to be known the world over. No church has been more favored of the Lord than this church. Not long after they had settled down in their new quarters the First African Baptist Church begun to bestir itself to put up a large brick building, to stand as a palace built for God to show His milder face. This was a great undertaking for slaves, but they were led by a great man, who was capable of undertaking great things, and who knew no such thing as fail. The church begun this hard task under adverse circumstances. It will be remembered that for about ten years there was no special things that transpired in the church worthy of note, except that the church grew and thrived under the faithful, pious and aged Andrew C. Marshall.

It was in the heart of Rev. Mr. Marshall to build a fine house of worship. For this purpose he begged money from his church and friends in Savannah, but seeing this was not sufficient and that he could not prosecute the work as rapidly as he wished, and seeing that the church was greatly put to it to raise money, Rev. Mr. Marshall went North to beg money. He had some success, but nothing like what he had hoped, perhaps. This trip was taken in 1856. He was cordially received by Northern Baptists and invited in the leading pulpits of New York, crowds greeting him wherever he preached. But declining health and old age caused him to return homeward. Not being able to procure a passage on the steamer, owing to a law of the free States that a slave could not return to a slave State, he had to undertake the trip by land and such conveniences as that day afforded. He got as far as Richmond. Va., and there breathed his last, full of years, faith and good works. Rev. Mr. Marshall hoped to finished the church building with the finishing of his days. But God called him to his reward without letting him return to see his people and report the results of his labors. When he died the work kept right on.

God had a man prepared to take up the work where Rev. Marshall laid it down, and whom the people would love just as much, and who would wield the same. if not greater. influence over them. A man of practical judgment and wonderful executive ability. That man was Rev. William J. Campbell. Under him the work did not lag. He did not leave the city to raise money to any great extent, but so great was his influence that he raised money at will. The building cost twenty-six thousand dollars ($26,000).' It was completed in 1859. It being the only brick building owned by negroes in the city, or in the State, it attracted great attention. It was called the brick church, and by many is still known by that name. The building is a plain, neat one. There is nothing showy about it. Not a brick is put in it that might have been left out. Economy and taste were displayed in the erection of this edifice. It was built simply for the glory of God and He blessed their efforts. The church continued in favor with God and man. Anything she undertakes never fails. It is true that Rev. W. J. Campbell was not so able as Rev. A. C. Marshall, but somehow he had an unbounded influence over people. They simply obeyed him as king. The church was orderly and dignified.

The building has a basement in which services are held during the week and prayer meeting early Sunday morning, and Sunday school Sunday afternoons. The main audience room has a gallery running around the front and both sides. In this room is preaching at 11 o'clock on Sunday morning and at night. On the first Sunday in the month, at 3 P. M., the Lord's Supper is celebrated here also, and on the third Sunday in each month, at 3 P. M., the Church Conference is held in this room. Otherwise this room is not used except on special occasions, such as marriages, concerts, etc. The church has a large choir and a large pipe organ, which afford music morning and night on Sunday. The building is surrounded by an iron railing, except the rear, with the inscription, "First African Baptist Church, Rev. W. J. Campbell, Pastor." It stands a lasting monument to the greatness of Revs. A. C. Marshall and W. J. Campbell. As this building was completed in 1859 it stood until 1888 without any remodelling.

Rev. W. J. Campbell was a wise planner. He knew how to

divide his forces and to concentrate them whenever this was necessary. When the church decided to tear down the old frame building and to erect a new brick edifice he appointed a building committee, of which he was chief director. As best we can learn, this committee consisted of Deacons Murry Monroe, C. L. DeLamotta, John Verdier and James M. Simms. These were members of the church and took personal interest in the work. The work was executed with great pride, exquisite taste and energy. Many men and women worked at night free of charge, and hence the work was pushed forward with wonderful rapidity. "The people had a mind to work." Mr. James H. Hooker, now a deacon of the church, boasts of having laid the first and last brick when the church was built. Many of the members loaned the church money on this occasion.

CHAPTER VIII.

Rev. George Leile—His Work in Savannah and Departure to Jamaica.

Rev. George Leile was born in Virginia about 1750; removed to Georgia and settled in Burke county some time before 1773. About 1773, after six months distress of mind and inquiring the way of life (or what we call "seeking the Lord"), he was happily converted, and was baptized by Rev. Mathew Moore (white). He was soon licensed to preach the Gospel, which he did with fine effect. His ordination followed very soon. From plantation to plantation he went bearing the olive branch of peace. Benedict says he preached at Brampton and Yamacraw, in the neighborhood of Savannah, for three years. He was owned by a Mr. Henry Sharp, who was very kind to him and gave him his freedom. One of the heirs undertook to rob him of his freedom after the death of his kind master, but God spared it to him. About 1781 he baptized Rev. Andrew Bryan, his wife, and two others. About this time the British armies were leaving our shore and Rev. George Leile decided to seek a home in the West Indies. He was led by the loving hand of a smiling Providence, though he knew it not. He had not the money with which to pay his passage, yet he was to plant the Gospel in Jamaica. God put it in the heart of Col. Kirkland to lend him the money. Led by the Spirit he sailed for Jamaica about the close of 1781 or the first of 1782. He put to work to pay back the money he had borrowed from Col. Kirkland just as soon as he reached Jamaica. In two years he had paid back the last cent. He was a farmer by trade. He had a wife and four children. He was busy preaching the gospel of Christ while he was making money to pay his debt.

In 1784 he had organized a church on the island and had gathered around him many anxious hearers. He is not content to organize a church, but he set to work to build a decent house for God. The Lord blessed his effort and some good Baptists in England were interested in his behalf, and by their contributions he erected a nice house of worship in that place. He organized the first Baptist Church in Kingston, Jamaica, and baptized the persons with whom the first Baptist Church of color was organized in Georgia. He is an important man, both in our history in Georgia and in the history of the Baptists in Jamaica. He was an able man of his day, if we may judge from his letters to Dr. Rippon, of London. In 1791 he wrote that he had baptized about 500 persons. He was very industrious, working with his own hands for the support of himself and family, either farming or driving a wagon hauling goods from one place to the other. He was a man of great practical judgment. He was neat in his dress and humble in his manners. He won the highest respect and admiration of the people of the island, white and black. The slaves loved him and their owners honored him. He was the friend of both. He handled skillfully the sword of truth and drew crowds after him wherever he preached the gospel. When he had established a church in the towns he made for the interior to unfurl the gospel banner to those who were sitting in darkness and in the region of the shadow of death. He never forgot his brethren in Georgia—frequent letters passed between them. He was anxious to know how the brethren here fared with whom he had labored, and some of whom he had led to Jesus and baptized. We subjoin a copy of a letter from Rev. Leile to Dr. Rippon which will show somewhat of the character of the man. It was written in 1791:

"I cannot tell what is my age, as I have no account of the time of my birth; but I suppose I am about 40 years old. I have a wife and four children. My wife was baptized by me in Savannah, and I have every satisfaction in life from her. She is much the same age as myself. My eldest son is 19 years, my next son 17, the third fourteen, and the last child a girl of 11 years. They are all members of the church. My occupation is a farmer, but as the seasons in this part of the country are uncertain, I also keep a team of horses and wagons for the carrying of goods from one place to another, which I attend myself, with the assistance of my sons, and by this way of life have gained the good will of the public, who recommend me to business and to some very principal work for Government. I have a few books, some good old authors and sermons, and one large Bible that was given me by a gentleman. A good many of our members can read and are all desirous to learn. They will be very thankful for a few books to read on Sundays and other days. I agree to election, redemption, the fall of Adam, regeneration and perseverance, knowing the promise is to all who endure, in grace, faith and good works to the end, shall be saved.

"There is no Baptist church in this country but ours. We have purchased a piece of land at the east end of Kingston, containing three acres, for the sum of £155, currency, and on it have begun a meeting-house, 57 feet in length by 37 in breadth. We have raised the brick wall eight feet high from the foundation, and intend to have a gallery. Several gentlemen, members of the House of Assembly, and other gentlemen, have subscribed towards the building about £40. The chief part of our congregation are slaves, and their owners allow them, in common, but three or four bits per week for allowance to feed themselves, and out of so small a sum we cannot expect anything that can be of service from them; if we did, it would soon bring a scandal upon religion; and the free people in our society are but poor, but they are all willing, both free and slaves, to do what they can. As for my part, I am too much entangled with the affairs of the world to go on, as I would, with my design in supporting the cause. This has, I acknowledge, been a great hindrance to the gospel in one way; but as I have endeavored to set a good example of industry before the inhabitants of the land, it has given general satisfaction another way. And, Rev. Sir, we think the Lord has put it in the power of the Baptist Societies in England to help and assist us in completing this building, which we look upon will be the greatest undertaking ever was in this country for the bringing of souls from darkness into the light of the gospel. And as the Lord has put it in your heart to inquire after us, we place all our confidence in you to make our circumstances known to the several Baptist churches in England, and we look upon you as our father, friend and brother. Within the brick wall we have a shelter in which we worship until our building can be accomplished.

"Your letter was read to the church two or three times, and did create a great deal of love and warmness throughout the whole congregation, who shouted for joy and comfort to think that the Lord had been so gracious as to satisfy us in this country with the very same religion with our beloved brethren in the old country, according to the Scriptures: and that such a worthy............of London. should write in so loving a manner to such poor worms as we are. And I beg leave to say. that the whole congregation sang out that they would, through the assistance of God, remember you in their prayers. They all together give their Christian love to you and all the worthy professors of Jesus Christ in your church at London, and beg the prayers of the churches in general and of your congregation wherever it pleases you to make known our circumstances. I remain, with the utmost love. Rev. Sir, your unworthy fellow laborer, servant and brother in Christ.

"GEORGE LEILE."

"P. S.—We have chosen twelve Trustees, all of whom are members of our church, whose names are specified in the title: the title proved and recorded in the Secretary's office of this island."

*From Benedict's History of the Baptists.

This man doubtless has long since finished his labors and has entered the saints' rest. We have no date of his death. nor the latter end of his work. But he will be remembered. and his name honored, both here and in Jamaica while memory holds its place. Whatever the negro Baptists here and in Jamaica are, they owe it to his humble beginning. And whatever may be written of either of us. it cannot be complete if his name is left out. His record is here. there and in heaven. Nothing is known of any of his family—whether any are alive or not.

CHAPTER IX.

Rev. Andrew Bryan and His Pastorate.

This faithful servant of God was born at a place called Goose Creek, about sixteen miles from Charleston, South Carolina, somewhere about 1716, and was baptized by Rev. George Leile about 1781. He was ordained to the office of the gospel ministry January 20th, 1788, by Rev. Abraham Marshall (white) and Rev. Jesse Peter, and was consequently 72 years old when he became pastor of the church. He learned to read about 1785. He was persecuted for preaching the gospel. He was whipped until he bled most profusely. But while bleeding, and the cruel lash yet falling upon his naked back, he held up his hand and said to his vile persecutors: "You may kill me, but I will preach the gospel. If you would stop me from preaching, cut off my head. I rejoice that I am worthy to suffer for Jesus." This was said with such Christian courage and humble boldness, and with a wonderfully powerful and sweet voice, that his inhuman and ungodly persecutors were dumbfounded. This touched the hearts of the white people and excited their sympathy for the persecuted saints, who declared that such treatment would have been condemned even among barbarians. Then Mr. Jonathan Bryan, the master of Rev. Andrew Bryan, interceded for him. His intercession was late, but better late than never. We are disposed to believe that the sympathy of the community excited in favor of the persecuted disciples moved him rather than the magnanimity of his own heart. Where was he when all this persecution was going on? Could his negroes, who were doubtless living on his premises, have been taken and almost martyred without his knowledge? Would white men in those days have treated each others' negroes with such extreme cruelties without their permission or knowledge? Verily, we think, no. Benedict says: "Jonathan Bryan, Esq., the kind master of Andrew and Samson, interceded for his own servants and the rest of the sufferers, and was much grieved at their punishment." While we thank God that help did come, we feel that this statement is highly colored. We lived in the days of slavery and saw and felt some of its ungodly hardships. We know that this was a remarkable case if Mr. Jonathan Bryan could not have prevented this diabolical treatment of these humble, defenseless Christians, his slaves, but God's freemen. If this was done without his knowledge he could have sued for damage, we think. Benedict does not tell us that he did. If he did, doubtless Benedict would have been delighted to have informed us at length about it. We thank God, however, for what Mr. Jonathan Bryan did. He might have done much worse.

After this terrible whipping, Rev. Andrew Bryan was given the use of his master's barns at Brampton, three miles southwest of Savannah, for the purpose of preaching Jesus to the negroes. Here for several years he preached the glorious gospel of Him who was born in a manger to anxious hearers in a manger. The blessing of Almighty God rested upon his efforts, and He honored his humble preaching in this humble place with the power of the Holy Spirit. Their number wonderfully and rapidly increased. They soon silenced and shamed their bitterest enemies, unarmed them and made ardent admirers of them. Rev. Andrew Bryan was a faithful, earnest and simple preacher of the New Testament. His simple, earnest preaching at Brampton's barn attracted attention and he was visited by distinguished men of that day. In course of time he procured a site in Yamacraw and there erected a church and preached very successfully the gospel.

He was given a place upon which to erect a house of worship

by Edward Davis, Esq., in Yamacraw. This was soon taken from them. The corporation of the city gave them a lot in Yamacraw upon which they erected a house 42x49 in 1792. It seems that they lost this too.

About this time Rev. Andrew Bryan bought himself and family and very rapidly accumulated property. He was worth before his death upward of five thousand dollars. The site the First Bryan Church sits on to-day was owned by him, and in 1797 he sold it to the First African Baptist Church. He wielded an immense influence. He was beloved and honored by white and black. He was pastor of the First African Baptist Church from 1788 to 1812—a period of twenty-four years. On October 6th, 1812, he breathed his last, full of faith, hope, honor, years and good work. He went to live with that Jesus for whom he suffered. Distinguished white men delivered eulogies at his funeral. Thus ended the wonderful career of this grand, good man, the father of the Baptists in Savannah, on the coast, and in Georgia. As a man he was humble and fearless. As a preacher he was faithful and true. Whatever was duty was supreme with him. As a pastor he was loving, tender and sympathetic. He loved his members as children, and they reverenced him as a father. When he died it was considered as a calamity by the whole community. One of the best men that ever lived had passed from labor to reward. In life he was beloved by all; in death bemoaned by all. He was an ornament to society and a blessing to mankind. He was followed to his last resting place by not less than five thousand persons, and addresses were made at his grave by three distinguished white men. He was a great man.

CHAPTER X.
Rev. Andrew C. Marshall.

Rev. Marshall was born about 1775 in South Carolina. He was the nephew of Rev. Andrew Bryan. He was, it is said, pastor of the First African Baptist Church for forty-four years, but this is hardly correct, for from the death of Rev. Andrew Bryan to the death of Rev. Marshall was just forty-four years. It is more than likely that some time elapsed before he was installed as pastor at the death of his uncle. The statement respecting Rev. Marshall is very conflicting. The above reference to his birth is according to Dr. Cathcart. We subjoin a statement that was written by a friend who claimed to have been acquainted with the facts in the case and who lived in the days of Rev. Marshall.

"Rev. Andrew C. Marshall was born in Bryan county, Ga., December 25th, 1745. In 1785 he became a member of the church, being baptized by his uncle, Rev. Andrew Bryan, pastor of the First African Baptist Church. A few years after he was licensed to preach the gospel, after which he was ordained as an evangelist. He preached in the Second African Baptist

Church for nine years. In the year 1808 he took pastoral care of the First African Baptist Church, in which he had been pastor for forty-eight years. From the time of his conversion he was used as an instrument in the hands of God of doing much good. He heard the conversion of 4,000 concerning the faith of the Lord Jesus Christ; he baptized 3,776; he married 2,400; he buried 2,040.

"Andrew C. Marshall was born a slave. He has traveled over a great part of the United States. He has by industry succeeded in purchasing himself and done many benevolent acts among his color, and has given to different institutions several thousand dollars. The venerable Father in Israel, Andrew C. Marshall, died in Richmond, Virginia, December 7th, 1856, while returning from the North to the people of his charge. For nearly or quite half a century he was a laborious and indefatigable workman in the vineyard of his Master. For many years he was the leading religious spirit among his colored brethren and maintained what he so well deserved, the respect and confidence of the whole community. Full of years, however, and full of honors, he has obeyed the welcome summons, 'Come up,' and died at the age of 110; and up to the time of his death he could discharge his duty as pastor of the church. His remains were brought to Savannah at the expense of the congregation, the funeral sermon was preached by the Rev. Thomas Rambeau, and deposited in his own vault. He is now succeeded by one of his own students, Rev. William Campbell."

Rev. Marshall must have been born later than 1775. If Cathcart's account is true that he was body guard to George Washington while in Savannah during the war, the war commenced in 1775 and lasted eight years, so Cathcart's account of the birth of Rev. Marshall can not be true. In fact, little if anything he says about this church is true. Rev. Marshall must have been born about 1745, as said of him.

Cathcart says he became pastor of the First African Baptist Church in 1808, and yet he says that "Rev. Andrew Bryan continued its pastor until his death in October, 1812." This is very contradictory. It is said on Rev. Marshall's epitaph in the church to-day that he was pastor of the First African Bap-

---

1. The reader will observe the contradiction in the place and time of the birth of Rev. A. C. Marshall.
2. It will be seen also that the First African Baptist Church was not organized when Rev. Marshall is said to have been baptized (1785), having been organized in 1788.
3. It is clear that Rev. Marshall was never pastor of the Second African Baptist Church. If he preached in said church nine years and resigned it in 1808, it will be seen that he took charge of said church in 1799, which was three years before the Second African Baptist Church was organized, being organized in 1802.

tist Church for forty-four years. If he was pastor of the First African Baptist Church in 1808, having served the Second African Baptist Church nine years, this would make him begin his pastorate with the Second African Baptist Church in 1799. This was quite three years before the Second African Baptist Church was organized. It was organized December 26th, 1802, and Rev. Henry Cunningham was ordained January 1st, 1803, and called to be its pastor. He served it continuously until 1831 or 1832, a period of twenty-eight or twenty-nine years. Hence Rev. Marshall was never pastor of the Second African Baptist Church since he served the First African Baptist Church from about 1812 to 1856, and since Rev. Henry Cunningham preceded him to the saints' reward about twenty-five years. Rev. Marshall bought himself and accumulated property very rapidly. He was a man of a large heart, iron will and an unflinching courage. He feared nothing and nobody that stood in his way to right. He had many good books which he read. His information was broad. He comprehended the precepts of the gospel, thought for himself, and never feared to proclaim his views. He understood the government of the Baptist Church and by that he was willing to die. He had much trouble, as our readers must have discovered ere this. He built a large brick house on Bryan street, in Yamacraw, and had much trouble about it from the report that he bought stolen bricks. The prejudice was very high against him and the church was closed for six months on account of this. In 1825, Rev. Marshall preached all of his spare time from his church as missionary to the negro Baptist Churches in the bounds of the Sunsbury Association and refused pay when it was offered to him. He was a great preacher, and controlled the people as if by magic. His people were willing to die with him. Wherever he went to preach crowds, white and black, flocked to hear him. His preaching was of the old school order, purely textual and abounded in numerous quotations. He believed the Bible was its best interpreter, and hence he always strove to make scripture explain scripture. He seemed to have eaten up the Bible. His voice was strong and powerful and at his perfect control. He could make it so pathetic as to melt his congregation to tears at will. He was humorous and wonderfully witty and extremely eloquent. Those who went to hear him never regretted it, and could never forget him. He preached extensively in Georgia—at Augusta, Macon and many other places. The Georgia Legislature adjourned a session and invited him to address the body. As a friend he was true; as an antagonist he was powerful and foxy; as a planner and debater his equals were few in any country, among any people; as a financier he was successful; as a gentleman he was upright, and as a Christian he was humble and forgiving.

After the split of 1832, when the disaffected members had withdrawn and formed the Third African Baptist Church, now the First Bryan Baptist Church, his people were more attentive to him, obeyed him unhesitatingly, and loved him more as the years passed by. He possessed a wonderful knowledge of men and had a strange influence over them. He saw much of the excitement of the Revolutionary war and was honored as body servant of George Washington while he was in Savannah. This we get from Dr. Cathcart's Encyclopedia of the Baptists, the accuracy of which is, at least, questionable. Yet if he was born in 1745 he would have been old enough.

We have found several of his statements contradictory. He says that Rev. Marshall became pastor of the Second African Baptist Church in 1806, and we think it clear that he was never pastor of that church. Many of the members who were baptized by Rev. Marshall, and a deacon who served under him, are still alive, who affirm that he was never pastor of that church. There never has lived a negro in Savannah who was the equal of Rev. Mr. Marshall. Through his skill and wonderful executive ability the site at Franklin Square was paid for, and he laid the foundation for the present beautiful edifice. While men loved him, they feared him and quaked before him. Little preachers in that day who could do passably well otherwise would cave in in the presence of Rev. Marshall and make a complete failure. Yet he was friendly, sympathetic and kind. But as kindness generally breeds fear, he was possessed of much kindness and hence was feared accordingly. When he had well nigh strained his people for money he went North for the purpose of begging money to complete his church. His success is not known. Returning he got as far as Richmond, Va., where he died, full of honors, full of good works, full of hope and full of faith. The church sent Rev. W. J. Campbell to bring his remains to Savannah. His sorrowing people honored in every possible way the remains of this venerable father. Many white people followed this aged saint to his last resting place. Thus ended the long and useful life of one of the greatest men in the American pulpit.

1st. If Rev. Marshall was born in 1775 he could not have witnessed much about the exciting events of the Revolutionary War, which commenced in 1775.

2d. If he was born in 1775 he may have been "converted and joined the church in 1785," as Dr. Cathcart says, but it was very rare in those days for negroes to join the church at ten years of age, and certainly he could not have been "licensed to preach not long after." The Dr. is mistaken.

We insert from Sprague's Annals of the American Baptist Pulpit the following:

ANDREW C. MARSHALL—1786-1856.

[From the Rev. J. P. Tustin, D. D.]

CHARLESTON, S. C., January 15, 1859.

Rev. and Dear Sir:

My ecclesiastical connection with Andrew C. Marshall and his church placed me, for several years, in constant communication with him. Having also to act as a legal security to meet the municipal ordinances of Savannah and the State of Georgia, with regards to colored preachers, I had much to do in matters of counsel and discipline in his church. The sources of information relative to the following memoir have been often attested by communication with the older members of the Georgia Historical Society, and with many of the oldest and most respectable citizens of that State. I am happy to be able to give you these memorabilia of one of the most remarkable colored men who have appeared in our modern times.

Andrew C. Marshall, late pastor of the First African Baptist Church in Savannah, Georgia, has deservedly become a celebrity in the annals of the American Baptist Church. During the last quarter of a century his name gradually attracted public attention, until at length it was known in distant parts of the country, and even across the Atlantic. Several of the most lively sketches of him which appeared were given by authors whose works are current in various languages. Among these is the account of Sir Charles Lyell in his volumes published after his second scientific tour in the United States. Miss Fredrika Brenner, in her American tours, has presented a striking portraiture of him. Within the last few years of his life, almost every intelligent stranger who might be visiting Savannah, was likely to seek out or to hear this venerable preacher, and the sketches thus frequently produced were widely circulated by the religious press of various denominations, and some of the leading secular papers in Northern cities had occasionally contributed to spread his fame.

The most noteworthy fact which made Mr. Marshall so celebrated in his later years, was his reputed great age. During his visit through the Northern States in the summer and fall of 1856, the last year of his life, the previously received version of his extreme age was extensively repeated, and has not been discredited. Some years previous to that time I had, as a tribute to the cause of science, attempted to collect and sift the evidence about this story, which, if only apocryphal, would mislead persons engaged in ethnological and historical researches. Literary and scientific gentlemen had frequently made reference to Mr. Marshall, as an important physical phenomenon.

With no wish to detract from a story of popular interest, but, nevertheless, with a strong desire to arrive at perfect accuracy, I sought all the sources available to myself for testing the question of Mr. Marshall's age. Several lines of investigation were followed, which partly tended at first to fix his age from ten to fifteen years below what was commonly assigned to him, and claimed by himself.

One of these lines of investigation was in the personal recollections of the late Hon. John Macpherson Berrien, so well known as United States Senator and Attorney General of the United States. Judge Berrien was educated for the bar by Judge Clay, of Bryan county, Georgia, by whom Andrew C. Marshall was owned as a slave, while Mr. Berrien was a member of the family. Mr. Berrien was born August 23, 1781, and after graduating at Princeton, commenced the practice of law in Georgia at the age of eighteen years, which was near the time when Mr. Marshall began his efforts at preaching.

With his great name for integrity and accuracy, Judge Berrien would not be considered likely to give countenance to any opinion which was unsupported by valid evidence. His recollections of Andrew C. Marshall's appearance could hardly be reconciled with the account which must have made him a person of fifty years of age when Mr. Berrien first knew him as a coachman. But it was at most a matter of impression with Mr. Berrien, that Andrew was at that period not more than a middle-aged man. Judge Berrien's impression can be accounted for by the fact that this remarkable African always carried his age so remarkably well, even at a century.

The late venerable Mr. Miller, familiarly known in Georgia as "Cotton Miller," from his having been the first person who sent the first bale of cotton to Savannah for shipment, was also of the opinion that Mr. Marshall's age should have been placed several years below what was commonly assigned to him, and by him. Guided by such cautious and accurate men, who thus seemed to discredit a popular and universally received version, it fell to my lot, some years ago, while acting as one of the Secretaries of the Georgia Historical Society, to examine Mr. Marshall more closely than ever, as to his personal history, and to compare the results of these interrogatories with other collateral evidence. Being charged with the duty, in behalf of the literary representative and grandson of Gen. Nathaniel Green, of the Revolutionary army, of identifying the spot where that hero was buried in Savannah, I found Andrew C. Marshall to be a most useful adviser on points which put at once his veracity and his accuracy of recollection to the closest tests. Some of his statements as to his age at the time of Gen. Greene's death, which occurred in 1786, at first seemed to confirm the impression of Judge Berrien and Mr. Miller, already referred to. On a review, however, of that case, it appears that these interrogatories were conducted too much in the manner of a cross-examination by a special pleader; and Mr. Marshall's confusion of mind or apparent inaccuracy as to dates, could be sufficiently explained by his want of familiarity with the published literary chronicles of the times in question.

It is, therefore, a concession which is now cheerfully made, that the doubts which I once published as to Mr. Marshall's being truly a living centenarian, may not be justified. No one who intimately knew the venerable subject of this sketch would suspect him of wishing to deceive in any important matter. The only abatement which any one would feel, arises from the well known propensity of colored people in all parts of the Southern States to make themselves older than they really are, after they reach to some advanced period. The deference accorded to age; the freedom from labor which aged servants enjoy, and the consideration received from those of their own race—these are among the inducements which lead aged Africans to over-estimate their years, sometimes by a very considerable difference.

It is possible that Mr. Marshall may have been deceived, not only in regards to his years, but also as to some other facts in his history. And yet it is proper to remark that his means of knowing were better than any others possessed. It must be allowed that his statements were not questioned by the oldest and most respectable citizens of his own city and region, and gentlemen now living can certify to more than fifty years' knowledge of him.

If any other question besides his age should be raised as to his accuracy or competency of opinion concerning himself, it would be as to the amount of African blood. In his conformation and general appearance, he would probably pass for a true mulatto. But some scientific gentlemen, accustomed to the refined test which the hair and other criteria of physiology seem to have settled in ethnological researches, have formed a decided opinion that Mr. Marshall was more of an African than would follow from a white father and a black mother.

His own account, so often repeated, and so widely known and believed, in lower Georgia, will now be mainly followed. He always referred his birth to the year 1755, being the time of General Braddock's defeat by the French and Indians. This, he said, had, from his early recollections, determined the year of his nativity. As informed by his mother, who was an unmixed negress, his father was an Englishman acting as an overseer in South Carolina, where Andrew was born. The father left for England where he died not long after the birth of the child. It was asserted by Andrew that he had been entitled to his freedom from his birth, as his father had arranged with a mulatto person by the name of Pendarvis, before going to England, that the negro mother and two children which she had borne him were to be provided for, and the children educated, and that upon his return the father would secure their freedom. His premature death becoming known, the mulatto overseer managed to enforce a claim against the estate of the father, and the mother and children were seized and sold as slaves. Andrew was sold to John Houston, Colonial Governor of Georgia, who died when Andrew was about 21 years of age.

Andrew Marshall was twice married; the first time at 16 years of age. By his two marriages he had twenty children, only one of whom now survives. He was separated from his first wife after the death of Governor Houston, by whom he had been bequeathed his freedom on account of having one time saved his master's life. The executors, however, failed to carry out the will, and Andrew was again sold, being then parted from his first wife. He evaded the decision by running away, and was sold while at large, becoming the property of Judge Clay, as already mentioned.

While in the service of Judge Clay, he accompanied his master, who several times visited the Northern States in the capacity of a member of Congress, and perhaps on some other occasions also. In these visits, Andrew's position as coachman enabled him frequently to see General Washington, of whom he was fond of relating several striking incidents. At a later period General Washington visited Savannah, and Andrew was honored with the appointment of body servant to the President. He was constantly near the General's person during his brief stay in the city, acting as his driver, and waiting upon him at a public dinner. Andrew said that Washington was uniformly grave and serious, and that he was never seen to smile during his whole visit, though he was always calm and pleasant.

The congruity of Mr. Marshall's recollections seems to be

verified, especially in regards to his age, in connection with the opening period of the Revolutionary war. The embargo having taken effect at Savannah, fifteen merchants of that city agreed to give him a purse of two hundred and twenty-five dollars, on condition that he should carry word to a number of American vessels lying in a bay on the lower seaboard and destined for Savannah. In this achievement he was successful. The vessels were enabled to escape to Spanish protection, before the courier, previously sent, had informed the fleet of their danger.

Mr. Marshall was an eye-witness of many of the stirring events which occurred in Savannah and its vicinity during the Revolutionary war. He was a trustworthy servant, especially when honored with any unusual promotion and responsibility. Even in the last war with England, he was employed, for a period of six weeks, by officers of the government or the army, on some important business, and for this he refused any compensation, as he always claimed to be a true American, and cheerfully shared in the toils and sufferings of the white population, though never with any unseemly pretensions on his part.

He had distinct personal recollections of General Nathaniel Greene. His account of that hero's early death agrees with the traditions which have been carefully attested by gentlemen familiar with historical researches. General Greene, immediately after the war, was rewarded with valuable grants of land near Savannah, to which he repaired with his family in 1783. Owing either to some disputed title, or to rancor and envy at the hero's valuable possessions, he was not allowed to enjoy them long. He was exposed to so much personal danger that he was obliged to ride armed with pistols, in going to and from his plantation near the city, and he could travel only in full daytime. Thus exposed in the midst of the summer's heat, he was suddenly smitten with inflammation of the brain, and died on the 19th of June, 1786. Andrew C. Marshall could recall all these events with the distinctness of an eye-witness. His account of the hero's funeral, in Savannah, is the only apparently faithful picture which can now be furnished, whether from written chronicles or from personal traditions. He described the surprise, grief and indignation of the people of the city at the early and untoward death of General Greene, and their willing minds but ineffectual desires to stand up for his honor and defense. The town and region around were summoned to the funeral, and tubs of punch and barrels of biscuits were placed along the road near the cemetery to refresh the wearied multitude. Andrew declared that he could pace off the distance from the gate of the old cemetery on South Broad street to within half a dozen steps of the spot where the General was buried. But his aid in verifying this locality had been too long deferred, when an investigation was attempted a few years ago, especially as it was then established by sufficient evidence that the remains of General Greene had previously been exhumed and removed to a spot which cannot now be identified.

Mr. Marshall's force of character seemed to have been chiefly expended on worldly interests, until he was about 50 years of age. He evinced, even to the last a lively sympathy in the welfare of the country, and was especially careful to maintain the cause of law and order in the social relations by which he was surrounded in his own city and vicinity. Not far from the time of his conversion, he also acquired his emancipation. He was at that time owned as a slave by Mr. Bolton, whose family name is honorably known among the merchant princes of Savannah. The father of Mr. Bolton had been the special friend of the Countess of Huntingdon while she was patronizing Mr. Whitefield's mission in Savannah, and the orphan house at Beulieu. The Bolton name is associated by marriage with the family of the late Rev. William Jay, of Bath, in England. The business partner of Mr. Bolton was the late venerable Mr. Richard Richardson, who purchased Andrew, and, with the view of effecting his emancipation, advanced him two hundred dollars, in order to purchase himself. With his previous earnings, and with diligence and economy, under the encouragements of his master, he saved enough to pay for himself and his whole family, then consisting of his wife and four children, his wife's father and his own step-father. Shortly after his conversion he began to preach, and in 1806 he became pastor of the Second Baptist Church* in Savannah, which was a colored church, in distinction from the First or the White Baptist Church, then recently formed by the distinguished Henry Holcombe, D. D., who afterwards died as pastor of the First Baptist Church in Philadelphia. About a thousand colored members then belonged to Mr. Marshall's church, and subsequently the number increased to some three thousand, when it was thought best to divide them. Accordingly the colored church was formed, which some time afterward purchased the old house of worship which the White Baptist Church vacated

---

*This cannot be true. The Second African Baptist Church was organized December 26th, 1802—the First African Church January 20th, 1788. The first was never known as the Second African Baptist Church in distinction to the White Baptist Church.

when they built their new brick meeting-house, under the pastorship of the late Rev. Henry O. Wyer, and which now formed a part of the large house of worship known as the First Baptist Church in Savannah. The church which Mr. Marshall thus formed took the name of the First African Baptist Church, and he remained its pastor till the day of his death.*

During the long period of his ministry Mr. Marshall was careful to preserve tolerably good memorials of his ministerial acts. His mere recollections seemed nearly as accurate as if they had been written and publicly certified. He had baptized about thirty-eight hundred persons, and he supposed that over four thousand had professed to be converted under his ministry. His personal influence extended over the plantations through several counties around Savannah, and the planters were generally satisfied with the beneficial effects of his labors. He was often sent for to preach and to perform funeral services at great distances, and such visits were often urged by the planters and the white people at large, as well as by the blacks. Whenever he visited any of the larger cities his appearance in public ministrations was greeted by great multitudes. He occasionally preached in Augusta, Macon and Milledgeville, as well as in Charleston, and even as far off as in New Orleans. On some occasions his audiences were composed, in large part, of the most respectable white people, and the Legislature of Georgia at one time gave him a hearing in an entire body. The winter before he died he visited Augusta and conducted a protracted meeting, which resulted in the addition of over three hundred and fifty persons to the colored church in that city. With all these immense results to his ministry, Mr. Marshall preserved a strict and salutary discipline, at least, such was the constant effort and rule of his proceedings. He was jealous of mere animal excitements, and generally unfriendly even to protracted meetings in his own church, or in others where he officiated. He relied upon the appointed and ordinary means of grace; and in his own church, there were seldom any efforts used beyond special prayer and the faithful ministrations of the word. He, however, was so deeply interested in the temperance cause, that he encourged, among his people, those methods of organizations for this object which are somewhat kindred to the plan of the Odd Fellows. There were also societies among his flock for mutual

---

*Mr. Marshall did not form the First African Baptist Church. The First African Baptist Church was formed by Rev. Abraham Marshall (white) and Rev. Jesse Peter (colored) January 20, 1788. The First African Baptist Church is twelve years older than the Savannah Baptist Church (white). They were never together and hence the colored church could not have come out from the white church. The First African Baptist Church worshipped in Yamacraw before the white Baptist Church was in existence.

benefit; and in these ways the poor and the infirm, especially among the free people of color, who had no legal masters to care for them in their old age were greatly benefited. Mr. Marshall was so strong in his opposition to drunkenness that no colored person would, by this indulgence, willingly incur his censure. There is no doubt that, in this respect, he accomplished much for the cause among the blacks, and thus for the public welfare generally.

The superiority of Mr. Marshall's character and talents especially appears in the methodical manner in which he conducted his own business, as well as in the discipline of his church. Long after he became a preacher, he had but a small and precarious support from any pecuniary rewards for his ministry. He supported himself and his family as a drayman; but his great capacity soon asserted itself, even in respect to his material means of prosperity. He conducted the portage and draying business on a considerable scale, at one period having owned a number of drays and teams, and even the slaves who drove them. He owned the large brick dwelling house in which he had lived for many years previous to his death; and was at one time rated in property as high as twenty-five thousand dollars, though this was probably too high an estimate. His property was diminished very considerably in his latter years. With his increasing infirmities he began to fear that he might yet be scarcely saved from the necessity of out-door duties and that he might have to give up the easy carriage and horse which he had so long enjoyed. He related that, on one occasion, he had advanced twenty-five hundred dollars to purchase a family of twelve persons, to prevent their separation, and that he never received back the money, except a mere trifle, which he had thus paid. His church, however, were abundantly able and willing to provide for him; and though they did not pay him a fixed salary, they made regular contributions, which amounted to a handsome sum annually, and which in any extremity could doubtless have been increased by several hundred dollars. Prominent native citizens were always among his tried friends: and some of the most respectable gentlemen in Savannah, of different denominations, acted as trustees for his church, to protect their real estate and other property.

Mr. Marshall possessed elements which would of necessity have made him a leading character anywhere. His Anglo-Saxon temperament made him superior to his African race. His strength of character showed itself in his indomitable perseverance, his calm self-possession, his practical sagacity, and a discretion which never failed him. Withal he had a genial and even humorous temper; and his countenance bore the finest lines of expression. He was entirely free from superstition, and gave no countenance to marvellous relations of experience, even in a work of grace. He could penetrate beneath disguises, and few men, white or black, of any age, could surpass him in reading human character. The deference which he always showed for the laws and institutions of the country was combined with a high measure of self-respect, and frequently with a decision and inflexibility which might be taken advantage of by unprincipled white persons. There was a period of about two years—from 1819 to 1821—when Mr. Marshall became somewhat unpopular with the white people of his own denomination, on account of his extreme views of theology, which at first bordered on Antinomianism, and at length receded to the opposite extreme of Sacramentalism in Baptism, as held by Alexander Campbell. During that time, and while engaged in his secular avocations, he had violated the laws by contraband dealings with negroes. He had made purchases from slaves having no tickets with leave to trade and sell; and, though many white people had laid the foundation of large success in business before, as others have since, by contraband with blacks, advantage was taken of Mr. Marshall's inadvertency, and happening together with his temporary unpopularity, he was prosecuted and sentenced to be publicly whipped in the marketplace. The kindness of his former master, Mr. Richardson, and the feelings of many of the best citizens, would not allow him to suffer; and personal witnesses of the scene, yet living, can attest that the whipping was only a semblance—the constable receiving instructions not to scratch his skin or to draw blood—his old master also being at his side to see that these precautions were faithfully and humanely observed. While Mr. Marshall was unvarying in his deference to white people, and was never distrusted for any disloyalty to the public peace; and while he was decided in asserting the necessity and advantages of the present institutions in the South, he yet never hesitated to make a firm and respectful declaration of the rights of conscience in matters of religion. He sometimes alluded to his celebrated uncle, the Rev. Andrew Bryan, who was a colored preacher of nearly as great reputation as ever Andrew C. Marshall possessed, and who died at an extremely great age, as pastor of the colored church in Savannah. In one of the turbulent outbreaks of religious bigotry among the baser sort of people, which happened before the demoralizing effects of the Revolutionary war had been followed by better morals and manners, this old preacher, Andrew Bryan, was silenced from preaching, and, upon his assuming again to preach, he was publicly whipped. But, after this flagellation, he declared that he could not stop preaching, even if at the cost of a martyr's sufferings. This old man seemed ever to have been the model of a true preacher, with Andrew Marshall; and when he died, his nephew and successor caused a beautiful mural tablet to be raised in his church, and an other large tablet of marble over his grave, in which were recited the events of his life, not omitting the whipping and persecution he had endured for righteousness' sake. The monument will probably long remain in the colored cemetery at Savannah.

The bent and tone of Mr. Marshall's mind was of the old Calvinistic order. His clear intellect was equal to the best distinctions in theology: and though he was rather too fond of sometimes saying in public that he never had a day's learning in his life, yet he had much of the discipline which every superior mind acquires and asserts for itself, by the very necessity and outgrowth of self-education; for every mind that is truly educated, when we look at the last analysis, educates itself.

He owned a considerable number of books; and among those evidently the most used were Dr. Gill's Commentaries. In his treatment of a subject in some of his pulpit performances there was observable the grasp of a mind which would be deservedly called great. Very often indeed, he intermingled incidents of his personal experience, and then would seem to run into a style; but even these discursive qualities served to keep alive the attention of his simple flock. But a man who could make some of the high mental efforts which Andrew Marshall at times displayed, would be pronounced as fully equal to any subject which he would find occasion to meet, if allowed opportunity for preparation.

The tones of his voice seemed rather to make his preaching of the conversational order, while yet there was really a unity of plan and a purpose, and a progress, in the whole deliverance. In his large house of worship, the soft tones of his voice would reach the farthest corner, and penetrate every ear. He never used notes in preaching; but his self-possession never failed him. His voice was so deep, sonorous and tender, that its capacity for the expression of pathos was unsurpassed. In his Scripture readings and in reciting hymns his power was always felt. His favorite hymns and selections of Scripture were sometimes pronounced with such effect that the most highly educated and discriminating person would never forget the impressions of such readings.

His appearance was commanding, though he was neither

stout nor tall, compared with the average of well-formed men. His African skin and hair compensated by a face of intelligence superior to the limitations of his race. His hair was of the clearest white, and, though truly African, it rose in unwonted profusion, giving him the presence of a venerable patriarch. His teeth were sound and beautifully clear; his sight and hearing as good to the last as in middle life, and his lower limbs only began seriously to fail him on reaching his one hundredth year. In some of his glowing pulpit efforts his face and whole person were irradiated with intelligence, and one could not hear him at such times without feeling himself within the influence of a superior mind.

In the last year of Mr. Marshall's life, it became an object of extreme desire with him to erect a new and better house of worship for the church which he felt he soon must leave. The old house (being built of wood) had become much dilapidated, and the city ordinance would not allow another wooden building to be erected on that spot, which was really an eligible one. Feeling the importance of his cause, after making some progress in Savannah and its vicinity, Mr. Marshall resolved upon another journey to the North, which he had frequently visited in the days and in the presence of Washington. He was accompanied by his wife, and he hoped also to receive some benefit by consulting physicians there for his infirmities, which neither nature nor medicine could much longer resist. He was respectfully received by some of the most prominent of the New York clergy of various denominations. He preached with acceptance in several of the Baptist pulpits,—among them Dr. Cone's and Dr. Magoon's,—and in those of other denominations, one of which was that of Dr. Krebs; and very soon he received in that city about six hundred dollars for his object.

But his race was run. He was soon admonished to return home at once, if he wished to see his own people again and to die among them. Extremely weak, and every day becoming more unwell, he reached Richmond in his journey by land, and thence he could proceed no farther. Having a letter to the Rev. B. Manly, Jr., President of the Richmond Female College, he desired his direction to some place where he could stay. Mr. Manly promptly and cheerfully provided for him at his own house, where the old man lingered for more than a month, evincing the same gracious affections and the same superior traits of character which had crowned and graced his life for so many years. Here, on the 8th of December, 1856, he breathed his last. His remains were carefully conveyed to Savannah, where his funeral took place on Sabbath, the 14th of the same month. The demonstrations of interest on this last solemn occasion of his earthly history were unequaled by anything of the kind in that city or region where a colored person was concerned. An immense procession of about a mile long, with fifty-eight carriages—either loaned by families in the city to their servants or other colored friends, or occupied (as in many instances) by respectable white people themselves,—followed him from his church to his grave. His funeral sermon was preached by the Rev. Thomas Ronbeau, pastor of the First Baptist Church in Savannah. Not more than two or three funerals, whether civil or military, and those of the most distinguished citizens of the place, have witnessed so large a collection of people in the course of the present century in that city as followed to the last resting place the remains of the centenarian, Andrew Marshall.

Yours respectfully,
J. P. TUSTIN.

CHAPTER XI.

Rev. William J. Campbell—His Long and Useful Life—A King among His People.

Rev. William J. Campbell was born January 1st, 1812. He was born a slave. He traveled extensively with his master, and thereby had an opportunity of learning much by traveling. He was baptized by Rev. Andrew C. Marshall, about 1830, and licensed to preach by the church on February 4th, 1855. He was assistant to Rev. Andrew C. Marshall, and when Mr. Marshall went North to beg money for the church he left Mr. Campbell in charge of the church. When he died in Richmond, on his return, Mr. Campbell was appointed by the church to accompany his remains to Savannah. Soon after this he was ordained by the Executive Board of the Sunsbury Baptist Association and called to the pastorate of the First African Baptist Church. This was in 1857. He immediately entered upon the work which the venerable Father Marshall had laid down. He tore down the wooden building and erected the beautiful brick edifice which was in the heart of Father Marshall to do before he left the walks of men. The people rallied to him with the same earnestness and love (if not greater) as they did to Father Marshall. No man ever had more influence over a people than Reverend Campbell. He, however, had his troubles, too. He was accused of stealing cotton on the Bay about this time. It had a bad effect upon the church, and gloom once more spread her drapery over this great church. This, however, was proven to be false, and the sun of peace and prosperity again leaped forth from his hiding place and shone with resplendent brilliancy and glory upon a heavy-hearted people, and kissing away their sorrows they went on their way rejoicing.

Rev. W. J. Campbell was a man of keen foresight, iron will, and a wonderful executive ability. He was a good preacher. He had read much, and well remembered what he read. His preaching was on the running commentary order, often taking a whole chapter for his subject. He had a peculiar sonorous voice, and spoke to the hearts of men. If a person once heard him line out a hymn he would not soon forget it. His prayer meeting lectures were sublime. Bishop Holsey said of him: "The grandest lectures I ever heard were Reverend Campbell's prayer meeting lectures." The people were satisfied to see him in the pulpit. His people would rather hear him give out a hymn than hear anybody else preach, let him be never so eloquent. He was as black as he well could have been, but he was neat, handsome, polite, and extremely dignified. Whatever he felt like saying in the pulpit he said. He was not afraid to tell the truth as it was in Jesus. He was for many years a deacon and a member of the choir. He was a good singer, and therefore enforced good singing in his choir. He was as much beloved by the white people almost as by the colored. Sinners quaked before him. The church soon ran up to 4,000 members. He controlled the surrounding country. He controlled from Savannah to Darien, Brunswick, and all the country adjacent to Savannah. His praise was on the tongues of everybody, and especially the saints. His people would do just what he told them to do. When he spoke it was law. If he said a thing was wrong, all the world could not make his people believe otherwise. It would have been an insult to have attempted it.

Reverend Campbell was widely known and equally respected. The church usually gave him three months' vacation each year, and sent a servant with him. He received as a salary $100 per month and everything he wanted. He was a favorite of Northern visitors; they preferred going to his church to any other in the city. He was in the organization of the Zion Baptist Association, the Missionary Baptist Convention of Georgia, and the Mount Olive Baptist Association. In all of these he played a conspicuous part. The people around the coast would hail his coming among them as a priest. He had twelve or fourteen prayer houses connected with the church, which were as large as many churches. Over these he appointed leaders, who reported to him monthly their condition and collections. To these societies—for by that name they are known—he would go at his leisure and they would always prepare a great feast for him. He was kind and loving to his officers, and controlled the church, absolutely, for twenty-three years with a four page constitution. In most things he was law to the people, and from his decision no one dared appeal. As he grew older, he was troubled with an impediment in his speech. He finally got so he could not speak without much difficulty. About this time a serious trouble broke out in the church: for this emergency too much of his strength had been spent and old age and paralysis had done their work too well. That powerful voice the people had long obeyed was now so palsied that it fell without effect, and the enemies had decidedly the advantage and they never failed to use it. An awful trouble broke out in the church, such, perhaps, as few churches in all ages have ever witnessed, or need ever have. It was not the fault of Rev. W. J. Campbell. When the trouble started he was in Griffin, Ga. If there is any blame upon Mr. Campbell it is that he left the church. The church never turned him off; the church could not have had the heart to do that. He was accused of taking sides with Deacon Robert P. Young, his spiritual child, who was accused of stealing money from the church. Rev. Mr. Campbell was true to a friend, and if he is chargeable at all it is due to his disposition to be perfectly true to a friend.

Reverend Campbell baptized several thousand persons. He was purely a gospel preacher, and gave his attention to nothing else. His house was a place of peace and comfort. He was brought up with rich white people and had a remarkably good taste. As a ruler he was strict and able. As a pastor he was attentive and loving. He understood men, and there was no fear of them in his composition.

He lived to a good old age, and he will be remembered with tenderest affection while memory holds her place or saints in Savannah live. We will refer to him again in another chapter in considering the church trouble.

CHAPTER XII.

The Great Trouble of 1877—The Cause—Its Fierceness—The Split—The Call of Rev. Gibbons and the Death of Rev. W. J. Campbell, and the Final Settlement.

In 1877, while Rev. W. J. Campbell was away on his vacation, the great trouble began. The cause of this trouble was the report that Deacon Robert P. Young had stolen money from the church. There is doubt about the correctness of this charge when all things are calmly considered. Mr. Willis Harris saw Deacon Young put the money in front of the organ, and after his back was turned took it away. Deacon Young, after the communion was over, reported to Deacon F. M. Williams what had occurred. · Deacon Williams told him to say nothing about it; perhaps some one had taken it to tease him; but if he did not get it to make it known to the brethren on finance night, which was Tuesday night following. Deacon Young took the advice of Deacon Williams, but on Monday the news of this occurrence was all over the streets. Mr. Willis Harris brought the money to the church the next following Thursday night and attempted to give it to the church, but was prevented by Deacon Richard Baker, who opposed it, and to avoid trouble on that night the money was kept and presented to the church in a special conference on the following Sunday. There were $22.32 in the basket. Mr. Harris reported that he caught Deacon Young stealing money. This very naturally created quite a sensation, and intense excitement prevailed.

While it is not clear that Deacon Young meant to steal the money it must be acknowledged that his conduct was very suspicious and justly aroused the displeasure of the church. He should have made the matter known to all of the brethren while they were counting the money, and a search for the missing basket should have been inaugurated; and should that have failed, announcements from the pulpit would have been in order. From the fact that this was not done rather weakened Deacon Young's case. While Deacon Young was decidedly wrong, Mr. Willis Harris was decidedly wrong also, and his action was totally at variance with the precepts of the gospel. It was his duty to have gone to Deacon Young and labored with him as the gospel enjoins before it was in order to tell the church. Twenty-two dollars and thirty-two cents were but a trifling affair as compared with the harm which came out of this case. Then, besides, Mr. Willis Harris himself was a most notorious thief.

The truth of the matter seems to be this: Mr. Willis Harris had not been long deposed from the office of deacon, and supposing that Mr. Young wielded a deal of influence in bringing about his deposition, he watched for and coveted every opportunity to get even with him. It is more than likely that he craved an opportunity to vent the prejudice of a malignant heart upon Deacon Young. Since he was actuated from improper motives his testimony in this case should be viewed in that light. It is not strange that this report should have excited the members. The deacons should have acted wiser.

Deacon Robert P. Young was tried before the church and made an humble christian apology, and his carelessness in handling the church's money was pardoned. He explained rather than confessed. It was not required for him to confess stealing the money. Deacon Richard Baker contended that Deacon Young ought not to make the apology. Whereas he had been requested by the church to resign, and had promised to do so, Deacon Baker contended that he should continue to discharge the duties of a deacon. Deacon Young attempted to carry out the instructions of Deacon Baker. This started the war in right earnest. The lay brethren then determined that Deacon Young should not pass the sacrament. This was well caucussed.

In the Conference of October 22, 1877, Mr. J. C. Williams moved to reconsider the motion passed in the August Conference pardoning Deacon R. P. Young. This was ruled out upon the ground that he made the motion to expel in August and voted in the negative.

Mr. J. C. Habersham then made the motion that Mr. Williams' motion be sustained, and it was carried. This brought Deacon Young back under the discipline of the church. This was wrong, of course, as no member should be pardoned by a church at one meeting and tried at another meeting for the same offense, except some new developments had come to the knowledge of the church. However, the motion of Mr. Habersham was a virtual appeal from the decision of the chair. This is generally admissible, but on this occasion it was at variance with every principle of justice and decidedly wrong.

The Conference adjourned at this stage, leaving Deacon Young under the charge from which the church had once freed him. The first Sunday in November being the communion, many of the brethren had decided that Deacon Young, being under a charge, should not carry around the communion. Several of the lay brethren waited on the officers that morning at prayer meeting, informing them that they had learned that it was the intention of some to have Deacon Young carry around the sacrament in the afternoon, and urged the officers to wait on Rev. Campbell and beg him not to allow Deacon Young to officiate in the communion. At 3 P. M. of the same day, when Mr. Campbell called the officers to pass to them the bread, Mr. James B. Lewis and Mr. Joshua Hicks arose and in open church said: "Mr. Campbell, you cannot give the communion to Young to pass around because he is under the dealing of the church." Mr. Campbell said to Deacon Young: "Go on, if they want to stop you, let them do it." Deacon Young took the communion and went to the choir, where he was accustomed to carry the communion. Mr. Alexander Rannair, according to a previous understanding of his followers, shut the door of the choir and said to Deacon Young: "Young, you know you are under a charge, and we don't want any bread from you up here." This created quite a sensation and not a little confusion in the church. Mr. Rannair had no earthly right to take this step in the church of the Lord Jesus Christ. If he did not want to accept the wine at the hand of Deacon Young he had the privilege that never has been denied a man—to refuse it. Nothing can justify this rash and inconsiderate course. Neither had Mr. James B. Lewis nor Mr. Joshua Hicks the right to take any such steps as they did, calling their pastor in open church and affirming that Deacon Young should not carry around the communion. It showed that the excitement had been worked up to a very high pitch. It is true that Mr. Campbell was wrong in giving the communion to Deacon Young under the then existing circumstances. If there was a charge against him he had no right to call him to pass the holy communion to those who held him charged. No wise apology can be given for this indiscretion. The proper way for them to have done was to have refused accepting it, and brought the matter up in the next conference. Deacon Young, if he had the proper christian spirit, would not have attempted to pass around the holy eucharist, knowing that a large number of the membership opposed it and entertained doubts as to his innocence of the charge of stealing money. This course of procedure upon the part of some of the members showed that the heretofore powerful pastor was rapidly losing power over his people. If the pastor had taken a second sober thought he might have acted a little more cautiously, and thereby have averted this dreadful storm. It should have been evident to him that he would not have the strength to pull through it.

On Tuesday, of the same week, Deacons Richard Baker. P. H. Butler and R. P. Young swore out warrants against the following brethren: March. Haynes, John E. Grant. John C. Habersham, Alexander Rannair and Samuel Roberts. These were tried; but Messrs. Alexander Rannair, Joshua Hicks and James B. Lewis were found guilty and fined $10 each: the others were acquitted. This did not settle the trouble. These brethren were only more determined in their fight. This was wrong in the deacons, and only served to make bad matters worse.

At the conference of November 19th, 1877, these deacons, having been notified to be present, and failing, were expelled. This was rather hasty. It was now evident that the war had begun. The brethren gave bond and employed counsel and went to law. This case created almost universal excitement. The courts were baffled for five or six years, and finally recommended a compromise upon the introduction of a bill of equity by the followers of Rev. W. J. Campbell.

The day he left the church can never be forgotten. When many who were in the church ceased to hear him and honor his gray locks, he arose and said: "My children, all who are with me follow me." He left the church, and as might be expected some of the best members of the church followed their aged chieftain. Old age and paralysis had done their work on him, and he was rapidly fading away. The party that had possession of the church met in rapid succession to make sure their position. The followers of Mr. Campbell were none the less assiduous and determined. They had caucuses in rapid succession. The leader on Mr. Campbell's side was R. P. Young. He furnished the brains for the party, as the pastor was now almost an invalid. This was a feast for the lawyers, and they harvested richly from the disaffection of the First African Baptist Church. As men do not generally care how long a good paying position lasts. it is quite natural that the lawyers had no special objection to the continuation of the case in court.

On the 17th of December, 1877, Rev. W. J. Campbell left the church. He had been requested to take the chair and preside over the conference, but declined, whereupon Deacon F. M. Williams was called to the chair. After the minutes of November 19th, 1877, were read, he (Mr. Campbell) arose and said: "That is all I come for, to hear that minute." Deacon F. M. Williams begged him not to leave, but this was useless.

When he had made up his mind to do a thing remonstrances were useless. He simply commanded his followers to follow him, and many of them did so. When he was going out, Mr. Peter Houston, who had some difference with Mr. Campbell because he had been expelled some years prior for issuing a warrant against one of the sisters, met him at the door and said: "Mr. Campbell, what did I tell you; when I would be coming in you would be going out." Mr. Campbell replied: "Do, Houston, for God's sake let me alone." Mr. Houston told him this years ago when he was turned out of the church, and did actually live to see it. But his (Houston's) end was not at all glorious. He was one of Mr. Campbell's shrewdest and ablest opposers. But he came to his death in a mysterious, inglorious way. It is not positively known whether he was murdered or committed suicide. He was, however, heartbroken by domestic troubles and disaffection. Mr. Houston's prophesy of Mr. Campbell came true, and so did Mr. Campbell's prophesy of Mr. Houston come true. Mr. Campbell said no good would follow Mr. Houston. For several years Mr. Houston had terrible family troubles. Many of the members of the church meant to have their way, but very few of them wanted Mr. Campbell to leave the church. Mr. Campbell went out into the square and addressed his followers. Mr. L. J. Pettigrew, a prominent character on the side of the majority, went out and begged Mr. Campbell to return to the church, but to no avail.

On Thursday night following this Conference Mr. Campbell, however, returned to the church, accompanied by Rev. James M. Simms and Rev. U. L. Houston. The brethren not knowing that he would return, had requested Licentiate John Nesbit to preach. Mr. Campbell not knowing this had invited Rev. U. L. Houston to preach. This Mr. Campbell stated to the church, whereupon Brethren Joseph C. Williams and Lewis J. Pettigrew objected, stating that Brother Nesbit had been invited to preach, and that they preferred to hear him to Rev. Houston, and Rev. Houston said that he would rather hear Brother Nesbit himself. This Mr. Campbell agreed to, and Brother Nesbit preached. When the services were over, Rev. James M. Simms stated to the church that he was invited by Mr. Campbell, his cousin, to be with him to-night, and expressing great sorrow for the trouble then existing in the church. Deacon R. P. Young, who was the clerk of the church, came forward to read out the letters for persons that had been sent in the care of the church, which was the custom, when Mr. March Haines and Mr. John E. Grant objected to his reading them as he was under a charge. This, of course, was wrong. There could have been no earthly objection to his reading the letters, since he was still a member of the church, and as reading out the letters was not performing any of his christian privileges. After this Mr. Campbell entered the church only once more. On that occasion Rev. U. L. Houston preached, and they did what they called "burying the devil," but as he was not quite dead his resurrection followed very soon thereafter.

On that memorable night Mr. Campbell sang this very appropriate hymn. He could line out a hymn as few men could, and it had a magic effect, but, alas! how soon forgotten:

> "Let-party names no more
> The Christian world o'erspread;
> Gentiles and Jews and bond and free
> Are one in Christ, their head.
> Among the saints on earth
> Let mutual love be found —
> Heirs of the same inheritance,
> With mutual blessings crowned.
> Thus will the church below
> Resemble that above,
> Where streams of endless pleasure flow,
> And every heart is love."

The singing of this hymn had such a wonderful effect that everything seemed all right, and that this grand old body was once more united, but not so. Satan had done his work too well. He was not so easily removed. The party that had left the church were holding divine services at Mr. W. G. Clark's house, on Margaret street in Yamacraw. They worshipped there for two months. There they held a conference and prepared all their minutes and wrote them up, dating them as if adopted at the First African Baptist Church on the following Sunday. They came to the church and after the close of the services one of their number moved to resolve into a conference. This, of course, was carried. While one of their number was down on his knees praying, Sexton Salbury Morse removed the table and their prepared minutes were grabbed by Alexander Miller, who fled with them. Deacon Young and others were arrested. This was a final opening of the great war. On both sides arrests were made. The whole city was most intensely excited. Rev. George Gibbons was the adviser of the party that held the possession of the church. Of course they were in the majority or they could scarcely have kept the church. There were many who had been turned out during the administration of the Rev. W. J. Campbell who rushed into the church at this terrible crisis. Of course they were not prepared to sympathize with Rev. W. J. Campbell, nor did they come in to help him. Mr. Campbell was losing more and more. From the house of

Mr. W. G. Clark they removed to the "Grits Mills" and for one year they worshipped there. Their increase was not very great, nor was the increase of the majority very great. From the "Grits Mill" they removed to the "Beach Institute." The Rev. W. J. Campbell was too feeble to give them much service in the way of preaching and scarcely any pastoral visits. Several efforts were made to get him back to the church, and one time it was thought that they had accomplished that end. The majority assembled in the church to welcome home their venerable father, their love for whom these years of bitter feelings, disaffections and many wrong doings had not effaced. But Deacon Richard Baker, R. P. Young and others would not allow him to return to his people, bringing his people with him. This would have put an end to the trouble. It appears that he did again enter the church. We insert the following report of the deacons of the majority, which speaks for itself:

OFFICERS' REPORT.

" We, your servants, in whose hands you have placed the affairs of your church to take care of and look after them, seeing the condition of your church at present, feel it our duty to present matters to you in their true light; the remedy is then with you as a sovereign church, and if you, as a church, fail to do your duty in the matter, then the fault lies at your own door. It is our duty to present the matter to you in its true nature, and your duty to act. In November last Rev. William J. Campbell, as pastor of this church, allowed himself to be accessory to the prosecution before the courts of the land of fifteen (15) members of this church in good standing, and did go into open court and swear to the fact that the members were guilty of crimes that we all knew them to be innocent of, placing them, according to his own testimony, virtually in the State's prison, depriving them of the comforts of their homes and the freedom of their religion. Responding to the call of men whom the church had rebuked for their misdeeds he again appeared before the magistrates in December last and openly disregarded the actions of this church by swearing that certain men were clerk and deacons of this church whom this church had expelled and whose expulsion was confirmed in his presence. He then appeared at our regular conference, held on the 19th day of December, and on being asked to take the chair refused, and after making some remarks in regard to taking names, picked up his hat and stick, and after saying that he would not give the snap of his finger for what the church was doing walked out. For each and all of these acts, which were extremely offensive to the church and unbecoming to the pastor of a church, the church demanded satisfaction.

"A committee was appointed to wait upon him, demanding satisfaction for the church. This satisfaction he failed to give. After the report of the committee was rendered it was decided by the church that his case be taken up at the regular conference in January, and he was so notified, and was also notified that he was to abstain from exercising the duties of pastor of this church until that time. On the first Sunday in January, after all arrangements had been made for the administration of the Lord's Supper, he sent a message to us by Brethren Jas. M. Simms and Robert Miflin, stating that in thinking over the case of Rev. Abram Burke he was led to feel that he was getting old and feeble, and as he did not know how long he had to live he wanted to come to peace with his church and commune with them on the first Sunday in the new year. The matter was taken before the church and it was decided to hear from the pastor. He then arose, and after stating his inability to do much talking, referred the matter to Mr. Simms, whom, he said, would speak for him. Mr. Simms then arose, and after stating what Mr. Campbell had said to him in regard to Rev. Burke, said that our pastor requested him to say to the church that he was sorry that anything had occurred to cause the church and himself to be at variance; but that he was here with the intention of coming to peace with his church, and that he desired that by-gones should be by-gones and that all old things should be buried forever.

"A resolution was accordingly offered and carried by unanimous vote that everything from to-day be dropped.

"In putting the motion, Rev. George Gibbons asked the pastor if he meant by what he said to recognize all that the church had done to be right, to which the pastor replied, Yes. The motion was then carried as above stated amid much shouting and gladness. The table was then turned over to him by Mr. Gibbons, when the pastor proceeded to administer the sacrament. He also appeared at the church on Thursday evening and confirmed what he said on the Sunday at the sacrament table, and said that he meant all that he said.

"In the week preceding our last communion he was waited on by two of our number to know what arrangements he had made about the communion. In reply to the question he wanted to know of them how could he give them the communion when they were under bonds. Desiring to indulge him as much as possible, another committee still was appointed to wait upon him. He told that committee that he did not recognize them as deacons, and that they had taken the advantage of him, and told them that he did not recognize what the church had done, and declares that he never did recognize their action, and told them that he would come and give them the communion but would not take it himself, and declares that he will never be satisfied with the church or come to peace until the church undo all that she has done in his absence by taking back all those that have been expelled and turning out all those that have been taken in. Then, he says, he will be satisfied and not before.

"As we have said at the outset, it is our indispensable duty to lay this matter before you in its true nature. In coming before the communion and saying and doing what he did, and then going right around and denying these very things, declaring that he did not do them, is an offence that should not be tolerated in a christian church. He has shown himself to be guilty of a willful falsehood. It is with great regret that we are compelled to present this matter to you in this manner, but we have no alternative. For to allow the matter to remain as it has been for the last three or four months would be almost to commit the unpardonable sin. We see our pulpit desecrated by slander and abuse, and even our communion table polluted by wickedness in high places, and all of it is simply because we have allowed our animal affections to get the better of us and cause us to flinch from our plain duty. The fan is in our hands and if we fail to thoroughly purge the floor then the sin lies at our own door. If we put the rod in the hands of another to scourge us, then we must bear the scourging without a murmur. As your servants, we have endeavored to do our duty. We lay the matter before you for your consideration and action, and can only say that unless some action be taken by you in regard to the matter we cannot be responsible for the peace and safety of your church. The points that we would have you more particularly look into are those running from the first Sunday in January down to the present time. Judge of the case and act upon its true merits."

Several efforts were made to have the matter amicably settled, but it seems that the fire of dissension had gotten too much headway. A council was called at the instance of both sides, consisting of Rev. T. Harley, Deacons Howard, Reid and Fairchild (of the white church), and Rev. Alexander Harris. But this council proved ineffectual, because some of the parties on the side of the majority opposed Mr. Fairchild, led by Deacon Joseph C. Williams, upon the ground that he was partial toward Mr. Campbell, and they feared that he would not do justice to Mr. Campbell's opposers. The day the majority gained possession of the church was a stormy day for this old church, and will long be remembered with interest.

Deacons Baker, Young and Butler had determined that no conference should be held that day and commanded the sexton not to open the church, and had engaged policemen to prevent the opposition from entering the church, charging that they intended a riot. But as the sexton was a secret disciple of the opposition they had him hid away near the church, and at a given signal he was to appear with the keys. Mr. J. C. Williams asked a policeman what he was doing there, who informed him that he was there to prevent a riot. Mr. Williams then asked him was he sent there to prevent the church from holding its conference? He replied, No. Then Mr. Williams asked him if he would arrest the man whom he saw creating the disturbance? He said, Yes. The sexton was then signalled to appear with the keys. As he came Deacons Young, Baker and Butler demanded the keys, and upon the sexton refusing to surrender them attempted to take them. Mr. Williams then called the policeman's attention, stating that these are the men who are creating the disturbance, and they were arrested, thus falling into their own trap. This gave the majority the possession of the church. They entered and forever afterwards held it.

Notwithstanding all this bitter feeling and wholesale expulsion so tender was the feeling for Mr. Campbell that he was never expelled. Deacon Joseph C. Williams contended that the pulpit should not be touched. Mr. Campbell could have re-entered the church at any time he wished without disciplinary action upon the part of the church. Mr. Joseph C. Williams deserves great credit for his wisdom and far-seeing sagacity in preventing the expulsion of Mr. Campbell. Had he been expelled perhaps the breach would never have been healed. This act shows the profoundest sympathy for the venerable father. Virtually Mr. Campbell died a member of the First African Baptist Church. He would, however, have been declared expelled but for Deacon Joseph C. Williams, who had a sacred reverence for the pulpit. Deacon Williams regarded Mr. Campbell as God's anointed, which he felt that should not be touched. He was willing to expel everybody else but the pastor. He kept the church from making a great mistake. The thanks of the church are due him. This proved him to be an able leader.

As harsh as the report from the officers is, no intimation of Mr. Campbell's expulsion is in it:

THE COMPROMISE.

"Richard Baker *et al.*, Complainants, and Peter Houston *et al.*, Defendants, to compromise and heal all dissension and division in the First African Baptist Church, which have existed for some time past:

"It is agreed that the portion of the membership of the church worshipping in the brick church, known as the First African Baptist Church, will invite the portion of the membership of the church worshipping in the "Beach Institute" to reunite with them as one body and congregation without any deprivation of any church privileges as members thereof, and without any disciplinary action whatever. That the officers of the First African Baptist Church worshipping in the "Beach Institute" voluntarily relinquish and resign such offices, and the said portion of the membership worshipping in the "Beach Institute" will accept the pastor, officers and trustees, and organization as it now exists, in the congregation in said First African Baptist Church building, and accept the invitation above extended to them.

"It is further agreed that this compromise be made the judgment of the court, if necessary; and that the same shall not be made by other party a precedent of church government, but as a settlement of this particular case."

This was agreed to and signed by the leaders of both parties.
In conformity to this wise conciliatory compromise the majority addressed the minority, as follows:

"SAVANNAH, February 8th, 1884.
"*To the First African Baptist Church, Beach Institute, Savannah, Ga.:*

"DEAR BRETHREN—At a special conference of the First African Baptist Church, Franklin Square, held last evening for the purpose of considering the recommendations as presented by the attorneys for both parties, in reference to the matter now pending between ourselves before the Superior Court of this city (of which you have a copy), was at this special conference read and confirmed by an almost unanimous vote.

"In conformity thereto, we hereby extend your Christian body a cordial invitation, requesting your presence at the next regular conference of the church, to be held on the 17th instant, at

3 o'clock P. M., at which time and place you will again have the opportunity of church privilege.
"Awaiting an early reply, we remain yours in Christ.
"REV. GEORGE GIBBONS. Pastor.
"Attest: C. H. EBBS, Church Clerk."

REPLY TO THE FOREGOING.

"SAVANNAH, February 10, 1884.
"*To the Pastor, Officers and Members of the First African Baptist "Church:*

"DEAR BRETHREN—At a special conference held by us on the above date, for the purpose of considering the recommendations as presented by the attorneys of both factions in reference to the matter that is pending between you and us in the Superior Court of this county, of which you have a copy of the same. We have adopted the document as agreed to by us in the matter, and also received your invitation requesting us to be present at your next regular conference of the church to be held on 17th instant, at 3 o'clock P. M., at which time we shall obtain privilege as members of one body again. Brethren, we will be present at the hour appointed with the books, deeds and titles of the First African Baptist Church according to our agreement made in the matter.

" Done in conference meeting.
"P. H. BUTLER, Moderator.
"Attest: R. P. YOUNG, Church Clerk."

This shows that each side had enough of the war. The few that stuck out were obstinate. Mr. Campbell, the leader, died October 11th, 1880. Doubtless his troubles came upon him too severely for his advanced age. It had much to do with hurrying the end. The crowd that followed him stuck to him till the last. Mr. Campbell's desire was to be buried by his people from his church that he had labored so hard to build. When he died his faithful followers made the fact known to the church. The church was willing to have him buried from his old home, but Rev. George Gibbons, who was pastor of the majority, objected to large nails, it is claimed, being driven in the pulpit and in other places in the church. But it does seem that a compromise as to the size of nails could have been easily effected and tacks substituted for the nails, or even strings might have been used. If there was not a deep, bitter feeling underlying this on one side or the other, doubtless this course would have been pursued. Rev. Gibbons being a gospel minister, it would seem, might have advised these heart-broken friends that the nails were too large, and that they ought to get tacks. This could have been done in such a tender way that would have won eternally their affectionate sympathy and coöperation. Then there would not have been any chance for the idea to gain foothold that Rev. Gibbons did not want the church draped for Mr. Campbell as though he was pastor, and as he was yet alive he felt that he was pastor, and no one had the right to be honored as such. It was most natural that a man should feel this way. Human nature is human nature, even in a Christian minister. Those who went to drape the church should have exercised more patience and doubtless they would have accomplished their purpose. In the heat of excitement the body of the venerable dead man was carried to the First Bryan Baptist Church in Yamacraw, having obtained permission from Rev. U. L. Houston, the pastor.

The parties concerned should have taken more pains to try to unite in doing honor to this grand old man. If there was no objection to this old servant being buried from the church for which he toiled so hard for years, all petty differences might have been waived and becoming honor done to this man of God. It is quite natural, also, that those who wished to drape the church were rather sensitive and most any act of Rev. Gibbon's would have been severely criticised. In fact, they felt sore toward him, and rather looked for unkindness, presuming, of course, that Mr. Gibbons was unfriendly to Mr. Campbell, their father and leader in Christ Jesus. Had Mr. Gibbons suggested the manner of draping the church for the noted dead, it would have tended greatly to unify the people and have generated better feelings. It would not have destroyed one whit of his power or eclipsed in the least his glory, but might have tended more to the glory of God. This act was perhaps inconsiderate. Rev. Frank Quarles, of Atlanta, was wired, who reached Savannah time enough to preach the funeral sermon of Rev. W. J. Campbell. He was followed to his last resting place by a host of heart-broken weepers. Thus ended the life of the most influential man that has ever lived in Savannah.

After his death frequently members from the Beach Institute returned to the old church. It was evident that the war was over. The minority continued out until February 17th, 1884, when they returned in a body, surrendering all claims of offices and the church waiving all discipline in their cases. That rainy Sunday can never be forgotten. Just before they reached the church they sung in a most solemn manner—

> "Blest be the tie that binds
> Our hearts in christian love;
> The fellowship of kindred minds
> Is liked to that above.
> Before our Father's throne
> We pour our ardent prayers;
> Our fears, our hopes, our aims are one,
> Our comforts and our cares.
> We share our mutual woes,
> Our mutual burdens bear,
> And often for each other flows
> The sympathizing tea'," &c., &c.

The entrance into the church was hailed by a large, joyous and weeping congregation. Deacon Baker did not return and perhaps never will. Four years have now passed since that day and he has not been even to the church. Deacon Young was soon restored to the choir and made its president. During the six years of trouble several of the societies of the church had been organized into churches. The grand body being once more united a more pleasing future was opened up to the grand old body. God helped her.

The following is inserted for the information of the reader, which will show some of Mr. Campbell's troubles in his early ministry and the split of 1859:

"SAVANNAH, GEORGIA, } To all whom it may concern.
"Chatham County. } Greeting:

"Know all men by these presents that we, the First African Baptist Church of Savannah, and State of Georgia, influenced as we trust by the grace of God, through our Lord and Saviour Jesus Christ, did in the year of our Lord one thousand eight hundred and fifty-five see, with deep regret and submission to our God, that our father, Andrew C. Marshall, for many years our pastor, laboring with us in the gospel ministry, had become very feeble and needed some help in the gospel ministry, thought it expedient to call to his assistance our Brother Wm. J. Campbell, whom, after being duly examined upon his sound doctrinal faith and belief in the church by the Rev. Henry O. Wyer, Rev. Thomas Rambout and T. J. Thelkeld, and found to be such an one as have been taught by the spirit of God, did farther, on the twenty-fourth day of February, A. D. one thousand eight hundred and fifty-six, call the assembly of the people together and in their presence and before Almighty God see him ordained to the gospel ministry. Our beloved brethren Rev. Henry O. Wyer, R. W. Winston and J. B. Stiteler officiated in this most solemn ceremony, the ordination of our beloved Brother Wm. J. Campbell. He labored with us, assisting our beloved father and shepherd, Andrew C. Marshall, until our God was pleased to call our Father Marshall to Himself in heaven to rest from his labors. In December, A. D. one thousand eight hundred and fifty-six, he died, and on the 18th day of February, A. D. one thousand eight hundred and fifty-seven, this church, after prayer to Almighty God for Divine instructions, called our beloved Brother Wm. J. Campbell to the pastoral care of this church, whom we do pray our God to keep in his useful and prosperous ministry for many and fruitful years is the prayer of his brethren always. Amen.'

"This document was ordered to be drawn by the officers of this church now acting in the deaconship, to-wit: Brethren R. McNish, John Burney, Samuel Miller, Friday Gibbons, London Small, Murray Monroe, George Gibbons, Cæsar Verdeir and James Simms.

"Done in Conference, February 19th, A. D. 1860.
"R. S. HARDWICK, Moderator.
"JAMES M. SIMMS, Clerk."

"FIRST AFRICAN BAPTIST CHURCH OF SAVANNAH,
"TUESDAY NIGHT, April 20, 1858.

"Certain causes growing out of differences of opinion among the members of the First African Baptist Church of Savannah having resulted in the interference of the civil authorities in so far as to impose certain restrictions embarrassing to the customary religious rights and privileges of said church, His Honor Richard Wayne, Mayor of the city of Savannah, to the end that the differences in said church be reconciled, and that said restrictions be removed, under his seal of office issued the following note, viz.:

"'MAYOR'S OFFICE,
"'CITY OF SAVANNAH, 17th April, 1858.

"'If the following named gentlemen will attend the First African Church to-morrow, Sunday, April 18th, 1858, at half-past 12 o'clock P. M., the restrictions now hanging over said church will be removed for the time being. The object is to have a final settlement of the difficulty in the church. The said gentlemen not to interfere, that is, to take sides with either party.
"'R. WAYNE, Mayor.

{ SEAL } "'Attest: EDW'D G. WILSON, Clerk of Council.

"'To the following gentlemen, Executive Committee of the
"'Sunbury Baptist Association, viz.: General Rabun, Rev.
"'Mr. Winston, Rev. Mr. Daniel, Rev. Mr. F. R. Sweat,
"'Lewis C. Tebeau, J. H. H. ———.'"

"In accordance with the said note (his Honor the Mayor having subsequently issued an order changing the time of holding the meeting from Sunday noon to Tuesday night) a special conference was held in the church on Tuesday night, April 20th, 1858. The Rev. L. G. Daniels and Mr. James G. Hogg, members of the Executive Committee of the Sunbury Baptist Association, were present, the other members of said committee, as named in the foregoing note of his Honor the Mayor, were absent, they having in a note to the Mayor declined attending the meeting.

"A motion being made and seconded, it was unanimously voted that Mr. R. L. Hardwick take the chair, and that Mr. L. J. B. Fairchild act as secretary of the meeting. Mr. Hardwick in the chair, the meeting was opened with prayer by the Rev. L. G. Daniel. The minutes of the regular conference, held March 21st, 1858, were read and confirmed by a unanimous vote. The following resolutions were regularly proposed and adopted by a unanimous vote of the church, viz.:

"'*Resolved*, That this church respectfully, but positively, declines accepting or adopting the constitution, covenant, confession of faith and by-laws referred to in the minutes of the conference held in this church on March 21st, 1858.

"'*Resolved*, That our brethren, Robert McNish, Robert Verdier and John Burney be a committee to prepare a constitution, covenant, confession of faith and by-laws for the future government of this church, and that said committee report the same to our next meeting.'

"John Burney, a member of the church, in a few appropriate remarks touching the want of harmony between the pastor and deacons, suggested the propriety of the resignation of both pastor and deacons. Whereupon the pastor, Wm. J. Campbell, responded in terms expressing a desire to do anything in his power to assist the church in her efforts to be released from embarrassment and to promote the religion of Christ, and yielding to the suggestion made, resigned his pastorate of the church. Robert Verdier, the only deacon of the church present, also replied to the suggestion in like terms and resigned his office as acting deacon. A motion was made and seconded not to accept the resignation of William J. Campbell as pastor of the church, and the vote being taken the motion unanimously obtained. It was also moved and seconded that the resignation of Robert Verdier as an acting deacon of this church be accepted, which vote unanimously prevailed.

"The following preamble and resolutions were read and adopted. On taking the vote it appeared there was one dissenting vote:

"'WHEREAS, There is an evident want of a happy coöperation between the deacons and pastor of this church touching the management of the affairs of the church generally, and whereas a hearty co-operation between a pastor and his deacons is essential to the peace and prosperity of the church, and whereas a suggestion has been made that both pastor and deacons resign in their office, in the view that the church might have freedom to select by her vote a pastor and deacons that would be more likely to consummate the desires and interests of the body at large, and whereas only our pastor and one of our deacons have responded to the suggestion of resignation, the rest of the deacons being absent from this meeting, when, in the judgment of this meeting, it was their manifest duty to be here, thus showing no disposition to be reconciled and to fraternize with pastor or people,

"'*Be it therefore resolved*, That our brethren Patrick Williams, Jerry Burke, —— Butler, Benjamin King and Robert McNish be considered as no longer occupying the place and office of acting deacons of the church, or at least until such time as it may be the pleasure of the church to reëlect them to the same. It being at the same time fully understood that nothing in this preamble and resolutions is intended to discredit or impair their standing as members in common.

"'*Be it further resolved*, That when this conference adjourns that it be adjourned to meet next Sabbath afternoon, for the purpose of filling the vacancies in the office of deacons occasioned by the action of this meeting.

"'*Resolved*, That as a church we will devote the hour allotted for worship on next Sabbath morning to humble prayer to God that he will direct us in our choice of brethren for the office of deacons, desiring as we do to have humble, God-fearing men, those who will be vigilant in the duties of the office, and seek the promotion of true and vital piety in the church, and thereby promote the glory of our Lord.'

"The following resolution was regularly adopted, there being only one dissenting vote:

"'*Resolved*, That as a church we place ourselves under the watch, care, guidance and direction of the Savannah Baptist Church, and that said church be requested to appoint a committee of three of her members to attend our conference and other business meetings, to the end that these meetings in future be conducted in an orderly and christian-like manner, and that we may have aid and witnesses to the same.'

"The preamble and resolution following was offered and unanimously adopted:

"'WHEREAS, This church has been informed that the book containing the records of the church could not be readily obtained when called for for the purposes of this meeting; be it therefore

"'Resolved, That the moderator of this meeting be requested to take the custody of the same.'

"It was also

"'Resolved, That the members of the Executive Committee present, viz., the Rev. L. G. Daniel and Mr. James E. Hogg, together with Mr. A. Champion, a visitor, be requested to add to the Secretary's report of the proceedings of this meeting their written testimonial as to the manner in which the business of this conference has been conducted, and of the aspect of the meeting generally.'

"It was also

"'Resolved, That the moderator and secretary of this meeting be requested to furnish his honor, the Mayor, and also the trustees of this church, a correct copy of the proceedings of this conference.'

"The business of the meeting closed with the following resolution:

"'Resolved, That as a church we tender our sincere thanks to our white brethren for their kindness in aiding us in the transaction of our business.'

"After singing, the meeting adjourned, to meet on Sabbath afternoon, April 25th, 1858.

"Adjourned.

"L. J. B. FAIRCHILD, Secretary.

"Tuesday Night, April 20, 1858."

"WHEREAS, Certain differences of opinion have existed among us, which prevented the affiliation of pastor, deacons and members, and whereas these differences, while they existed, were reasons why the ministers of the gospel of the Sunbury Association refused to sign such a paper as was necessary to secure our pastor his license in terms of the law, and whereas at our adjourned conference, held on the 25th of April, all of our difficulties were happily adjusted, as can be shown from our minutes of that day; be it

"*Resolved*, That we, as a church, earnestly and respectfully request three or more ministers of the gospel of said association to sign such a paper as will be necessary to enable our pastor, William J. Campbell, to obtain his license from the proper authorities, that we may have the gospel preached to us and the sacrament administered in the church.

"*Resolved, further*, That the secretary of this meeting, Mr. Fairchild, make out a certified copy of this preamble and resolutions, and the moderator, Mr. N. J. Hardwick, and Mr. G. W. Wylly present it to three or more of the ministers of the gospel, as aforesaid, and procure their written recommendation to the Superior Court, and then with this written recommendation to the Court procure said license.'

"There being no further business, after singing and prayer the meeting adjourned.
"L. J. B. FAIRCHILD, Secretary *pro tem*.
"Confirmed June 20th, 1858."

"The Rev. Mr. Willis, a gentleman engaged in the missionary labors of the Sunbury Baptist Association, feeling a deep interest in this church as a constituent of said body, but more especially as a church of Christ, and sympathizing with her in her late embarrassments, expressed a desire to ascertain the degree of harmony existing between the church and her pastor, William J. Campbell, and to this end requested all of the members present, deacons and others, to give evidence, by their vote, as to their christian confidence in him as their brother and undershepherd, and called upon the church, each and every member, without reserve, to stand forth and testify in presence of all if they had aught or knew aught against his moral or religious character that would tend to disqualify him as a member or as a preacher of the gospel. Many of the members responded to this call in terms of the utmost confidence and brotherly affection toward their pastor, but none against him, whereupon the moderator, at the request of Mr. Willis, by a vote, took the sense of the church as to their desire to have their pastor's license renewed. The vote was taken, and it appeared that of all the very large number present there were but three dissenting votes.

"Mr. George W. Wylly, one of the committee appointed at the last conference in connection with Mr. Hardwick to procure our pastor's license, reported verbally to the church that said committee were stopped in the prosecution of their duty by the Rev. Mr. Winston's refusing to sign our pastor's (William

J. Campbell's) license papers, and giving as his reason that he believed Campbell a bad man, who had told a lie.

"Gen. Rabun also made the latter assertion: whereupon the following preamble and resolutions were unanimously adopted, viz.:

"'WHEREAS, It becomes the duty of this church to investigate the charges made against our pastor, William J. Campbell, to the end that we may know whether he is guilty or not: be it

"'*Resolved,* That this church invite a presbytery of all the ministers of the gospel of the Sunbury Association who have not been connected in any way with the late difficulties and troubles of this church, and any others whose services can be obtained, to sit as a presbytery in the case of William J. Campbell, and determine on his guilt or innocence.

"'*Resolved,* That 3 o'clock on the third Sabbath in June, in this church, and in the presence of the members thereof, be the time and place of meeting, and that a copy of these proceedings be served on the Rev. Mr. Winston and General Rabun, that they may have notice of the time and place of meeting, and this church respectfully invites them to be present and establish the allegations they have made.

"'*Resolved,* That his honor the Mayor of the city, the trustees of this church, and such other gentlemen of the city as the committee of white brethren appointed to aid us in our business may think proper, be, and they are hereby, respectfully invited to be present at such said meeting and investigation.

"'*Resolved,* That Mr. Fairchild, secretary *pro tem.,* make out a certified copy of these proceedings and furnish one to each minister invited, the trustees of this church, and the accusers of Wm. J. Campbell.'

"The moderator mentioned that a correspondence had been held between the committee and the Rev. Mr. Winston, referring to the charges against the pastor, which would be read at some subsequent meeting.

"The committee appointed April 20, 1858, to prepare a constitution, covenant, etc., for the future government of this church, submitted their report, which, by a vote, was laid over for further consideration.

"There being no further business, after singing and prayer the conference adjourned.

"L. J. B. FAIRCHILD, Secretary *pro tem.*

"Confirmed June 20, 1858."

Following is the correspondence with Mr. Winston, the enemy of Mr. Campbell:

"SAVANNAH, May 22, 1858.

"Dear Brother Winston:

"You gave as the reason why you would not sign William J. Campbell's license papers that you believed he was a bad man, that he told a lie, or you believed he had, we are not certain which expression you used. The high and important position you occupy as a minister of the gospel is a guarantee to us that you would not have given such a reason without sufficient grounds for so doing, and if your allegations can be sustained he, Campbell, should not be licensed, and we would be as unwilling as yourself to aid in getting it done. But men should not be condemned without a hearing, although their skins may be black. We, therefore, respectfully request that you give us in writing the reason you have for believing Campbell a bad man, and in what particular he told a lie, and when and where. Justice to the position you take to Campbell and to ourselves, as well as the good of the church, demands this course. Campbell's license has been repeatedly renewed and no charge has been preferred against him, and we supposed that his christian character was good until you made the allegations herein referred to. We purpose instituting a rigid examination into the case, and if we find that your opinions are well founded, we will turn his case over to the proper tribunal for adjudication and abandon the prosecution of his license. Campbell is a man of color and incapable of defending himself against charges as a white man would be under the laws of the State as well as those of the church, but he is nevertheless entitled to justice, and which we are bound to believe you are willing to award to him. Give us your answer through the post office by 10 o'clock Tuesday morning.

"Yours respectfully,

"R. L. HARDWICK,
"G. W. WYLLY."

THE REPLY.

"SAVANNAH, May 24th, 1858.

"Gentlemen:

"Your letter, in which you call upon me to give my reasons for some opinions I lately expressed in an interview with yourselves respecting Wm. J. Campbell, I have just received.

"I regret the necessity you have laid me under, by thus catechising me, of speaking to you with that plainness which I think the nature of the case demands. I must say, then, that I

African Baptist Church.

do not recognize your authority in behalf of the First African Church, or any other church or body you may represent, to interrogate me in regard to any opinion I may have expressed or may hold concerning the individual referred to by you. Looking upon you, as I do, as having assumed and exercised powers that do not belong to you, in your late interference with the officers of the First African Baptist Church, I utterly repudiate and reject the idea that you have any right to address me, in behalf of that church, upon any subject whatever.

"And, if I must speak as I think and feel, I will say to you that for you to affect to hold me to account for my opinions in regard to Campbell, I regard as a piece of unmatched impudence.

"Yours, &c.,
"M. WINSTON."

How signally has God blessed this church against the mightiest foes. Because Mr. Campbell was a negro, this Mr. Winston presumed that his mere opinion and assertion was sufficient to dethrone a pastor of more than a thousand souls, and felt highly insulted because his word was not taken as absolute proof against this man of God. Mr. Campbell conquered through Christ, and the church marched on.

CHAPTER XIII.

Rev. George Gibbons—His Call, Pastorate and Death.

Rev. George Gibbons was born in Thorny Island, Barnwell District, S. C., November 13th, 1819. He was a slave and belonged to Mrs. Telfair, who was very kind to him. He was baptized by Rev. Andrew C. Marshall in 1844. He was elected a deacon of the First African Baptist Church, January 29th, 1860. He was licensed to preach by the First African Baptist Church about 1870, and he was ordained in 1871, and served as an assistant of Rev. W. J. Campbell in the pastorate. He was called to the pastorate of Bethlehem Baptist Church of Savannah about 1875 or 1876. He was much beloved by said church. He was a man of pleasing manners, dignified bearing, refined culture, and was a model christian gentleman. He was humble and very polite. He was brought into prominence by the call to the First African Baptist Church in 1878. He was called at the time when great excitement prevailed, and it was next to impossible for his administration to have met with much success. He had as much as he could do to keep what

African Baptist Church.

he had. He could not have been expected to make advances on the world when the church was not united. The old pastor (Rev. W. J. Campbell) was still alive and his influence was still living, and all militated against Rev. George Gibbons' success. The friends of Mr. Campbell were the enemies of Mr. Gibbons, and *vice versa*. Rev. Gibbons served the church under these disadvantages for six years. He had not been visiting the annual sessions of the Baptists and hence knew very few of the brethren and practically nothing of the workings of the Baptists outside of Savannah. He had been so confined at home with the affairs of the old white people who raised him that he knew next to nothing of what was going on among the negroes in everyday life. Therefore, he was unprepared to deal with them successfully in church as a pastor. He did not know enough about them. He had traveled extensively with these white people, having visited Europe. He had a fine mind and possessed sublime thoughts. No one could justly point the finger of blame at Rev. George Gibbons. Everybody united in calling him a good man. Even those who disliked him for filling the pulpit which they felt justly belonged to Mr. Campbell would unhesitatingly call him a nice man. His home was very happy, quiet and dignified, and everything he wished for he had at his hand. He was a man of means. The white ladies with whom he stayed died and left him more than seven thousand dollars. His estate is worth upward of twelve thousand dollars. He had a great, generous heart, and was a friend to mankind and an honor to society. In 1884 his health began to fail him, having been undermined by his laborious work and perplexity of mind. The church granted him leave of absence to travel in the up-country for his health. He visited Columbus, Rome, Marietta, Atlanta and Athens, and returned in Ocber, 1884. He was thought to have improved greatly, but this was only imaginary. On his arrival he expected to enter with vigor upon his work. On Thursday night, November 12, 1884, he undertook to preach, and selected for his text, Psalm XVI, 11: "Thou wilt shew me the path of life: in Thy presence is fullness of joy; at Thy right hand there are pleasures forever more." He read very distinctly his text once and read it a second time, and his hands fell by his side, his mouth closed, and he never spoke again in life. It was evident that his work was over. He had been shown the path of life and would be soon ushered into the presence of the King. He was taken home, where the best medical aid was summoned, but his case baffled medical skill, and after nine days' suffering he breathed his last. He was buried on Sunday, November 23d, 1884. Rev.

Alexander Harris preached his funeral sermon. Revs. A. Ellis, U. L. Houston, S. A. McNeal and E. K. Love also took part. The funeral was very large, being attended by not less than five thousand people. This good man ended gloriously the life he so well lived. Mr. Campbell only preceded him four years one month and eleven days to the saints' rest, where they would make no more mistakes. Rev. Bryan preceded Rev. Marshall forty-four years, one month and one day. Rev. Marshall preceded Rev. Campbell twenty-three years, eleven months and four days, he also having died in October. It is a little singular that all of these great men died about the same time of the year. The church never had a better man than Rev. Gibbons, so far as quietness, gentleness and pleasing manners are concerned, but all were abler preachers than he was. He was a living example of the gospel which he preached, and had a high sense of honor and right. He did not believe in worldly amusements and had no patience with the idea of begging money for the cause of Christ, nor giving entertainments to raise money for the church. He believed that people ought to give from a sense of duty and from a principle. He was an hundred years ahead of the age in which he lived. Perhaps his ideas of that dignified order of christian work may be realized in the next hundred years. His idea of church work was on the most dignified order. It could hardly have been otherwise, owing to his cultured rearing. He was progressive in church work and in church order. He was actually at one time opposed to accepting, upon the part of the church, $70 from a party of sisters because it was raised from a supper given for that purpose which had music. He contended that the gospel did not warrant raising money in that way for the church, and instead of accepting the money he was in favor of expelling the sisters. This created quite a sensation, and for a while made him unpopular with many. If he could have enforced his ideas he would have had a model gospel church. But this was at least an hundred years too soon for the inaugurating of such plans. It would have been like rooting up the tares in the wheat, which would have done more harm than good. The day must come, however, when his ideas must be adopted. When this grand man died the church had just cause to mourn.

CHAPTER XIV.

Rev. E. K. Love, D. D.—His Call and Pastorate.

[By Rev. S. A. McNeal, of Augusta, his friend.]

Rev. Emanuel K. Love, was born in Perry county, near Marion, Alabama, July the 27th, 1850. He was a slave and reared on a farm. His parents were poor and uneducated. They were unable to educate him. He had a burning desire to get an education. He was converted in the spring of 1868 and baptized in July of the same year by Dr. W. H. McIntosh. He was baptized in the afternoon and tried to preach that night. He was soon afterwards given permission to preach and won great distinction in the country places as a preacher. He soon left the farm and became a ditcher. In 1871 he entered Lincoln University, Marion, Alabama (having studied very hard for six years privately, getting instruction from white persons on farms who were kind enough to give it to him), where he studied for five or six months, winning great distinction as a hard and wonderfully apt student. When his money gave out he was compelled to leave school. He went to ditching. At this he made money very rapidly. But unfortunately he loaned this out to friends and relatives who were farming. The church to which he belonged, the first Sunday in November, 1872, decided that he should go to a theological school and prepare for the ministry. This he knew nothing of until the matter was brought up in the church meeting. At the time he had only eight dollars and fifty cents in ready money. The farmers to whom he had loaned his money had failed, and it was now evident that he could not hope to collect a dollar of his money. After the church meeting he went seven miles into the country to see what arrangements could be made to collect the money, as he had only two weeks. On Monday, the next day, a farmer came to town in search of a ditcher. Some how some friends recommended Mr. Love, though many ditchers were in town. He went out at once to see the gentleman and took the job, completed it in ten days and cleared one hundred and twenty-two dollars. It was finished on Friday, he settled up his business on Saturday, preached his farewell sermon on Sunday and left for Augusta, Georgia, on Monday, arriving there on Tuesday, November 19th, 1872, and entered the Augusta Institute on Wednesday, November 20th, 1872, from which he graduated with first honors June, 1877.

He had many hardships in school. His money gave out several times, when he was compelled often to go several days without anything to eat. He has broiled meat skins on the coals, ate crusts and drank water for days. He had no bed nor bedding, save one quilt and one sheet, the gift of his mother when he left home. In the winter he was compelled to build a fire in the class room and sleep on benches to avoid freezing. As great as his suffering was he always stood head in his classes. He was the best bible scholar ever graduated from the school. He taught as assistant teacher in the school under the venerable Dr. Joseph T. Robert, D. D., LL. D., for several years. When Dr. Robert was sick or absent Mr. Love would take charge of the school and deliver lectures on theology to the school, which he did to the satisfaction of the scholars.

He was ordained to the gospel ministry by Revs. W. J. White, Dr. Jos. T. Robert, Henry Watts, E. V. White, Henry Morgan, Aaron Green, G. Arrington, Henry Jackson and Geo. Barns, December 12, 1875. at the Harmony Baptist Church, by request of his church at Marion, Ala. He taught county public schools at Newton, Appling and Camilla, Ga. In 1876 he served his mother church in Marion, Ala., for six months, and declined a unanimous call to be its permanent pastor, and returned to Augusta to finish his studies. He was appointed missionary for the State of Georgia under the Home Mission Board, of New York, and the Georgia Mission Board (white). He served in this capacity until July, 1879, when he resigned to take charge of the First African Baptist Church, at Thomasville, Ga. Here he rebuilt the house of worship and baptized 450 hopeful converts. The church, under his administration, took its stand along by the side of the best churches in christian work and finance in the State. On the 1st of October, 1881, he resigned this church to take charge of the Sunday school mission work of the State of Georgia, under the American Baptist Publication Society of Philadelphia. In this work he continued for four years, winning great distinction as an efficient missionary, and was called the best missionary of the South. He gave perfect satisfaction. After serving in this sphere to the unanimous satisfaction of all concerned, on the 1st of October, 1885, he resigned to take charge of the First African Baptist Church of Savannah, Ga. This church is the most famous in the world among negroes, and it is not at all surprising that Mr. Love would want some time to prayerfully consider the grave responsibility invited upon him. Mr. Love was a young man, being only 35 years old when he was called. There were great fears even among good people that he would not succeed. The church had never had a young pastor. She had been accustomed to old men, whose age the people would respect as well as their position. Rev. E. K. Love was intellectually the superior of his predecessors.

Mr. Love had long been the favorite of the church. In February, 1878, Deacons J. H. Brown and L. J. Pettigrew heard him preach the missionary sermon before the Florida Baptist Convention, at Monticello, Fla., and were so carried away that they invited him to Savannah to preach the same sermon, and in March of the same year he visited Savannah. His visit was hailed with large congregations, and always after that it had only to be hinted that Rev. Mr. Love would be in the city and seats in the church would be at a premium. Rev. Geo. Gibbons became his friend and made him welcome to his home. As Mr. Gibbons was not a revivalist, every once in a while the church would send for Rev. Mr. Love to give her a series of sermons. When Rev. Gibbons was stricken with paralysis, Rev. Love had just finished a series of meetings and had been gone not yet a week. When Rev. Gibbons died he was telegraphed for and came to the funeral. He knew his name would be put forward for the pastorate and therefore ceased to visit the city. He soon found out that there were some who opposed his being called, and several falsehoods were trumped up, which his friends vigorously met and successfully refuted. The church invited Mr. Love to hold a series of meetings in the last of May, 1885, running up to the first of June. This he did with some success, and on the first Sunday in June, 1885, baptized ten converts and administered the Lord's Supper. There was one brother who so bitterly opposed Mr. Love that he would not allow his daughter to be baptized by him, though she was a candidate for baptism. There was much talk and many aspirants. Many subterfuges were resorted to to prevent the call, but the friends of Mr. Love were competent for the task and met every emergency.

In the conference of the third Sunday in August an attempt was made to call Rev. Mr. Love, but his friends seeing the situation and having consumed the time in meeting objections, moved to adjourn the conference until the fifth Sunday in August. This conference was very largely attended. Mr. L. J. Pettigrew moved that Rev. E. K. Love, of Thomasville, be called pastor of the First African Baptist Church. About fifty persons, male and female, seconded the motion at once; seven hundred persons voted for him, and seven against him. The objection of these seven persons was of a three-fold nature. First, that he had made, some years before, some undue familiar advances toward a prominent female member of the church, which proved to be utterly false; yet there was a vile conspiracy in it. Second, that Rev. Gibbons had not been dead long enough, and that the church ought not to take down its mourning for the late pastor under a year. Third, that he was too young. Over all these objections Rev. E. K. Love was made pastor by a large majority August 30th, 1885. He was then 35 years old, and was at the time missionary of the State of Georgia. He was wired the result of the election at Washington, Ga., September 1st, 1885, and the letter notifying him officially was sent to him at Eatonton, Ga., where he was in attendance on the Middle Georgia Association. Following is the letter of notification:

"SAVANNAH, GA., Sept. 3, 1885.
"*The First African Baptist Church, Savannah, Ga.,*
To Rev. E. K. Love, Thomasville, Ga.

"BELOVED BROTHER: As a committee appointed for the purpose, we take more than ordinary pleasure in conveying to you the (to us) most pleasing information that at an adjourned session of the regular Monthly Conference of the First African Baptist Church, held on the 30th day of August, A. D. 1885, you were called to the pastorate of the above named church.

The number of those who voted in the affirmative upon the question of the call was such as to make us feel safe in assuring you the hearty support of the church in your labors among us, and leaves no doubt as to the directing hand of Providence in the result. The salary has been fixed at seventy-five (75) dollars per month, with December 1st, 1885, fixed as the date for you to assume the duties of the office. We send herewith the warmest feelings of christian love and prayer of the church.

"Awaiting your reply, we are yours in the bonds of love.
"J. H. BROWN,
"C. H. EBBS,
"L. J. PETTIGREW,
"Committee."

When it became known throughout the State that Rev. E. K. Love, D. D., had been called to the pastorate of the First African Baptist Church of Savannah, the brethren all over the State regretted to lose him from his post as missionary of the State. He was the favorite of Georgia. The brethren generally called him "Bishop." They still very generally call him by this name. He regretted to leave the brethren. He loved the mission work. He finally accepted.

The following is Rev. E. K. Love's letter of acceptance:

"ATLANTA, GA., Sept. 12, 1885.
"*Messrs. C. H. Ebbs, L. J. Pettigrew and J. H. Brown,
Committee First African Baptist Church, Savannah, Ga.*

"DEAR BRETHREN: Yours of the 3d instant, informing me of your great church's choice of me as pastor, to hand. I can but view the circumstance as the most flattering in my history. Your church is an old, influential body, and I feel most forcibly the grave responsibility invited upon me in your call. Feeling, as I do, the magnitude of this work, and the able pastors who have preceded me, and appreciating the learning and profound research and wonderful executive ability he must possess who is your leader, I would most respectfully cry unworthy and decline, but for the conviction, after a prayerful consideration, that your call voices the will of God. For His service I live, and in it I hope to die; hence, I regard as a rule the voice of the people as the voice of God. When this is so I bow to them as to their Master.

THE WORK OF THE PASTOR.

"There is no more responsible an office to which men can be possibly called than that of a pastor. To his care is committed the training of the people spiritually. Praying for the sick, standing around the bedside of the dying, watching over the spiritual interests of the church, looking out for the good of the community generally, rebuking sin and wickedness in high places, to throw his influence on the side of temperance, waging an uncompromising war against whiskey, to fight never ceasingly for right, to work untiringly for education, and to preach faithfully the word of God in such a manner that the whole people might hear him gladly. The work of the pastor is the most sacred and responsible under heaven, and angels would gladly engage in the pastor's work. The privilege to pray for the suffering and distressed is certainly sweet to the minister called of God to preach the gospel of His son.

THE RELATION OF THE PASTOR TO HIS PEOPLE.

"The man who deals with the spiritual affairs of a people must be most dearly and tenderly related to them. He who teaches the souls of a people must enter and live in their souls. His soul should be large enough to take all of his people into his heart of hearts. The pastor is a member of every family circle in his congregation. All of the people are his people, and he is the servant of all. He can not afford to have any enemies who can give a just cause for their opposition. If possible, he must live peaceably with all men, and endeavor to have all men to live at peace with him. He is the spiritual overseer of the church of God, and is the adviser of the church in all of its concerns.

YOUR DUTY AS A CHURCH.

"I can not hope to succeed without your coöperation and hearty support. I am not ignorant of the fact that a people can defeat the work of their pastor or make it a grand success. It will, as you know, be your duty to assist me by your presence, support, prayers and sympathy. For this I shall look most anticipatingly. I need not invite your attention to the domestic part of your work. A parsonage, I believe, is generally acceded to be the duty of the church, and the minister be left free to give himself to study, prayer and the ministry of the word.

THE TIME NAMED BY YOU.

"It will be necessary for me to tell you that the work which I am now doing is important to the State of Georgia. The Baptists of Georgia have given me their united support, and it is with profoundest feeling that I resign this work. The American Baptist Publication Society, in whose employ I have served for four years, has been very kind to me, and has treated me with the utmost deference and will regret to lose my services. You name December 1st as the day to commence the work. Perhaps you did not know that my year expires with October 1st, and that it would be much easier and smoother for me to resign at the end of the year. Your time seems to necessitate the loss of two months. If this cannot be remedied I shall submit.

"The salary you offer I hope will be so fixed as to put myself and family on equally as good living terms as in my present position. You cannot afford to do less.

"You owe me your prayers; pray for me, dear brethren. I feel so much my unworthiness and inability to discharge the duties of so high a calling. Having been duly, officially, informed that on the 30th of August, 1885, I was duly elected as pastor of your great church, and regarding the voice of the people as the voice of God, I, Emanuel K. Love, of Thomasville, Ga., in the thirty-fifth year of my age, do, in the name of Almighty God, in the name of His Son, Jesus Christ, and in the name of the Holy Spirit, accept, looking to Him for guidance, protection, and an understanding heart.

"And now, may the great head of the church, the Shepherd and Bishop of our souls, even the Lord Jesus Christ, bless you in all things for good.

"I am your humble servant, in His name,
"EMANUEL K. LOVE."

THE INSTALLATION.

When the letter of acceptance from Mr. Love was read before the church, the church at once changed the time from December 1st, 1885, to October 1st, 1885, to suit Mr. Love's convenience. This showed that the pastor elect already had influence with this noble people. At a mere hint from Mr. Love that either January 1st, 1886, or October 1st, 1885, would suit him best the church embraced the opportunity of getting him at the first convenience. October 1st, 1885, was set for the installation.

Rev. Love was installed by Revs. U. L. Houston, J. S. Habersham, John Nesbit, W. L. P. Weston, of Savannah, E. R. Carter, of Atlanta, C. T. Walker, T. J. Hornsby and S. A. McNeal, of Augusta, T. M. Robinson, of Harlem, and G. H. Washington, of Quitman. Rev. C. T. Walker introduced Rev. E. K. Love in the following eloquent speech:

"It is with no small degree of pleasure that your humble speaker appears before this august assembly on this auspicious occasion. I am gratefully sensible of the honor done me in selecting me to speak on this important occasion. You gather to-night on no ordinary occasion; you come not to witness the inauguration of the chief magistrate of the nation; you come not to your regular church services as you usually do on this night; no, you are here to meet the leader, the shepherd of the flock that God has sent you. The ministry is of divine appointment, and is such a sacred and holy calling God has reserved the right of appointment to himself, and by the influence of the Holy Spirit he has urged you to call to the pastorate of this great church Emanuel K. Love. Christ, the great shepherd of the sheep, the bishop of our souls, has committed His people to the instruction and guidance of faithful ministers.

"While this noble church has had a number of eminent preachers, such as Andrew Bryan, Andrew C. Marshall, William J. Campbell and George Gibbons, who have erected monuments to their noble deeds, yet I assure you that the cause will not suffer in the hands of the present incumbent. He, by the fervor of his appeals, the force of his argument, the glow of his eloquence, the beauty of his piety, his familiarity with the Scriptures, and his sincere devotion to the Master's cause, will edify and delight his christian hearers. Though the duties of the pastoral office be arduous and responsible, you have made choice of one who will discharge them with fidelity and ability. He will give effective service and meet your highest expectation. Only give him your prayers, sympathy and hearty co-operation. Rev. E. K. Love, as a student, was earnest, apt, diligent, thorough-going, and always led his classes. He has reached the degree of a well-developed manhood and of a richly-cultivated intellect. He served as missionary under the Home Mission Society, New York, and the Home Mission Board of the Georgia Baptist Convention (white), and gave entire satisfaction. He was afterward called to the pastorate of the Thomasville Baptist Church. This church building was quite dilapidated, the flock scattered and the Baptist cause at a low ebb in that city; but during his pastorate the church was tastily beautified and embellished, and 450 added by baptism. He was called from that field of labor to become the Spurgeon missionary under the auspices of the American Baptist Publication Society in Philadelphia. He won their confidence and respect, and was styled by them the best missionary in all the South. He is known all over Georgia; his friends are legion. He won the confidence and respect of his denomination. He is

African Baptist Church.

known and loved in this State and treated kindly. He resigns a prosperous work to obey your mandate. He comes to this field with experience and executive ability. He comes to the call of his heavenly Master. He comes, burdened with the responsibility devolved upon him. He comes a christian gentleman. Gentle with all men and clothed with the raiment of a meek and quiet spirit. He is eminently social and will be the friend of the unlettered peasant as well as the erudite scholar. The most humble in the church will find in him a friend—generous, noble-hearted and kind. His liberality is greater than his purse. He has learned what few ministers have—to esteem another better than himself, and in honor to prefer his brethren. In my friend and brother you will find an experimental preacher, natural and impressive. He is up with the times. The age in which we live is one of mental activity, busy, progressive, and calls loudly for men of character, doctrine and education. Not altogether excellence of speech, to gratify the curiosity of the people, rhetorical strains or philosophical essays, but men who will know nothing among men save Jesus Christ and him crucified. I present to you a christian gentleman who will, to-night, enter upon his work with a solemn appreciation of it, and with an earnest desire to do it ably and faithfully. His unselfishness, his broad charity, his marked sincerity, his simplicity and scholarly attainments, coupled with the grace of God, all fit him preëminently for the office he is to fill. And, dear church, I bespeak for him your sympathy, confidence, support, love, coöperation and prayers. I ask for his most excellent, devoted, praiseworthy, christian wife your respect and generous consideration.

"And now, beloved brother, in entering upon this new field of labor, may the Lord bless thee and keep thee; the Lord make His face to shine upon thee, and be gracious unto thee. The Lord lift upon thee His countenance. The Lord give thee peace. May you, by good work, write your name on time as legibly as the stars on the brow of the evening. And when you stand upon the interlacing margin of eternity may you hear the shout of your welcome borne from afar: Well done, good and faithful servant."

Rev. S. A. McNeal then addressed the church in the following most timely speech:

ADDRESS TO THE FIRST AFRICAN BAPTIST CHURCH.

"*Dear Brethren and Sisters, Friends and Well-Wishers:*

"I am glad to answer this honor you have conferred upon me. I regard it as no small matter to be called upon to address you upon so auspicious an occasion as this. You have assembled here to night to see publicly installed the man whom you, of your own volition and deliberate choice, have called to serve you as your leader, your counsellor and your shepherd. In this act you have taken upon yourselves solemn obligations that the great head of the church will hold you answerable for. It is no small thing for a church or people to call a minister of the gospel from his God-given field of usefulness to take charge of its work. For being, as he may be, settled in his Master's vineyard, where he is succeeding, and where he knows how to succeed, to come among a new people, to discontinue his usefulness, to run the risk of being successful or to be disappointed may be for life. It is no small thing to do this, but, on the other hand, an awful thing. For this man you have called is doing a great work, and in fact he has done the greatest work that has been done by any one in the mission in this State. The truth is, he is a man who will succeed in any field, if only allowed. As an organizer and builder he is the acknowledged leader in this State. As to his intellectual ability you have been truthfully told by the brother who introduced him to you. I have been appointed to speak of the relations to exist between you as church and pastor. I wish to say, by way of emphasis, that whatever a pastor may do or be very greatly depends upon what that church is, or what that church may be capacitated for. The pastor is expected to draw the line of campaign and furnish the brain and the people or church to execute. If the church grows intellectually or morally that very greatly depends upon the leadership of the pastor coupled with its own willingness to attain these high and lofty things.

"Then the first thing that the church is required to do in order to get these blessings is to have great confidence in the pastor and hold him in high esteem. For in order that we may follow any one we must first have faith in such an one. The second thing is to love him; for there will be times when you will be called upon to bear very much with your leader, and if you don't love him you can't bear the burdens that may be put upon you. The third thing is to be willing to obey your pastor, for the good book informs you that obedience is better than sacrifice. The next thing is you must pray for your pastor; you must at all times remember that he needs your prayers.

I will repeat here what I heard once told having happened between a church and its pastor. He, it was said, was a young man, and having preached for some time to the church was about to fail, when the members of the church met to discuss the matter and do something thereabout. When they had fully ventilated the matter, one brother moved that the pastor be asked to resign; but just before they voted one old man arose and asked, with tears in his eyes, that as the pastor was a young man, and there was much to hope for, the church pray for him for one month, and at the end of that time they had quite a revival in their church, and from that day the church began to grow and became the largest and most flourishing church of that day, and in all that country was their praise. So I would urge you to pray for your church and pastor and great results will follow.

"Then I want to tell you what you must not do yourselves, nor allow anyone else to do in your presence—speak disrespectfully of your pastor; but always have a good word for him. When he preaches a good sermon, tell him so, and it will help him to do better the next time. If he does or speaks a thing you do not understand, do not go around criticizing and complaining, but wait for an opportunity and speak to him kindly about the matter, and always feel that you have pleasant access to him. And even when you disagree with him, allow it to be between you two, and don't go all over the town tattling and making partisans of yourself and others. This will injure the church, the pastor, others and yourselves. Then the time will come when you may learn that, after all, he knew best and acted wisely. And not at all times are you to know what the true minister of Jesus Christ does. He has nothing at heart but the good of Zion and the glory of God.

"I have known Mr. Love most intimately for the past thirteen years, and I tell you I don't know any man for whom I would swear quicker than for the Rev. Emanuel K. Love, who has been called to serve you. He is a good man, a noble man, a man whose heart is as broad as the world and as deep as the sea. He is as true as steel, and a man who cannot go back on a friend. I know no man so well as I know E. K. Love. He cannot be more honest than he is. Deception is not in him.

"And I pray that this call, which he has felt moved by the Holy Ghost to answer, has been of God. Then if it has been of God no man can overthrow or hinder him from going to a grand success. Hoping that this old patriarchal and historical church may be made all that the dear Lord would have her be, and that my dearest friend and your beloved and newly-elected pastor and his grand church may do all they may desire to do, and be, through him that loves the church and gave himself for the church, more than conquerors; that he might present to God, the Father, a pure church, without spot or blemish, or any other such thing, is the humble wish of your brother, for Christ's sake. Amen."

Rev. E. R. Carter then charged the pastor in a most touching manner.

REV. LOVE'S ADDRESS.

"*Dear Brethren, Sisters and Friends generally:* This demonstration of your interest, both in me and in the work to which I have been called by this people, makes me feel more keenly than ever my unworthiness and inability to discharge the duties of this high office. Were I to consult my feelings in this matter I would be forced to the conclusion that this task might have been consigned to more competent hands than mine. But as God has spoken through his people, as his servant, I should disregard my feelings and hear what the Lord, my God, saith. His word is much plainer and clearer of fault than my treacherous feeling; to his word I bow. If God chooses to work through me in this field, I think I should make no objection. I yield, therefore, and throw myself upon the merit of His grace, assured that He is with me 'alway, even unto the end of the world.' I come among you as one that serves. I give you my unqualified word to-night, in the fear of God, that I have no friends to reward nor enemies to punish. I shall look upon every man in this church as my brother and every woman as my sister, provided I find them worthy. I shall place every man upon his merit: Whatsoever he soweth that shall he also reap. I shall rebuke sin in whomever and wherever I find it, regardless of the consequence. I put in this night to get on with you, and I want you to make it up in your minds that we have got to get on together. There is no good reason why we should not get on together. I have not come here to fall out. I pity a christian that cannot live in peace with a christian. The religion of the Lord Jesus Christ is a system of peace, and those who do not make peace have not the spirit of the Lord Jesus Christ. I feel very grateful for the complimentary terms in which my reverend brethren have spoken of me to-night. I assure you, brethren, that you, together with this occasion, shall be carefully and sacredly stored away in my fondest recollection. Whatever ability I may possess shall be devoted to the promotion of Zion and the truest interest of this whole people. They shall take part in all of my thoughts. My heart shall be burdened with their sorrows and elated with their joys. I shall live for them, and hope to live in them. I may commit errors. Who is free from them? I shall make them as seldom and as far between as possible. They shall always be errors of the head. It is not my desire to do wrong. Pray for me that God may help me to do right and teach you the same. I want to prove myself a workman that needeth not to be ashamed right here in this field. May God grant me grace to do this work to His honor and glory.

"Allow me to say to you before I finish that I shall try my best to be your pastor, and I wish you to try equally as hard to be the members. Treat me as I treat you and I ask no more. I deserve no more. I expect you to attend church as regularly as the doors are open. Let us start with each other in a way that we can hold out. If we start right we can hold out, for right breeds right. Let us remember that one night's confusion in the church will do more harm than we can remove by months' preaching. As it is easier to go down than up, we should hold every notch we make and struggle for the next one. The attention of the country is turned toward this church. Look at the representatives you have here to-night from nearly all over Georgia. Let us appreciate our surroundings and act accordingly. If there be any who have made it up in their minds to make this administration a failure, I persuade you, in the name of God, to change your minds. Be admonished by your friend and brother to unite with the whole church to carry on the work of God. It is not our cause, it is God's cause, and let us not insult our Master because He does not do business to suit us. He is working for our good; He knows best who He wants to watch over his people. Do not contend against the army lest you fight against God. If God, whose cause we espouse, can put up with a man in His vineyard, it does seem that you might be able to stand it. I must congratulate you upon the almost unanimity of your call. Many churches have split nearly half in two by calling a preacher. You have steered clear of this, be it said in praise of the church.

"I shall deliver my inaugural discourse on Sunday night. That discourse will be an index to my administration. I, therefore, urge you to turn out in full and hear it."

This short address had a wonderful impression upon the people. The reader misses the fervor, ease, grace and earnestness with which it was delivered.

THE PAPERS ON REV. LOVE.

The Thomasville *Times* said of him when he resigned the church there:

"Rev. E. K. Love has resigned the pastorate at Thomasville and enters the service of the American Baptist Publication Society as Sunday School missionary. The following is the action taken by the deacons of the church in reference to the matter:

"'*Resolved*, That it is with great reluctance that we are constrained to accept the resignation of our beloved pastor; that the ties which have so long bound us together are indeed hard to sever;

"'That in thus severing the relation of pastor and people we recognize the hand of God calling him to a more useful and extended field;

"'That we will follow him with our prayers wherever he goes, praying that He will care for him and his while he goes forth to do the bidding of the Master;

"'That his faithfulness and earnest labors with this church entitle him to a warm and lasting place in our hearts and memories;

"'That we commend him most heartily and cordially to our brethren all over the State as an able and devoted minister of the gospel;

"'That the doors of this church, and the hearts of our people, will always be open to him when he returns in his rounds of labor;

"'That we, as a church, in bidding in our brother adieu at the same time bid him God-speed on the high and holy mission to which he has been called.

"'(Signed)

"'ROBERT PONDER,
"'S. SMITH,
"'AARON JONES,
"'S. M. WILSON,
"'ANDREW HUGERSON,
"'JAMES A. HAWKINS,
"'Deacons.'"

The *Times* said, in an editorial:

"Rev. E. K. Love has the entire confidence and respect of the citizens of Thomasville, white and black. He has stayed here long enough for them to know his sterling worth. Georgia is a big field, but if there is a man who can work it up, that man is E. K. Love."

Rev. T. J. Hornsby in The Defense, May 24, 1884.

"HEPZIBAH, GA., May 19th, 1884.
"*Editor Defense:*

"Please grant us space to speak a word about the man who is styled the 'Bishop of Georgia,' Rev. E. K. Love, the Sunday School missionary of the American Baptist Publication Society. This very able divine visited the Spring Hill Baptist Church on the 17th ultimo and delivered one of his supremely eloquent sermons upon the unpardonable sin. It certainly was a masterly effort, and we would be glad if all the world had heard it. He conducted an institute meeting at Smith Grove Church on the 18th and 19th ultimo. We assure you that it was timely, instructive and pleasant. He certainly is the right man in the right place. As you know, he is not only enthusiastic but really logical at the same time. He seems to have such extraordinary and commanding powers, and can preach or teach with so much propriety that when we get it altogether we can well afford to call him the 'Bishop.' The gentleman handled all of his subjects with great credit to himself and incalculable benefit to his audiences. Well may the denomination boast of her gem and Georgia exult on his account. It has been some time since a missionary visited us, therefore we cannot refrain from talking about it The meeting indorsed the God-sent man and his work in very commendable terms, which we forwarded to the *Georgia Baptist*, which I have been taking nearly ever since its existence, with request to publish, which must have gotten into the scrap basket before they were published, for three weeks have passed since and we have not seen them. As the resolutions were long may be this caused them to be left unpublished. Accept many thanks for space.

"Respectfully,

"T. J. HORNSBY."

Rev. Love and the *Georgia Baptist* were not on good terms at this time, and hence nothing in praise of him could find its way into the columns of that paper.

Echo, Savannah.

The Baptist Foreign Mission Society of the First African Baptist Church Sunday School, said of Mr. Love in the *Echo:*

"The regular meeting of this society will take place at the First African Baptist Church this (Sunday) afternoon at 3 o'clock. Rev. E. K. Love, of Thomasville, Georgia, will preach the regular missionary sermon, which will certainly prove quite interesting, as Mr. Love is decidedly one of the ablest divines in the State. The collections at this mission meeting are for sending the gospel of Christ to the poor heathens in Africa, and it is hoped the attendance will be large and the contributions liberal. Mr. C. L. De Lamotta is one of the leading agitators in this work in the Forest City whose efforts in its behalf is undoubtedly commendable in every particular."

The *Sentinel* said of him:

"The election of the Rev. Editor Love, as pastor of a great Baptist church in Savannah, is a well merited compliment both to the church itself and its new pastor. Rev. Love is acknowledged, we believe, to be the ablest biblical scholar among the young colored men of his State. As a pulpit orator he has no superiors and few equals among Georgia's clergy. As a writer and thinker on general topics he stands among the foremost. We bespeak for pastor and flock a happy association."

Camilla Clarion (White).

"Rev. E. K. Love has been called to the pastorate of the First Baptist (colored) Church in Savannah and will make that city his home. He taught and studied in Camilla for several years, and we know his record and his abilities. He is indeed a very intelligent and able man and the church has done well to secure his services. Withal he is pious and devoted to his work. We congratulate all parties."

Savannah Morning News (White.)

"Rev. E. K. Love has recently been called to the pastorate of the First African Baptist Church of this city to fill the vacancy occasioned by the death of the late Rev. George Gibbons. He was installed on Thursday night. This young divine is a graduate of the Atlanta Baptist Seminary and is one of the foremost men in the denomination. For three years he was missionary of Georgia under the Home Mission Society, New York, and the Georgia Baptist Mission Board (white). He resigned that position to take charge of the Thomasville Baptist Church and served that church three years, during which he baptized 400 converts and greatly added to the material interest of the church. He resigned the Thomasville church against the earnest solicitation of the people and accepted the missionary position under the American Baptist Publication Society of Philadelphia, which position he held for four years. He gave entire satisfaction, and resigned that position to accept the call to the church of this city. He was at one time editor of a paper published in Albany, Georgia, known as the *National Watchman*, and is at present second editor of the *Weekly Sentinel*, a negro paper published in Augusta, Georgia."

Augusta Sentinel, Sept. 12th, 1885.

PASTORATE FIRST AFRICAN BAPTIST CHURCH.

"The above-named church is one of the largest and most prosperous churches in Georgia. It has been pastored by such worthy men as Bryan, Marshall, Campbell and Gibbons, all of whom are now in the enjoyment of infinite rest. The church has more than 3,000 members, and is noted for her benevolent missionary spirit. Rev. Emanuel K. Love has been called to the pastorate of this noble church and the church made a wise selection. He is a diligent student of the Scriptures, well educated, a sound theologian—all his sermons bear the stamp of his iron genius. He is in full vigor of a well-developed manhood and of a richly-cultivated intellect. As a preacher, he is able, instructive and powerful; his views vast, profound, original, and his sermons practical. As a pastor, he is sympathetic, vigilant, benevolent, and devoted to missions, and will faithfully discharge the duties of that responsible office.

" During his pastorate at Thomasville the church was strengthened greatly and reached a high degree of prosperity. Now, as a missionary under the auspices of the Publication Society of Philadelphia, his perseverance and devotion in that work has caused him to be styled one of the best missionaries in the South. He has qualifications that fit him preëminently for the position he has been called to fill; he brings to it the best of executive and organizing powers, combined with unquestioned consecration to his Saviour and His cause. He is kind, generous, noble-hearted, and possesses germs of genuine greatness. There is no man in Georgia to-day more interested in the work of his denomination than E. K. Love. C. T. W."

The Sentinel.

"On next Thursday night, at 8 o'clock, Rev. E. K. Love, the Baptist Sunday School missionary and evangelist of the State of Georgia, will preach at Thankful Baptist Church. Rev. Love needs no introduction to the people of Augusta. On this

occasion he proposes to preach the grandest sermon of his life.
Let everybody turn out to hear him."
Rev. Love made no such intimation as above.

The following is the introductory sermon of Rev. E. K. Love
on entering upon the pastorate of the church:

INTRODUCTORY SERMON

*Of Rev. Emanuel K. Love on Entering the Pastorate of the First
African Baptist Church, Savannah, Ga., Preached Sunday
Night, October 4th, 1885. It is Published by the Unanimous
Request of the Church, expressed by a Vote.*

"This very able and instructive sermon was delivered by Rev.
Emanuel K. Love on entering the pastoral duties of the First
African Baptist Church of Savannah, Ga., the first Sabbath
night in October, 1885. The spacious and magnificent auditorium of the grand old church was crowded to its utmost capacity,
and many could not gain admittance.

"The author is a sound theologian, strikingly original, and has
reached the degree of a well-developed and richly cultivated
intellect. It is by the unanimous request of this time-honored
church that the sermon appear in print.

"It is replete with wholesome advice, helpful suggestions,
and is capable of elevating and edifying each christian soldier.

"It is hoped that this evangelical gospel sermon will be carefully and prayerfully read, and that the pastorate of our dear
brother may be richly fruitful of good.
"C. T. WALKER,
"Pastor of Tabernacle Baptist Church, Augusta, Ga."

"Acts, x, 29: 'Therefore, came I unto you without gainsaying
as soon as I was sent for: I ask, therefore, for what intent have
ye sent for me.'

THE SERMON.

"I have very often preached to this church for six or seven
years, and although I could not have done so more earnestly,
I've never attempted to preach to you in the capacity which I
now attempt. Before I have taken up the burden only for a
short while—for a night, for a day, and never for longer than a
week or two, though I've carried you in my heart, for God
had assured me years ago that I would be your pastor. I was
not responsible for your perpetual instruction, the order of your

house, nor the peace of this flock; I'm invited now to a constant burden, and for your welfare I must shoulder the responsibility. I feel it needful, therefore, to have a plain talk with you to night, hence I have selected this text to ask you for what intent did you send for me. You will recollect that the angel told Cornelius to send for Peter, and that the Lord told Peter that he had instructed Cornelius to send for him; yet Peter asked Cornelius why he sent for him. It may not be out of place, therefore, for me to ask you for what intent did you send for me. Let us notice the person sending for the preacher:

"I.—Cornelius had been praying. This was the proper time to send for a preacher, after prayer and after he had received God's answer. Such persons are always ready to hear words of God from His ministers. A church should never presume to call a preacher until it has consulted God in prayer and his answer returned. You will observe that the whole matter of a choice of a preacher was left with God. God chose the preacher, named the man and told where he was. Cornelius prayed before sending for the preacher. He did not call together a select few and discuss personality and raise objections; he prayed. He did not hunt up his parliamentary guide to make trap motions, call the previous question, or move to lay on the table; he prayed. He did not make a long, cunning speech and have some one posted to second his motion; he prayed. He did not rise to a point of order, a privilege question, or a question of information; he prayed. There was no confusion about whom he must call, about the majority ruling or the sovereignty of the church; he prayed. I have no sympathy and less patience with rings, tricksters, family connections and party ties or aristocracy in the church of Christ. Let us stand on the same hallowed plain of brotherly love and friendship, remembering that one is our Master, even Christ, and that we are all brethren. It will be noticed again that Cornelius sent a committee of three to inform Peter of his call and to accompany him on his way. This committee went both in the name of God and in the name of Cornelius. They informed Peter that Cornelius had been praying, and that in answer to his prayer God had instructed him to send to Joppa for him. As though it was necessary for Peter to understand the character of the man who had sent for him to enter his house, they proceeded to give a brief history of the life of Cornelius, and recommended him very highly to the preacher. It is not out of place, therefore, for preachers to know something of the churches that seek them, and to have a good report of them. God recommended Peter, and he needed nothing more. It is too common among

us to accept a church with merely a 'majority.' The sooner
this custom dies out the better it will be for our churches. I
doubt any man's fitness or call to the gospel ministry who will,
for the sake of getting a church, accept the call to be its pastor
with merely a majority, and encourage confusion and disaffection among the brethren. It must be noticed again that Cornelius made himself responsible for the preacher's congregation.
He did not expect the preacher to come there and preach up
his own congregation. He had gone around or sent and invited
his neighbors and relatives, and having his own family present.
When the preacher reached Cornelius he found his congregation
in waiting. This is so unlike the majority of our churches.
They send for the preacher and expect him to gather the congregation, do the preaching, do the praying, do the singing, lead
the prayer meetings, teach Sunday school, make the people do
right, and keep the spirit in the church. If the church gets
cold and converts are not coming in they charge it up to the
preacher, and hence they mourn, sigh and pray for a change of
preacher. It must still be noticed that Cornelius did not content himself with having sent for the preacher and congregated
his hearers, but as soon as he heard that Peter was coming went
out himself to meet him, and embrace him, and extend to him
that christian welcome that only those can give whose hearts
are aglow with the love of God. This, too, is so very much
unlike the most of our churches. Too many of our members'
interest end with the call of the preacher. They are not there
to embrace him, coöperate with him, and sympathize with him
in his work. It is oftentimes true that those who are foremost
in calling the preacher are furthest behind in supporting him.
But I think better things of you. The shake of hand is stiff,
slack and cold, destitute of love, and there is no religion in it.
There is so much depending upon the encouragement the
preacher receives from his people. It must be noticed that
Cornelius announced himself and his people ready for the
preacher and his message. Verse 35: 'Now, therefore, are we
all here present before God to hear all things that are commanded thee of God.' This is not always the case with our
congregations. In the first place all are not there, and all of
those who are there are not there to hear all things commanded
the preacher of God. Some things they would much prefer not
to hear. And still, let us observe that Cornelius took the
preacher into his house and cared for him. He did not try to
put him off on somebody else or send him to a hotel. He was
willing to take God's message into his heart and God's messenger into his house. He was willing to provide for the man who

brought to him the bread of life. This should teach us a lesson. 'I ask, therefore, for what intent have ye sent for me?'

II. THE PERSON SENT FOR—THE PREACHER.

"The minister is God's chosen instructor. God sends men to teach men; He has always employed men to teach men, though men have not always been willing to be taught by the men God has sent them. They have spoken evil of their teachers, persecuted them, imprisoned them, and put them to death in every conceivable way. This is the terrible history of the world.

"A milder form of persecution now exists—it is slander, evil-speaking and refusing to pay the preacher. When the preacher fails to suit them, they resort to some one or all of these methods. It is very often that the preacher finds those of his congregation who presume to teach him. With these he must contend. There are those in this congregation who can teach me about merchandise, carpentering, sampling cotton, printing, painting, laying bricks, plastering, machinery, and many other trades, but I've come to teach you the bible—the word of God. I've come to teach every one of you. God has called me through you to teach you this word, and I have come to do this work. Is that the intent for which you have sent for me? Then pray God to help me do this great work to His honor and glory and your edification and truest interest. Israel thought quite often that they could teach Moses. God teaches in mercy through his ministers, or teaches in wrath himself. When Saul failed to hear the prophet he taught him in death. Our Saviour has said to his ministers, 'Go ye, therefore, and teach all nations, baptizing them in the name of the Father, and of the Son, and of the Holy Ghost. Teaching them to observe all things whatsoever I've commanded you; and lo! I am with you alway, even unto the end of the world. Amen.'—Matt., xxxviii, 19, 20.

"'And he gave some apostles, and some prophets, and some evangelists, and some pastors, and some teachers.'—Eph., iv, 11. We see, therefore, that the teacher is divinely appointed. God has always had them. We read in Isaiah xxx, 20, 21: 'And though the Lord give you the bread of adversity and the water of affliction, yet shall not thy teachers be removed into a corner any more, but thine eyes shall see thy teachers, and thine ears shall hear a word behind thee saying, 'This is the way, walk ye in it, when ye turn to the right hand and when ye turn to the left.' It will be observed that the teacher is to point out the way to the people and urge them to walk in it. The people are not to point out the way to the teacher, but the teacher is to point out the way to the people. God enjoins the duty of teaching the people upon the ministers.

"Again, it will be observed, that the minister is God's leader. Too many of our churches presume to lead the preachers and some of them are led, and they fall, and great is the fall. The preachers should be first in labors of love; first in the mission work; first at the bedside of the suffering, when in his power; first in matters that concern the public good, and, so far as he is able, first in matters that elevate the people intellectually and every other way. If I should be asked to name some things and places which he should be last in or not at all in, among the many I would name politics, bar rooms, shows, excursions, and last, but not least, *debts*. To owe is either to be a slave or dishonest. A debt is a curse. The preacher should be as an Æolian harp, catching the faintest breeze of heaven's air, and resounding in thunder tones to his flock—he stands nearest to God and should hear Him first. Indeed, he hears when no one else hears. God has promised that the preacher should hear the words from His mouth and warn the people from Him. Our Saviour has said, in Luke 10, 16: 'He that heareth you, heareth me; and he that despiseth you, despiseth me; and he that despiseth me, despiseth Him that sent me.' This should make us be very careful how we treat God's leaders. He says again: 'He that receiveth you, receiveth me.'—Matt., x, 40. I have trembled for people when I have seen them mistreat God's servants. The insult is not to the servants, it is thrown in the face of his Master. Better for that people had they never been born than to meet a God who pleads the cause of his servants. I wonder how they expect to meet God and answer for this insult before him. The people should follow the preacher as he follows Christ. I would ask again, for what intent did ye send for me? There are those in the church who are ready to follow after anybody else than the preacher, and after anything else than righteousness. This is not confined to a few and not confined to the poor and unlearned. There are those who are unable to attend church, but get perfectly well to attend any entertainment of a worldly character. We should know that our religion is following: we shall know if we follow on to know; we are commanded to learn of Christ: his ministers are the teachers: the church is the school house and the Bible is the text book, and the people are the scholars. The angel told Cornelius that Peter would tell him what he ought to do. This is the burden of the preacher's mission to tell people what they ought to do in spiritual matters—in matters that pertain to their everlasting salvation. I am glad that the preacher is not expected to make people do, but to tell them what they ought to do. If he was to make them do, the entire responsibility of their salvation would rest upon the preachers, and every one that was lost, his damnation would be charged up to some poor preacher. He is appointed to tell people what they ought to do. I ask, therefore, for what intent have ye sent for me?

"The minister is God's embassador. An embassador is the highest commissioned officer; he is usually sent to a foreign country; his duty is to represent the power that commissioned him; he must, therefore, be somewhat in character as the commissioner; he must understand the burden of his message, the laws of the country he represents, and he must either understand the laws and language of those to whom he is sent or must have an interpreter. The Spirit of God is his interpreter. God has sent him out on a mission of peace. The world is his field; the minister is God's overseer; he is to watch over the spiritual interest of the church of Christ; he is called the angel of the church. Christ is the shepherd and bishop of our souls, and the minister is the under-shepherd; he is to feed the church of God which he has purchased with his own blood. There is no one who can supply the place of the preacher; no one on earth is over him. He is the only overseer in the church. God made him overseer, and any effort made to change him is an insult to the power by which he is appointed. He is clothed with the power of God and he is to beseech men in Christ's stead to be reconciled to God. 'I ask, therefore, for what intent have ye sent for me?' The message which he is to deliver is glad tidings of a reconciled God to the children of men. In this work he does not always meet with encouragement; yet his business is to preach faithfully the gospel of Christ, leaving the result and his own provision and life in the hands of his Master who commissioned him. I have heard many preachers complain of it being harder to preach on Sunday night than at any hour during the day. I have often felt it a strain myself. I have wondered why. I used to think that it was because there was a much larger crowd and more heat and diversity of minds to deal with and endeavor to control. But this reason does not seem to hold good. I have lately concluded that it is due to the fact that our congregations are too much given to visiting and street promenading on Sunday, that when night comes they find themselves too much fatigued to enjoy and take in a sermon. When a person has been engaged in visiting, laughing, talking and having a good time during the day, when night comes he is not prepared to sit an hour and listen to a discourse without having a chance to throw in a word occasionally and laugh quite heartily frequently, or get up and take a drink of water once in awhile. His mental and physical powers have both been excited, and if he doesn't go to sleep he will feel like it; but most generally he will get at it. He will, at any rate, get tired of the sermon, and call the most masterly effort 'a poor thing.' He is not prepared to take it in; nature wants rest; the fault is his own. What effect has this upon the preacher? Well, just this: As the congregation is, so will the preacher be; he cannot carry all asleep, he can lead them all awake. Energetic, earnest hearers, the bright countenances, sparkling eyes and attentive ears, all conspire to enthuse the man of God to deliver his message. How will we remedy this? Well, if our people will not do, and will do, we will soon see that it will be as easy, if not easier, to preach on Sunday night as at any other hour during the day. If our people will not do so much visiting on Sunday, and will not engage in such light employment and that of a worldly character on Sunday, and will stay home during church service intervals and will read their Bibles and meditate on the law of the Lord, and will sing or hum praises to God, and will pray as did Cornelius, they would come to the church prepared to hear all things of the preacher commanded of God, and would, indeed, worship God. A praying congregation makes an earnest minister; an appreciative, interesting and weeping people make an eloquent preacher. So, my hearers, if God has called your pastor, revealed His Son in him and committed to him this glorious gospel, you have the privilege to improve him. You can make him just what you want him to be. You can make him profound by asking him questions that have puzzled you; you can aid him in piety by praying for him. This you ought always do. You can make him study by studying yourself and supporting him. You can make him love you by loving him; you can make him tender by being tender yourself. Many farmers have made poor land rich; many poor horses have been made fat by good attention. You have the ax; grind it. Nobody can tell how much it helps a preacher to do his work when his people encourage him but a preacher, and may be he cannot tell himself just how much it aids him. 'I ask, therefore, for what intent have you sent for me?' God's preachers love their work. I had rather be a preacher than be the world. I had rather be a preacher than to be any one or all of the stars. I had rather be a preacher than to be the sun. I had rather be a preacher than to be an angel. Did God count me worthy to commit this glorious work to me? God wanted me to be a preacher, hence He called me and revealed His Son in me. This Son I have come to preach to you. Is that the intent for which ye have sent for me? Then God forbid that I should know anything among you save Christ and Him crucified.

"III.—The preacher should go to the people to whom he is called just as soon as he is convinced that it is the will of God, and doubt nothing. Again, while Cornelius had been praying Peter had been praying too; hence, both were prepared for their work. Cornelius was prepared to hear and Peter was prepared to preach. In order to be prepared, each must pray. Both saw a vision. The same God appeared to both. Cornelius said we are all here before God to hear, and Peter said, I came without gainsaying as soon as I was sent for to preach. He had no doubt. God had assured him that it was his duty to go. The obedient servant will not question his work when the Master has spoken. Indeed, when God calls a servant to a work his provision is all right. God will see that he is supported, protected and guided. There is nothing to fear in the God-selected field. He may not always have encouragement in his field, but if he is ready to preach the gospel of Christ he must be willing to bear the conflicts of the gospel and to endure hardships as a good soldier of Jesus Christ. He must through tribulations enter heaven, and lead others. His way is marked through tribulations, and to shun them is to leave the hallowed way. Even those to whom he preaches will at times turn against him. This was the case with his Master, the prophets and apostles. He will meet his hardest trials among his own people. They will be willing to pull out their eyes for him to-day, and be ready to pull out his eyes to-morrow; but he must bear the toils, endure the pains, supported by the word of his Master. The minister must be ready to preach the gospel under all circumstances. His Master has not promised him that he would have no trouble, but has warned him of trouble and advised him to beware of men. Though he is to preach to men he is warned of them. While he is preparing a sermon for them they are making a trap for him; while he is praying for them they are finding fault with him; while he is outing the fire of dissension they are busy kindling it; and, as Judas, they grumble at every charitable deed. Yet, in all this, the preacher must be ready to preach the gospel to them. To preach to them is his own food, and to refuse to do which is to starve himself. He must eat of the same food which he deals out to others. Their dish is his dish, and their diet is his diet. Hear his solemn charge: 'I charge thee therefore before God, and the Lord Jesus Christ, who shall judge the quick and the dead at his appearing and his kingdom; preach the word; be instant in season and out of season; reprove, rebuke, exhort with all long suffering and doctrine.'—II Tim., iv, 1-2. To this our congregations will object, especially the part that tells the preacher to rebuke. In I Tim., 4, 16, he is told: 'Take heed unto thyself, and unto the doctrine; continue in them: for in doing this thou shalt both save thyself, and them that hear thee.' In Acts xx, 28, it is said: 'Take heed therefore unto yourselves, and unto all the flock over which the Holy Ghost hath made you overseers, to feed the church of God, which he has purchased with his own blood.' These passages point out very clearly the preacher's duty; he cannot mistake his way; let him take the word of God as a man of his counsel and have simple faith in God. In order for the preacher to be ready in season and out of season, he needs always to pray for the Spirit of God to assist him in preaching the gospel. He should go to his people ready to share their joys, sorrows and troubles. He should be ready to mourn with them who mourn, and weep with them who weep, and pray with them who pray. It is the most fearful responsibility under heaven to be a pastor—the most sacred trust and the highest honor. I am officially informed that I have been chosen of God and called by his people to be the pastor of this church. Regarding the voice of the people as being the voice of God, I do therefore, in the name of God, accept the same. I accept, not ignorant of its weight and cares. I shall expect you as a church to do your part, remembering that whatever you mete to men it shall be measured to you again. Let it be the controlling object of our whole life to win souls for God and for heaven. It is our business to lead sinners to Jesus. I put the sinners of Savannah on notice this night that I have come for you, I have come to lead you to Jesus. I have come to hold Christ up to you as the fairest among ten thousands and altogether lovely. I have come to hold up Jesus Christ to you as the only name given under heaven whereby you might be saved. I have come to beg you in Christ's stead to be reconciled to God. I have come to beg you to make friends with God. I have come to be your friend and to teach you to love him who first loved you and gave himself for you. I have come to invite you down in Jordan to be cleansed of the leprosy. I have come to beg you to get ready to die. You are swiftly passing away to the great judgment day, and I have come in the name of my Master to beg you to make some arrangement for your soul. Oh! I beg you in the name of high heaven to-night to commence even now, to make some arrangement for that precious soul that must always live in heaven or hell. Dear brethren. is this the intent for which ye have sent for me? Then do help me to preach this word: help me to show the sinners of Savannah the beauties that are in Jesus Christ. God help us do this in order that our garments might be clear of their blood. It is all of our business to see to it that sinners are properly informed of Christ. Let us speak well of Jesus. I have come to Savannah to speak well of the plan of redemption and of Jesus, its author. I have come among you as the friend of education, the advocate of economy and industry, as a worker in the Sunday schools, a promoter of peace, a law-abiding citizen, and the untiring and uncompromising enemy to whiskey. I want to be understood to-night as being the terror of whiskey and its votaries, so far as my power goes. I shall speak, write, preach, fight, work, pray and vote against it at every opportunity that may be afforded me through the entire journey of my life. Dear brethren, is this the intent for which ye have sent for me? Then can I depend upon you to support and help me do my work? The christian's life should be so sublime; his life should be a living reality of the joy and blessedness of the life beyond; he should live so that he might be able to say, I know upon whom I have believed; I know that my Redeemer lives. 'O, what a blessed hope is ours while here on earth we stay.' Let us live and work as become children of the light and our death will be as sweet as it will be sublime, and heaven will be our eternal home. Let us covenant to walk together in Christ from this very night. As we walk together here we shall live together over the river upon the shining shores of that blessed country whose builder and maker is God, where pastor and people shall be gathered with everlasting joy and singing; where death never comes; where victors are crowned with Eden's wreath; where they shall sorrow no more; die no more; cry no more: thirst no more and hunger no more, for the lamb upon the throne shall feed them. For this let us labor, watch, pray and wait till Jesus comes and we will be gathered home. God help us for Jesus' sake. Amen."

Very soon after Mr. Love took charge of the church he found it necessary to preach upon going to law, this being prevalent:

GOING TO LAW.

"I. Cor., vi, 1: 'Dare any of you, having a matter against another, go to law before the unjust and not before the saints?' I am not ignorant of the fact that I have a delicate and difficult subject to handle to-night about which much has been said, written and thought. If I should carelessly speak to-night untold harm might be the result, which would be just the opposite to what I aim at and wish so much to accomplish. I am also aware that this subject is as a two-edged sword, capable of cutting both ways.

"Believing it better to let two guilty men escape justice than to punish one innocent man. I proceed to discuss this subject to-night in the fear of heaven, relying upon the guidance of the Holy Spirit to assist me in so fearful an undertaking. I am outgrowing the idea that the truth should be kept from the people for fear that they will abuse it. I think the better way would be to have the whole truth and let the results be what they will. The common interpretation of this scripture will tend to make religion objectionable and church membership an unreasonable burden. The religion of Christ is based upon common-sense reasoning. We have hold of the chain of reason, the opposite end of which is centered in the eternal bosom of God. Religion requires us to live a common sense, practical life. Our Saviour rebuked the Pharisees for misinterpreting the law and binding heavy burdens, and grievous to be borne, upon the people. Religion requires us to adopt a common course of justice with our fellow-men. There is as much logic in the idea of keeping the whole truth from the people for fear they will abuse it as there would be in the idea of keeping freedom from a people for fear they would abuse it. The better way would be to let the people have freedom, which is right, and then teach them the proper way to enjoy it. There is no privilege but that it has and can be abused. The principle is right, nevertheless. Water and food have made persons sick, yet it is not denied that they are good to take in. Some persons marry and do not get on well together, yet it is admitted that marrying is right. One man quits a woman upon the ground that he can not live with her, and yet another man marries her and lives happily with her.

"It must be admitted also that there are exceptions to all general rules. It is so in the Bible as well as in other books. God has shown this in his dealing with the children of men. Hence the origin of miracles. The rule for entering heaven is marked through repentance toward God and faith in His son, yet none of us doubt the salvation of infants. who can not do either. The rule is that a star does not stop, and yet one stood over the manger where the young child was. It is the rule that fire will burn, yet the Hebrew children went through the fiery furnace without the smell of fire upon their clothes. It is a rule that men die, yet Enoch and Elijah were translated. It is a rule that iron sinks, yet the prophet caused it to swim. In this light we must view many scriptural precepts. It was not lawful for the disciples to enter the corn field and eat on the Sabbath, yet Christ defended them, and said he was Lord even of the Sabbath. With the foregoing remarks we can more practically discuss this much disputed subject.

I.—IS IT RIGHT TO GO TO LAW WITH A BROTHER?

"We would say that it depends largely upon the character and nature of the subject in dispute. As a rule it is not right to go to law. If every body would do right we would have but little, if any, use for the courts. But from the fact that we are not predisposed to do unto all men as we would that they do unto us, God has appointed judges. The judges that sat in the gates of the city were to discern between the people. It is not good for church members to be contentious, because it does not reflect favorably upon christianity. It would not reflect creditably upon members of the same family to be contending in the courts with each other. If brother goes to law with brother, where is the evidence that the grace of God is sufficient for all things, and that we love each other and are made perfect in one? As a rule the saints should judge points of difference between saints. As they shall take part in judging the world they might be intrusted with the matter of deciding points of difference between brethren with whom they shall be associated in deciding the destiny of the world, for the apostle says:

"I. Cor., vi. 2, 3: 'Do ye not know that the saints shall judge the world? And if the world shall be judged by you, are ye unworthy to judge the smallest matters? Know ye not that we shall judge angels? How much more things that pertain to this life?'

"This instruction is evidently for personal differences. In cases of personal misunderstandings the church should interpose, and only the church. If a member is personally injured or aggrieved, he should, after proper gospel steps, tell it to the church. This principle is laid down by our Saviour in Matthew, xviii. 15–18: 'Moreover, if thy brother shall trespass against thee go and tell him his fault between thee and him alone: if he shall hear thee, thou hast gained thy brother. But if he will not hear thee, then take with thee one or two more, that in the mouth of two or three witnesses every word may be established. And if he shall neglect to hear them, tell it unto the church: but if he neglect to hear the church, let him be unto thee as an heathen man and a publican.'

"In Leviticus, xix, 17, 18, we read: 'Thou shalt not hate thy brother in thine heart: thou shalt in anywise rebuke thy neighbor, and not suffer sin upon him. Thou shalt not avenge nor bear any grudge against the children of thy people, but thou shalt love thy neighbor as thyself: I am the Lord.'

"As the Israelites were just emancipated from Egyptian bondage, and were freemen going to live together in a free country, it was necessary that they should know their obligation to each other as the chosen of the Lord and as fellow-citizens. We read again in Luke xvii, 3, 4: 'Take heed to yourselves: if thy brother trespass against thee, rebuke him; and if he repent, forgive him. And if he trespass against thee seven times in a day. and seven times in a day turn again to thee, saying, I repent, thou shalt forgive him.' These passages point out clearly the course to pursue in general matters. Respecting personal offenses, I wrote Dr. J. E. L. Holmes, of this city, asking him if a man who is a member of the church should assault your wife or daughter could you take such a a case to law? This is his reply:

"'January, 11, 1886.

"'I should find it difficult to decide. The circumstances under which the assault was made would have much to do with the right or wrong. Might there not be reparation, apology? Ordinarily personal difficulties are better settled privately, and if carried into court give a notoriety to all concerned which is not in the interest of good order or wholesome influence. I rather think the apostle would have discouraged going into court in this case.'

"It seems that the christians at Corinth habitually went before the heathen courts for every trifle about which they disagreed. The apostle is rebuking them for this, and gives them to know that this course is wholly repugnant to the genius of christianity, and that by it they could not hope to impress the heathens with the loving influence of the christian religion and thus win them to Christ. A contentious spirit is at variance with the spirit of religion and does not add a salutary influence to the church of Christ. Matthew Henry says on this subject: 'Here the apostle reproves them for going to law with one another before the heathen judges for little matters, and therein blames all vexatious law suits. In the previous chapter he had directed them to punish heinous sins among themselves by church censures. Here he directs them to determine controversies with one another by church counsel and advice, concerning which observe: 1. The fault he blames them for, it was going to law. Not but that the law is good, if a man use it lawfully. But brother went to law with brother—one member of the church with another. The near relation could not preserve peace and good understanding. The bonds of fraternal love were broken through. And a brother offended, as Solomon says, is harder to be won than a strong city; their contentions are like the bars of a castle. Christians should not contend with one another, for they are brethren. This duly attended to would prevent law suits and put an end to quarrels and litigations. They brought the matter before the heathen magistrates; they went to law before the unjust, and not before the saints: brought the controversy before unbelievers and did not compose it among themselves, christians and saints, at least in profession. This tended much to the reproach of christianity. It published at once their folly and unpeaceableness; whereas they pretended to be the children of wisdom and the followers of the Lamb, the meek and lowly Jesus, the Prince of Peace. 'And therefore,' says the apostle, 'dare any of you, having a controversy with another, go to law, implead him, bring the matter to a hearing before the unjust?' Christians should not dare to do anything that tends to the reproach of their christian name and profession. Here is at least an intimation that they went to law for trivial matters, things of little value, for the apostle blames them that they did not suffer wrong rather than go to law, which must be understood of matters not very important. But in matters of small consequence it is better to put up with the wrong. Christians should be of a forgiving temper. And it is more to their ease and honor to suffer small injuries and inconveniences than seem to be contentious.'

"This all seems to be striking at personal matters—matters of small moment. All seem to admit that this is the general rule—that the church should intervene to settle such matters between its members. Any matter that affects us as individuals in the shape of individual insults, assaults on our character or persons, may be adjusted by the church, and should by all means be kept out of the courts. There is only an individual feeling or grievance at stake. In this case the censure of the church is sufficient. Now let us be very careful as we notice the exceptions to this general rule. Let us pray that the holy spirit might give us a door of utterance, and that he also might prevent a misunderstanding of this scripture.

II.—IS THERE NO CIRCUMSTANCE UNDER WHICH A CHURCH MEMBER MAY TAKE A CASE TO LAW?

"We answer, most certainly there is. To say there is not

would be to most fearfully pervert the spirit of the scriptures and open a door to the dishonestly disposed for the most unmitigating frauds. Too many dishonest church members would borrow money from church members with no intention whatever to pay it, and hide behind this scripture: 'Dare any of you, having a matter against another, go to law before the unjust and not before the saints.' It must be considered that the christians at Corinth were living in a heathen land and subject to heathen magistrates. We do not live in heathen lands and are not presided over by heathen rulers. We are citizens of a common country and are in honor bound to support the laws of this country. Many of our rulers are members of the christian church, and many of their christian lives are irreproachable. The laws of our country are based, for the most part, upon the Bible, which book is the guide to the christian church. It must be acknowledged, therefore, that the circumstances under which the christians at Corinth lived and the circumstances under which we live are decidedly different, and hence the exceptions to this general rule. I have taken pains to write some of the most learned men of our denomination on this subject; men whose ability is not questioned, and who are authority on Baptist usage. I give you extracts from their letters:

"Dr. J. E. L. Holmes, of this city, writes me:

"'JANUARY 11th, 1888.
"'*Dear Brother Love:*

"'I think we must take several things into consideration in interpreting I. Corinthians, vi, 1: 'Dare any of you, having a matter against another, go to law before the unjust, and not before the saints?' The point of the apostle's answer is found in the fact that they went 'to law before the unjust,' that is, before the heathen tribunals. And this not because they could not hope for justice from heathen rulers, nor because the heathen rulers were not to be respected. The apostle is careful to teach them to respect and be subject to the authorities that be. See Romans, xiii, 1–8: ('Let every soul be subject unto the higher powers. For there is no power but of God: the powers that be are ordained of God. Whosoever, therefore, resisteth the power resisteth the ordinance of God: and they that resist shall receive to themselves damnation. For rulers are not a terror to good works, but to the evil. Wilt thou then not be afraid of the power? do that which is good, and thou shalt have praise of the same: For he is the minister of God to thee for good. But if thou do that which is evil, be afraid; for he beareth not the sword in vain: for he is the minister of God, a revenger to execute wrath upon him that doeth evil. Wherefore ye must needs be subject not only for wrath, but also for conscience sake. For this cause pay ye tribute also: for they are God's ministers, attending continually upon this very thing. Render, therefore, to all their dues: tribute to whom tribute is due; custom to whom custom; fear to whom fear; honor to whom honor. Owe no man anything, but to love one another: for he that loveth another hath fulfilled the law.') Titus, iii, 1: ('Put them in mind to be subject to principalities and powers, to obey magistrates, to be ready to every good work.') But he saw that the effect of such litigation would be unfavorable to christianity. The Jews were known to be a contentious people. They (christians) must so act as to prevent creating such impression about the christians, most of whom, at least at first, were Jews. Besides it was a sorry sight that these christians, who were called of God and the heirs of heaven, should be going to these less favored to decide questions which they could so easily decide. I think we get the impression in reading the context, and especially the seventh verse, that the matters in dispute were of little consequence, involving no principle, and likely to produce no great injury one way or another. Notice, then, first, that we are not situated just as they were. Our judges and rulers are not heathen, but often our own brethren; our laws are based for the most part upon the principle taught in the New Testament. There is, then, no such scandal in going into court as there was in the days of the christians of Corinth. But it may be wrong, nevertheless, to go to law, if by going to law we make it apparent to the world that while professing to be christians we have not the spirit of Christ, or worse still, if the world (as represented in civil government) should be led to think that the spirit of contentiousness was the spirit of Christ. Better suffer some injustice than do the cause an injury by furnishing cavilers occasion for talk. Brethren should settle their difficulties by appeals to brethren, and with the advice and assistance of brethren. Romans xii, 18: 'If it be possible, as much as lieth in you, live peaceably with all men,' is a fine illustration of the apostle's way of setting forth a great principle, with the limitation which our weakness makes necessary. If it be possible, that reminds us that there are exceptions to the rule. And now having noticed the principle, let us notice the exception. Are there not matters of difference which the church cannot decide? Ought not the church to relieve a brother of embarrassment in this regard (sometimes by putting an unworthy brother out of its pale)? Is a brother to suffer the loss of property, or to be otherwise injured in his person or family, because some one claiming to be a brother is presuming upon his connection with the church, while the first brother has no redress? To ask these questions is to answer them. A man who is capable of a great wrong has no claim to a brother's privileges, and the one who has been thus grievously wronged is under no law to treat him as such. Matthew, xviii, 17, might apply in such a case. It is the duty of the church in such a case to relieve itself of the odium attaching to a life so wholly at variance with the teaching of Christ. In the case you suppose, I should say that the banker might, without violating the spirit of the scripture, go to law.' [This was in answer to the question whether a banker could by law recover his money or not.]

"'The last case seems to me clear, if arbitration has first been tried. And the right to property may depend upon a legal technicality. In the first and last cases it is true there is a matter of personal feeling, but of right under the law. Can a member of the church go to law under any circumstances? I should greatly regret having to go into court, but I should most certainly do so before I would allow the support of my family to be taken from them: before I should allow myself to suffer any great injury. Paul did not hesitate to appeal to Cæsar when he saw that in this way alone could he have his rights and secure a fair trial. When the cause is manifestly just, when a principle is involved of real moment, and the rights such as depend upon the existence of government, I believe we may rightly make exceptions to what ought to be the rule. If all brethren were as they should be, of course secular courts would not be needed for christianity, but this is not an ideal state, and the Bible recognizes the fact.'

"As to going to law, Dr. Mell writes, January 11, 1886:

"'*Rev. E. K. Love:*

"'DEAR BROTHER—Can one church member sue another at law? This is one of those questions on which there will always be an honest difference of opinion; for, 1st, courts in this country cannot be characterized as essentially and by their own constitutions and materials 'unjust' and unbelievers. They are partly based on the christian religion. The Bible is used in its administrations, and often large portions of its individual members are exemplary christians.

"'2d. There are many legal questions that honestly spring up between brethren that none are competent to decide except those learned in the law. Very few, if any, of our churches are competent to adjudicate such questions. It would seem then that, with or without first obtaining the consent of the church, brethren may amicably and candidly submit such cases for the arbitration of the courts without violating the principles of the gospel law—especially if they would refrain from the use of strategy so often employed by counsel. Sometimes delay, caused by the slow intervention of the church, affords opportunity to a dishonest church member to make away with his property to the great injury of the one who has a just claim against him. I see not why there should be any hesitation in invoking the courts in the two cases you refer to, since no church could consistently hesitate to expel the parties at the first opportunity.'

"We call next on the stand that distinguished theologian and scholar of the first order, Rev. Dr. J. M. Pendleton. He writes from Bowling Green, Ky.:

"'JANUARY 13, 1886.

"'*Brother Love:*

"'I do not understand I. Cor., vi. 1, as forbidding christians in any circumstances to go to law with another. There may be cases in which it is necessary to bring suit with a view to settle points that can not otherwise be settled, deciding, for example, land titles, etc. Such suits may be brought in a friendly manner. I give this illustration to show that it is not wrong, in all circumstances, for brethren to go to law.'

"In answer to a question that I put to him, that if a man borrows money at the bank and gave property as collateral, and refused to pay the bill, could the banker sue for his money—presuming that both are members of the church? He answers:

"'If there is proof of dishonesty in the borrower, then he should be excluded from the church and be no longer regarded as a brother. When this is done, there is nothing in the way of bringing suit.

"'Your second question refers to an assault on some one's wife or daughter by a church member. You ask if in such a case may there be a resort to law. I answer, Yes; but the first thing is for the church to exclude the member. In case of scandalous crimes, no church trial is called for. The exclusion should be prompt, as you may see from I. Cor., v. After the exclusion there may be an appeal to law; but in many cases it is better not to have such a matter ventilated in the courts. The course to be taken should be determined by the circumstances in each case.'

"As to a dispute about property, he says:

"'I do not see how the matter can be settled out of court; but there should be no unfriendly feeling, only a simple desire for justice to be done.'

" We once more quote the distinguished commentator Matthew Henry:

"'In matters of great damage to ourselves and families we may use lawful means to right ourselves. We are not bound to sit down and suffer the injury tamely, without striving for our own relief.'

" We would still put up another important witness. He is the first preacher I ever heard of in my life. He baptized my mother and father and most of my relatives. He seems as a grandfather to me. He is a ripe scholar and a safe theologian. That beloved, distinguished man is Dr. J. H. DeVotie. He writes me from Griffin, Ga., January 15th, 1886:

"'*Dear Brother:*

"'In the simplest form I answer your questions in your note of January 5th, 1886. The 6th of I. Cor., i, 5, does not forbid under *all circumstances* members of the church from settling their differences by an appeal to the laws of the country.

"'*Question A.*—I answer yes, he ought to be made to pay it. They have made it a transaction governed by law. They have made legal papers, and there is a legal tribunal. The church should exclude the man who will not meet his honest engagements, and who will not listen to the committee of the church who deal with him according to the scriptural rule. He should be to the church 'as a heathen man and a publican.' and be dealt with according to the laws of the heathen and the publican.

"'*Question B.*—I do not know what you mean by wife or daughter being assaulted by a member of the church. If you mean an attempt to commit rape, or something kindred to that. why certainly he ought to be indicted and punished according to law.

"'*Question C.*—The two members of a church who hold. each of them, a deed to the same piece of land must settle it by law. The law creates the title. I cannot conceive of two *good* deeds to the same piece of ground. There must be a legal and an illegal deed. The law alone can decide. Brethren may interpose. but they can never say justly that the illegal deed must hold the land.'

"And last, but not least, we call to the stand a scholar and safe theologian, and successful and experienced pastor. He is my father in the gospel; by him I was baptized, and from him I received my first impressions of gospel truth. That dear man is Rev. W. H. McIntosh, D. D. He writes me from Cedartown, Ga., Jan. 21, 1886:

"'*Dear Brother Love:*

"'I can only give the scriptural law applicable to the case. I. Cor., vi, 1, forbids brother to go to law with brother. I know of no exception in the New Testament. This law is not designed to screen one member of the church from paying an honest debt to another member. If it is evident that he is seeking to defraud his brother of a just claim, the church should arraign him for dishonesty, and when they have excluded him then the aggrieved brother can appeal to the courts for redress; the offender is to him 'as a heathen man and a publican.'—Matt., xviii, 17. Such cases are apt to be complicated and to prove troublesome to the church, and it is sometimes wise to get the parties (creditor and debtor) to submit the matter to arbitration before it comes before the church. You see the danger is that the friends of each party may take sides with their favorite, and parties be raised in the church that may be perpetuated for years and for evil. The same principles apply to the case of two members each holding a deed to the same property. In the case of assault by a member of the church upon the person of the wife or daughter of another member, if you mean an attempt upon her virtue, the offender should be arraigned before the church and, if convicted and excluded, as he should be if guilty, the husband or father can and ought to prosecute him.'

"It is remarkable that all of these divines agree in substance upon this scripture. They are not biased, as they knew not what I wanted to teach. They gave honest statements. In the mouth of two or three witnesses every word shall be established. They do not give it as a result of consultation with each other; every one wrote from a different place and from his standpoint, without knowing that anybody else had been consulted.

"This subject has caused a great deal of trouble in the church of Christ. Many unworthy persons have taken advantage of this scripture, which the church is endeavoring to honestly obey, to be dishonest and perpetrate the most glaring frauds upon each other. For a church to insist that a member can, under no circumstances, go to law, is to license men to commit the most terrible crimes, the atrocity of which common sense and civilization will scorn. If the church continues at this, the young element will revolt and leave the church of their fathers. If men honestly owe debts, and have property out of which those debts can be paid, it is common justice that they pay them. If they will not pay those debts, the church should be no screen to protect dishonesty, and the courts should interpose to defend the rights of a citizen. If a man can pay a debt and will not pay it, and as the church cannot make him pay it, the courts should be invoked. There are numbers of church members sitting down in the church who owe debts, and upon the presumption that you dare not go to law, wilfully refuse to pay them. What is the remedy? Let the member so suffering report the case to the officer whose duty it will be to labor with the debtors, and if they still refuse to pay, let the officers tell it to the church, and if they still refuse, let the church expel them, and then the suffering member can take legal steps to recover his money. This should only be done when everything else has failed. No church can consistently keep in its fellowship a dishonest member, and no person is honest who can pay a debt and will not do it. We are not bound to respect dishonest persons.

APPLICATION.

"I have known judges and lawyers and jurors in our courts to be preachers of the gospel. Would we call a court of that make-up 'heathen,' 'unjust' and 'unbelievers?' There is perhaps, in many instances, as much honesty and justice in the decisions of the courts as in those of the churches. As a rule, homestead is dishonest and a screen from justice. Our property ought to be subject to our debts. The church very often makes sad mistakes in its dealings with its members. This is because she is not infallible. The sweet thought is that we will get home by and by, where mistakes will be impossible. There will be no conferences nor arbitration of the courts. Jesus Christ will hug us to his holy bosom and our joy will be as pleasing as it will be eternal. Then shall we know as we are known, and having everything in common, we shall join the countless number of harpers harping with harps, and throughout the countless ages of eternity we shall bathe our weary souls in seas of heavenly rest, and not a wave of trouble roll across our peaceful breast. Then, as we stand upon the sea of glass mingled with fire we shall make heaven's arches ring as the flightless ages of eternity roll. God help us. Amen."

Shortly after the delivery of this effectual discourse Rev. Love delivered the following discourse to a densely-packed house. The congregation was intensely interested, and it is confidently believed that great good followed from this discourse. During its delivery Rev. Mr. Love held his hearers spell-bound. The fact that so many members of the church and citizens generally felt that they could break the nuptial tie at will, and since they obtained a divorce from the courts that all was well. Mr. Love felt called upon to raise his voice against it. After the delivery of this sermon the church took a strong stand against unscriptural divorce:

THE SERMON.—SCRIPTURAL DIVORCE.

"There is nothing which strikes so essentially at the very root of society as the tampering with the marriage institution. If this is corrupt, society is degraded, happiness is destroyed, morality is debased, virtue is gone, civilization is crippled, christianity is hindered and gloom spreads her drapery over our land, the garden spot of the globe. For the family circle is the seed-bed of society, the fountain-head of civilization, the birth-place of tranquility, the cradle of prosperity, the moulding-place of character, and the reservoir from which streams of joy or misery flow. As the family circle is, so will society be. Clandestine marriages and divorces seem to be the special curse of this age. It would seem that the further we get from the primeval state of man the more remote are we removed from the proper observance of the matrimonial institution. In Massachusetts for every fourteen marriages there is one divorce. In proud Maine there are 478 divorces a year. In these Southern States it is simply alarming. In the New England States there are 2,000 divorces in a single year. What must all these grass widows do? Do you believe that they will live pure? Is not this an alarming state of society? Is it not time that the church was waging war against this flood-tide of immorality? Can society rest at ease when a restless worm is eternally gnawing on its tap root? Should not the watchmen on the walls give the alarm when they see the enemy coming to destroy the city and take away the inhabitants captive? How long will it be before we will reach the point when it will not be safe for anybody's daughter to follow a man off if this thing continues? How long will it be before parents should mourn for their daughters as though they were dead when they give their hand in marriage to a man? How long will it be before there will be more grass widows than there will be young girls who have never been married? How long will it be before young men will be obliged to pick their choice from among the grass widows or wait till some more girls grow up? How long will it be before the girls will have to inquire after every young man who makes a polite bow, tips his hat and wishes to see her to church, 'Is he a grass widower?' Considering this appalling state of society, we beg your prayerful consideration to-night of

SCRIPTURAL DIVORCE.

"Mark, x. 9: 'What therefore God has joined together, let not man put asunder.'

"We are called upon to consider another one of those delicate subjects that gives endless trouble in the christian church and in all this land. I can scarcely hope that this feeble effort will be wide spread and do anything like universal good; but I can and do hope that it will do good in my immediate congregation. The prevalence of divorce, clandestine marriages, and separation is simply alarming. The ignoring of the sanctity of the nuptial tie in this country is a great scandal to civilization and the cause of christianity. The church should be aroused to throw all of her influence against this flood-tide of immorality and save this nation from this sin and shame. The marriage rite is of God, and His book alone is authority for its government. Civil government did not originate the matrimonial institution, and should not interfere with it further than His law allows. The Bible is the foundation of all just and wise laws, and no courts should presume to forego its teachings. God is the author of all of our being, and his laws should govern us all. They were given in divine wisdom, and we should not presume to improve upon them. We are not allowed to amend them. They are as everlasting as He is eternal. His own Son came to earth and denied that he had a right to change them, but that he came to explain and fulfill them. His laws should be sufficient for his children. The wisdom of men and angels combined could not produce such a book, and hence the folly in trying to make better laws than it contains, or wickedness in refusing to abide its teachings. Marriage is a religious rite, and the Bible is the book governing religious rites. Whatever the courts do in this regard that is not in accordance with that blessed book is sinful and wrong, and must work hurt to the cause of morality, christianity and civilization. They differ only from heathens in that they know better; and hence their wrong is the more inexcusable.

I.—WHAT GOD HATH JOINED TOGETHER.

"The sacredness of the matrimonial relation is at once put forth in the fact that God joins together. He who opens and no man can shut, and shuts and no one can open, joins together man and woman as husband and wife, and puts His seal upon the union that 'no man put asunder.' The sacredness of the relation is further seen in that God made them at first twain. They were the only two, and, therefore, must stay together. They fell together and were driven out of the garden together. There was no other woman for Adam to take and Eve could not get another husband. It seems that if God had meant for man to have more than one wife he would have started him with more than one. He said that man should cleave unto his wife and not wives. The Bible says that woman should obey her husband, not husbands. There is nothing more wonderful and sacred than the flowing together of two human lives. Can we conceive of a thing more wonderful than that a man who is born and reared a thousand miles from Savannah, comes here on a visit, gets acquainted with one of our girls, falls in love with her, letters begin to pass between them, and by and by their lives are flown into one. He lives for her and she lives for him. Their destiny is one and their interest is common. Their love is one, their joy is the same, and through the vicissitudinous cycles of time they are to live as one, for better or for worse. A union that is so sacred, so wonderful, and so sublime as this should not and can not be dissolved at will.

"It is not strange, therefore, that the most stringent laws are thrown around the holy rite of matrimony. The more sacred a thing is, the more rigorous the laws concerning it, and the more severe the punishment in case of violation. The Saviour described His intimacy with His church by the relation of husband and wife. The name woman means pliant, and implies that she leans upon man. If man falls she cannot stand, and if she falls she carries him with her. This is plainly shown in the fall, and in all subsequent history. Though Eve was the first to fall, she carried Adam with her. They were one in interest and in destiny, and the one could not stand after the other had fallen. Adam's only excuse to God for his sin was, 'The woman whom thou gavest to be with me she gave me of the tree, and I did eat.' They alike were cursed, for they were one. They went out of the garden alike and together. 'Unto Adam also and to his wife did the Lord God make coats of skins and clothed them. In all of God's dealings with the children of men this fact of the union of husband and wife is recognized. The limit of the union is marked by Him. His limit is the only legal one. There is nothing on earth that is a purer picture of heaven than the family circle. There is nothing that more clearly illustrates the love of God for His church than the nuptial tie. It is not strange, therefore, that it is said that God joins them together. All true marriages are just as truly joined together by God as the church and His Son are joined together by Him. And He has just as complete control of the conjugal relation as over the union of the church and His Son. He sustains the same relation to both: God over all and blessed for evermore. The woman is said to be 'the better half.' See that infant boy as he comes into the world unconscious of his existence, and still every effort seems to be a struggle for his 'lost piece,' his better half.' The girl is the same. Every smile and graceful look seems to indicate that she is in search of something that she would be delighted to find. It is a husband with whom she wishes to cast her destiny. It is nature seeking its own. See them battling with the ins and outs of life until they come to years when the dreams of infancy are o'er and the visions of childhood are ended, and they refuse longer to remain under the parental roof. There is something without that suits them much better. It does not matter what attraction the parental home may possess, it does not matter what wealth the parents may have, nor what may be the culture and refinement the family home present, 'there is a gentle voice within calls away.' He goes up to a man and looks him in the face and asks him for his daughter with as much grace as a Jew would invite you into his store. Generally the father says yes.' He asked once himself. How can he refuse? It is the young man's wife that God has made for him and the father has been holding her in trust simple until this young man comes for her and asks that their lives be poured into one. As a rule, it is the father's duty to surrender his guardianship just as completely as if she had died.

"Their lives henceforth is to be a life. God has joined them together and he seals the union with heaven's stamp that 'no man put asunder.' If it be argued that all marriages are not joined together by God, I answer, neither are all persons' union with the church sanctioned by God, but they say so, and we take their word and receive them, for by their word they shall be judged. In the church we deal with hypocrites and true christians by the same rule. We call them all brethren and sisters because we do not know any better. They are responsible to God for their internal qualification. No mistake is admissible before His righteous bar, before which we will be tried. God has made us intelligent beings capable of making a choice, and he holds us accountable for the choice we do make. I believe it is everybody's duty to get married. I believe it is a divine duty. The God of our being, who knows every particle that goes into our make up, said it was not good for man to be alone. He made us help meets one for another. That woman's life that cannot pour into some man's life is cloddy, spongy and sticky. Lumber that can not be worked is knotty and refused, it matters not how good it may look. You very often hear persons say that the reason that they do not get married is that they can't find anybody to suit them It is just as often true that there is nothing of genuine greatness in them to be suited. The union of husband and wife illustrates finely the union of the believer and Christ. 'My beloved is mine, and I am his.' 'I sat down under his shadow with great delight, and his fruit is sweet to my taste.' 'His left hand is under my head, and his right hand doth embrace me.' 'My beloved spoke, and said unto me, rise up, my love, my fair one, and come away.' 'I am my beloved's and his desire is toward me.' 'Set me as a seal upon thine heart, as a seal upon thine arm : for love is strong as death.' These quotations are from the Song of Solomon, that all admit to be a figure of Christ and his church. If we are Christ's by redemption and the gift of the Father, His life and our life are one, and the life which we now live is not ours, but we live by faith that is in Him. When the hearts of Christ and the believers have been joined together by the Father, then, and not until then, can we see the force and beauty in the expression of Paul: ·For to me to live is Christ, and to die is gain.' We come now to consider the separation.

II.—LET NOT MAN PUT ASUNDER.

"This restraint is put upon man individually and collectively. The restraining injunction is issued by the court of heaven against individuals, societies, courts and churches for anything other than God's law doth allow, and that thing is adultery or fornication. If we would come back to the old landmark the marriage institution would be purer, social order would be more sacred, and human happiness would be sublimer and the standard of morality would be raised higher. If our courts would conform to the divine law in divorce cases they would do lasting good to the cause of civilization and promote the cause of christianity. The courts have established the following legal grounds for a divorce:

"I. Inter-marriage.—That is where a man marries too near a relative—a half-sister, cousin, etc. Such a marriage the courts would declare null and void.

"II. Mental Incapacity—*Non compos mentis.*—That is a person who is so crazed as to be unfit to discharge the marriage duties. In this case the courts would declare the nuptial relation invalid and would grant a divorce to the plaintiff, putting them asunder.

"Impotency.—That is weakness, whether of mind or body; some disease of body or mind that makes a person incompetent to do the duties of a married life, or too disagreeable to live with. This the courts would declare sufficient grounds for divorce and the contracting parties would be set at liberty.

"IV. Forced Marriage.—That is where a person is forced to marry by others, by outside influence or for fear of losing life. The courts would say that the parties did not contract and hence the marriage is illegal. The parties would be declared free.

"V. Pregnancy of the wife before marriage unknown to the husband at the time of marriage.—This is tantamount to adultery after marriage. This, the courts would decide a legal cause for divorce, and hence it would be granted and the parties set free. But if the man knew it when he made the contract, he would be held responsible and not be allowed a divorce.

"VI. Simple adultery is a legal ground for divorce by the courts.—Upon this the laws of God and of man are agreed.

"VII. Willful and continued desertion of either contracting party for three years.—The courts would decide the marriage vow broken and, therefore, the contract a nullity, and grant a permanent divorce, freeing the parties.

"VIII. Conviction of either party of crime involving moral turpitude and sentenced for two years in the penitentiary.—This the courts would deem a sufficient cause for divorce. Then, again, the courts have what they term discretionary grounds for divorce. Under this head is cruel treatment and habitual intoxication. For these the courts leave themselves free to grant or refuse as they may see fit. Now have not they plausible grounds to set at naught the law of God? What can look more abominable than an earthly court sitting in judgment upon the court of heaven, reviewing its decisions, reversing and setting at naught its judgment, the lower court reviewing the higher court, men correcting God? The Supreme Law Giver has allowed but two things to put asunder what He has joined together—they are adultery and fornication. The one is unforeseen by the contracting parties, the other can't be helped. Jesus has said that if a man puts away his wife for any other cause except adultery or fornication causes her to commit adultery, and he that marries her that is put away also commits adultery. This is the gospel order and the gospel church is morally bound to support and contend for the gospel order. It does not matter, therefore, upon what ground the courts may grant a divorce the church cannot recognize it, except it is granted upon the principle laid down by our Saviour and for the cause named by Him—adultery.

"All other divorces are unscriptural, and the parties so obtaining them are guilty of adultery, and therefore unfit for membership in the christian church. A married couple is bound by the law of God as long as they live, except fornication or adultery separate them. Neither is free while the other lives, unless the cause be scriptural. If the cause be scriptural, the innocent party may marry again, after a divorce is had, and remain a wholesome member of the church, but the guilty party cannot marry again and be a member of the christian church. Though, if there is evidence of genuine repentance, the guilty party might be restored to church fellowship, but not allowed to marry again.

"In cases of abandonment, or 'willful continued desertion,' as the courts put it, the parties might be allowed to separate and be retained as members of the church, provided they are reconciled to each other, but not be divorced from each other—not allowed to marry again, from the fact that the church cannot make laws. Her laws are made by Christ, and He has allowed only two causes for total divorce, and they are adultery and fornication. A thousand men have no more right to put asunder what God has joined together than one man has. It is no more legal, in the sight of God, for twelve men to put asunder man and wife than it is for one man to do it; and the church should regard it no more than if one man had done it.

"The Apostle Paul says, in I. Cor., vii, 10, 11: 'And unto the married I command, yet not I, but the Lord, that a wife depart not from her husband: But and if she depart, let her remain unmarried, or be reconciled to her husband: And let not the husband put away his wife.'

"Here is no intimation of divorce, for she is told to remain unmarried.

"In the twelfth and thirteenth verses, the apostle lays down the rule for the government of marriages of believers and unbelievers. He says, if a man has an unbelieving wife, and she be pleased to stay with him, he must not put her away. The same is true of a woman with an unbelieving husband.

"At the fifteenth verse he seems to strike another key. He says that 'If the unbelieving depart, let him depart. A brother or sister is not under bondage in such cases.'

"The apostle is not contradicting the general principle laid down by the Lord. Christ dealt with a general matter, and the apostle is dealing with a special matter. Christ laid down the general rule, and the apostle is applying it. We would need to consider the circumstances for which the apostle is giving this special rule, for we all know that it is one thing to lay down a general rule, and quite another to apply it.

"The converted wives of pagans were subjected to many difficulties and temptations. These christian women had learned to look upon idolatry with horror, and still the kitchen hearth was consecrated to false gods. These gods were to be worshipped by the family circle. How could a christian woman conscientiously do this? And how could she have peace if she refused? When they sat down to a meal, libation, as worship, was poured out to some false god, 'and on joyous occasions the pantomimic dance and profane song were required.' What christian could take part in such worship, so wholly repugnant to the religion of Christ? It is said that the 'reign of Venus was coextensive with that of Jove.' There were many heathen worships that the wife would be subjected to by marrying a heathen man that would make her life miserable. Under these circumstances the apostle wrote. Yet he does not tell her to leave him, 'but if he depart, let him depart,' and after he departs she is not told to remarry, but remain unmarried.

"Respecting cruel treatment, it seems that this same rule would apply. If life is endangered by living together, a temporary separation may be in order, but never a remarriage. Whenever the parties became reconciled they might again resume their nuptial relation.

"So with drunkenness. The wife might resort to every honorable means to cure a drunken husband, but never separate from him except it be absolutely necessary to save her life. And then she is positively forbidden to marry again. That same drunken man is her husband until he dies.

"So with willful and continued desertion. If he still lives he is her husband, and the scriptures do not justify a divorce. It must be remembered that they married 'for better or for worse.'

"I believe that either party guilty of the offense named by the Saviour is bound to divorce the other when apprized of it. It is not in their province to forgive this offense, for it just as virtually dissolves the union as death. If they remain together after this both are guilty of adultery and unfit for membership in the christian church. A man marrying a woman that is divorced, and professing Christ afterward, cannot join the christian church so long as he lives with this divorced woman. You will see, therefore, that a divorced person is never capable of marrying again. She is forever retired from the matrimonial world. To the marriage rite she is dead, and a man has no more right to contract marriage with a divorced woman than with a dead woman. If he does, he dies with her, and the church must regard him as dead and turn him out of her pale to mingle with the dead. The courts have what they call discretionary powers, but the church has none. The Bible is her code; to its teachings she must bow and say amen.

"The cause of so many separations and divorces is because persons have gone into the matrimonial rite heedlessly—without mature thought, and, worse still, without love. Persons have been persuaded to marry by their friends who had no higher idea of marriage than to accept the advice of a foolish, deceitful friend. Many persons have married because the woman looked well, dressed well and talked well. With no higher aspiration than to get a good looking wife. Some girls have married a man to spite the other girls, or because her parents didn't want her to marry him. Some girls, I'm sorry to say, have married to get away from their parents because they were so unreasonable and cruel. They hadn't time to think of love. They were in the fire and the quickest way out was the best way to them. Some parents seem never to think that their girls are of age until they marry. Some girls have simply married a fellow because he had something; some, still, married one man and loved another. The parents objected to to their choice, and hence the man married another to abuse her, and the girl married another to disobey and deceive him. It is a fearful thing to trifle with a person's love. Many parents will find it hard at the bar of God. To all of those who have gone into marriage thoughtlessly, yea, to you unfortunates, I have this word of consolation for you: You have made your bed hard, lie hard—God's word does not grant you a divorce. Try to so live that you will get over it when you die. That is the end of your suffering. You will not have to live with him as husband in heaven, for there they neither marry nor are given in marriage. But they do always behold the face of the

Father, and Jesus Christ the Lord. Then it will all be over and heaven will yield you sweeter rest. It is pleasing to know that when this life of suffering, abuses and disappointments is over that we have the promise of a better life beyond—that is free from mistakes or anything that defiles a man. The hope of that heavenly home is sweet. If a single thought that I have expressed will urge you to purer lives and to think more highly of Jesus and the glorious doctrines of the cross I am satisfied. May the holy spirit impress these truths upon your hearts, for Jesus' sake. Amen."

Rev. Love was earnestly requested by some of his members to preach a sermon upon the "Keys of the kingdom, and binding and loosing," which he did to the satisfaction of the church, a true copy of which is here reproduced, with the hope that it will do much good. We charitably hope that it will be read with interest and profit. Those who read it may not be so highly favored as those who heard it considered themselves, yet the blessing of God is prayed upon it that it may prove a blessing to the reader too :

LOOSING AND BINDING.

"Matthew, xvi, 19—'And I will give unto thee the keys of the kingdom of heaven : and whatsoever thou shalt bind on earth shall be bound in heaven: and whatsoever thou shalt loose on earth shalt be loosed in heaven.'

"I appear before you to-night to discuss another one of those difficult subjects about which there is a diversity of opinion even among scholars. I do not delight in discussing difficult subjects, but it is needful for me to suggest a few thoughts from this text which I hope will be useful to you. This text is very much quoted and equally as much misunderstood. The blessed Saviour's intimacy with his church is declared in the text. The Saviour organized the church and left His seal of approbation upon it, with the promise that whenever they met in His name and agreed, that their meetings and doings should be clothed with divine authority, and that heaven would sanction whatever they did in His name as His representatives. This is what makes apostolic examples as binding on us as the words of our Saviour. They were inspired to act as well as to say. They did what the Saviour would have done, and said what He would have said. Jesus, on entering Cesarea Phillippi, asked His disciples what did men think of Him. Peter said that some thought he was John the Baptist, some thought he was Elias, some thought he was Jeremias, or some of the prophets. The Saviour then put the question directly to them, to which Peter answered, 'Thou art Christ, the Son of the living God.' Upon this truth confessed by Peter the Saviour promised to build His church, to which He gave Peter the keys, that he might unlock it to Jews and Gentiles. This was not to put Peter above the other disciples. As he had nearly always spoken for the crowd, being characteristic of his nature, so he represented them in the reception of the keys.

I.—AND I WILL GIVE UNTO THEE THE KEYS OF THE KINGDOM OF HEAVEN.

"A key is an instrument for opening a door. He who has it has the privilege of entering at will. The keys referred to in the text mean authority, power, divine appointment. This authority has not been given to Peter alone, but in some respect to every minister of Jesus.

"If to Peter alone was given this power and divine sanction we might justly be alarmed, unless we can find the family through which the transferring of the keys have passed from St. Peter. If we should fail in this, then we should find no open door into the kingdom. There is no evidence in the scriptures that St. Peter was promoted above his fellow-disciples. Paul withstood him to his face for he was to be blamed. This Paul would not have done had he recognized Peter as ruler. For Paul more than once taught that we should obey them that had rule over us, and that whoever resisted the rulers resisted the ordinances of God.

"If St. Peter was recognized as chief of the church of the apostolic age, it is strange that none of the documents bear his signature approved as such. It is more than strange that he on no occasion issued a proclamation to the churches as such. Every other person claiming to be chief on certain occasions has issued proclamations or documents bearing their signature as chief. The logical conclusion, therefore, must be that so far as apostolic supremacy is concerned there was none, and all of the apostles were equal.

"The power was given alike to all of them. The presentation of the keys to the apostles reminds us of a husband going away and turning over the keys to his wife, to whom he entrusts all of his business. After giving her full instructions about the business, and ample directions in every part of it, he tells her that whatever she does, according to the directions given, he will approve it, for it would be as if he had done it. Or as a master going off delivers his goods into the hands of his servant, with orders and promises to approve whatever he does according to the orders given. Christ is under no promise to endorse what He has not ordered, and what the Bible does not contain He has not ordered and will not endorse. The presentation of the keys to His disciples indicates His loving intimacy with the church. Where a loving intimacy exists between two parties there also exists power of the one over the other. For intimacy breeds power, confidence and approbation. This is what makes the church the most powerful institution under heaven. She enjoys intimacy with Christ. She has His approving smiles. No other organization could have come through the bloody and fiery persecution, increasing as it marched, but the church, the Lamb's bride. Her intimacy with the King gained His favor and protection. The intimation to St. Peter here is that he would be the first to open the door of the visible kingdom—the church—to both Jews and Gentiles. This was fulfilled on the day of Pentecost, and at Cornelius' house. The kingdom evidently means the christian church. It must be remembered that no intimation is here or elsewhere given that Christ gave Peter the keys of heaven. For in that event every one who wished to enter heaven would be obliged to consult Peter. Peter would indeed be the proper being to whom prayer would be due, since upon him would hang our chance for entering heaven; in this case it would be evident that Christ had transferred his power to Peter, and hence prayer to Christ would be improper and a violation of contract. It will be remembered, also, that Christ appeared to John many years after this with the keys of authority in his own hands, showing that he had not transferred them to anybody. Our Lord has arranged it so that we can go to the throne direct and have no right or business to consult men, departed saints nor angels. We can come boldly for ourselves to a throne of grace and speak directly to the King. We have as much right to the keys of heaven as Peter had, or anybody else. We rejoice to know that God will answer our prayers as quick as He will anybody else's. That which guarantees the answer to prayer has always been the same, and that is faith. The prayer of faith has always been answered. By this means the door of heaven is opened. Whether this is the key or not, it is not important to know. It opens or it influences him to open who has the keys. In either case the result reached is the same. There need not be any miscarriage in our petitions, for we can carry them ourselves directly to the King. If we have not the keys of the kingdom of heaven, we have the keys of authority to approach His Majesty in the name of Christ, the Lord. This intimacy is encouraged by the Lord, and He is still the head of the church and hugs her to His bosom as His bride and approves her as His own.

II.—BINDING ON EARTH AND IN HEAVEN.

"This at once sets forth the seal of approbation upon the church of Christ the Lord. But this is conditioned upon the presumption that the church has complied with the contract. The word 'bind' among the Jews was used to denote a thing declared—a doctrine taught. It must be remembered that 'loose' and 'bind' were used only among the Jews, and refers to things and not to persons. So that the Saviour meant that whatever thing or censure ye inflicted upon a person, or in the church, according to the rule I have just given you, shall be ratified in heaven. Let us not forget that the Saviour quotes this Jewish phrase just after he had given direction how to deal with an offending person. The language used by Christ is found only in Matthew, who is supposed to have written his gospel in Hebrew for the Jews and afterward translated it into Greek.

"It will be seen that the Greek 'osa' is neuter and refers to a thing, and that 'desete' was used among the Jews as referring to the declaration of a doctrine or any article of restraining or granting. They generally meant that it is lawful to do or not do, as the case might be, by 'loose' and 'bind.' Now, then, the conclusion must be that Christ meant to teach them that whatever law they enacted or censure they inflicted according to His law He would approve of it. A sweet thought is intimated here that the doings of the church on earth are reviewed by the church in heaven. The decision of the court below is subject to the court above. If the court below meets in the name of Christ, and censures one of its members for crime or obstinacy, the court above confirms the decision of the court below and the censure is valid. Such a member is turned over to Satan to be buffeted for a season until that member shall have learned to behave and acknowledge the authority of the church. The court regards the censure as being just. Just how such a member is regarded by the court above we may not learn until we shall have been made members of that holy and infallible tribunal. If from prejudice, ill feelings, unfairness or strategy a member is turned out, the censure is unjust, the judgment of the court below is reversed. It is not 'bound' in heaven, not 'loosed' in the court of the righteous Judge of all the earth.

"It must be noticed, also, that the apostles were inspired and therefore less likely to make mistakes. No church and no minister would presume to read the hearts of their members as Peter did Anania's and Sapphira's. That power was granted only to the pioneers of the christian religion. It is not now used because it is not now needed. People are more capable of reasoning now, and hence we resort to reason, for the days of miracles to convince men of the power of the christian religion are over. Where Paul found the people prepared to reason, as at Athens, no miracles were performed. The approbation of Christ upon His church is to make men fear and love the church as they would Him. It is intended to have the enemies of the cross to know that He espouses the cause of His church and will defend her. He made Paul understand that the punishment that he was inflicting upon His church was upon her Lord. 'Saul, Saul, why persecuteth thou me,' was the strange inquiry. He has said, 'Inasmuch as ye have done it unto one of the least of these, my brethren, ye have done it unto me,' and that one had better be in the sea with a millstone about his neck than to offend one of these, my little ones. Such passages should make the enemies of the cross stand in awe. If you insult the church you insult her Lord. Who can behold the wonderful accomplishments of the church without learning that she must have been supported by hands divine? Who can, after examining the victories of the church, fail to see that she was defended by an eternal arm? Who can learn the history of the church and notice her powerful enemies without feeling that a supreme being must have guided her. Criticise the church as severely as you may, but you will find fewer mistakes in her acts than in any other institution under heaven. Examine her literature and learned men and no other institution presents such an enviable front. In question of purity where is her equal? In doctrine, what institution touches her purity, justness and sublimity? In liberality and virtue she occupies the highest plane. All this shows that she is guided by the eternal eye and kept by grace through faith. As the church associates with Christ she will naturally contract His habits, imbibe His doctrines and gather strength from Him. Therefore He has promised to endorse what she does in conforming to His will. It does not mean that if the church receives an unconverted person into her fellowship that heaven accepts him. This would be inconsistent with the charter of the gospel church—regeneration.

"There are many things which the church does that are not 'bound' in heaven. This does not mean that if the church should owe an honest debt and 'bind' not to pay it, that it will be 'bound' in heaven. The Bible tells to her to 'owe no man.' This does not mean that should the church 'bind' not to support the mission work and spread the gospel that it shall be 'bound' in heaven. She is told to preach the gospel to every creature. It means that whatever the church does that is right, that the author of right will endorse it; that whatever she does that He has commanded He will approve of it. God will approve of the right in everybody and reward them accordingly. He will show her the path of life and bring her in His presence where there is fullness of joy, and set her on His right hand where there are pleasures for evermore. If the church would have the approving smiles of her Master, let her strive to do right and all will be well. His smile eclipses the frowns of all the enemies combined. It is day if He smiles upon us in the midst of ten thousand frowning worlds. In the scorns, contempts and darkness of the world, like the children of Israel in Egypt, there will be light in our house under the approving smiles of Christ, our Lord, and amid the persecutions and fierce battles of life we may sing amid the tempest, 'Praise the Lord.' Notice further:

III.—LOOSING ON EARTH AND IN HEAVEN.

"It is also true of this loosing. It is a seal of approbation; but it is a seal of approbation of the right, and not of the wrong. In neither case is it meant that there is a turning out of heaven. The primary meaning is that the acts of the church are endorsed by heaven. It is fair to presume, therefore, that since the church makes mistakes many of her decisions are reversed by the supreme court. Many whom the church censures do not rest under the divine censure, because the church is wrong; and many whom the church acquits still remain under the divine censure, because they are guilty. But if the church justly declares non-fellowship with a member, Christ approves it as being just. This is what is meant by 'loosed' on earth and 'loosed' in heaven. This further shows the intimacy between Christ and his church. Whatever she hates, He hates, and whatever she declares is wrong and unholy, He declares is wrong and unholy. It does not mean that whoever is turned out of the church is turned out of heaven. This is not what the Saviour is driving at. If when they are turned out of the church they are turned out of heaven, then when they wish to make their return, they must first be taken into the church before they can be received back into heaven. This argument would place the church before heaven, and strike the death-blow to the doctrine taught by John, that we must bring forth fruit meet for repentance. The soul should first get right with its God, and then with His people. It is often the case that when God has forgiven a sin that the church is still grumbling about it. It is also true that God has forgiven many sins before the church has found them out, and hence the church in some instances works too late. The rule is nevertheless good that when the church condemns sin God approves it, and when the church accepts a true penitent God sanctions it. In neither case does the church act before God does.

"Dr. P. H. Mell says on this subject: 'The Saviour promised the apostles to give them plenary inspiration. That he would see that they should make no mistake in any doctrines they announced, or in any gospel institution they might organize. That they should adopt (or bind) on earth what already had been decided upon in heaven, and reject (or loose) on earth what had already been rejected in heaven. This makes apostolic examples as binding on us as apostolic precepts.'

"Dr. J. M. Pendleton says on this subject that 'we are to understand 'bind' in the sense of forbid, and 'loose' in the sense of permit, and the meaning of the passage is that what a church does in accordance with the law of Christ is approved and ratified in heaven.'

"Dr. DeVotie says: 'It must be very clear to you that no one can be bound in heaven or on earth by a decision against Him contrary to the gospel.'

"Dr. Holmes says: 'It is said that the words 'bind' and 'loose' were frequently used by the Jews in the sense of enjoin and permit as applied to the teaching of their rabbis, both practical and doctrinal. That may be the sense in which 'bind' and 'loose' are used here.'

"Matthew Henry says: 'Here is a warrant signed for the ratification of all the church's proceedings according to these rules. What was said before to Peter is here said to all the disciples, and in them to all the faithful office-bearers in the church, to the world's end.'

"We are to be very sure that our sentence is pronounced according to the gospel rule, or we are more censurable than those whom we attempt to censure. Or it would be true '*clave erranti*'—the key turning the wrong way. The keys are as a two-edged sword, which cuts those who handle it if it is turned the wrong way.

APPLICATIONS.

"It must be very evident that the apostles did not have absolute power to 'bind' and 'loose' on earth, or there would be no need to 'bind' and 'loose' in heaven in ratification of what they did on earth. It must be clear from what has been said that their acts were not final, from the fact that they were to be reviewed by heaven and 'bound' and 'loosed' there before they were valid. The decisions of no court are final that are subject to review. The church is the highest court on earth, and therefore can be reviewed by no earthly tribunal. It must be apparent that the church is a branch of the government of heaven and is answerable alone to headquarters. It cannot be doubted that whatever the church endeavors to accomplish that is right God will see to it that she prevails. Right is immortal and will ultimately prevail.

"I have been inexpressibly pleased to see that the success of the prohibitionists has been unanimously charged up to the church. She 'bound' on earth, and it was 'bound' in heaven. In a certain city in Georgia, where the fight against whisky was hot, a Baptist minister got on the fence and the prohibition army failed. Though the frowns of every good citizen in that community rest upon him, and though ladies, white and colored, hiss at him as he passes through the streets, he can assuage his sorrow by drinking to their health of the best whisky in that town free of charge, and in the magnanimity of his drunken soul pass their vituperation by without a rejoinder for the next two years. Then shall the Babylonian garment and the golden wedge be dug up, and Achan and his family stoned by the army of the living God, and Israel shall go up in the strength of their God and take Ai without the loss of a man. Then shall the enemies of the cross know that there is a God in Israel who pleads the cause of his church and will utterly destroy all of her enemies and build up Zion on the ruins thereof. This can but show in either case the influence of the church. The church rocked in her cradle science, dandled on her knees civilization, and from her bosom came the noble God-like spirit of liberty that has pervaded this land. She revolutionized the world and she is determined to rule it. From her rostrum comes the law that has divinity in it, before which mountains melt to flames and the king of righteousness without a rival reigns. The warp of her flag is truth, the woof is righteousness, and upon it is spangled, with divine symmetry in gorgeous beauty, the stars of holiness, peace, mercy, temperance and virtue. Under its golden fringes the blood-washed army march, cognizant of the fact that upon the flag under which they march is inscribed in golden letters 'the kingdoms of this world for our God and his Christ.'

"It is not disputed that the church has always been and is destined to be successful in whatever she undertakes that tends to advance the kingdom of Christ and promote the truest interest of mankind. It is to be lamented that many churches have been used by wicked designing men and some have been frightened from the path of duty by the boastful howling of the wicked. Sometimes by those who happen to be in authority. Ministers have shrunk from duty for fear of unpopularity. This will never be endorsed by heaven. We should do what we know to be right with a conscience void of offense towards God and man. Offend all the world a thousand times rather than to offend God once. That popularity that God frowns upon is eternally dangerous. Let the church do her duty and God will see to it that she is defended, guarded, protected and led. Let humility, union and love characterize all of our acts and we have nothing to fear. The Lord our God shall fight for us and we shall hold our peace. Let the church 'bind' that no unrighteous man shall have rule over us, and it will be 'bound' in heaven. And when we shall finish our session of 'binding' and 'loosing' on earth, the church on earth shall go up to join the church of the first-born in heaven, where congregations never break up and Sabbaths have no end. There we shall spend a never-ending eternity in the glorious presence of the King. And with the redeemed and sanctified we shall praise Him who died for us and by His blood purchased our pardon. To Him, the head of the church, the shepherd and bishop of our souls, be all the glory, now and forever more. Amen."

These discourses show somewhat of the abilities of the man a sketch of whom I have attempted to write.

Rev. E. K. Love was honored with the degree of D. D. by the Selma (Ala.) University May 31st, 1888. The following is an editorial in the *Baptist Leader*, June the 7th, 1888:

REV. E. K. LOVE.

"The Board of Trustees and Faculty of Selma University conferred upon Rev. E. K. Love the degree of D. D. We know of no man more deserving the title than the one mentioned above. He is a scholar and a christian gentleman of undisputed ability, and posesses the qualities that make up the true man. Alabamians will enjoy this information and hence address Rev. E. K. Love, D. D."

The notice of this honor came while the convention was in session in Mr. Love's church and the brethren spoke in the highest terms of the Doctor and praised the University for this deserved honor.

African Baptist Church. 141

At the session of the Missionary Baptist Convention of Georgia, May, 1888, Rev. E. K. Love, D. D., was unanimously elected Vice-President of said convention.

He has the entire confidence of the brethren throughout the State. He is friendly, sociable and loving, and to know him, is but to love him.

CHAPTER XV.

Rev. Dr. Love's Administration.

The church was very much divided in heart and sentiment when Rev. E. K. Love took charge. He soon found that the bad feeling and distrust occasioned by the split of 1877 had not entirely disappeared. He set to work very wisely to unite the hearts of his people. The friends of Rev. W. J. Campbell had been long struggling to erect a monument to his memory. They had no help, and hence the work lagged. Rev. Dr. Love took hold of it heartily and the church united with him, and very soon a very handsome monument was erected to the memory of this faithful servant of God. This monument was unveiled January 1st, 1886. Revs. J. M. Simms, E. K. Love, Deacon J. H. Brown and others made very appropriate addresses. This convinced the followers of Rev. Campbell that they had a friend in Rev. E. K. Love, and that they need have no fears that Mr. Love would not have respect for the labors of their sainted father and do full justice to his memory. This step led rapidly to the healing of the breach and closing the vacuum between the two heretofore contending parties, and Mr. Love became the favorite of both parties, and union very soon followed, to the well-being of the church. The increase in the collections and the large congregations showed that there were better feelings in the church—the collections scarcely ever falling below $400 a month. The church was never more prosperous than under the leadership of Mr. Love.

In the spring of 1886 the church had a glorious revival, and the first Sunday in May, 1886, Rev. Mr. Love baptized 110 hopeful converts. The time consumed in baptizing these was only 23 minutes. The first Sunday in June, 1886, he baptized 70 hopeful converts in 13 minutes, and the first Sunday in July 25 in 8 minutes; on other occasions less. In these meetings the members took an active part. The sisters had prayer meetings daily at 4 P. M. under leadership of Mrs. M. C. Johnson, one of the best women in the world. On the first Sunday in October, 1886, Mr. Love baptized 155 persons in 33 minutes; on the first Sunday in November, 1886, he baptized 89 in 23 minutes, and on the first Sunday in December, 1886, he baptized 39 persons. Up to this time he has baptized more than 1200 persons. The church is very much devoted to him and so is he to the church.

NEEDING ROOM.

Often the church was crowded to its utmost capacity and still many went off who could not gain admittance in the church at all. There were often as many that could not get into the church as could get into the building. The Savannah *Morning News* substantially said of this church during one of its revivals: "The church is filled every night to its utmost capacity; all around the iron railing is crowded by anxious listeners and the square in front of the church is crowded with persons anxious to hear the eloquent preacher through the windows. The church was worked up to an interest in the salvation of souls seldom witnessed by any church."

It was now evident that the administration of Mr. Love would be a success and that the church had not made a mistake in its choice of him as pastor. Winning the confidence of the better class of people, the church increased beyond the most sanguine expectation of Mr. Love's most ardent admirers. Room could not be obtained in the church after the hour for regular services to begin. This necessitated the enlargement of the building. In order to do this it was necessary to buy the property in rear of the church. This was quite an undertaking, but the church was competent to the task.

At the July Conference in 1886 Mr. John E. Grant, a prominent member of the church, made a nice speech and motioned to buy the property in rear of the church. This was carried. A purchasing committee was appointed with plenary power, consisting of Deacons J. H. Brown, chairman; C. L. DeLamotta, Alexander Rannair, March Haines, F. J. Wright, and Mr. R. P. Young. The property was bought for five thousand eight hundred and sixty-seven dollars and forty-five cents ($5,867.45). This was engaged in August, 1886, and the last dollar paid on the 6th of April, 1887. Every note was met without any delay whatever.

The property having been purchased the church was advised by the ironed-will pastor to commence work. The wisdom of this was doubted by the officers except Deacons F. J. Wright and E. C. Johnson. Deacon Wright contended publicly and privately that the work could be done. He was a great comfort to the pastor. Urging him not to be discouraged that the work could be done and that the people would raise the money and that he would find no trouble in accomplishing the work. The third Sunday in October, 1887, the first collection was taken for the building, and every third Sunday thereafter until the third Sunday in April, 1888.

The church passed a resolution on the third Sunday in February, 1888, that work should commence the latter part of February, 1888. The building committee consisted of Brethren A. M. Monroe, chairman; C. H. Ebbs, Richard Butler, Richard Maynor, David Jackson, John Byrd and Sandy Rhett. This was an earnest, competent and whole-souled committee. Deacon J. H. Hooker was chosen foreman of the brick work, Deacon F. J. Wright foreman of the wood work, and Deacon F. M. Williams to do the painting. The work commenced on the 21st of February, 1888. Deacon J. H. Hooker laid the first brick. The extension is 28 feet 6 inches long and consists of a bay window for the pulpit, a pool and an arch gallery, forming into an o. g. before it reaches the walls of the west end of the church, in which is the pulpit. The pulpit has two doors and two handsome windows of stained glass and arched, with the photographs of Revs. Bryan, Marshall, Campbell and Gibbons. A flight of stairs leads from both sides of the pool in the pulpit to rooms in the basement, and also a flight from each door of the pulpit outside for the pastor. There are dressing rooms where persons descend for the purpose of dressing after baptism—one for ladies and the other for gentlemen. There is a third room in the basement for the use of the pastor. All of these rooms will be used for Sunday school class rooms also. The third room is under the pulpit formed by the bay window and will be for the pastor's dressing-room. This arrangement adds much convenience and comfort to the church. The discipline meetings of the officers are held in these rooms, and also other committee meetings of the church.

The cost of the extension was $12,000, making the valuation of the church not less than $75,000. Adding to this $5,000 of societies' prayer houses, will make $80,000.

The members were divided into clubs for the purpose of raising money, both for the church extension and the centennial celebration. The following is a list of clubs and the amount each gave for the church extension.

Rev. George Liele Club—Deacon J. H. Brown, President; Mrs. Nancy Gibbons, Vice-President; Miss L. L. Carey, Treasurer; A. M. Monroe, Secretary. These were children from the Sunday School. They gave for church extension $7.00.

Rev. Andrew C. Marshall Club—Rev. E. K. Love, D. D., President; Mr. Freeman Trotty, Vice-President; A. G. Brown, Secretary; Mrs. Susie O. Graham, Treasurer. They gave for church extension $819.46.

Rev. W. J. Campbell Club—Deacon F. J. Wright, President; Deacon E. C. Johnson, Vice-President; Mr. John H. Davis, Secretary; Mrs. Mary A. Wyly, Treasurer. They gave for church extension $750.88.

Motto Club—Rev. W. G. Clark, President; A. M. Williams, Vice-President; Deacon J. H. Brown, Secretary; Deacon March Haines, Chaplain; Mrs. L. A. Beatty, Treasurer. They gave for church extension $430.55.

Rev. George Gibbons Club, No. 1—Mrs. D. W. Gibbons, President; Mrs. Phyllis Jenkins, Vice-President; Mr. D. W. Gibbons, Secretary; Mrs. Mary Brown, Treasurer. They gave for church extension $49.95.

Rev. George Gibbons Club, No. 2—Deacon John C. Habersham, President; David Blake, Vice-President; Mr. W. B. Jenkins, Secretary; Mrs. Leah Garvin, Treasurer. They gave for church extension $464.89.

The Rev. E. K. Love Club—Deacon R. H. Johnson, President; Richard Law, Vice-President; James Brown, Secretary; Mrs. Hannah Glen, Treasurer. They gave for church extension $155.92.

The Harmony Club—Deacon Alexander Rannair, President; May Hunter, Vice-President; James Small, Secretary; Mrs. Lydia Small, Treasurer. They gave for church extension $92.55.

Ruel Club—Miss S. C. Jenkins, President; Mrs. J. C. Wade, Vice-President; Mr. R. B. Heggs, Secretary; Mrs. J. C. Love, Treasurer. They gave for church extension $98.76.

The M. C. Johnson Club—Mr. M. S. Anderson, President; William Boyd, Vice-President; Mrs. Sarah Burke, Secretary; Mrs. M. C. Johnson, Treasurer. They gave for church extension $65.65.

The M. L. Jackson Club—Mr. Henry Minis, President; Mrs. E. F. Brown, Vice-President; Benjamin R. Young, Clerk; Mrs. Sarah Butler, Treasurer. They gave for church extension $62.10.

The Mount Zion Club—Deacon F. M. Williams, President; Deacon P. A. Glenn, Vice-President; Mr. Richard Jenkins, Clerk; Mrs. S. R. Williams, Treasurer. They gave for church extension $263.20.

The C. L. DeLamotta Organ Club—Mrs. Matilda M. Monroe, President; Miss Lula Hines, Secretary; Miss L. L. Carey, Treasurer. They gave for church extension $36.65.

The Daughters of Zion Society—Deacon J. C. Habersham, President; L. J. Pettigrew, Vice-President: C. H. Ebbs, Clerk: Mrs. S. R. Williams, Treasurer. They gave for church extension $62.00.

The Young Men's Christian Association—B. C. Creamer, President; L. A. Washington, Clerk: Henry Emory, Treasurer. They gave for church extension $65.00.

The Mungin Centennial Club—Dittsmersville. They gave for church extension $27.00.

The Glassco Jackson Centennial Club, Southville—W. G. Clark, President. They gave for church extension $3.00.

The Ladies' Laurel Branch Society—D. Mitchell, President: L. J. Pettigrew, Secretary. They gave for church extension $15.00.

Ladies' Zion Watchman Society—Mrs. Claranda Jenkins, President; Mrs. Amanda Pettigrew, Vice-President: Mrs. Amelia Bing, Treasurer. They gave for church extension $10.00.

Zion Watchman Society—L. J. Pettigrew, President: J. H. Coffee, Secretary. They gave for church extension $5.00.

The Baptist Christian Circle Association Society—Mr. Chas. Green, President; Mrs. Betsy Williams, Vice-President: Mr. Albert P. Williams, Secretary; Mrs. Ella Mulligan, Treasurer. They gave for church extension $20.00.

The Ladies' Union League Society—Mr. William Logan, President; Mr. E. Collins, Vice-President; Mrs. Rachel Logan, Treasurer; ———, Secretary. They gave for church extension $15.00.

The Sons of Zion Society—Deacon F. M. Williams, President; Deacon J. C. Habersham, Vice-President; Deacon J. H. Hooker, Treasurer; Deacon A. Rannair, Secretary. They gave for church extension $20.00.

The Lone Star Cadet Branch Society—Mr. Abram Bowens, President; Mr. H. F. Griffin, Vice-President; Mrs. Bina Lewis, Treasurer; L. A. Washington, Secretary. They gave for church extension, $10.00.

The United Tie of Brotherhood—Mr. S. Bowman, President: Mr. James A. Williams, Vice-President; Mr. George Bacon, Treasurer; Mr. James P. Green, Secretary. They gave the church $10.00.

Capernaum Society—Mrs. Anna Gibbons, President; Mrs. Phiby Butler, Vice-President; D. W. Gibbons, Secretary; Mrs. Mary Brown, Treasurer. They gave the church $20.00.

The Ladies' Union of St. Paul Society.—Mrs. D. Grant, President; Mrs. Amelia Bing, Vice-President; Mr. Peter Denigal, Secretary; Mrs. Rebecca Richards, Treasurer. They gave the church $35.00.

Sons and Daughters of Abraham Society gave the church $5.00.

The Lilie Union Society—Mrs. R. Quarterman, President; S. A. Nichols, Vice-President; B. R. Young, Secretary; Mrs. Caroline Low, Treasurer. They gave the church $5.00.

The S. C. Mutual Aid Society—Mrs. M. A. Wylly, President; Mrs. Julia Winston, Vice-President; Mrs. Charles Lewis, Secretary; Mrs. Charlotte Fields, Treasurer. They gave the church $20.00.

Building Club No. 1—Mrs. Sophia Verdier, President; A. M. Williams, Secretary. They gave the church $47.00.

The Benevolent Association gave the church $2.00.

The Benevolent Aiding Association—M. E. Nichols, President; B. R. Young, Vice-President; J. A. Nichols, Secretary; S. Bizzars, Treasurer. They gave the church $2.50.

The Mechanics' Branch gave the church $5.00.

The St. James Macedonia Society gave the church $5.00.

Savannah Light Infantry Branch gave the church $2.50.

The Ladies' Brick Layer Society—John Jackson, President; Maria Loyd, Vice-President; Samuel Loyd, Secretary; Lydia A. Jackson, Treasurer. They gave the church $1.50.

The Ladies' and Gentlemen's Social Society—Mrs. Annie Jackson, President; Rebecca Brox, Vice-President; Mr. Robert H. Lewis, Secretary; Mrs. Hester Haynes, Treasurer. They gave the church $10.00.

Brampton Club—Bro. Wm. Moore, President. They gave for church extension $21.95.

The Children's Israelite Society—Mr. March Houston, President; Mrs. Annie Burk, Vice-President; Mr. A. G. Brown, Secretary; Rev. E. K. Love, D. D., Treasurer. They gave the church $10.00.

The Young Ladies' Select Branch of the Israelite Society—Mr. March Houston, President; Mrs. Mira Miller, Vice-President; Miss Lou Hines, Secretary; Mrs. Mamie Hines, Treasurer. They gave the church $2.50.

East Savannah, Thunderbolt and Zion Hill Societies gave their moneys through the Mount Zion Club, already referred to. Southville and Dittsmersville gave their moneys through the George Gibbons Club, No. 2, already mentioned. Each and every club vied with the other as to which would do most for the church.

This wise division of the church into clubs so inspired the members and united their hearts and efforts in the work that they did the work with an ease surprising to themselves and to the whole community. This generalship will class Rev. Mr. Love with the ablest pastors of the country. Mr. Love contended that the church was able to do her work without begging a dime out of the city, and that he did not mean to beg out of Savannah, nor to beg a single church in the city. He kept his word and the work was done and paid for without a day's delay in the hands getting their money or the work suspended. When the work was completed the church owed but a trifle. The pleasure of the members at the leadership of Mr. Love was indescribable. During Mr. Love's labors to enlarge and beautify the church, his amiable christian wife rendered him incalculable service. She was an earnest, faithful, able, loving and punctual Sunday school teacher. Whoever else might be absent, Mrs. Love was sure to be present. She was a conspicuous member of the Ruel club, and was its treasurer. She entered heartily into her husband's work, sharing heroically his sorrows and his joys. She was humble, loving, faithful and obedient as a wife, and it is doubtful that a minister ever had a better wife. She was converted in April, 1879, in Thomasville, Ga., and was baptized by Rev. E. K. Love the first Sunday in May, 1879, and on the 28th of October, of the same year, they were married. She is a devoted christian, mother and wife.

Mr. Love inaugurated a children's day, on which he preached to the children at 11 A. M. He had young boys for deacons who were members of the church, and boys and girls in the choir, most of whom were members of the church. Little Etta Monroe, the daughter of Mrs. M. M. Monroe, was organist, and little Mary C. Johnson, Jr., was leading soprano singer. Her voice was remarkably sweet. This soon became the most interesting service of the church, and perhaps did more good than any other service of the church. The elder people were asked on this day to go up in the galleries and the children occupied the main audience room. In this way Rev. Dr. Love endeavored to impress the parents that they would ere long be in heaven and looking upon their children filling the places which once they occupied while on earth, and to impress the children that their parents would soon be gone and that they would have to take the place of their parents and carry on the work of the Lord, but that their parents would be watching them from the balconies of heaven.

Too much can not be said in praise of Mrs. M. C. Johnson for organizing many of the young boys and girls into a society known as "The Young Christian Workers." This society did a noble work for the church, and acquired thereby the habit of giving and making for the Lord. Mrs. Johnson was in full sympathy with Rev. Dr. Love, and did as much, if not more, to help him in his work as any other member of the church. She said but little, but she worked much and brought forth much fruit.

The church under Rev. Dr. Love's administration did more mission and educational work than ever before in its history. In 1886 the church sent up to the convention that met at Quitman $404, and in 1887 to the convention at Brunswick $342. In 1886 it sent up to the Mount Olive Baptist Association $91.96, and in 1887 $64. This was $901.96 in two years. Adding to this incidental missionary collections and what was given to churches for building and liquidating debts and to traveling preachers will go far towards swelling the amount to $2,000. Besides this, the church provides for many of her poor saints and buries them. And still, besides this, her current expenses are more than $200 per month. This church has not a superior in liberality in existence. This church prides itself in taking care of its pastor. Whatever he wants, he has only to hint it. Its financial record can not be excelled. It usually pays all of its debts monthly without any strain.

The congregation is orderly during service, and it is the rarest thing imaginable for the preacher to have to call for order. This is due to the early training of the fathers.

The church building is kept neat. The sexton, Mr. James Richards, is as attentive to the church as a loving wife to a sick husband.

The administration of Rev. Love has been mainly characterized by peace and good feeling. The Gibbons people, about 100 in number, who went off during the trouble of 1877, and who were organized into a church about seven miles from Savannah by Rev. U. L. Houston, without letters and at the emphatic protest of the First African Baptist Church, returned under the administration of Rev. Dr. Love. The so-called church was dissolved, and the brethren returned to the church again. It was a day of rejoicing. Many others that had not returned with the body on the 17th of February, 1884, returned under the administration of Rev. Dr. Love, amounting to several hundred. This showed Rev. Dr. Love's ability to win the hearts of men. The members were never more attentive.

CHAPTER XVI.

The Societies of the Church—Their Membership—The Value of Their Property and Their Condition.

THE SOCIETIES OR PRAYER HOUSES OF THE CHURCH.

East Savannah Society (prayer houses they are properly, but they are called "Societies") is about three miles east of Savannah. It has about one hundred and fifty members. Mr. James Lawry is leader of this society. He is a faithful, earnest leader, and is very much beloved by the people. This humble man watches over the people of this society in love and keeps before them the duty they owe to the church. He takes monthly collections and turns them over to the church through Deacon P. A. Glenn, who visits them once a month. This is a strong liberal society. Their property is worth $900. Mr. L. J. Pettigrew and Miss Rebecca G. Houston keep up a flourishing Sunday school at this house of worship.

Eastville Society is about two miles east of Savannah. It has 38 members. Mr. John Byrd is leader of this society. He is an humble, faithful, loving and God-fearing man. He is also a member of the choir of the church. He is very active and attentive. From this little society he brings in more money to the church than any other society connected with the church. He took a deep interest in the extension of the church, and enthused his people with the same burning zeal that was ablaze in his own bosom. He is a great help and comfort to the pastor. Mr. Byrd keeps this society peaceable and quiet and they give the church very little trouble. This society reflects credit upon the church and the church has just cause to be proud of it. The property is worth $350.

The Thunderbolt Society is about four miles from Savannah. It has 125 members. Mr. Morris Pray is leader of this society. This is a quiet society and causes the church very little trouble. The people of this society have a very good house of worship, which is worth $1,000. It is in a beautiful location. They do well and come into church on communion days. They have a flourishing Sunday school. Misses Marion E. Houston and Rosa L. Brown go out on Sundays and assist Superintendent F. McIntosh in teaching.

Lover's Lane Society is about two miles from Savannah. It has 60 members. Mr. Adam Houston is the leader of this society. He is a faithful, earnest man. He is very dutiful and attentive to the church. The society is lively and at times very troublesome to the church, the members (many of them) being often before the church for fighting. Mr. Houston is a good leader and faithful to both the society and to the church. This society has been of great service to the church in its work of extending the church edifice. Deacon F. M. Williams visits this society, and its monthly collections are turned over to the church through him.

The Dittsmersville Society is about two and one-half miles south of Savannah. It has 50 members. Mr. John Morrel is leader of this society. It is a very earnest, energetic society. Mr. Morrel has proved a success as a leader. The success of this society is largely due to Deacon J. C. Habersham and Licentiate W. G. Clark, who very often visit it and exhort the people to active church work and pious lives. Mr. Clark also keeps up a flourishing Sunday school there.

Sand Fly Station Society is six miles from Savannah. Mr. Tony Giles is leader of this society. This society has 13 members. It is a quiet, loving band and gives the church very little trouble. Deacon F. M. Williams visits this society, and its monthly collections are turned over to the church through him. The church is proud of this society. Mr. Giles, as leader, exercises a great influence over the members and is very much beloved by them. He is faithful and attentive to the church. The property is worth $150.

Wheat Hill Society is four miles from Savannah. It has 20 members. Mr. A. Houston is leader of this society. Deacon J. H. Brown visits this society. It is a quiet society, and very seldom has any cases for church discipline. They send in their monthly collections through Deacon Brown. The property is worth $250.

South Valley Society is fourteen miles from Savannah. Mr. David Solomon is leader of this society. It seldom, if ever, has any cases for discipline. They are few in number, and are quiet and loving. They don't give much money because they are very generally poor, but out of the little they make they give the church some. It has 35 members.

Zion Hill Society is about six miles from Savannah. Mr. J. Jordan is leader here. The society numbers 65 members. They have but little trouble among themselves and are an earnest and faithful band. The property is worth $300. They are liberal and give money to the church quite often. In the work of church extension they aided nobly. Deacon F. M. Williams watches over this society as deacon, and also visits them occasionally. Mr. Jordan is an earnest man, and very much beloved by the members.

Sabine Field Society is three miles from Savannah. Mr. Richard Gibbons is the leader. The old man is also a licensed preacher of the church. For years he has been a licensed preacher and leader of this society. He is a good man, and the members are devoted to him. This society numbers 150 members. It does not give very much money to the church, but it is a quiet, loving band. The property is worth $125.

Brampton Society is three miles from Savannah. Mr. Isaac Charlton is leader of this society. It numbers 65 members. The property is worth $200. It was at this place, one hundred years ago, that the First African Baptist Church was organized. The old spot is very dear to the church. It has not been out of the possession of the church as a place of worship for one hundred years.

Southville Society is two miles south of Savannah. It numbers about 50 members. Mr. Jack Jackson is the leader of this society. The property is worth $300. Deacon J. C. Habersham watches over it, and Licentiate W. G. Clark does great service out here also. The members here are very quiet and give the church very little trouble. They are liberal and did well in giving the church money during its efforts to extend its building. The money was reported through Deacon Habersham.

Gibbons Society is seven miles from Savannah. Mr. January Mack is leader of this society. This society was famous for its noble deeds in the days of Rev. W. J. Campbell. These good people were captured by Rev. U. L. Houston, and without letters from the First African Baptist Church, were organized into a church during the troubles of the church, which began in 1877. They returned to the church in 1888, and upon dissolving the so-called church and making christian confession they were restored. They number about 200 members. The property is worth $900. Mr. Mack is a faithful man and is very much beloved by the church and the society.

The Richmond Society is seven miles from Savannah. Mr. James Nial is leader of this society. This society numbers 15 members. The property is worth $75. Deacon Alexander Rannair visits this society and watches over it. It is a quiet, loving band and causes very little trouble. According to their means and number, they gave quite liberally to the church in its endeavor to extend its edifice.

These societies are all members of the church, but are united simply to hold regularly prayer meeting, because of their distance from the church. The members are expected to come into the church on every first Sunday to communion, and on third Sunday to conference.

The total worth of the property of these prayer houses is ($5,000) five thousand dollars.

The First African Baptist Church, because of its liberality to the State work, was voted the banner church of Georgia. It was given a beautiful banner in token of the appreciation in which the church is held by the State.

CHRISTIAN BANNER.

Prepared by Rev. C. H. Lyon for the occasion of presentation of the banner to the First African Baptist Church.

Tune C. M.

This banner, love, is Christ the Lord's,
 And in His name we hoist
Aloud the battle cry against
 All hostile to our host.

This army terrible shall be
 While under this banner led;
And in this sign shall christians prove
 Triumphant through their head.

This blood-stained banner is unfurled,
 Upheld by faithful hands,
In true defense and great display
 Of the pure gospel band.

This mighty army of our God
 Shall wave their banner high,
'Till Satan's army vanquished be
 And christians' reign be wide.

The following sermon by Rev. C. H. Lyons, corresponding secretary of the Missionary Baptist Convention of Georgia, on presenting the banner to the church, was very interesting and filled the church with great joy.

THE CHRISTIAN BANNER.

A Sermon Delivered on the Occasion of Presenting the Prize Banner to First (A.) Baptist Church, Savannah, Ga., Feb. 28th, 1888, by Rev. C. H. Lyons, Pastor Mount Olive Church, Atlanta, Georgia.

There are three words of Hebrew origin of a kindred nature expressing different shades of meaning of a banner. *Oth* represents a small sign or banner; *nes* an ensign, a token of a thing; and *degel* a flag, a banner; a standard from the verbal form, *dagal*, to cover, to glitter and to shine, or lift up a banner; and the Latin *vexillum* is also expressive, which is rendered a military ensign, said to be a red flag placed in front of the general's tent, indicating to march forward.

The important and emphatic stress placed upon our subject is brought out forcibly in the three significant passages here alluded to.

"Lift ye up a banner upon the mountain."—Isa., xiii, 2. The wrath and fury of God threatened against Babylon are here indicated. God gives a banner to those who fear him to secure their triumph and betoken his approving presence with them.

In the name of our God we will set up our banner as an inspiration to wage war in defence and in honor of the name and cause of God, and acknowledge that all possible success depends upon the name and power of God.

The described nature of this banner evidently portrays divinity. His banner over me was love. God is love. Terrible as an army with banners, for the Lord thy God is among you; thy God is terrible.

Each army must have its panoply, leaders and uniforms and flags or banners. Jesus Christ is all these to His army.

I. Let us now consider the symbolical signification of the banner.

'Tis not merely the indication of war.

1. But 'tis a sign of distinction and protection of the army. We have defined the original to mean to cover. All under this banner, whether soldiers or caravans, are covered, defended, distinguished from other armies or dangers. The twelve tribes had each a small banner styled standard, owing to its smallness, but each three tribes had a banner, when combined, which defended and protected them both as a caravan and an army.

When his banner was hoisted all soldiers and travelers of like color and aims assembled under it in loyalty to their commanding chief. In our late civil but bloody war the flags marked distinctions between the secessionists and unionists above anything else; and in our christian war Jesus Christ was His people's ensign; keeps the differentia intelligible from all other forms of religious creeds. All are known and distinguished as christians, not by their form or profession, but by their likeness and imitation of and their identity with Christ alone. For by their fruits ye shall know them. This army and caravan are covered and protected by Jesus.

And any cause of distinction between any heterogeneous and homogeneous elements or classes is a virtual protection and defence of the merited parts. Distinction of colors and principles makes each more valuable and admirable. Therefore the distinctive doctrines and principles of the Bible should be more systematically taught and urged. The distinguishing of truth from error, wrong from right, is the great mental and moral project of this host, and all needed protection and distinction are found in a wise and proper assembling under this gospel banner.

The Jewish army and caravan apprehended neither defeat nor danger as long as their Shekinah was visible over them. The christian army has no just fears while it trusts and owns Jesus, its loving and glorious ensign or banner.

2. It means to illuminate and attract the army to the center or union. The significance of the word as alluded to means to glitter, to shine.

The people of that day traveled mainly by night to avoid the fearful heat of the sun; therefore, had banners prepared to burn wood like a stove, to give light by which to travel, which burned and shone all night. The beacon lights were placed on hills and mountains to aid the caravans and armies. These lights were of vast importance to the physical eye. But this banner more effulgently reflects the divine light upon the path of heaven. 'Twas said of one of the banner-bearers that he was a burning and shining light. Jesus, our banner, is the light that lights every man that comes into this world; and His light is the life of men. Jesus said, as long as I am in the world, I am the light of the world. What a glorious and luminous banner! It penetrates thick and repugnant darkness, and it cannot seize it. 'Tis incomprehensibly wonderful.

Light naturally and officially attracts all tangible to it. The sun's light marshals the world by his brilliant beams by day and reflected rays by night. The revolution and vegetation of the earth are the resultant effects of his light. Our world is animated and influenced by light from the highest to the lowest order. Is it at all surprising that all in the mental, moral and religious world should be vastly more influenced and benefited by holy and divine light.

Yea, however scattered and varied, all christians center their hopes and actions in Christ. When Moses beheld Jehovah in the burning bush, he drew to him. When the Magi saw the bright morning star, they came in diligent and immediate search of it. When the introducer of the christian dispensation preached repentance, faith, baptism and the remission of sins, all Judea and adjacent countries came to him. Jesus, our banner, says: "If I be lifted up from the earth I will draw all men unto me."

Moses said unto Him, "Shall the gathering of the people be?" Let this Baptist army rally around this banner till every foe quits the field and Christ becomes Lord indeed. What a marvelous, attractive and brilliant banner.

3. It is a sign of inspiration to war-like actions. A banner which distinguishes, protects, illuminates and attracts its army will doubtless serve as a most powerful incentive to aggressive actions. In the greatest vicissitudes it brings courage and prompts fortitude. It is a most effective dissuasion against all infidelity of the trust so sacredly committed, and a very predominating buoyance over all temptations to cowardice and relaxations of warlike gallantry. It was common for the Spartan mothers to exhort their sons going to war to bring home their shields or be brought home on them.

A champion soldier said, if they could not fight in the sunshine that they would fight in the shade. Those who love and honor their banner die to prevent its trail in the dust or suffer defeat. Let us, O army of God, fight very mightily and manfully under our banner. If we can't contend earnestly and properly for that old, sacred and saving faith, once for all delivered to the saints under favorable circumstances, we will fight under unfavorable, for we will fight the good fight of faith. As long as the drum and bugle of war are heard, this spangled banner seen, the heroes will never yield their forts nor quit the field. We will wave this gospel banner high into victory grand, Satan and his host defy, and shout for Daniel's band.

II. The banner awarded to this army.

God gives a banner to them that fear him as a token of his love for his army!

He brought me to His banquet house, and His banner over me was love. The prophet declared Jesus to be an ensign which should be set up for his people. Solomon described the banner of the church love, and the same to be chief among 10,000 and altogether lovely. John taught, in his sublime and safe instruction, that Christ was love, and they that dwell in love dwelt in him. How clearly and beautifully is Jesus declared the banner of the church. The banner over me is love. God loves His church, and with an everlasting love He draws it. He loves the gates of Zion more than all the dwelling places of Jacob. The church is His peculiar and royal people; therefore he gave them Jesus as a banner. What incomprehensible love and grace bestowed upon those that reverence Him! Christ loves His church as a man his wife, and gave Himself for it that he might redeem it and wash it by His blood and word. Christ is the manifestation of God's love for his army, which cannot be misunderstood or over-estimated. He found His elect as of a hidden treasure and went and sold His heavenly pleasures and privileges and bought them. Paul says, "For ye know the grace of our Lord Jesus Christ, that, though he was rich, yet for your sakes he became poor, that ye through his poverty might become rich." What interest, sympathy and love for us! Greater love have no man than this: that a man lay down his life for his friends, and no less maximum of love is displayed in giving the immaculate of heaven, the only begotten Son of God, to this army. What wondrous love is this!

1. In token of his presence and identity with His army.

The Bible is made increasingly mysterious in attempting to affirm and describe the intimate and indissoluble union between Christ and His people. "He that believes into me shall be saved."

Christ says, "As I am in the Father and the Father in me, even so are you in me and I in you." "I am the vine, and ye are the branches." "Abide in me, and let my word abide in you; then ye shall ask whatsoever ye will, and it shall be done unto you."

Christ and His church are identified in suffering. For he that suffers with me shall reign with me. In His crucifixion we were crucified together with Christ. In His death and resurrection; for as we have been in the likeness of his death, even so shall we be in the likeness of His resurrection. Christ is all and in all for and to His army. The psalmist has this delightful description of His identity and interest in His church: "God is in the midst of her; she shall not be moved; God shall help her, and that right early."

The way and dealings of God are in His sanctuary. Jehovah promises never to leave nor forsake His people. Christ assured His disciples that where two or three gather together in His name, "I am in the midst of them." This army is aggrandized and made victorious and invincible by the omnipotence, omniscience and omnipresence of Christ, our banner. God was with Adam prior to his fall and caused him to superabound in every imaginable felicity. His potent hand was visible in the history of Noah in the deluge. He manifested himself in Jacob and elevated Joseph to the second power of the Egyptian kingdom, and educated Moses in all the learning of that place and day to qualify him for the leadership of his people from captivity to freedom and the promised inheritance.

And the stupendous exhibition and identity of himself in the fiery pillar by night and the cloudy pillar by day to lead and protect them. The apostles were sent to preach with this glorious guaranty, Lo, I am with you alway even to the end of the world. Christ is not merely identified with His people, but is their banner, implement of war, their panoply.

2. To make His army terrible.

Who is she that looks forth as the morning, fair as the moon, and as clear as the sun, and as terrible as an army with banners? The progressive periods of the church have been aptly described in the above figures. She was of the vigor and brightness of the morning in the patriarchal periods. She was of the fairness of the moon in the typical and Mosaic dispensation, and in the christian dispensation was the clearness and brilliancy of the sun; when the sun of righteousness arose, when the scheme of redemption and benign designs of the gospel are consummated, she shall be terrible as an army with banners. Then shall she be beautiful and comely like Jerusalem and terrible as an army with banners. Then shall she become more than a conqueror through the defensive presence of Christ.

The Jewish army with four banners looks appalling, but how much more vastly frightening shall the whole army of God, out of every nation, kindred and people, be when their white horses and riders will be both indicative of victory and innocence in achieving it.

Her four chariots, hailing from between mountains of brass, with her horses colored in destructive and dreadful descriptions, how terrible! The enemy of this army captured, and their kingdom subdued and made loyal to this terrible army, all heretics and their books shall be priced and consumed.

Before this army shall old Lucifer fall like lightning. Gog and Magog shall be conquered. The old dragon and his angels shall be cast into hell.

The old harlot and all who bear her image will be judged and put into unquenchable fire, there to wail and gnash their teeth. This army is so terrible that it subdues kingdoms, wroughts righteousness, obtains promises, stops the mouths of lions, quenches the violence of fire, escapes the edge of the sword, out of weakness becomes strong, waxes valiant in fight, and turns to fight the armies of the aliens.

III. The banner hoisted by this army.

In the name of our God we will set up our banner, indicative of their aggressiveness to battle. There may be questions and problems of such nature and magnitude that neither our philanthropy nor our magnanimity can effect a satisfying solution without the force of war. Then our flags, declaring war, are raised; but our causes of conflict are always such as to render the christian war unavoidable and unceasing. There can be no retreat nor suspension of arms upon any compromise whatever.

We shall have christian liberty and victory or death in pursuit of them. This trumpet of war has been heard with no less distinctness through all generations from the first assault till to-day. There are entreaties for peace and cessation of war, but our lifted banner declares there shall be neither peace nor cessation but as achieved through the defeat of the devil and destruction of his kingdom.

The prophetic trumpet was engaged in arousing Zion to awake and put on her warlike dress and strength. The apostolical council was, acquit yourselves like men; be strong, fight. We are importuned to fight the good fight of faith and war a good warfare.

As the seven nations preoccupied the land of Canaan, promised to Israel, so vice, immorality and demons in high places obstruct our prosperity ; therefore the war is inevitable, for the stronger and greater must occupy.

As Joshua, the champion warrior, led his army to victory and emancipation, much more completely will Jesus, our Joshua, lead this army into the defeat of Satan, destruction of sin, victory and everlasting freedom. The implements, ammunition and causes of war are the same. Let the war-cry be heard aloud : "To war! to war ! ye army of the living God, to war !" Never think the victory won, nor lay thy armor down, for thy arduous work will not be done till you obtain your crown or prize.

Then fight on, my soul, agonizingly till death relieve you from the field. What means this uncompromising outcry and excitement of battle and out-spread banner to be displayed because of the truth ?

A certain renowned man declared that in comparison with all things truth is the most weighty; in weight, therefore, all things are chaff compared with truth, and in nature, all things fiction ; truth underlies every virtue, crowns all the worthy and is the chief constituent of every grandeur. God is truth ; the infinite attribute of Deity is truth ; the Bible is the revelation of divine truth ; the christian church is the ground and pillar of the truth ; Christ and the Holy Spirit are the prolific source and expounders of the truth ; Paul teaches that we can do nothing against the truth, but all for the truth; therefore we have set our banner in defence of this glorious cause. A battle pitched under this banner is actuated by the greatest combination of inspirations. The raising of this banner means the exultant triumph of truth and the cause of the church, of the Bible and of God.

The existence, handiwork and dealings of God have been so perfectly, confutingly established and acknowledged that the opponents of these doctrines have underrated themselves in the estimation of this progressive and religious world. It is claimed by this class of opposers that science so antagonizes religion that much of religious truth is false, scientifically considered. This is false in both theory and practice, for one poet has said, "For truth is truth to the end of reckoning."

The divinity and mystery of religious truth may be classed preposterous when alone scanned through scientific medium.

But this is a frank confession of the imperfection of the human mind to conceive or account for the actions of the divine. The truth of the Bible does not always nor essentially foreshadow visible phenomenon any more than positive precept presents their reasons for demands. All the ever-existing phenomenon for the deluge is now. But 'tis not for science to explain why the flood does not repeat itself.

But the God of science has decreed and declared it in His word.

In these and many other things the scientists overrate themselves and the philosophers are deluded with sophistry. All truth is truth whether discovered from a scientific or religious standpoint.

And each scientific discovery will corroborate each religious doctrine in proportion to their designs and the perfection of man to draw correct conclusions from scientific phenomenon.

The deluge is denied on so termed philosophical and scientific basis. But is this position supported scientifically and historically?

Is there more scientific phenomenon for the swimming ax than for the deluge? Any more for the dry passage of the 3,000,000 through the Red Sea than for the deluge? Any more for the water becoming wine without scientific means or fermenting operations than for the deluge?

Are all these false because they are not your deduction from scientific phenomenon?

Is it any part of erudition or wisdom to conceive everything false and absurd which we cannot understand the philosophy of? The great truth is, there be that intimate relation sustained by natural and religious science, that the better we understand pure science the better we appreciate religion and God.

The Bible is the text and law book of the church. The unity, oneness and consistency of this church would be a foregone conclusion should its precepts and principles alone be adhered to. For the oneness, unity and victory of this church we have set up our banner, builded our fortification and sacrificed our lives and freedom to wage war till all come to their required combatableness.

We claim that there is no want of fullness nor explicitness of Bible teaching on all subjects upon which we differ; that our difference on baptism is due to positive ignorance or disregard of divine authority on this subject, for there is no passage of Scripture, in fact or figure, taken in its proper connection, that either teaches or supports sprinkling or pouring as baptism.

There is no text of sacred Scripture approving or authorizing the final apostacy of the saints.

These doctrines are false, ruinous and insulting to the dignity of the army and of God. From one cause two opposing effects can't come. Therefore these unholy divisions among professing christians are the effects of heresy. For, says Herrick, 'twixt truth and error there is this difference known: error is fruitful, truth only one. Truth establishes, protects only one; therefore all the others are the children of error.

Destroy the error permeating the heart and now adorning the profession of christianity, then the weight, beauty and efficiency of truth will result in the unity, oneness and harmony of the christian church; the widespread of the pure gospel, and the universal acknowledgment and predominance of the christian religion.

Our banner opposes all false doctrine, character and colors.

Our Captain warns the army to beware of the leaven of the Sadducees and Pharasees.

Beware of the false prophets which come to you in sheep's clothing, but inwardly they are ravening wolves.

Beloved, believe not every spirit. Try the spirit by the spirit, whether they be of God. Because many false prophets are gone out into the world. But there were false prophets also among the people, even as there shall be false teachers among you, who privily shall bring on damnable heresies, even denying the Lord that bought them, and bring upon themselves swift destruction.

He that modifies the truth of the Bible, either by addition or diminution, shall have his name erased and plagues added. Because he is a transgressor and has not the doctrine of Christ. John teaches that whosoever transgresseth and abides not in the doctrine of Christ has not God. He that abides in the doctrine hath both the Father and the Son. If there come any unto you and bring not the doctrine, receive him not unto your house, neither bid him God-speed; for he that bids him God-speed is partaker of his evil deeds.

We can't succeed in destroying false doctrine nor the pernicious influence of Catholicism as long as we are partial toward their branches. Let this army cry out, as indicated on their banner, that by thy precepts I get understanding: therefore hate every false way.

2. In the name of our God we have set up our banner; 'tis God's cause, God's army, God's banner. Therefore we have in honor of Him and hope through Him lifted up our banner. Whatever we do or say should be done in the name of God—the name of God is holy and is reverence. The things in His name must be holy and reverential. This name is, therefore, a safe defense and protection to this army. 'Tis a wonderful name; therefore wonderful will be the consequences through it. This name has God exalted above every name in heaven and earth. Therefore the army defended by this name shall be most triumphant. Before His name men and angels fall and devils fear and fly. David conquered Goliah through His name. The unsurpassed victories of Joshua were through His name. The holiness, invincibleness and superior excellence of his army are very astonishingly demonstrated in their dependence upon His mighty name for success. Through His name all miracles done by the prophets and apostles are wrought. The redemption and salvation of man effected, benedictions invoked and the churches' ordinances administered in this glorious name. 'Tis a grand, yea, peculiarly great display of recognition to be honored as the banner-bearer for more than 1,500 churches and more than 160,000 soldiers, and in recognition of deserving merit we regard it as a pleasure of no ordinary kind to present you this banner.

CHAPTER XVII.

Something About the Deacons of the First African Baptist Church.

Since the origin of the Deacon's office, as recorded in the sixth chapter of the Acts of the Apostles, this office has been very important in the christian church. It is true, however, that the office is greatly magnified to what seems to have been its origin. But if Stephen & Phillip must be taken as examples, it would appear that the office began to be magnified in the days of the Apostles, and under their eyes. Indeed, it appears that they endorsed this. The deacons, then, both preached and baptized. The Apostles didn't condemn this, but rather approved it from the fact that down in Samaria they simply imparted the Holy Ghost to those who had believed and been baptized by Phillip without questioning the validity of their baptism. We have no record that the deacons were ordained for other than serving tables, yet they preached and baptized. The office of the deacon is certainly a very important one. They can do a great deal of good or harm. If the deacons are wise and judicious men they will be of incalculable service to the pastor and will be greatly honored by the church. If they purchase to themselves a good degree and great boldness in the faith, they will prove a blessing to the church. The First African Baptist Church has changed deacons quite often. The church did not consider that, once a deacon always a deacon. She reserved the right to remove them when she pleased. This is a good thing for all churches to do. By this course they could command better officers. Of the early officers not much is known. Therefore, we will only be able to mention the names of many of them, and it may be possible that some of their names even cannot be given. The following is as near as can be had the list of officers from the organization of the church in January 1788 to June 1st, 1888:

DEACONS.

Sampson Bryan, Somerset Bryan, Dick Nethercliff, Charles Golosh, Trim Campbell, Sandy Waters, Thomas Campbell, Josiah Lloyd and Harrington Demere.

These were the first set who served under Father Bryan, and still in his day others served as deacons from time to time.

Deacons Adam A. Johnson, James Willis, Adam Sheftall, Paul Hall, Cajo Ross, July Ward, Solomon Hall, Robert McNish, Samuel Cope, Abraham Wallace, Balfour Roberts, Jack Simpson, James Baily, Cuffee Williams, Ratio Frasier, Bing Frasier, Joseph Marshall, James Wilkins, James Butler, W. J. Campbell, Benjamin Ring, Joseph Clay, Anthony J. Baptiste, Charles Neufville, Patrick Williams, Jeremiah Jones, Robert Verdier, Cæsar Verdier, James M. Simms, Samuel Miller, Murry Monroe, Patrick A. Glenn, Sandy Jordan, James Richard, Friday Gibbons, George Gibbons, London Small, March Davis, Charles L. DeLamotta, Paul Demere, Ishmael Stevens, Edward D. Brown, July Boles, David McIntosh, Frank M. Williams, Peter Williams, Randolph Bolden, Richard Baker, John Nesbit,

Robert P. Young, P. H. Butler, Dennis Mitchell, Willis Harris, John H. Brown, J. C. Habersham, J. C. Williams, L. J. Pettigrew, J. H. Hooker, March Haines, Peter Houston, R. H. Johnson, E. C. Johnson, Alexander Rannair and F. J. Wright. The first named, Deacon Sampson Bryan, was a brother to Rev. Andrew Bryan. He, as his brother Andrew, was baptized by Rev. George Leile about 1781. With his brother he was imprisoned and, like him, whipped until his back was torn and his blood puddled by his side on the ground in the sight of his vile persecutors. But he would not deny the Jesus whom he loved, nor consent to cease speaking of His goodness. He shared with his brother the bitter persecution that the church was called upon to suffer in those days. Though missiles most terrible from the enemy's camp were hurled against the church, this good man never faltered. He "purchased to himself a good degree and great boldness in the faith." He was much beloved by the church. He served the church faithfully until he fell asleep in Jesus early in the nineteenth century.

DEACON ADAM JOHNSON.

Deacon Johnson may have served as deacon under Rev. Andrew Bryan. He was contemporary with Rev. Andrew Marshall. He was the ablest deacon connected with the church during his day. He was baptized by Rev. Andrew Bryan about the close of the eighteenth century, and was called to the office of deacon about the close of Mr. Bryan's administration, or about the first of Rev. Mr. Marshall's. He was a diligent student of the Bible. He was younger than Rev. Marshall. He waged the terrible war of 1832 against Rev. Mr. Marshall for adhering to the doctrine of Rev. Alexander Campbell. To him is due more than to any one else the split of the church in 1832. He must be credited with waging one of the most disastrous wars that has ever disgraced a christian church. He was, however, contending for what he believed to be "the faith once delivered to the saints," and doubtless fought with a clear conscience, believing that he had right and truth on his side. He was true to a principle, and hence his tenacity to what he believed right is not inconsistent with all that went to make up this grand man. He led the crowd that opposed Mr Marshall. His following, however, was not very large. When the final split occurred he had only 155 to acquiesce with him, while 2,640 agreed with Rev. Mr. Marshall. Deacon Johnson will always be remembered in Savannah. He was always, after the split, the leader of the Third African Baptist Church (now the First Bryan Baptist Church), which was the result of the split and which was organized under him as leader about the last of December, 1832, or the first of January, 1833, and in November of 1833 was entered in the Sunbury Baptist Association as the Third African Baptist Church of Savannah. As a christian, Deacon Johnson was pious and upright. He thought for himself and never feared to express his thoughts when the cause of Zion was concerned. He lived to a good old age, and full of years, honors and good works he fell asleep in Jesus March 18th, 1853, and was gathered to the saint's rest.

DEACON ADAM SHEFTALL.

Deacon Sheftall served as deacon, it appears, under Mr. Marshall and took sides with Deacon Johnson against Mr. Marshall. He was deacon at the time of the split or elected very soon afterwards. He was quite prominent in the split and immediately afterwards. He was almost always chosen delegate to represent the "Third Church" in the association after the split.

DEACON JACK SIMPSON

was a very pious, humble deacon of this church. He was a coadjutor of Deacon Adam Johnson, and did valiant service in the war of 1832 against Rev. Mr. Marshall. He believed that Deacon Johnson was right and, therefore, when the church split he went with the 155 which was constituted into the Third Church.

DEACON ROBERT M'NISH.

Deacon Robert McNish was born in Camden county, Ga., June 19, 1808. He was converted in 1825, and baptized in the fellowship of the First African Baptist Church by Rev. Andrew C. Marshall. He was elected a deacon of this church about 1835. He was perfectly devoted to Rev. Mr. Marshall, and was much beloved by the church. He served as a deacon under Rev. W. J. Campbell and became as devoted to him as he was to Rev. Marshall. When the split of 1832 came he cast his lot with Rev. Marshall, and in the split of 1877 he cast his destiny with Rev. Campbell and stuck by him until his death, in October, 1880. He returned with the body of members of this church from the Beach, February 17th, 1884. As the terms of agreement upon which the trouble of 1877 was settled provided that the officers of that portion of the church at the Beach Institute should relinquish their claims to offices in the church, he, upon the reunion of the church again, was thereby deposed from the office of deacon. He still lives, an honored, consistent member of the church. The old man's presence in the church is inspiring. His hair is perfectly white and he has a patriarchial appearance. Everyone calls him "Father McNish."

DEACON W. J. CAMPBELL.

Deacon W. J. Campbell was born January 1, 1812. He was baptized by Rev. Andrew C. Marshall about 1834, and elected deacon about 1840. He served in this office faithfully until he was licensed to preach in February, 1855. He became pastor of the church about January, 1857. The foundation of his great influence was laid deep and strong while he was a deacon, and he is undoubtedly remembered with more tender affection than any man who has ever lived in Savannah.

DEACON JAMES M. SIMMS.

Deacon Simms was born in Savannah, Ga., December 27th, 1823. He was converted in March, 1841, and was baptized into the fellowship of the First African Baptist Church the first Sunday in April, 1841, by Rev. Marshall. He did not remain long in the church. He was expelled for continued neglect of christian duties, and remained out of the church until 31st of October, 1858. He made several attempts, however, to get back, but Rev. Marshall seemed not to have been in a hurry to restore him. He was very presumptuous and defiant. On one occasion when he tried to return, and, having got wet, remaining out doors for his turn to be called, as the custom was, and being disappointed, as the conference adjourned without calling him, he said to Dr. Marshall : "When I ask you all to take me in again, you will do it." He left the church and went to fiddling and numerous other sins, and never returned during Mr. Marshall's life. When Mr. Marshall died, this statement returned with great force to him, and he was one of the bitterest weepers at Mr. Marshall's funeral. But he remained out two years longer, when he returned to the church and was restored. He was elected clerk of the church December 19th, 1858. His push and pluck made him prominent rather than the wish of the people to have him as officer. He was appointed one of the building committee of the church. He was a very fine workman, and had charge of the wood work of the church. This he executed with remarkable good taste. He was very intelligent for that day. He bought himself in the year 1857 for $740. He was licensed to preach by the First African Baptist Church in March, 1863. He was elected deacon January 29th, 1860. He was detected teaching the children of his race April, 1863, for which he was fined $50. When the war broke out between the North and South, he ran the blockade and went to Massachusetts, leaving Savannah on the 2d of February, 1864, and returning on the 2d of February, 1865. During his twelve months' stay in Boston, Mass., he was ordained to the office of the gospel ministry by the Twelfth Street Baptist Church, Boston, Mass., April 17th, 1864, by Rev. Leonard A. Grimes; Reymond, of New York; Rev. Thompson, of Boston; Randolph Charlton, of Boston.

When he returned home, Rev. W. J. Campbell, the pastor of the First African Baptist Church refused to recognize the ordination of Mr. Simms, claiming that no church had the right to call to ordination one of the members of his church. In this Mr. Campbell was quite right. Mr. Simms had a commission from the Home Mission Society to labor among the negroes in this part of Georgia and in parts of Florida. Mr. Campbell appears to have written the society that Mr. Simms was not regularly ordained, and the society withdrew the commission. This drove Mr. Simms into politics, there being a Freedman's Bureau in the city, which gave him employment. From this time on he entered fully into politics. He was elected to the Legislature of Georgia, and served several terms. He was an able member of that body. He was appointed a judge by Governor Bullock, but did not hold court anywhere because the office was abolished very soon after its establishment. Judge Simms took a letter of dismission from the First African Baptist Church and joined the First Bryan Baptist Church. Rev. U. L. Houston, pastor of said church, recognized the ordination of Mr. Simms. This enraged Rev. Mr. Campbell with Rev. Houston, which bitter feeling lasted for years. Rev. Simms' ordination is counted irregular by the First African Baptist Church till this day. In 1885 Rev. Mr. Simms took a letter of dismission from the First Bryan Baptist Church to join the First African Baptist Church, but the church refused to accept it, and returned it to him, when he carried it back to the First Bryan Baptist Church, where he is still a member. It is just to state that Mr. Simms is not properly a gospel minister, having never been properly ordained, and should not be admitted into the pulpit of any orderly Baptist church. He has been in several very questionable law suits which reflected seriously upon his character. Mr. Simms, all told, is among the ablest men the church has ever produced. He is stubborn and possesses an iron will. He has been pastor of several country churches, but has continued with no one of them very long at a time. He has left politics and is giving himself wholly to the ministry, preaching at several country churches and wherever else a door is opened to him. But his manners are repulsive to the people, and as a preacher he does not succeed.

DEACON MURRY MONROE.

Deacon Monroe was born in Liberty county, Ga., July 16th, 1818. He was baptized into the fellowship of the First African Baptist Church in 1844 by Rev. Andrew C. Marshall. He was very much attached to Mr. Marshall. He loved him as his own father. Mr. Monroe named his oldest boy after Mr. Marshall. That boy is Andrew Marshall Monroe and is an earnest, faithful, consistent member of the church to-day. Mr. Monroe was elected deacon of the church May 16th, 1858. He served most faithfully and acceptably for years, when he resigned because of business engagements which prevents him from giving the office his time. The church hated to part with him. He was a man of considerable means and unbounded liberality. He reared his children right, and had as nice and respectable a family as any in the city. He was one of the building committee who superintended the erection of the church in 1859. In all things he has been a faithful, upright and consistent christian gentleman. He was an example of christian piety, fidelity and devotion. He was quick to forgive and forget an injury. He still lives and aged, faithful member of the church. He is very feeble now, and cannot attend on divine service as in former days. He is universally beloved and honored. Deacon Monroe can never be forgotten by the members of the First African Baptist Church. He has served the church faithfully and long, and has never put the church to any trouble. As a man Deacon Monroe has a pleasing address, gentlemanly bearing and dignified manners. He is polite, affable and kind, and has great reverence for his church and pastor. He is naturally polished and his countenance bespeaks truth, honesty and sincerity. He is withal a good man.

DEACON PATRICK A. GLENN.

Deacon Glenn was born near May River, S. C., in 1817. He was baptized into the fellowship of the First African Baptist Church about 1835 by Rev. Andrew C. Marshall. He was called to the office of deacon May 16, 1858. He was for awhile deposed from office, and remained out until the split of 1877, when he was restored to office. He took sides against Rev. Campbell in the church fight, and was vigorous in his opposition to him. Deacon Glenn still lives, an aged and honored member of the church. He has a large circle of admiring friends, and is quite influential, in the country places especially. He is now feeble, but manages to get out to church and attend to his duties as a deacon. He is very industrious and has some good property.

DEACON JAMES RICHARD

was born near Hilton Head, S. C., August 10, 1820, and was baptized into the fellowship of the First African Baptist Church about 1844 by Rev. Andrew C. Marshall. He was elected deacon May 16, 1858, and served for seven years, when he resigned. He was very diligent and active and served his church most faithfully. He is an humble man, full of faith and love, and everyone regards him with much tenderness and affection. He is the faithful sexton of the church, and takes great pride in his work, and the church is kept perfectly clean. He is perfectly devoted to the church and pastor. Anything left in the church through mistake, or lost, is perfectly safe in his hands. No one has a harsh word to say of Mr. Richard. He is polite and has a pleasing address, and has always had a wonderful influence. He is noted for meekness and great patience. He still lives, a loving, consistent member of the church.

DEACON FRIDAY GIBBONS.

Deacon Friday Gibbons was elder brother of Rev. George Gibbons. He was born in the year 1809, and was baptized by Rev. Andrew Marshall about 1830. He was called to the office of deacon January 29th, 1860. He was an active deacon, and won the confidence of the church. Those who opposed him as deacon acknowledge his uprightness and faithfulness as a servant of God. He fell asleep in Jesus December 26th, 1874, full of years and full of good work. He is very tenderly spoken of by the members of the church.

DEACON GEORGE GIBBONS

was born on Thorny Island, Barnwell District, S. C., November 13th, 1819. He was converted to God about 1844, and baptized into the fellowship of the First African Baptist Church by Rev. Andrew C. Marshall. He was elected deacon of the church January 29th, 1860. He was an humble, active, loving deacon, and won the confidence, admiration and love of the entire church. He was licensed to preach, and was therefore promoted from the position of deacon. He became an assistant to Rev. W. J. Campbell in the pastorate. He became pastor of the Bethlehem Baptist Church, which he served very acceptably until he was called to the pastorate of the First African Baptist Church during the troubles of 1877.

DEACON C. L. DELAMOTTA.

was born in Charleston, S. C., in the year 1822. He was converted to God about 1844, and was baptized into the fellowship of the First African Baptist Church by Rev. A. C. Marshall. He was elected deacon of the church October 12th, 1862. He was very stubborn when he took a stand. He opposed the call of Rev. W. J. Campbell, and for a while made it very unpleasant for him. He was very quick to beg pardon when it appeared that he would be expelled. If the church gave him time to talk, his pitiable pleading and humble attitude would preclude the possibility of expulsion. He was, however, expelled in 1858 for his opposition to the pastor, and again in 1876 for his opposition to the pastor and deacons. He was the faithful and loving superintendent of the Sunday school. He was greatly beloved by the scholars and teachers. They were willing to stand by him under almost any circumstance. When the State Baptist Convention met at Columbus,

Ga., he sent the Sunday school letter by Rev. Alexander Harris, pastor of the First Bryan Baptist Church, West Broad street, notwithstanding Deacons R. P. Young and P. H. Butler were delegates from his own church. To this, these two brethren took exception and reported the matter to the church, upon which Deacon DeLamotta was expelled. Rev. Campbell, the pastor, endeavored to get Deacon J. H. Brown to take charge of the Sunday school as superintendent, but he, being true to a friend, and true to an understanding of the matter before hand, declined. Deacon R. P. Young was appointed superintendent. The teachers refused to serve under Deacon Young, which was rightly construed to mean contempt of the church, and therefore Superintendent DeLamotta with all of his teachers, seventeen in number, were expelled. Most of these remained out until the trouble of 1877, when they rushed in and swelled the number of the majority, which was then arraigned against the pastor. Mr. DeLamotta was restored to the office of superintendent and deacon. Some of these teachers continued to commune in some of the churches where they were permitted to do so, notwithstanding they were expelled members. It is hard to conceive how people who had the intelligence these teachers had could be guilty of so gross an error as to commune with the Lord and his people when they were not reconciled with the church into whose fellowship they had been baptized, but such is the fact. It is hardly natural to suppose that they would be prepared to sympathize with Rev. Mr. Campbell, whom they charged with being the cause of their expulsion. It tended, however, to show the hold Mr. DeLamotta had upon the hearts of these teachers. The Sunday school was perfectly devoted to Mr. DeLamotta and he was equally devoted to the Sunday school. Whenever anything concerning the Sunday school came up he would be sure to do his part. He had no children of his own, but he had such a big heart that he could and did take in everybody else's children. There has never been a deacon connected with this church, perhaps, who has done as much good as Deacon DeLamotta. While he did his duty as a deacon of the church, his labors among the children knew no bounds. The majority of the people of this church now owe their christian information to Deacon C. L. DeLamotta. He can never be forgotten in Savannah. He was as humble and obedient to his mother as a child. At the convention in Cartersville May, 1885, in a Sunday school mass meeting, after the congregation had sung, "Hold the Fort for I Am Coming" in a most feeling manner, he rose and said: "Children, while you are singing 'Hold the Fort for I am Coming,' my soul rejoices, though I cannot help you sing that part. I have been here too long to sing that as you do. I have most gotten through with my work here. I will soon be gone. I rejoice that God has raised you up to hold the fort that I have been trying to hold for so many years. Therefore I shall sing to you, ' Hold the Fort for I am going ' " This had a wonderful effect upon the congregation, and melted many to tears. Deacon DeLamotta opposed the call of Rev. E. K. Love, and became so naughty that he was deposed from the deacon's office and narrowly escaped expulsion. He, however, very soon made friends with him and co-operated with him in his work. Rev. Love stood by him to the last, admiring him for " the very work's sake." Rev. Love restored him to office and found in him a faithful officer. He died December the 30th, 1886, full of good works Before he died he sent for Deacon J. H. Brown and other teachers and had them to sing some of his favorite songs, and then committed the school to Mr. Brown, saying, "John, I must die, take care of the school— take care of my children." He sent for Rev. E. K. Love, his pastor, and told him, " I cannot live; I must die. Tell the people I love Jesus I know I have done wrong in many things, but it is all well, now. Tell the church I am going home to rest. I love Jesus, and he loves me." Very soon after saying this he calmly fell asleep in Jesus. Rev. Alexander Harris, his life-long friend by his side The church bore his funeral expenses, and a very large crowd of weepers, together with the Sunday school, headed by Deacon J. H. Brown. followed him to his last resting place, January 1st, 1887.

DEACON DAVID M'INTOSH

was born in Savannah, Ga., about 1843, and was converted to God about 1866, and baptized into the fellowship of the First African Baptist Church by Rev. W. J. Campbell. He was called to the office of deacon January 31st, 1869. He was a faithful deacon. He stood by Rev. Campbell in the trouble of 1877, and when the church split he went with him to the Beach. He returned to the church, awhile before the body did, February 17, 1884, and remained a faithful, active member until his death. He was murdered by Frederick Wright, who also was a member of this church, July 22d, 1886. Mr. Wright suspicioned Mr McIntosh of criminal intimacy with his wife, and unceremoniously shot him down. Mr. Wright's suspicion prove to be unfounded, and he was found guilty of murder and recommended to the mercy of the court. He was sentenced to life-time imprisonment. Deacon McIntosh stood well in the church and well in the community. Nobody believes him guilty of the awful crime for which he lost his life. A good man was thus rashly removed from us.

DEACON FRANK M. WILLIAMS

was born in Beaufort, S. C., May 10th, 1842, and was converted to God May, 1866. He was baptized into the fellowship of the First African Baptist Church by Rev. W. J. Campbell. He was called to the office of deacon January 31st, 1869. He is an humble, meek, loving man, and is much beloved by the church. He took sides with the majority against Rev. Mr. Campbell in the trouble of 1877, and was moderator of that memorable conference when the split occurred. He is regarded a senior deacon of the church, though comparatively a young man. He is chairman of the finance committee, and is almost always made moderator, when the pastor is absent. He goes in the water with the pastor on baptism days. He has a sweeping influence. He still lives, and exerts a wonderful influence in the church. Mr. Williams has been moderator of several memorable conferences. He was moderator when Rev. E. K. Love was called. He has always reflected credit upon the church. He is treasurer of the Mount Olive Baptist Association and several other important societies, with all of whom he stands well. He is very kind, and treats the members with the utmost tenderness and becoming politeness.

DEACON RICHARD BAKER

was born in Savannah about 1820. He was converted to God about 1838, and was baptized into the fellowship of the First African Baptist Church by Rev. Andrew C. Marshall. He was elected deacon of the church September 25th, 1865. He had a great influence, and in power stood next to Rev. W. J. Campbell, the pastor. He was perfectly devoted to the pastor, supporting him unqualifiedly in whatever he undertook. In the trouble of 1877 he took sides with the pastor, who was unfortunately with the minority. Indeed, Mr. Baker was more largely responsible for that trouble than any other man connected with it. Had Deacon Young not taken the advice of Deacon Baker, it is quite probable that the trouble would not have assumed so serious a magnitude. Deacon Baker mistook his strength in the church and undertook to carry things his way, and hence the terrible clash. He entered the first indictment against the brethren for disturbing public worship, and started the law suit. Had he exercised more of a Christ-like, forbearing spirit, this law suit would not have been, and the matter would have been much more easily settled. He became chief prosecutor on the other side. When the split occurred, he, of course, went with Rev. Mr. Campbell. He remained with him until his death. Mr. Baker did not return with the people from the "Beach," February 17th, 1884, nor has he returned yet. He seems to have taken a vow that he would not come back. He still lives an alien and stranger to the church and almost forgotten by the members. His name is never heard in the church and very rarely among the members. Though he lives, he is dead. Had he died during the trouble he would have been spoken of more kindly, and his memory would have been more respected. He will probably never return to the church, but the church has forgotten him and is moving grandly on to a glorious success.

DEACON JOHN NESBIT

was born in Charleston, S. C., about 1828. He was converted about 1858 and baptized into the fellowship of the First African Baptist Church by Rev. W. J. Campbell. He was elected deacon of the church January 31st, 1869. He was licensed to preach by the church in 1874. When Rev. George Gibbons was called pastor of this church and resigned the charge of Bethlehem Baptist Church, Mr. Nesbit was called to ordination and elected pastor of said church in 1879, where he still labors successfully.

DEACON ROBERT P. YOUNG

was born in Savannah October 25th, 1842. He was converted to God in 1861 and baptized into the fellowship of the First African Baptist Church by Rev. W. J. Campbell. He was elected deacon of the church January 31st, 1869. He was active, intelligent and pious. He was a favorite of Rev. Campbell. He was also clerk of the church. The trouble of 1877 is traceable to him as the starting point. He was the person charged of misplacing the money of the church. He acknowledged being careless with the money, but stated that he had no intention of stealing the money. This statement was accepted and his carelessness pardoned. Mr. Joseph C. Williams motioned to expel him, but Deacon Baker made a substitute motion that he be rebuked and forgiven. The substitute prevailed. At the next conference Mr. J. C. Williams motioned, on the confirmation of the minutes, that the motion which pardoned Deacon Young be reconsidered. The chair very correctly ruled this motion out of order. Mr. J. C. Habersham moved to sustain the motion of Mr. Williams. This motion prevailed. This was virtually an appeal from the decision of the chair. This erroneous motion started the ball to rolling. But for this motion, it is hard to see how the church would have split at that time and for that cause. This laid the foundation for the objection to Deacon Young carrying around the communion, and for Mr. A. Rannair barring the door of the choir to prevent him from entering the choir with the holy eucharist which laid the foundation for the indictments of disturbing public worship, and this laid the foundation of the bitterest hostilities ever occurred in the history of the church. This unsavory motion was the prolific parent of all these troubles. The church finally split, and Deacon Young cast his lot with those who stood with Rev. Mr. Campbell. He was their intellectual leader. He prepared the papers that were used in court for his side. He stood by Rev. Campbell until his death. He led the army back February 17th, 1884. He surrendered the books to Rev. George Gibbons and every other right save that of a member. But he was very soon placed back into the choir and made its president. In this position he remained until he died. When he was about to to die, he sent for his pastor, Rev. E. K. Love, and said to him: "Parson, I have sent for you to tell you what to do with my body. I have decided to die; I know I cannot live; I will take no more medicine; I would rather die; I am at peace with God and all men; tell the church I am going to heaven; tell them to meet me there; I have done many things wrong, but it is all well; take charge of my body and lay it away decently and pay my board bill for me; the Masons and longshoremen will bear my funeral expenses; may God bless you." Shortly after this Deacon R. P. Young fell asleep in Jesus in April, 1887. He was followed to his last resting place by several thousand persons. Deacon Young was a meek man and full of faith, and will always be remembered with interest.

DEACON POMPEY H. BUTLER

was born in Whitehall, Bryan county, Georgia, December, 1841. In April, 1853, he was converted and united with the Macedonia Baptist Church into the full membership, of which he was baptized the following July by Rev. Mr. Fuller Harmon, who was a missionary preacher laboring in Whitehall and other portions of Bryan county.

In 1865 he went to Savannah, where he placed himself under the watchcare of the First African Baptist Church, over which Rev. William J. Campbell was then presiding. One year later, in 1866, he drew his letter from the Macedonia church and became a full member of the First African Baptist Church.

Here he won the respect and confidence of all, and was in due time promoted from the ranks of the laity to official standing. January 31st, 1869, he was chosen deacon, which position he held continuously fifteen years and one month, discharging his duties faithfully and acceptably.

By the unanimous consent of the church he was licensed to preach September, 1885. Feeling the need of some preparation for his work, he went to the Atlanta Baptist Seminary, where he devoted some three years to earnest study, and made decided progress.

Polite, affable, he makes a favorable impression, and wins friends wherever he goes. He was intimately associated with the pastor, by which he became very influential. He went with the pastor whenever and wherever he went on his vacation. He enjoyed the fullest confidence and the most tender love of the entire church. He was away with the pastor when the memorable trouble of 1877 begun. Hence, he was not concerned in it, but took sides with the deacons and pastor. This was most natural for him, under the circumstances, being with the pastor and being himself a deacon. He took an active part in the trouble and became one of the prominent characters in the prosecution. He stood by Rev. Campbell till his death. He, with Deacon Young, brought the church back from the Beach. He lost his office in the compromise, but was very soon licensed to preach the gospel. Mr. Butler stands spotless in this community. He possesses pleasing manners and is very friendly. If he is as successful as a preacher as he was a deacon, the church will have great need to be proud of him. Mr. Butler is widely and favorably known. The brethren love him.

DEACON PETER WILLIAMS

was born in Bryan county, Ga., in the year 1832. He was converted to God in 1867, and was baptized into the fellowship of the First African Baptist Church by Rev. W. J. Campbell. He was called to the office of deacon in 1875. He was an humble officer, active and pious, and greatly beloved of the church. He won the highest confidence of the entire church. He was very much devoted to Rev. Campbell, his pastor, obeyed him absolutely, and was willing to die with him. He took sides with Rev. Campbell and went with him to the Beach. He stood by him until his death. He returned to the church February 17, 1884, with the body of members from the Beach. By virtue of the compromise he lost his office and became a private member. He has since been elected deacon but declined acceptance. He is still a consistent member of the church, a man much beloved by the people. Deacon Williams' life is worthy of imitation. He is a good man.

DEACON MARCH HAYNES

was born in Pocataligo, S. C., March 4, 1825. He was converted to God in April, 1838, and was baptized into the fellowship of the Wilmington Baptist Church, April, 1838, by Rev. Jack Watry. He was elected deacon of said church in 1849. He removed to Savannah in 1858 and joined the First African Baptist Church, of which he became an active deacon in December, 1877. He is a faithful officer and enjoys the entire confidence of the church and community. He enlisted in the late war on the Union side and did valiant service. He was active in putting many of his race over on the Union side, where they enjoyed freedom. He was a brave soldier. In attempting to get some of his people from Savannah over on the Yankee side he encountered the enemy, who commanded him and his faithful few to halt. This command was given to the wrong man. He was willing to meet death rather than obey that command. He knew it was death to obey and could but be death to disobey, hence the war began between them, in which he was terribly wounded. He made good his escape, however, to the Union soldiers. He is still alive, but unable to work from the effects of the wound he received on that occasion. He is pensioned by the United States, but not near so much as he should be. He is an humble man, meek and full of faith, and is beloved by the entire church. He is one of the most polite men in the world. Whatever duty is assigned to his hands will be done with promptness and accuracy. There is not a deacon or a member connected with the church that has suffered more for his race than Deacon Haynes. He is a true man, and would have been a leader in any age and of any people. He is a natural detective, and as a shrewd man he has few equals. As a friend he is true, lasting and tender. He is forbearing and extremely kind, and is an honor to our church and race. He loves to work for his Master, and, though wounded, always does his part. He is possessed of indomitable courage and great zeal, coupled with a clear judgment and profound discretion.

DEACON JAMES H. HOOKER

was born in Savannah, Ga., January 30th, 1835, and was baptized into the fellowship of the First African Baptist Church January 2, 1862, by Rev. W. J. Campbell. He was elected deacon of the church November 25th, 1877. He was the same day elected treasurer of the church. He was elected trustee of the church December 16th, 1877. As a deacon Mr. Hooker is blameless, humble, loving and very kind. He reverences the church of Christ. He has a good report by them that are without. The members have unbounded confidence in him. No man in Savannah stands higher than Deacon Hooker. He is a man of few words, but of a princely, large heart. He was with the majority during the church trouble. During this time he was elected to offices already mentioned. He comes as near as frail man can meeting Paul's requirements of a deacon. As a treasurer, he is pure, and not even a whisper of his ever having done wrong with the money of the church. Every cent was accounted for to the fullest satisfaction of the church. He would be treasurer to-day but for a severe attack of pneumonia and nervous prostration, which the doctors declared unfitted him for any responsible office; that he could not stand the care of this office, and so he resigned, to the regret of the church. As a trustee, he is honest, wise and faithful. The interest of the church cannot suffer in his hands. He believes that God ordained that he should fill these offices, and hence he fills them as in the sight of God. If all of our officers in all the churches were to feel this way our churches would be a power in the world. He was ordained as deacon December 6th, 1885, by Revs. E. K. Love, U. L. Houston and S. A. McNeal. Deacon Hooker is still alive, exerting a powerful influence for good. He is a man of means and rules well his own house. He scarcely finds time to visit any other church when his church is open. Deacon Hooker owns a fine brick residence, and lives in comfort and ease.

DEACON L. J. PETTIGREW

was born in Scriven county, Ga., April 9th, 1847. He was converted to God in July, 1867, and was baptized into the fellowship of the first African Baptist Church by Rev. W. J. Campbell. Mr. Pettigrew was elected deacon of the church October 22d, 1877, during the great trouble of the church. He was an active and conspicuous character in the trouble of 1877, and took a strong stand with the majority against the deacons and pastor. There was not a person more prominent in the whole affair than Mr. Pettigrew. He was very shrewd and crafty, and much of the planning is due to him. He was, prior to this trouble, one of Mr. Campbell's most trusted friends, and his not going with him must have taken the old man with great surprise. Mr. Pettigrew was also clerk of the church. He was, therefore, one of the most important men in the conflict after the matter reached the courts; much depended upon him for documentary evidence. This duty was well performed. He was very active in supporting Mr. Gibbons for the pastorate of the church. He resigned the offices of deacon and clerk in 1882. However, he still wielded a wonderful influence in the church. He was largely instrumental in securing the call of Rev. E. K. Love. He was Dr. Love's fast friend. Mr. Pettigrew is a man of keen foresight, quick perception, and ready argument. He is kind-hearted, friendly and generous. He still lives, a member of the church, with a host of friends. He is generally successful in whatever scheme he undertakes in the church, being very artful.

DEACON JOSEPH C. WILLIAMS

was born in Jefferson county, Ga., May 15, 1843. He was converted to God in May, 1868, and was baptized into the fellowship of the First African Baptist Church by Rev. W. J. Campbell. Mr. Williams was a very prominent character in the great trouble of 1877, and was elected deacon in that year. He stood by the church against the old deacons and pastor. It was rather surprising to the old man that his spiritual son Joe should go against him, but such was true. Deacon Williams took a strong stand and contributed no little to the planning of the majority; he was fearless and outspoken; he was generous and kind-hearted, cheerful in the discharge of his duties, and had a large following. Mr. Williams supported Mr. Gibbons for the pastorate of the church. He was not a warm supporter of Mr. Love, and resigned the office of deacon about the time Mr.

Love was called. He still lives, a member of the church. Mr. Williams is naturally intelligent and well suited to lead. He is dignified in bearing, affable and polite in manners, and he is generous and kind. As a friend he is tender and true, and he has a large and tender heart. He is shrewd and much given to technicalities. He is artful in debate, pointed in argument, and bold and fluent in speech. He is a leader among men. He was much opposed to Mr. Young about the money affair. He believed him guilty and contended that he should be expelled. To this opinion he stuck. Mr. Williams might be made still more useful than he is. To him is due more than to any living man the fact that Rev. Campbell was never expelled. This makes him the wisest and safest leader on the side of the majority. But for him the trouble would have been fiercer.

DEACON JOHN H. BROWN

was born in Savannah, Ga., August 5th, 1855. He was converted to God in the year 1873, and was baptized into the fellowship of the First African Baptist Church by Rev. W. J. Campbell. He was elected deacon in the year 1875. He was assistant superintendent of the Sunday school under Deacon C. L. DeLamotta, and acquiesced with him in his action respecting the Sunday school letter already referred to. He was urged by his loving pastor to accept the superintendency of the Sunday school, vice Deacon C. L. DeLamotta removed, but he stubbornly refused and suffered himself expelled for contempt of church. This was suicide. There could have been no righteous agreement between him and Mr. DeLamotta which would have made it ungodly for him to accept this responsible position to do good in his Master's vineyard. But he did not see duty in this light, and for several years he remained out of the church. During this period he spent his time visiting the white churches. Intellectually, he was greatly benefited. In the trouble of 1877 he put in his appearance time enough to put in some telling work against Rev. Campbell. He was, educationally, the ablest man on the side of the majority. Every single document of any note during that time was his production. He is still among the ablest men connected with the church, intellectually. When he was restored, he became deacon again and assistant superintendent again. He was elected vice-president of the Missionary Baptist Sunday School Convention of Georgia in 1881, and was elected president of the same in 1882. He has since filled that office with honor, dignity and ability. He has for many years been secretary of the Mount

Olive Baptist Association. He was elected clerk of the Missionary Baptist Convention of Georgia in 1886, which office he has since filled most satisfactorily. He is a member of the State Centennial Committee, and is its clerk. Whatever office he is elected to, he will fill with credit and satisfaction. He is superintendent of the First African Baptist Church Sunday School. In this sphere he is still doing great good. His great fault as a leader is that he is universally tardy, and seldom ever reaches any meeting, church or otherwise on time.

DEACON WILLIS HARRIS

was born about 1842. He was converted to Christ about 1867, and was baptized into the fellowship of the First African Baptist Church by Rev. W. J. Campbell. He was elected deacon of this church about 1874. Shortly afterwards he was deposed from this office. He doubtless cultivated a dislike for Deacon Robert P. Young and Rev. W. J. Campbell, whom he decided were instrumental in getting him out of office. Hence he set in to watch them to see what he could see. He appears to have been determined to get something on them or make it. He saw Deacon Young put a basket of money (already described in a previous chapter) under or on the pedals of the organ in the choir, and told the sexton about it and had him to remove it. He scattered it over town the next day that Young had stolen a basket of money. Deacon Young, however, had told Deacon F. M. Williams of the incident before leaving the church. Deacon Young affirmed that the basket was removed before he could get it to bring down. Mr. Harris certainly did not act the part of a christian nor of a wise detective. As a christian, he should have labored with Deacon Young to reclaim his erring brother. If Deacon Young heard him, he had gained his brother and the matter should have ended there. As a detective, he should have waited for Mr. Young to return for the money and let him have attempted to leave the church and then have found the money on his person. He seemed to have been so anxious that he did neither of these things. It is clear that he meant mischief, and he caused the church to reap a terrible harvest of bickering, disaffection, sorrow and heartaches for seven weary years. He brought the money to the church a night or two after this and attempted to present it in open church, affirming that he had caught Mr. Young stealing it. Not long did vengeance suffer him to go free. He was caught stealing from a Mr. Douglass, in whose employ he was. The extent of his stealings has never been determined. He had many dollars' worth of goods hid about the church (being at the time sexton of the church) and many more at his home. He was arrested, found guilty and sentenced to seven years in the penitentiary at hard labor, where he is still. This was a righteous retribution for the troubles and heartaches he caused in Israel. The frowns of Almighty God seem to have rested upon the man.

DEACON JOHN C. HABERSHAM

was born in McIntosh county, Ga., April 20th, 1838. He was converted to Christ and baptized into the fellowship of the Bryan Neck Baptist Church in 1852 by Rev. J. H. Edwards. He joined the First African Baptist Church of Savannah in 1866. He was elected deacon of this church October 22d, 1877. This was during the troubles of 1877. He was a conspicuous character in that trouble, taking a strong stand on the side of the majority against the pastor and deacons. He is strong in the faith; of determined resolution and of iron will. He is very popular and has a large influence among the membership. He loves his church most ardently, and whatever tends to advance its interest he is found in the foremost ranks. His motion to sustain the motion of Mr. Joseph C. Williams against Deacon R. P. Young, after he had been forgiven by the church, is largely responsible for the continuation of the terrible church trouble which begun in 1877. Perhaps he had no idea of the heartaches and sorrow that little motion would breed. He still lives, and is exerting a good influence. He is active and pious and full of faith. He possesses, in a large measure, the gift of preaching, and should he enter the ministry he would be acceptable to the people and would do great good in the vineyard of the Lord. There is a sweetness in his voice that wins the attention of his hearers. He has studied well the Bible, and may yet do good service in the ministry. Mr. Habersham is a very determined man. Whatever he undertakes he goes into with all of his soul, and never fails. He is a born leader. In every contest of the officers for prizes for popularity, or raising money otherwise, for the church, he always beats, hence it must be that he has more influence than any of them.

DEACON PETER HOUSTON

was born in Savannah, Ga., about 1820. He was converted to God about 1840, and was baptized into the fellowship of the First African Baptist Church by Rev. Andrew C. Marshall. He was clerk of the church for quite a long time. As a clerk he was faithful and punctual. He was one among a very few who were able to take minutes before the war. He was a slave, yet he managed to acquire some education. He was a useful member. Whatever Mr. Houston said could be relied upon. He was as true as steel. As a man he was fearless and perfectly honest. He was outspoken and friendly. He was expelled for taking a sister to law. He did not feel that his expulsion was justifiable, and never returned to the church while Rev. Mr. Campbell was pastor. He remarked to Mr. Campbell when he was expelled : "Never mind, when you will be going out, I will be coming in." This proved to be absolutely true, though it was said, evidently, in a bad spirit. The day Rev. Campbell went out of the church, Mr. Houston met him at the door and called his attention to his phophecy years ago, to which Rev. Campbell replied : "Do, Houston, for God's sake, let me alone!" The old man prophesied in return that no good would follow Houston, which proved to be equally as true. Mr. Houston was in 1877 made deacon of the church. He was a very efficient deacon, and had more influence than any other man on the staff. The people believed him absolutely. He was an upright, virtuous christian gentleman, and stood perfectly fair in the community. He did not favor Rev. Mr. Gibbons for pastor. He was, it is believed, assassinated. The prevalent opinion is that he was smothered and thrown in the river. This occurred one Saturday night in 1883. He had just finished the erection of a prayer house in Southville, where he lived, and it was to be dedicated by Rev. Gibbons on the next Sabbath. Mr. Houston was missed at the time, and a great concern was felt. The people suspicioned that something had happened, as Mr. Houston was a very punctual man, and as there was a case to come up in the United States District Court on Monday in which Mr. Houston was a witness, and as he had told the parties that he would tell the truth, and as the truth would injure the parties concerned, it was suspicioned that he was killed. Hence a party was organized to drag the river for him. The suspicion proved to be true, as he was found in the river some days afterward. The guilty parties escaped justice as it could not be determined who perpetrated the atrocious deed. The whole church mourned for this good man. The church lost an able and faithful deacon and the community a good and useful citizen. There is an opinion of the minority of the people that he committed suicide because of domestic troubles. This is hardly true, as this trouble had been going on for some time and as he had faithfully promised to conduct the dedication of his prayer-house the next day. This man was greatly beloved of the church.

DEACON MOSES L. JACKSON

was born in Savannah, Ga., in 1837. He was converted to Jesus in 1858, and was baptized into the fellowship of the First African Baptist Church by Rev. W. J. Campbell. He was an active member of the church and was always influential. He was appointed deacon of the church in 1877, and was prominent in the famous church troubles of that year, taking sides with the majority against the deacons and pastor. He was one of Mr. Willis Harris' witnesses in the R. P. Young case, and testified that Mr. Willis Harris did, on the first Sunday afternoon in August, call his attention to the fact that Young had concealed a basket of money in and about the organ. Deacon Jackson became one of the most useful and influential deacons in the church, and was of incalculable service to the pastor. The poor had in Mr. Jackson a special friend. He would walk the city over in visiting the poor and praying for the sick and burying the dead. In fact, Mr. Jackson knew more about the members than did the pastor. He was very much beloved and wielded an immense influence in the church. He had a large number of spiritual children over whom he had almost absolute control. He taught a private school, but got his living mainly from his spiritual children. He was licensed to preach the third Sunday in October, 1885. Mr. Jackson, as a preacher, was not very logical, nor profound nor accurate, but his earnest and tender devotion quite atoned for this with the people. He loved to preach, and always did so with a most graceful smile. He was quite gentlemanly and dignified, and a faithful servant of God. The church greatly misses him, and his place is hard to fill. He died of dropsy in September, 1887, and was followed to his last resting place by a multitude of mourners. Mr. Jackson's good work was not confined to the city, but he delighted to go into the country places, scattering seeds of kindness for his reaping when he would be gathered to the saint's rest in glory. He was a man of a large heart. His work follows him, and he is remembered with much tenderness. He died in the full triumph of the christian faith, and with a smile on his face he bade this world farewell. There never was a deacon in the church nor pastor who did the visiting and praying Mr. Jackson did. He knew almost the entire membership and they knew him. A faithful man has been gathered home.

DEACON ALEXANDER RANNAIR

was born in Savannah, Ga., October 9th, 1846. When he was seventeen years old he embraced the christian religion, and in September, 1863, was baptized at Guyton, Ga., by Rev. Sweat, having been carried there by his owners. He returned to Savannah in 1864, and became a member of the First African Baptist Church. In 1866 he became a member of the choir, in which he has sung for twenty-four years. In January, 1886, he was elected deacon. Mr. Rannair was the person who barred the choir door against Deacon Robert P. Young, and told him that the choir did not want any communion from him. From this rash act of Mr. Rannair the terrible law suit begun. Mr. Rannair was indicted for disturbing the public worship and fined ten dollars, together with several others. He became, therefore, a prominent figure in the trouble of 1877. Mr. Rannair is quite intelligent, and it is passing strange that he should have taken such an unwarranted and unwise course. Surely $23.32 could not have been the cause of this feeling when it is not quite certain that Deacon Young meant to steal the money. It seems that the spirit of the Lord Jesus Christ would have taught more christian forbearance and patient investigation. However, Mr. Rannair was backed by a large majority of the church, and his conviction in the courts amounted to nothing with the church. Deacon Rannair is still very popular and stands well with the church. He is a faithful member and very much devoted to his church. He is beloved and trusted by his brethren. Mr. Rannair has a very pleasing address and dignified manners. He is still a live and active member, full of promise. His character is good.

DEACON R. H. JOHNSON

was born near Savannah, Ga., December 17th, 1845. He was converted to Christ January, 1873, and was baptized by Rev. George Gibbons into the fellowship of the First African Baptist Church on the first Sunday in February, 1873, the Rev. J. W. Campbell being sick. He was not very officious in the trouble of 1877. He is a man of few words and very pleasant manners. He is very kind and polite. He is a most devoted member of the church. He is kingly in his appearance and earnest in his work for the church. He is never absent, unless he is sick, or some other providential hinderance. Mr. Johnson has a very winning way and the members love him devotedly. Mr. Johnson was elected deacon of the church in January, 1886.

He proved to be a faithful officer and an invaluable help to the pastor. He favored Rev. E. K. Love as pastor of the church and did all in his power to secure his election as pastor. No deacon of the church is more active than Deacon Johnson. He loves his work and takes pleasure in visiting the sick and poor in his ward, and has very few cases of discipline from his ward. As a man and as a christian Deacon Johnson stands well and has the fullest confidence of the church and community. Deacon Johnson is unassuming, humble, patient and full of the holy ghost and faith. He has filled his office with honor to the church and credit to himself. The church has a just cause to be proud of him.

DEACON E. C. JOHNSON

was born in Bryan county, Ga., November 20, 1850, and was brought to Savannah when quite a child. He was converted to Christ July 20, 1870, and was baptized on the first Sunday in August of the same year by Rev. W. J. Campbell. He was elected deacon of the church in January, 1886. Deacon Johnson is a quiet, dignified, upright christian gentleman. He is blameless, a man retired in manners and of very few words—absolutely has nothing to say in church conferences except circumstances force him. Whenever he does speak he is pointed, brief and powerful, and his words well selected and never fail of force upon the people. His life is always an eloquent appeal in his favor. He has the entire confidence of the church and community and is greatly beloved. He was elected treasurer of the church in the latter part of 1886, vice Deacon J. H. Hooker resigned. The finances of the church have been perfectly safe in his hands, and have been faithfully and ably managed. The church could not have elected a better man were it to try it over a thousand times. Deacon Johnson is a faithful man, pious and upright, and loves his church and pastor devoutly. He was a warm supporter of Rev. E. K. Love for the pastorate, and has always stood ready to assist and protect him. The church is his delight, and nothing is too great for him to undertake for Zion. He is kind to everybody and is beloved by all good people. He is active and energetic, not easily discouraged, and is full of faith and hope. He has "purchased to himself a good degree and great boldness in the faith."

DEACON F. J. WRIGHT

was born in Charleston, S. C., December 24th, 1857. He was brought to Savannah while quite young. He embraced Jesus in 1879, and was baptized into the fellowship of the First African Baptist Church July 6th, 1879, by Rev. George Gibbons. Mr. Wright grew up in the Sunday school. He is still a faithful and efficient teacher in the Sunday school. He is honest and fearless. He was an ardent admirer of Rev. E. K. Love. He was made a deacon of the church January, 1886. He was stubbornly opposed by quite a number of the members, but was elected by a handsome majority. Several points were raised upon his character, but these all proved futile. Mr. Wright's patience was greatly tried and his character subjected to the severest scrutiny. All this he bore in an humble, Christ-like manner, which won the commendation of even his enemies. Mr. Love was accused of favoring Mr. Wright and even planning for his election. The charges purported to have come from Mr. A. M. Monroe. Upon investigation they proved to be true and Mr. Monroe was expelled. The objections raised against Mr. Wright were at the instance of Mr. Toby Loyd (a member of the church) who accused Mr. Wright with criminal intimacy with his wife. These were not sustained and Mr. Loyd begged the church's pardon. A man of iron will, indefatigable courage and christian devotion to the church. He has won the confidence of the church and is regarded as one of the most honest, straightforward men in the church. He stood by Mr. Love when other officers, nearly all of them, doubted the wisdom of undertaking the extension of the building. He urged that the work could be done. He gave very liberally of his personal money for the work. He is the youngest officer in the church.*

The officers about whom nothing is said is due to the fact that nothing beyond their names could be learned of them. Indeed, it was no easy job to get the facts in the lives of those who are still alive. This is due to the fact that they came along in the dark days of slavery when their owners kept the records.

REV. JAMES J. SEVORRES

was born in Charleston, S. C., December 18th, 1853. He was converted to Christ in 1869, and baptized into the fellowship of the Tabernacle Baptist Church, Beaufort, S. C., by Rev. Peter White in April, 1869. He was licensed to preach by the Mount Zion Baptist Church in April, 1883. He joined the First African Baptist Church of Savannah by letter from the Mount Zion Baptist Church November, 1884. He was called to ordination by the First African Baptist Church, and was ordained by Revs. E. K. Love, D. D., U. L. Houston, and S. A. McNeal, December 6th, 1885. Rev. Mr. Sevorres is an intelligent young man, quite gentlemanly, honest and upright. He attended the Atlanta Baptist Seminary for a short while, and made very commendable progress in his studies. It was very much regretted by his friends that he could not spend more time there, as he certainly would have made a much more able man. He was for a short while missionary of the Mount Olive Baptist Association, and did earnest work in its service. He loves his Master's work, and slights no opportunity to speak for Jesus. He is a pretty fair preacher for his opportunities. He is well known to the country churches where he so much delights to preach Jesus to the people, and the common people hear him gladly. Mr. Sevorres is an earnest, forcible preacher. As a man he is reliable and upright. As a member of the church he is faithful and humble, and has the entire respect and confidence of the people.

---

*Since the above was written we regret very much to say that Deacon F. J. Wright has proved to be a failure as a deacon. He is vulgar in the extreme and double-tongued. He has been expelled from the church and is now at large in the wild world. He abused the pastor most shamefully and several other of the members. He could not stand the honor and promotion and got entirely beside himself and the patience of the church ceased to be a virtue and he was expelled. We hope that the spirit may force him to repentance. The prophecy of many of the old members that the church would regret electing Mr. Wright a deacon proved to be true to the chagrin of his friends.

MR. W. G. CLARK,

Licentiate W. G. Clark was born in Columbia county, Ga., September 17, 1843, and while quite young was brought to Savannah. He was converted May 8, 1869, and was baptized into the fellowship of the First African Baptist Church June 5, 1869, by Rev. W. J. Campbell. Mr. Clark was one of Rev. Mr. Campbell's strongest supporters in the trouble of 1877, and went with Mr. Campbell to the Beach, remaining with him until he died, when he returned to the church. Mr. Clark is an earnest worker for Christ. He grew up in the Sunday school, and has for years been a faithful teacher in it. His work is not confined to the city, but he delights to go into the country among the poor and forsaken and publish the news of salvation. He visits the hospital and prays for the sick and tells them of Jesus. He was licensed to preach May 15, 1887. He is of great service to the pastor and church in visiting the sick and attending funerals. For his chances he is a good preacher, and give promise of great usefulness in the pulpit. Mr. Clark stands perfectly fair in the community and is much beloved by the church. He is an upright christian gentleman, very polite, forbearing, dignified and kind. He is well acquainted with the scriptures and his sermons abound in apt illustrations. He always preaches on the practical order, never making any attempt at oratory or eloquence. He puts those to thinking who hear him. He is a straightforward, honest man, and no one can say aught against him. He delights to do right and is always willing to do something for his church. As a man Mr. Clark is true; as a friend he is constant. He is a first-class man.

BROTHER JOHN E. GRANT

was elected deacon of the church in January, 1886, but declined. He is a whole-souled man and passionately devoted to the church. He made the motion that the church undertake the purchase of the property in rear of its building. This was grandly successful, to the fullest satisfaction of the church. He did much personally for the accomplishment of this end, and can never be forgotten. He was with Deacon Haynes when he got shot. Mr. Grant did valiant service on the Union side during the late war and was active in help freeing his people. He is highly respected and has the entire confidence of the church and community. Mr. Grant is a man of determined will and indefatigable courage. He is a true and tried citizen. He never fails to fill his seat in the church, except for good reasons. He is a very good man, with faith, zeal and very good judgment.

MR. C. H. EBBS, CLERK,

was born in Savannah, Ga., March 17th, 1854. He was converted to God December 26th, 1865, and was baptized into the fellowship of the First African Baptist Church of Savannah by Rev. W. J. Campbell January 7th, 1866. He was elected clerk of the church January 6th, 1878. Mr. Ebbs is a fine penman and infinitely the best clerk the church ever had. He is faithful, accurate, loving and kind. He is a member of many societies, and is the clerk of nearly every one of them. Mr. Ebbs has served the church for ten successive years. The church could not elect a better clerk. Mr. Ebbs is very friendly and polite. He has a great deal of patience and great meekness. No man in the church is more humble than Mr. Ebbs: in conferences and other deliberative bodies his voice is seldom heard. Mr. Ebbs is a self-made man, and withal is real intelligent. Whatever duty is assigned to his hands, will be done with precision, accuracy and promptness. Mr. Ebbs is very useful to the church.

MRS. M. M. MONROE, ORGANIST,

was born in Savannah, Ga., September 5, 1857. She was converted to Christ December 22, 1871, and was baptized into the fellowship of the First African Baptist Church the first Sunday in August, 1872, by Rev. W. J. Campbell. She was elected organist in 1874. She is a true Baptist, a consistent member of the church, and is faithful and punctual, never being five minutes late. She spares no pains to raise her children in the fear of the Lord. It does not matter how the weather is, Mr. A. M. Monroe, wife and children are generally at the church. No member in the church has better trained children. She plays well and has a host of friends. She attended the Atlanta University for several years.

CHAPTER XVIII.

The Centennial Celebration of the Church—The Sermons, Papers, &c.

AFTER A CENTURY.

One hundred years have passed since the organization of the first negro Baptist church in Georgia, and, so far as history relates, the first in the United States.

In October, 1884, in the city of Milledgeville, Rev. E. K. Love called the attention of the Executive Board of the Missionary Baptist State Convention to the fact that we were nearing our centennial, and offered a set of resolutions looking forward to the celebration of the happy event. (He was then missionary of the State of Georgia, and not pastor of the First African Baptist Church.) This fact, together with the resolutions, were reported to the Missionary Baptist Convention of the State of Georgia in its session at Cartersville, Ga., May, 1885. This was heartily endorsed, and a State Centennial Committee appointed, consisting of Revs. W. J. White, J. C. Bryan, E. K. Love, G. H. Dwelle, C. T. Walker, C. H. Lyons, E. R. Carter, T. M. Robinson, and Deacon J. H. Brown. At this session of the convention the name of Rev. S. A. McNeal was added to the Centennial Committee. These were appointed to raise means and to plan generally for the celebration. Rev. W. J. White was elected chairman; Rev. C. H. Lyons, treasurer, and Deacon J. H. Brown, secretary.

The committee employed Rev. J. C. Bryan as traveling financial agent. A better selection could not have been made. It was also determined to get out a book containing the history of the negro Baptists for the past one hundred years, of which Rev. E. K. Love, D. D., was appointed editor-in-chief; Rev. W. J. White compiler, and Rev. E. R. Carter and Deacon J. H. Brown appointed to gather historical data. This committee was composed of the ablest men of our denomination in Georgia, and notwithstanding they worked most assiduously they failed to get out the book. This was no fault of theirs. The undertaking was quite a great one and attended with much expense. It is still the determined resolution of the committee to get out the book, but this will require hard work, much money, time and patience.

At the session of the convention in Brunswick, May, 1887, the committee was enlarged by the addition of the chairman from each associational centennial committee. This was an increase of about fifty members. The congratulations of the denomination are due to this committee for the able, faithful and arduous labors which brought a pleasing success to our centennial celebration. The interest these brethren manifested in the work was simply wonderful. They have inscribed their names upon the pages of history as legibly as the stars upon the brow of the evening. Their names shall be enrolled upon the sacred scroll of history among those few immortal names which were born never to die. When they shall stand upon the interlacing margin of eternity and hear the shouts of their welcome borne to them by angelic harpers from the other golden shores, they may rejoice in the consoling fact that their brethren upon this terrestrial globe are not less silent in their praise while they sing in human tongue in concert with the angels, "Blessed are the dead which die in the Lord from hence forth; yea, saith the spirit, that they may rest from their labors, and their works do follow them."

At the session of the convention in Brunswick, May, 1887, the following special programme committee was appointed: Brethren A. Harris, W. J. White, E. K. Love, J. M. Simms, J. H. Brown, D. Waters, J. C. Bryan, U. L. Houston, C T. Walker, E. R. Carter, S. A. McNeal. This Committee, led by Rev. Alexander Harris, chairman, did its work in an able manner, and reflects great credit on the denomination. They prepared the following programme:

CENTENNIAL CELEBRATION OF THE NEGRO BAPTISTS OF GEORGIA, TO BE HELD IN SAVANNAH, GA., COMMENCING WEDNESDAY, JUNE 6, AND CLOSING MONDAY, JUNE 18, 1888.

Committee—Rev. Alexander Harris, Chairman, Savannah, Ga.; Rev. U. L. Houston, Savannah, Ga.; Rev. J. M. Simms, Savannah, Ga.; Rev. David Waters, Savannah, Ga.; Rev. E. K. Love, D.D., Savannah, Ga.; Rev. C. T. Walker, Augusta, Ga.; Rev. E. R. Carter, Atlanta, Ga.; Rev. J. C. Bryan, Americus, Ga.; Deacon J. H. Brown, Secretary.

PROGRAMME.

Wednesday, June 6th—9 to 10 A. M.—Praise Service, led by Rev. Henry Way, Hawkinsville, Ga.

I.—10 A. M.—Welcome Address, by Rev. E. K. Love, Savannah, Ga.

African Baptist Church.

II.—11 A. M.—Opening Sermon, by Rev. C. T. Walker, Augusta, Ga.
III.—12 M.—History of the Church, by C. A. Clark, Brunswick, Ga.
IV.—3 P. M.—Baptist Doctrine, Rev. C. H. Lyons, Atlanta. Ga.; Rev. S. A. McNeal, Augusta, Ga., and Rev. J. M. Pendleton, D.D., Pa.
V.—4:30 P. M.—New Testament Policy. Rev. E. M. Brawley, D.D., Greenville. S. C.; Rev. W. E. Holmes, A. M., Atlanta. Ga.; Rev. A. F. Owens, Mobile, Ala.
Night Session, 8 o'clock—VI.—Peculiarities of Baptists that distinguish them from all other people, Rev. W. J. Simmons, D. D., Rev. C. H. Parish, A. B., Louisville, Ky., and Rev. C. S. Wilkins, West Point, Ga.
Thursday, June 7th—9 to 10 A. M.—Praise Service, led by Rev. E. W. Walker, Dawson, Ga.
VII.—10 A. M.—Baptist Church History, by Revs. W. J. White, G. H. Dwelle, Augusta, Ga., and Rev. W. H. Tillman, Atlanta.
VIII.—11:30 A. M.—Reminiscences of the Baptist Fathers and the Church during one hundred years. Revs. Levi Thornton, Greensboro, Ga.; J. M. Simms, Savannah, Ga., and Alexander Harris, Savannah, Ga.
IX.—3 P. M.—The Wants of the Colored Ministry, Rev. W. H. McIntosh, D. D., Macon, Ga.; Rev. Alexander Ellis, Savannah, Ga., and Rev. W. G. Johnson, Augusta, Ga.
X.—4:30 P. M.—The Relation of the White and Colored Baptists in the Past, Now, and as it should be in the Future, Rev. T. J. Hornsby, Augusta; Rev. G. S. Johnson, Thomson, Ga., and Rev. J. B. Hawthorne, D. D., Atlanta, Ga.
Night Session, 8 o'clock—Sermon by Rev. E. R. Carter, Atlanta, Ga.
9 to 10 A. M.—Praise Service, led by Rev. C. A. Johnson, Americus, Ga.
XI.—10 A. M.—The Home Mission Society and its Work for the Colored People, Dr. A. E. Williams, Crawfordville, Ga.; Prof. S. Y. Pope, Waynesboro, Ga.; Rev. G. A. Goodwin, Gainesville, Fla., and Rev. S. Graves, D. D, Atlanta, Ga.
XII.—12:30 P. M.—Woman, Her Work and Influence, Misses S. B. Packard, Atlanta, Ga.; J. P. Moore, New Orleans, La., and Rev. L. Burrows, D. D., Augusta, Ga.
XIII.—3 P. M.—The American Baptist Publication Society and its Work for the Colored People, Rev. E. K. Love, Savannah, Ga.; Rev. N. W. Waterman, Thomasville, Ga.; Rev. G. B.

Mitchell, Forsyth, Ga., and Rev. B. Griffith, D. D., Philadelphia, Pa.

Night Session, 8 *o'clock*—XIV.—Education, Dr. J. H. Bugg, Lynchburg, Va.; Rev J. A. Metts, Hightown, N. J., and Rev. J. A. Battle, D. D , Macon, Ga.

Saturday, June 9th.—9 to 10 A. M.—Praise Service, led by Rev. John Williams, Brunswick, Ga.

XV.—10 A. M.—The Bible as Believed by Baptists, Revs. J. C. Bryan, Americus, Ga.; H. N. Bouey, Columbia, S. C.; G. M. Sprattling, Brunswick, Ga., and P. S. Henson, D. D., Chicago, Ill.

XVI.—12 M.—The Authenticity of the Bible, Rev. David Shaver, D. D., Atlanta, Ga., and Rev. H. H. Tucker, D. D., Atlanta, Ga.

XVII.—3 P. M.—The Dignity of the Ministry and the Necessary Qualification to Fit Them for Their Work, Revs. E. R. Carter, Atlanta, Ga.; C. H. Brightharp, Milledgeville, Ga.; E. V. White, Thomson, Ga., and Dr. J. B. Broadus, Louisville, Ky.

Sunday, June 10th.—Divine Services.

Monday, June 11th.—9 to 10 A. M.—Praise Service, led by Rev. Floyd Hill, Athens, Ga

XVIII.—10 A. M.—The Duty of Baptists to Home Missions, Revs. W. H. McAlpin, Montgomery, Ala ; J. M. Jones, C. O. Jones, Atlanta, Ga., and E. J. Fisher, La Grange, Ga.

XIX.—12 M.—Temperance, Hon. J. W. Lyons, Augusta, Ga., and Rev. S. D. Rosier, Midville, Ga

XX.—3 P. M —The Duty of Baptists to Foreign Missions, Revs. J. E. Jones, W. W. Colley, and J. H. Pressly, Virginia.

XXI.—4.30 P. M.—Baptist Newspapers and their Influence, Revs. S. T. Clanton, D. D., New Orleans, La.; J. T. White, Helena, Ark., and Deacon W. H. Stewart, Esq., Louisville, Ky.

Night Session, 8 o'clock.—XXII.—Scriptural Divorce, Revs. A. S. Jackson, New Orleans, La., and C. O. Booth, Selma, Ala.

Tuesday, June 12th.—9 to 10 A. M.—Praise Service, led by Rev. Henry Morgan, Augusta, Ga.

XXIII —10 A. M.—Are We Advancing as a Denomination? Deacon J. H. Brown, Savannah, Ga.; Prof. M. J. Maddox, Gainesville, Fla.; Prof. M. P. McCrary, Valdosta, Ga., and Rev. T. Nightingale, Memphis. Tenn.

XXIV.—12 M.—The Bible as Suited to the Elevation of Mankind, Revs. J. E. L. Holmes, D. D., Savannah, Ga., and W. W. Landrum, D. D., Richmond, Va.

XXV.—3 P. M.—The Duty of the Pastor to the Church, Revs. J. W. Dungee, Augusta. Ga.; J. G. Phillips, Aiken, S. C., and E. W. Warren, D. D., Macon, Ga.

XXVI.—4.30 P. M.—The Duty of the Church to the Pastor, Prof. Isaiah Blocker, Augusta. Ga., Deacon R. H. Thomas, Savannah, Ga., and Rev. J. L. Underwood, Camilla, Ga.

Night Session, 8 o'clock.—XXVII.—Sermon by Rev. T. M. Robinson, Macon, Ga.

Wednesday, June 13th.—9 to 10 A. M.—Praise Service, led by Louis Williams, Washington, Ga.

XXVIII.—10 A. M.—What is Our Duty to the Baptist Institutions of the Country? Rev. A. Bings, Jr., Col. A. R. Johnson, Prof. H. L. Walker, Prof. T. M. Dent, Augusta, Ga.

XXIX.—12 M.—The Importance of Pure Baptist Literature, Revs. E. P. Johnson, Madison, Ga.; J. G. Ross, Jacksonville, Fla.

XXX.—3 P. M.—The Purity and Work of the Church, Rev. C. G. Holmes, Rome Ga.; Henry Jackson, Augusta, Ga., and J. B. Davis, Atlanta, Ga

XXXI.—4.30 P. M —The Deacons and their Duty, Revs. J. H. DeVotie, D. D., G. R. McCall, D. D., Griffin, Ga.

Night Session, 8 o'clock—XXXII.—Money as a Factor in Christianizing the World, Revs. W. R. Pettiford, Birmingham, Ala.; R. N. Counter, Memphis, Tenn., and Prof. J. G. Mitchell, Malvern, Ark.

Thursday, June 14th—9 to 10 A. M.—Praise Service, led by Rev. U. L Houston.

XXXIII.—10 A. M.—Baptist Church Government, Revs. J. L Dart, Charleston, S C.; H. J. Europe, Mobile, Ala.; H. A. D. Braxton, Baltimore, Md.

XXXIV.—12:30 P. M.—God as Revealed in Nature, Rev. H. H Tucker, D. D., Atlanta, Ga.

XXXV.—3 P. M —Christian Baptism, Rev. J. H. Kilpatrick, D. D , White Plains, Ga.

XXXVI.—4 P. M.—Independence of a Baptist Church, by Rev. W. L. Kilpatrick, D. D , Hepzibah, Ga.

Night Session, 8 o'clock.—Preaching.

Friday, June 15th.—9 to 10 A. M.—Praise Service, led by Rev. C T James, Baconton, Ga.

XXXVII.—10 A. M.—The Duty of Baptists to give the World the Gospel, Rev. W. L. Jones, Atlanta, Ga.; John Marks. New Orleans, La ; E. R. Reid, Valdosta, Ga., and Rev. A. S. Jackson, New Orleans, La.

XXXVIII —12 M —The Final Perseverance of Saints, by Rev. E. Lathrop, D. D., Stamford, Ct.

XXXIX.—3 P. M.—Our Duty as Citizens. Unassigned.
Night Session, 8 o'clock—Preaching.
Saturday, June 16th.—Devoted to Sunday school.
Sunday Morning, June 17th—Devoted to Sunday school.
Afternoon—Sunday, 3 P. M.—Dedication First Bryan Baptist Church.
Monday and Tuesday devoted to miscellaneous subjects.
The persons to whom this is sent, whose names appear on the programme for an address or sermon, will please signify their acceptance by addressing REV. A. HARRIS,
William Street, Savannah, Ga.

All these brethren did not come, and some of those who did come spoke extemporaneously. Those who spoke from manuscript their productions are given in this work. At the session of the Missionary Baptist Convention, May, 1888, just preceding the centennial celebration, Rev. W. S. Ramsey, of Columbus, Ga., stated that since the centennial celebration must be in honor of some church as the oldest, and that since both the First African Baptist Church, Franklin Square, Savannah, Ga., and the First Bryan Baptist Church on Bryan street, in Yamacraw, claim to be the original First African Baptist Church, it seemed befitting to him that a committee of judicious brethren should be appointed before whom the claimants should go in person and with papers. The convention then appointed the following brethren as that committee: Rev. F. M. Simmons, Stone Mountain, Ga.; E. J. Fisher, La Grange, Ga.; Rev. W. S. Ramsey, Columbus, Ga.; Rev N. B. Williamson, Quitman, Ga.; Rev. H. B. Hamilton, Walthourville, Ga., Rev. S. A. McNeal, Augusta, Ga., and Rev. C. H. Brightharp, Milledgeville, Ga.

Rev. James M. Simms, representing the First Bryan Baptist Church, gave notice that the representatives from said church would not appear before the committee. The committee, however, having the book he had just published purporting to be the history of the oldest Negro Baptist Church in North America, which book set forth his claims as cogently as he possibly could have done. Putting this book in evidence the committee proceeded to make the following report, which was unanimously adopted:

REPORT OF SPECIAL COMMITTEE.

We, your committee, to whom were referred the matter of priority of the First Bryan Baptist Church on Bryan street, in Yamacraw, or the First African Baptist Church at Franklin

Square, beg to submit the following report: Having the facts in the case, which we think are conclusive, we earnestly state that the conclusion to which your committee has arrived was caused solely from the facts at their command. We regret to state that one of the parties refused to appear before your committee, notwithstanding being urged upon, namely, Rev. J. M. Simms, for the First Bryan Church in Yamacraw. It does strike us that men feeling that they had a good case would not refuse to be examined. These brethren have openly and defiantly refused in the presence of this convention, to lay their case before you or the committee, declaring that you have nothing to do with it, and they had nothing for you to decide. Your committee proceeded to perform their work. Having seen the book written by Rev. J. M. Simms purporting to be the true history of the oldest colored Baptist church in North America, your committee feels that the book makes their case as strong as they could possibly make it. We find that the church organized at Brampton's Barn, three miles southwest of Savannah, January 20th, 1788, is the same First African Baptist Church to-day. This fact is admitted by the book which Rev. Simms has written. Until 1832 there was no dispute about the first A. B. Church, but in the year 1832 a great trouble occurred which continued for several months. Many councils were called, who advised again and again a course, which, if pursued, would restore peace to the grand old army, then numbering 2,795 members and divided into two parties, the one led by Rev. Andrew Cox Marshall and the other by Deacon Adam Arguile Johnson. Two thousand six hundred and forty following Rev. Marshall and one hundred and fifty-five following Deacon Johnson. It appears to your committee, from the evidence found, that before this trouble the church had contracted to buy the white Baptist church located at Franklin Square, hence, when the trouble occurred, Rev. Mr. Marshall and his 2,640 members went to Franklin Square, still owning the site on Bryan street, in Yamacraw. The white Baptist church of this city took a lively interest in the church, and tried to spare it of all this bitter pain and heartache, an accurate account of which has been carefully preserved in their church records, which has been in the hands of your committee and carefully read, which we now offer in testimony. We read from the minute book of the white Baptist church:

"In the conference of the white Baptist church, Dec. 24, 1832.

"An application was made that the minority of the First African Church be received as a branch of this church, when it was decided that it was proper that they first be formed into a church and afterward could come under the supervision of a committee."

They being refused admittance under the supervision of the white Baptist church, it appears quite clear that the white brethren began to labor with both parties, hence the following petition of the First African Baptist Church, January 4th, 1833. The First African Baptist Church addressed the following letter to the Savannah Baptist Church, white:

"We, the subscribers, of the First African Baptist Church, do solicit the aid and protection of our brethren, the Baptist church of Savannah. We propose to come under the supervision of a committee of your body, provided you will receive us on the terms and conditions following:

"1st. That we be independent in our meetings; that is, that we receive and dismiss our own members, and elect and dismiss our own officers, and finally manage our own concerns, independently; however, with this restriction: In case any measure is taken by us which shall seem to militate against our good standing as a church of Christ, we *shall* submit it to a committee of five members, whom we shall choose out of the Baptist church of Savannah, whose counsel we bind ourselves to follow, provided it be not contrary to the precepts of the gospel.

"2d. We agree to hold no meetings for discipline or other purposes until we have duly notified by writing, one member of the Baptist church, selected by said church, to be present and agreeing not to pursue any measure such delegated member shall deem improper until we shall have had council of the above named committee.

"3d. We agree to relinquish to the minority of this body all our rights and title to the old church so soon as they shall agree to give up and do relinquish to us all right and title to the newly purchased one, and when we are put in full and free possession of it and our trustees, viz.: William H. Stiles, Peter Mitchell and John Williamson, shall satisfy us that they have good and sufficient titles.

"4th. We agree to dismiss all members, and such as have been members of our church, that they may either join another or form a new Baptist church, and as soon as such church shall be satisfied with and receive them, then they shall be dismissed from us."

This being accepted by both parties, the minority of the First African Baptist Church was organized into the Third

African Baptist Church, for in the minutes of the white Baptist church January 28th, 1833, appears the following resolution:

"Resolved, That, inasmuch as the minority of the First African (now the Third) Church have conformed to the requirements of this church in constituting themselves into a church, be received under the supervision of this body upon the same terms as the First African Church."

The 155 was always after the trouble of 1832 called the minority of the First African church until they were organized into a church, when they became the Third African Baptist Church. To this name they offered no objection, nor for thirty years was the slightest protest offered of their being known and called the "Third African Baptist Church." In 1833 they entered the Sunbury Baptist Association as such, and their church was always recorded in their minutes as the Third African Baptist Church. The Sunbury Association expelled the First African Baptist Church in November, 1832, as the First African Baptist Church. Every reference to this church in public or in the minutes of the Savannah Baptist Church book is as First African Baptist Church. The Third church themselves complained against the First African Baptist Church as the *First African Baptist Church*. Rev. Simms, in his book, admits that the 155 above mentioned were organized as the Third church; that is, he admits a reorganization. Your committee has seen a sketch of the First African Baptist Church from its organization in 1788 till toward the close of the administration of Rev. W. J. Campbell about 1877, in Rev. Simms' own handwriting, without any reference to the First Bryan Baptist Church. It appears passing strange to your committee that if the First Bryan Church is the First African Baptist Church that they do not and have not called themselves by that name. The pastor of the First African Baptist Church has shown your committee the deed of the First African Baptist Church to the spot of ground which the First Bryan Baptist Church now occupies. With all of these facts and as many more which have come before your committee as candid, God-fearing men, we feel in honor bound to decide that the First African Baptist Church at Franklin Square is the original First African Baptist Church, organized at Brampton barn January 20th, 1788, by Rev. Abraham Marshall and Rev. Jesse Peter, whose centennial anniversary we have gathered to celebrate. We decide, therefore, that the claim of priority of the First Bryan Baptist Church, which has given itself this name since the emancipation and the claim of the book written by Rev. J. M. Simms, of being the oldest church (colored) in North America is without foundation.

Signed, your committee.   REV. F. M. SIMMONS,
Chairman.

The centennial celebration of the Baptists of Georgia, in honor of the First African Baptist Church, opened most solemnly on Wednesday, June 6th, 1888. The members of the First African Baptist Church met at their spacious church edifice at 9 o'clock in the morning and marched out to the Centennial Tabernacle. Rev. E. K. Love, D. D., and officers marched in front. Deacon March Haynes and Brother John E. Grant alternately bore the banner of the church. The procession was over a mile long. The Church entered the Tabernacle singing, "All hail the power of Jesus' name." When Rev. Alexander Harris, chairman of the programme committee, called the vast multitude to order, he introduced Rev. E. K. Love, D. D., pastor of the First African Baptist Church, who had been selected to deliver the welcome address. Rev. Dr. Love delivered the following appropriate welcome address, which was well received:

Dear Brethren: It falls to my happy lot to bid you welcome to Savannah, to our homes and to our churches on this auspicious occasion—the centennial anniversary of our church. From our church the Negro Baptists of Georgia commenced. After battling with sin and Satan for 100 years, scattered all over Georgia, we have returned as one family again around a common family altar to recount the labors of an hundred years, to rejoice over the victories achieved and lament our failures. As one army of the Lord we welcome you. The Baptist star which arose in the eastern part of this State an hundred years ago has been often covered by intense darkness, but which has been as often kissed away by the sun of righteousness assuring us that all was not lost, but that "behind a frowning Providence he hides a smiling face."

We invite you here as fellow-citizens of the household of faith. Our faith is your faith, we love the God you love, we were redeemed by the Saviour who died for you, we are journeying to the same celestial city to which you are going, we are traveling home to God with you in the way our fathers trod, and our home and glorious inheritance is the same.

It is very befitting, therefore, that we should welcome you. Our church was planted in blood. Rev. Andrew Bryan, its founder and first pastor, was whipped until his flesh was terribly torn. His blood ran freely and puddled by his lacerated body on the ground for no other crime than that he preached Jesus to Africa's sable sons and daughters enslaved in this country.

When he was commanded not to preach the gospel he raised his dusky hand, stained in his own blood drawn by his vile persecutors, and said with a trembling voice, with that manly heroism and christian courage that the grace of God alone can fan into burning eloquence, "If you would stop me from preaching, cut off my head." This humble statement from our father in Israel amazed and ashamed his ungodly persecutors. This humble slave, using the weapon of warfare which is not carnal, but mighty through God, conquered these human brutes and through Christ won a signal victory for the church. Our fathers planted the banner of the Lord here in sweat, tears and blood, around which their children have rallied for one hundred years.

Our troubles have been great, our trials many, but we have not yielded an inch of ground to the enemy. We have not compromised any part of the grand old principles that distinguish us as Baptists, and though missiles most terrible from the enemy's camp have been and are being hurled at us, we have not nor will we ever quit the field.

Our fathers suffered nor do we expect to shun the hallowed road which they have gone. The Baptists of Savannah, an hundred years ago numbered only four souls, now they number something over ten thousand.

We all make you welcome to our city. We make you welcome because you come to rejoice with us. We make you welcome because you come to speak words of peace and comfort to us, and we bid you a hearty welcome because you are our brethren. In retrospecting the ground over which we have come during the last century, we felt it becoming to invite you to rejoice with us for the train of mercies which has followed us *for one hundred years.*

THE FIRST HUNDRED YEARS OF OUR EXISTENCE.

The nineteenth century has been a most wonderful century. It begun upon an enslaved people, without liberty, without churches and without a knowledge of Christ. In this awful century our church was organized. The nineteenth century is characterized by wonderful inventions. Locomotives, telegraphs, telephones and many other inventions came into use in this century. In this busy and exciting century the Baptists of Georgia were born.

This century has witnessed a most remarkable change in this country. The slaves have been all set free and public opinion has been entirely revolutionized. Those who were once slaves now worship God under their own vine and fig tree, and no one dares molest or make us afraid. So wonderfully has God blessed us through these weary years, that we have felt it a great privilege as well as a pleasing duty to invite you here to celebrate our centennial anniversary. We could do naught else but welcome you. From the depth of our souls we welcome you. We want that you should feel at home for you are at home with your brethren around the old family hearth-stone.

From this time-hallowed shrine you begun. You have been spread over Georgia for an hundred years fighting for the right with heavenly weapons. You have not gone alone. A covenant-keeping God has gone with you and has prospered you in the land whither you have journeyed, and has added very largely to your number many happy recruits. After you have been gone for an hundred years, most of which time you have spent in the most cursed and disgraceful system of slavery that has ever spread sorrow, gloom, heartaches and wounds over a civilized country, you have returned to the old parental home to rejoice with the mother. The mother at times has had it hard; she has had untold sorrows and innumerable difficulties. Your countenance give signs of careworn and inexplicable anxiety and suffering which tell me that you have encountered Appolyon on your respective fields of labor in the vineyard of the Lord, but beneath it all I see blooming up in your countenances evidences of that joy and peace which only the grace of God can give.

From four, the Baptist family of Georgia has increased to 166,429. This is an average of 1664 29-100 a year. While we rejoice over these that the Lord has given us in the land wherein we sojourned as strangers we would humbly cry unworthy and ascribe our conquest to the Lamb, our victory to His blood and our life to His death. From one church, 1,500 have sprung up, an average of 15 a year. The joy belongs to us all. All the glory belongs to God.

We welcome you from our hearts. We feel that we have great need to rejoice that God has so wonderfully blessed us in letting our old fathers remain with us so long to give us their wise counsel. We should be thankful that the school doors have been thrown open and so many of our young men have been favored with educational advantages and are so much better prepared to preach the gospel than our fathers were. We invite you here after the close of an hundred years to rejoice over the advancement our people have made in the sciences, literary pursuits, in theology and in morality. The Baptists have been great gainers in all these virtues and attainments.

More than two-thirds of the educated young preachers in Georgia are Baptists. In welcoming you, we rejoice that among you are some of the best scholars in our race. We welcome you as able expounders of the sacred scriptures and eloquent preachers of the New Testament. We are glad to welcome many of you as professors of colleges and accurate teachers and newspaper editors. In welcoming you, we are glad to note that many of you are comfortably situated in your own homes and are moderately rich, and are raising dignified, interesting and happy families.

We are glad that while other denominations have made progress that the Baptists have not stood still. This denomination is more largely responsible to give the world the whole truth as it is in Jesus than any other. To the Baptist denomination the great commission was given to preach the gospel to every creature. No denomination can stand so flat footed upon the Bible as the Baptists. No denomination meets as few passages in the Bible which war with its practice as the Baptist denomination. As Baptists we have nothing to fear. We are gaining ground. We are proud to welcome you as Baptists.

Our ministry of to-day is of such that we can look upon with pleasing pride, both as men of letters, good morals, temperate, full of zeal and piety. We have not retrograded. Our young men have become learned and our old men have made very commendable progress.

Dear Brethren, let us pray and humbly trust that our meeting at the close of this century may so inspire, bless and lift up our people that we may be living afresh for the next hundred years. If we are not here in person, it may be our happy lot to be angel visitors to the next centennial celebration of the Negro Baptist of Georgia. Then, the Lord grant that it may be a thousand times more glorious than this one, and may the fruits be infinitely more plenteous, the victories be far more signal and God more glorified in his servants.

May heaven more gently and lovingly smile over our great denomination and its wonderful accomplishments at the next centennial celebration. God grant that there may be fewer if any destitute places in Georgia at that time. Then when our work on earth is done, God grant that we shall be gathered in peace to the saint's rest with our fathers, where congregations shall never break up and Sabbath never end. And with the redeemed and sanctified and the countless number of happy harpers, we shall have a never ending eternity in our Father's house,

> "The far away home of the soul,
> Where no storms ever beat on the glittering strand,
> While the years of eternity roll"

to ascribe ceaseless praise to the triune, God through Christ the Captain of our Salvation.

We welcome you here, but on your entrance into that glorious inheritance, uncorruptible and undefiled, you shall receive a more glorious welcome by the celestial choir which will voice in jarring hosannas the sentiments of heaven, and added to this will be the benignant smiles of God the Father and the plaudit of Christ the Son, "Well done, good and faithful servant, enter into the joys of thy Lord." Then will your welcome, borne to you upon the melodious songs of seraphs, be more pleasing, charming, inspiring and infinitely more lovely and rapturous. While we watch, wait, work, pray and hope for this, let me bid you thrice welcome to all of the joys and comfort in our power to give you now. In Jesus' name we make you welcome ye servants of the Lord.

Rev. C. T. Walker was next introduced to preach the introductory sermon.

The Rev. Mr. Walker opened the service by singing a hymn which he had prepared for the occasion. This hymn was sung by the vast multitude in such a way that the scene beggars description. The bosom of the air never bore off sweeter strains and the golden rays of the sun never kissed more pleasing faces. The following is the hymn:

CENTENNIAL HYMN.

BY C. T. WALKER.

Oh God, who hast Thy people led
  For these one hundred years,
A gospel table thou hast spread
  Amidst our flowing tears.

We've come through deserts dark and drear,
Through sorrows and through fears,
Of mercies past we've come to talk
And still renew our walk.

Our church was planted in this State
  A hundred years ago,
And at Thy feet we've learned to wait
  Until we've seen her grow.

Our fathers trusted in Thy name
  And built upon Thy truth,
Grant us Thy aid to do the same.
  And teach it to our youth.

Thy kingdom, Lord, is spreading wide
From mountain to the sea,
Still let us in Thy truth abide
Till all the world be free.

Oh God, we thank Thee for this day
That celebrates our birth,
May it inspire us on our way
Until we leave the earth.

Oh Thou, who hast Thy people led
Through these one hundred years,
Inspire our souls, dispel our fears,
Feed us on heavenly bread.

Rev. C. T. Walker then preached the following sermon:

Numbers xxiii, 23: "According to this time it shall be said, 'What hath God wrought?'" We stand to-day upon an eminence from which we may take a retrospective view of one hundred years' journey of our grand old denomination in Georgia. A glorious day. We have come to celebrate the progress and triumphs of a century. The cause we represent is a blessed one. We are here to speak of the vicissitudes through which we have passed, the conflicts we have encountered, the obstacles we have surmounted, the success attained, and the victories already achieved. We are here to pass up and down the line of march from 1788 to 1888.

Old fathers, worn and weary with the burden and care of a long and useful life, their heads whitened by the frost of many winters, infirm and superannuated, they have come up to shake hands with the century, to bid God-speed to their brethren, and, as Simeon of old, to exclaim: "Behold now, Lord, I have seen Thy salvation, now let thy servant depart in peace!" Young men have come to get inspiration from a review of the work of the fathers and to return to their various fields of labor stimulated, electrified and encouraged to make the second century far more eventful in the propagation of the gospel and subjugation of the world to Christ than the first.

The colored Baptist family of Georgia, representing 166,429 communicants have met in the Forest City of Georgia, at the close of one hundred years, to give thanks to God for what he hath wrought. The great leaders of the Israelites, Moses and Joshua, were very solicitous to implant in the minds of the people a perpetual remembrance of God's kindness. They, therefore, marked the stations and stages in their progress with monumental circumstances and objects. They erected monuments, built altars and anointed pillars to be memorials of some remarkable transaction. It is our duty to use every possible means of turning the past into lessons of solemn admonitions. A reflective, conscientious, serious spirit will exhibit the intense illuminations of divine truth that kept the old ship together all these years; we will have illustrations of divine guidance, and receive strong manifestations and enforcements of future duties and increased responsibilities incident thereto.

I. We shall discuss what God hath wrought in the permanent establishment of this church. The illustrious kingdoms of the world were founded by the world's renowned men. The Babylonian empire, the Grecian, the Medo-Persian and Roman empires owed their foundations to their kings and emperors. There is a prophetic description in Daniel of a stone being cut out of the mountains without hands—that is, without human agency, and that that stone smote the feet of the image, shattered it into fragments, and the stone became a great mountain, filling the whole earth. This stone rolled forth from Mount Zion and raised a dust which darkened the very heavens. It has rolled and demolished its most powerful antagonist,.and has become a great mountain that shall fill the whole earth forever. The founder of the true church is Christ. He is the Son of Abraham, according to the flesh, and He is also the true God and eternal life. Two natures and three offices mysteriously meet in His person. He is the blessed, bleeding sacrifice, the sanctifying altar, the officiating priest, the prophet of Israel, the prince of peace and the author of eternal life. He is the foundation of His church, the chief corner-stone, the law-giver in Zion. He hath given us a kingdom that cannot be moved. He is the king of Zion who liveth forever. He himself is the father of eternity. He began in Asia to ride in the gospel chariot, sent out twelve small boats, and on the day of Pentecost added 3,000 to the number, and in 1630 sent Roger Williams over to America. He, in the spirit of his master, planted churches in New England, and the stone continued to roll until it reached the sunny South. There the oppressed, rejected and enslaved brother in black, in A. D. 1788, for the first time in Georgia, lifted the Baptist flag under the leadership of Andrew Bryan; here the handful of corn was sown, not on the high, wild, rocky, uncultivated mountain, but on the seaboard, and the wind carried the seed to every part of Georgia, and the barren rocks and sandy deserts became as Jordans of the Lord. From the handful of corn have sprung more than 1500 churches, 500 ordained preachers, and 166,429 communicants. The little one has become a thousand to-day. She is the mother of thousands of children born in a century. While Satan has tried to destroy the true church of God because he sees in her the artillery of heaven playing upon his fortresses of idolatry, skepticism, atheism and infidelity, the captain of our salvation, in the formation of His church, laid the foundation deep and well. Having routed the powers of darkness, on Calvary captured the captain of the opposing host, he mounted the white horse of the gospel and will ride from conquer to conquer until he has put the last enemy under his feet: too wise to err, too powerful to be overcome. The cause he has espoused must triumph. Let the Baptist family of Georgia, on this auspicious day, break forth in the soul-inspiring song: "Arise, shine, for the light is come, and the glory of the Lord is risen upon thee. Gentiles shall come to her light and kings to the brightness of her rising. Her sons shall come from far, and her daughters shall be nursed at her side. The glory of the Lord shall be displayed and all flesh shall see it together." The progress of the Baptists in this country is due to the earnest, faithful and simple preaching of Christ crucified by the fathers. They did not preach philosophy, nor did they strive to reach the people with rhetorical strains of eloquence, but by preaching the truth. The gospel declared in its simplicity and truthfulness will make Baptists.

There is about one and a quarter million colored Baptists in the United States. In the "Story of Baptist Missions in Foreign Lands," by Rev. G. M. Hervey, and in "Jamaica, Past and Present," by Rev. W. M. Brown, M. D., all give an account of a noble colored preacher, by the name of George Leile, who was brought from Virginia to Savannah, Ga., where he remained until the close of the Revolutionary war. His master was a British officer, and when the British evacuated Savannah his master fled to a more congenial clime and took with him his servant George to the West Indies. They settled in Jamaica and George Leile began to preach in Kingston and vicinity, and founded the first African Baptist church ever established in the West Indies with five Afro-Americans, George Leile himself being one. No Protestant mission, except that of Monrovians, which had been formed in 1754 in Jamaica, but had made slow progress. Leile baptized 400 converts in eight years, and in ten years there were 500 members. It has been claimed that the first Baptist church in the West Indies was established by the first missionary of the Baptist Missionary Society of London; but George Leile was preaching in the West Indies, assisted by Moses Baker, George Gibbs and others, as far back as 1793, and when the missionary of the Society of London reached the island in 1814 there were not less than 3,000 Baptists on the Island. Bryant Edwards, the historian, gave him a contribution amounting to £900, which was spent in erecting a chapel. He was thrown into prison for preaching, loaded with irons and tried for his life. We find the following in "Jamaica, Past and Present:"

"Owing to the fearful state of Jamaica at that time they baptized and administered the Lord's Supper at night in unfrequented places, sought the swamps and grounds covered with trees and bushes to evade arrest; but they were found, and called to undue punishment, the bitter effects of the same spirit that kindled the fires of Smithfield and originated the cruelties of the inquisition. Jamaica has furnished as noble a band of martyrs to the truth as any part of the world of similar extent and within the same period of time since the sixteenth century."

These were *colored* martyrs, and among the first of the moral heroes of the pioneers was George Leile, a negro Baptist preacher from Georgia. George Leile lived until 1822, and went to his grave full of years and good works, like a shock of corn fully ripe in its season. Historians, blinded by prejudice, have tried to rob the brother in black of the honor conferred upon Leile. The honor can not belong to the Missionary Society of London, for it did not exist until 1792, and the Baptist membership in Kingston then was over 400. It can not be given unto the American Baptist Missionary Union, for it began in 1814. It can not be given to the Foreign Mission Board of the Southern Baptist Convention, for that began in 1845. It can not be given to the African Baptist Missionary Society, of Richmond, Va., for it began in 1815. But the planting of the first Baptist church in the West Indies, so far as human agency is concerned, was inaugurated by George Leile, the black apostle of Georgia, who planted the standard of christianity in the far-off West Indies, and despite opposition, oppression and persecution, he saw the church strengthened, prosperous and flourishing. So Georgia numbers thousands of sons and daughters in the West Indies who are bound to us by the triple declaration of one Lord, one faith and one baptism. Well might the church sing to-day, "Gird thy sword upon thy thigh, oh thou most mighty, and in thy majesty ride prosperously because of righteousness, truth and meekness." Our fathers had in mind the fact, as is beautifully expressed by the poet:

"A sacred burden is this life ye bear;
Look on it, lift it, bear it solemnly;
Stand up and walk beneath it steadfastly.
Fail not, for sorrow falters not for sin,
But onward, upward, till the good we win."

II. God hath wrought wonderfully in the foreign fields. God put the magnificent and stupendous enterprise of modern missions in the heart of William Cary a hundred years ago. Dr. Somerville says:

"In the case of William Cary we have the example of what a single laborer in Christ's field may effect. Poor in worldly circumstances, without academic culture, with nothing to prompt or guide him but the inspired word of God, without sympathy from churches, in the face of doubt, incredulity and disheartening apathy on the part of christian ministers and people, but with a courage that never blanched, a resolution that nothing could withstand, a faith that never faltered, and with a humility that made him the lowliest and loveliest of men, he set his face towards British India, which then, and long after, scowled all missionary enterprise. Thirty-four translations of the Holy Scripture fell from his pen, twenty-seven mission stations and hundreds of schools were established. He aroused the entire christian world to its duty to the heathen, and he has given an impulse to mission work that will never die. The Bible is being issued by the million in more than 340 languages. The ordained missionaries in the fields of heathenism and Mohammedanism exceed 3,100. More than 2,300 women have consecrated their lives to the work with woman's tenderness and affection, with woman's unswerving fidelity, and with woman's measureless love. So that the number of missionaries, British, American and Continental, exceed 5,000 with the 30,000 native helpers. All in a century. The Baptists of Georgia are helping by contributions to give the gospel to the heathen, and especially has the grand old First Baptist Church of Savannah acted nobly her part in disseminating the gospel. Behold what God hath wrought in this century. Nations will still fall down before him and empire upon empire will be conquered, and christianity will spread from clime to clime, and from pole to pole, until the knowledge of the Lord shall cover the earth as the waters doth the mighty deep, when there shall be one people and one God. The trump of jubilee shall sound and countless numbers of the redeemed shall sing aloud, Hallelujah, God omnipotent reigneth. This gospel, which is God's lever, whose fulcrum is the Rock of Ages, will lift up our degraded, sin-cursed earth and produce God's glory over the creation.

2.—WHAT HATH GOD WROUGHT PROVIDENTIALLY?

The history of my people.—This century was one of hardship, oppression, persecution and sore trial. We were slaves, enslaved bodies and enslaved minds. No moral training. no intellectual advantage. It was a crime to read a book, patrolled, Spanish-bucked, run by blood-hounds, whipped to death, put on the auction block, sold from parents like cattle, husbands and wives separated, must get a ticket to go to church, get permission to join the church, and in many instances not allowed to use your own choice about what church you should join.

Slavery was wrong. God was against it, and He who presides over the destinies of nations in His own good time removed the foul blot from the national escutcheon. Some attribute their freedom to Abraham Lincoln and the Union armies, but we received our liberty, like Israel of old, from the great God of heaven and earth. God's operations may be slow in the incipiency, but the triumph is sure and not distant.

After four years of the saddest, severest civil war, slavery fell, like Dagon before the Ark, and we were free. Emancipated without a dollar, without experience, without education, without friends and without competent leaders. Like Ishmael and Hagar turned out to die, driven into the wilderness. When Prussia emancipated her slaves they were given a start in life, and when the Queen Regent of Spain emancipated the Cuban slaves they were given something as a reward of their past faithfulness. We were turned loose, unaided as we were, were vested with the right of citizenship at a time when we were unprepared for it; but despite all obstacles the negro in Georgia has ten millions dollars' worth of property and has proven himself worthy of citizenship. Take our intellectual advancement. There are in the public schools of Georgia thousands of children, and two-thirds of them are Baptists. We have a number of high schools owned and controlled by our associations, besides the Atlanta Baptist Seminary and Spellman Baptist Seminary under the auspices of the American Baptist Home Mission Society. Our men will be found in the legal fraternity, the medical professions, professors in our colleges, in the legislative hall, or the list of authors, skilled musicians, polished scholars, journalists and theologians.

The Baptists of Georgia are placed under lasting obligations to the American Baptist Home Mission Society for their support and to the Baptist Publication Society for Baptist literature. The name and memory of the venerable Dr. Joseph T. Robert should be cherished by every Baptist in Georgia for the work he accomplished in preparing the leaders for the next century. God hath wrought wonderfully among us. God is still opening up a way for the spread and propagation of the gospel. The way has been opened for a great outpouring of the spirit on the Congo valley. We have come to a period of culmination. The cry is loud and long for consecrated workers. The harvest is truly great and the laborers are few. Take a retrospective view of the work accomplished in one hundred years under such adverse circumstances. This meeting should inspire every disciple to go to his field of labor with renewed energy and courage to extend this kingdom, disseminate the gospel until every knee shall bow and every tongue shall confess that Jesus is the Christ, to the glory of God the Father. I have three propositions to make:

1. Systematic work and giving.
2. Prayerfulness for the success of the work.
3. Earnestness in the proclamation of the truth.

1st. Systematic work and giving.—We are living in an age of mental activity; an age of invention and wonderful development; a busy, progressive age: a wonderful century. No century of the past has been so remarkable with results as the nineteenth. The church is the advance guard of civilization and must disseminate the word of life which is like a purifying bath and the gently distilling rain. The church has sufficient material resources but they are locked up, and system and order are necessary.

Christ in order to feed the hungry multitude with five barley loaves and two small fishes required order and system. He commanded them to be seated in groups or companies, and when there had been an orderly and systematic division of the multitude He said to His disciples. "Give ye them to eat." We are in the midst of a hungry multitude. The marvellous resources of the church are locked up within the domains of the church. The command of the Saviour is ringing out loud and clear, all along the line, "Give ye them to eat." The dark continent of Africa, with 192,000,000 of people, and only 2,000,000 have ever heard of Jesus. Stanley has traced the Congo from its source in Eastern Africa to the Atlantic, a distance of 2.800 miles, with 1,000,000 square miles of territory and a population of millions. What is this but a great door-way for christianity? Let the progress and success of the past give us fresh inspiration for the future. Let Christ's love for us, and our love for Him in return, and by our obedience to his commands, devotion to His cause, advance His kingdom by devising systematic plans to feed the hungry multitude and make ready a people for the coming of the Master. Hasten, Lord, the glorious time.

2d. Prayerfulness for the success of the work.—While the Council of Nuremburg was signing the edict that gave the Protestants their freedom, Martin Luther was away off in a room by himself praying for its accomplishment. Though there was no line of communication between the place where the council was assembled and the room where Luther was praying, yet Martin Luther suddenly arose from prayer and said: "It is accomplished. The Protestants are free. Victory! victory!" He received what he asked for. Like Daniel, we are to pray with our face towards Jerusalem. Like Stephen, looking up into heaven. Like the Publican, with our hands on our heart. I heard Mr. Andy Comstock, of New York, say last fall while speaking before the New York Baptist Ministers' Conference, that the night the Comstock bill was passed by Congress he was in his room at the hotel praying for its passage the very hour it passed, and though he was not informed of its passage until the next morning, he was conscious something would be done. Our own blessed Saviour, who entered fully into humanity, entered into our sorrows, our woes and agonies, prayed earnestly, tenderly, affectionately, and yet argumentatively, for the preservation of his people, for their unity and sanctification. Cold mountain and the midnight air witnessed the fervor of His prayer. If it became Him who was holy, harmless, undefiled and separate from sinners to spend whole nights in the mountain praying, how much more important is it that His followers spend much time in earnest prayer to God for divine guidance in discharging the weighty and responsible duties devolving upon them as representatives of their Master whose glory they must exhibit, and who must overcome the world by the blood of the Lamb through the word of God, and by the word of their testimony. Mr. Spurgeon says prayer is the rustling of the wings of angels that are on their way bringing us the boons of heaven. Even as the cloud foreshadoweth rain, so prayer foreshadoweth the blessing, even as the green blade is the beginning of the harvest, so is prayer the prophecy of the blessing that is about to come. So pray, brethren, pray.

3d. *We need earnestness and simplicity in proclaiming the word.*—Daniel Webster said he did not go to church to hear studied oratory but to hear the gospel. Our fathers were men of one book; they received power by prayerfulness, and proclaimed earnestly and plainly what they understood. Like Paul they said: "Though I preach the gospel I have nothing to glory of, necessity is laid upon me, yea woe is unto me if I preach not the gospel." The gospel is an intervention of Jesus Christ to save lost men and must be given to every creature. It is heaven's appointed remedy for man's malady, and the directions for taking the medicine must be so plain that the fool may take it assured of the fact that he will be healed. The gospel is a ship loaded with bread of life, and must be brought so near the landing that the hungry can reach forth and take the bread of life. The gospel is the announcement of reconciliation between God and the sinner, a message of mercy, the history of the advent of Christ, His life, miracles, death, burial, resurrection, ascension and intercession. The gospel is the Messiah's conquering, triumphal car. There is power and magnetism about. It is to be preached in its purity and its truthfulness. It is the gospel of which Christ and heaven are interested.

> "In heaven the rapturous song began,
>   And sweet seraphic fires
> Through all the shining legions ran,
>   And strung and tuned the harp.
> Swift through the vast expanse it flew,
>   And loud the echo rolled,
> The theme, the song, the joy was new,
>   'Twas more than heaven could hold.
> Down through the portals of the sky
>   The impetuous torrent ran,
> And angels flew with eager joy
>   To bear the news to man."

Man has been honored in being chosen of God to carry this holy message. Beginning a new century in the history of our denomination, let us carry this message with the same earnestness as did our fathers. Discourage inactivity, coldness, indifference, formalism, and this kind of spasmodic religion. . Contend earnestly for the faith once delivered to the saints. Contend for those principles that have been the very life of the Baptists. This gospel must go, like the sun shining in his strength, scattering all clouds from the face of the world until the moon and stars shall be lost in its effulgence. It must fly until, in the language of Christmas Evans, living waters flow through the channels of mercy in summer and winter, not frozen by the cold nor evaporated by the heat. It must go until the cause of Christ shall be preëminent in the estimation of mankind. It must fly until the instrument of war be turned into scythes and ploughshares, and nations learn war was no more. It must go until the ferocious wolf dwells with the innocent lamb, the furious leopard lay down with the kid, the cow and the bear feed in the same pasture, and the little child leads the lion by the mane. Onward, christian soldiers, on, on to victory. The struggles of a hundred years have ended in a victorious triumph. Hannibal and Hamilcar lead the armies of the Carthaginians; Victor Emmanuel led the armies of the Italians; Tamerlane led the armies of Asia; Gustavus Adolphus, Xerxes, Alexander and Washington led battalion after battalion. It is estimated that in all the wars from scriptural times more than thirty-five billions of men have fallen in battle. Soldiers and commanders have received honors from the world. Sky-towering monuments have been erected to their memory. But the men who have been engaged in a holy war, leading a crusade of virtue against vice, an army of righteousness against sin, the harbinger of peace, the bearer of good tidings, the watchman on Zion's holy mount, they were instruments in saving instead of destroying life. And yet their graves are unmarked, no tombstone marks the place where many of them rest. But "God, my Redeemer, lives, and often from the skies looks down and watches all their dust till He shall bid it rise."

Georgia owes it as a sign of recognition and appreciation of their services to erect a monument in this city to the memory of the Baptist leaders who fell during these one hundred years. Our captain is now riding on his white horse giving orders to the armies to move forward. He said to Andrew Bryan one hundred years ago, "Go forward." He speaks to all of you brethren as you move off in the second century. Go forward, let the universal moving of the footsteps of the army of Zion be heard in the camp of the enemy. In the language of Daniel Webster at the laying of the corner-stone of Bunker Hill monument: "Let it rise. Let it rise. Let it rise till it meets the sun in his coming. Let the early light of the morning gild it, and parting day linger and play upon the summit." So let the gospel star-spangled banner rise. Let it rise. Let it rise until its magnetic influence shall draw all men to Christ. Let it soar till the attention of the African shall be called from his devil-bush, the Arab from his tent and the Jew from his wandering. Let it rise until the shouts of our triumphs be borne aloft to the ear of the redeemed as they shout from their high citadel of triumph. We want angelic messengers who come as the representatives of heaven to this centennial celebration to report to the heavenly hosts we are moving forward; to tell Andrew Bryan, Marshall, Campbell, Kernel, Glen, McCrady, Golphin, Jacob Walker, Kelly, Lowe, Peter Johnson, Henry Johnson, John Cox, Joseph Walker, Rucker, Quarles, Frank Beale, George Gibbons, Henry Watts, Arrington, Allen Clark, John A. James, Arthur Johnson, Alfred Young, I. C. Houston, F. D. Williams, J. M. Jones, Henry Williams that we are holding the fort, and that they are still joined to us by all the glorious recollections of the past and the still more glorious anticipation of the future, and ere long we will take our places by their side, and we shall review the grand procession of the Baptists from the chancels of glory. at the close of another century, as our departed heroes reviews us to-day. Let the gospel banner rise. Let it rise! Let it rise!

A CENTENARIAN AT THE CELEBRATION—117 YEARS OLD.

Mrs. Mary Jackson, who was baptized by Rev. Andrew Bryan nearly an hundred years ago, was presented to the centennial celebration by Rev. E. K. Love, D. D., as a living witness of the organization of the First African Baptist Church. When she was asked did she know anything about when the First African Baptist Church started, she replied, "Yes; I was there the very Sunday evening it first started." "Well, mother, who baptized you?" asked Rev. Alexander Harris. "Daddy Bryan," was the prompt reply. "Where did he baptize you?" "In the river. If you will carry me there I will show you the place." "Who baptized old Daddy Bryan?" "A young man who was his friend, but things are so tangled up now I can't get 'em straight"—meaning that she could not remember his name. Mr. George Liele is the young man referred to, who was then about 37 years old. This is not at all strange, when it is remembered that he was not located permanently in Savannah. He was at work down the river, and very soon left for Kingston, Jamaica, in the West Indies. This old lady, has a vivid recollection of the organization of the church, being 17 years old at the time. She is well preserved for one of her age. She can remember and tell of every pastor the church has ever had. She was born on Bull Island, in South Carolina, in 1771, and belonged to Mr. John McQueen. Some of the old members were called, that it might be learned if they knew anything about her. They testified that they knew her over forty years ago, and thought she was dead forty years ago, as she then looked old enough to them to have been dead from old age. Many things tended to corroborate the old lady's statement. When she was asked where did Father Bryan live, she replied: "Right on the way as you go to the baptizing ground." She could tell of many old people who lived in that day. She could tell of Father Bryan's wife and his brother Sampson.

There are several persons still living who remember the old man. Among them are Mother Bryan and Mother Delia Telfair. The latter was 15 years old when Father Bryan died. Rev. Andrew Neyle was eight years old when the old man died, and remembers him quite distinctly.

But to Mrs. Mary Jackson, the subject of this sketch. She is living about fourteen miles from the city, a member of the First African Baptist Church, but she is unknown to the majority of the members. Even the old members thought she was dead over forty years ago. This, perhaps, is due to the fact that she lives in the country. It is possible that in a church of

5,000 members that many would not be known. So far as can be known she has lived a consistent, Christian life for 100 years. Having never been disciplined by the church she, however, would never have become distinguished but for her age. Her life has been of the humble, retired order. Having been a slave, she cannot be noted for great intellect, her greatest blessing being that God has spared her life for 117 years.

No wonderful event in her long life leads us to suppose any reason for its preservation. The only reason that can be given is it pleased God to do so. Her faith is strong in the Saviour. He has kept her for some reason best known to Himself. It was a source of great joy to the church to have a living witness of its organization and an eye-witness to its eventful career for one hundred years. She spoke of Rev. Father Marshall as "Young Marshall, who took old Dady Bryan's place when he died." She knew nothing of dates, when certain events transpired, but had a clear knowledge of certain things which prove conclusively that she is a centenarian. She remembers the trouble of 1832, and when "Young Marshall," as she calls him, carried the church from Yamacraw.

In connection with this living relic, Mr. Love showed the congregation the chair in which Rev. Bryan used to sit while presiding over his church conferences, the dish out of which he used to eat, and the table at which he ate, and a large oil painting of the venerable hero.

The occasion can never be described. The centennial celebration of our church can never be forgotten. The sermons, addresses and papers from the different brethren tended to incalculably indoctrinate and strengthen us in the faith. It was a feast of good things; it was a theological school to our preachers. There were five States represented—Florida, Tennessee, Pennsylvania, Alabama and South Carolina. There were services three times daily—morning, afternoon and night. Each of these services were pretty largely attended, the members of the First African Baptist Church forming the largest quota from the churches of the city. People for ages to come will point back to the great Baptist centennial. Children will date their birth from the centennial; lovers will date their acquaintance from the centennial; old men will date their marriage from the centennial year, and other great events will be spoken of as having occurred in the great centennial year.

So as a snow-ball the great Baptist Centennial will continue to increase in interest and magnitude as the years roll by, and what to us may seem but a trifling affair will be wonderful in the next centennial celebration. Again, this centennial celebration laid the foundation for the next one. Those who will be living at the next centennial will have what we have written of our church and the fathers, and it will then be dim with age, and will be all the more precious because of the age and having been transmitted to them from the fathers. Orators will then move their vast audience as they speak of us as the fathers. The youngest of us will then be called fathers. If any one who could remember this centennial should be there he or she would claim the profoundest consideration and receive the attention of an angel visitor. Indeed, we have done more than we are apt to think of at first. But as the ages pass by more learned men will write of it, and could we be here to the next centennial celebration we would be surprised to know how this centennial celebration had increased in every way. We would feel then that we had only been looking through a glass darkly.

In closing this part of our work upon the centennial celebration, the writer feels that he has not been able to remove the curtain just enough for those of us of to-day to get a peep into the future to even divine what the greatness of this celebration will be in coming ages. But having used the light that is given us, we shall feel content. It is not duty to do what one can not do—and since we can do no more, then we have done, our duty is performed. We feel that it was our duty to do what we could to guide those who are coming after us.

BAPTIST DOCTRINE.

BY REV. S. A. M'NEAL, OF AUGUSTA, GA.

To the President and Members of the Centennial Committee of the Negro Baptists of Georgia, and of this Grand Mother Church of Negro Baptists:

We are assembled here to celebrate the centennial anniversary of the negro Baptists of Georgia. All grand institutions that have ever accomplished great and grand results have had to pass through many fiery ordeals and encounter many conflicts upon life's tempestuous sea, which have put to the severest test their strength and durability. If their make-up had not been genuine, they would have gone to wreck. So it has been with this old gospel ship, which has been sailing on the ocean of time for an hundred years, and has weathered many storms. But to-day she stands safe and sound, and a thousand times more glorious than ever, though she has been buffeted. She is sailing still heavenward, whose colors are floating freely and grandly, praised and admired the world round, and her power for good is known and felt even where her colors are not seen. Her moral, religious and financial condition to-day surpasses any church among the negroes of this country, and is ahead of many churches of that race whose advantages have been superior to ours.

But, coming to the subject, let us ask why is all of this? How came she so safely through the perils and dangers of the past? I answer because it was first founded right. Its foundation was right, and hence its success. We are here to-day to speak on this particular line, "Baptist Doctrine." What other foundation could have given rise to this success but Baptist doctrine, or Baptist belief, or the doctrine as believed and practiced by the Baptists? Every grand and laudable institution has had at some time its grand days or great epoch, and so the church of Christ.

We are assembled as a great people to do Him honor who has safely led this grand church along through the past century. It is the grand doctrine of the Baptist church that has given rise to this grand church and great Baptist denomination of Georgia, whose churches are known by the hundreds, and whose communicants are numbered by the thousands. Her sons are now in the various parts of the known world, publishing the glad tidings of the blood-spattered cross—even Calvary. We speak of the doctrine of the church as its foundation, and greater foundation can no man lay than that which is already laid. We speak of the doctrine or principles of the church as the foundation, for it is the foundation that gives power and durability to the superstructure.

What the bones, sinews, nervous system and the blood are to the physical man, so are the doctrines to the church. What the roots of the tree are to the trunk, to the boughs and to all of its branches, so the doctrines are to the church. And as it is impossible for the building to stand the wreck and hardships of time, etc., without its foundation, so it is with the church. As the tree cannot bear fruit without its roots, so it is with the church. Had not the church been founded upon the foundation of God's word, which is the true principle of the divine Architect of the church, its grand achievement would not have been. But all of these grand results have come to the church because it was founded upon the foundation of Christ and His apostles, Jesus Christ himself being the chief corner-stone.

We wish to speak in particular of the Baptist doctrine as being identical with the word of God, for there is no creed nor even shadow of a creed of this church but that of the word of

God. It is the main doctrine of the Baptists to proclaim nothing but the Bible, and that pure and simple. Upon this every one who has risen against it has had this accusation, that we stick too uncompromisingly to the scriptures, and will admit of no modification or even shadow of turning.

The doctrine of the Baptists is the doctrine of the Bible. Upon it all of our fathers stood, fought, conquered and died. Upon it we are standing to-day. The stand which the Baptists have taken for the leading doctrines of the Bible has been as a beacon through all ages in giving and preserving the truth in the world and of keeping a pure faith and church. Though they have not always been known to bear the name of Baptists, there have always been those who have believed and practiced what the Baptists do.

It is quite encouraging to know these two things about God and His people, Christ and His word. The first is God's word—has always stood since He first spoke it. The second is since the days of Jesus Christ. His people have always been loyal to the truth as is believed and practiced by Baptists. Hence He has always had a church to worship Him on the earth and a people to believe His word just as He has given it to them.

Sir Isaac Newton says: "The Baptists are the only body of christians that have not symbolized with the Church of Rome." Jesus is the Son of God, hear ye Him. Christ is the head over the church and its law-giver. The New Testament contains his law which is our infallible guide and supreme standard by which all church doctrines and rites are to be tried. Those are christian churches strictly speaking that correspond with the New Testament pattern, and Baptists have always appealed to the New Testament as furnishing the only true authority for the faith and practice of the churches. The great Erasmus says: "It is not from human reservoirs pregnant with stagnant waters that we should draw the doctrine of salvation, but from the pure and abundant stream that flows from the word of God." And since Christ is our law-giver, whom shall we obey? Who is supreme, Christ or the church? Where did the church get the authority to substitute something else in the place of that which Christ has ordained? There we are to learn our duty in all things of faith, etc., that which He teaches is all-sufficient for all times and places. What He commands we are to do. From his decision there is no appeal. Apostles, ministers nor churches can not alter or amend, but must submit, and grace suggests that our submission be heartily and cheerfully. Since we have the law-giver and the law let us acquaint ourselves with that law of Christ, and say, in all things, "Oh God, Thy will be done."

Our principles of obedience to Christ make us first Baptists ourselves, and immediately set us to making Baptists of others. We become Baptists, and we become propagandists of Baptist views by one and the same almighty, creative acts through all ages. The Baptists have adhered most strictly to the doctrines that are taught in God's word. So that obedience has been ever the leading idea with Baptists. They hold that obedience is better than sacrifice. And upon that fact they have ever stood contending, and to-day they are conquering the world upon that ground. For the world is asking every day, "What says the Bible?" and when told, they are saying "It is better to obey God rather than man." And behold, many are coming into the grand army of the Lord every day. When you ask me why is this, I tell you it is because of that longing in the converted heart to obey God. So, to obey, the Baptists have always held to be a sacred duty. So very jealous are they of the obedience which they are disposed to render to their Lord and Master, should they find in their book one page, one chapter, one sentence, or even one word that did not in every way comply with the sacred word of God, they would cast it out and leave that space vacant. If asked about it, they would with great delight give their reason for its abstraction. Then they would even go beyond that. They would brand the writer as ignorant or a heretic. What Baptists mean, so far as in them lies, is to go to heaven through obedience to God and faith in His word. Our fathers did it in all of their ignorance. And what else can we, as their children, do? Our fathers had masters who were Episcopalians, Methodists, and even Catholics, but they turned their backs on their masters' religion and profession, even when it was more convenient for them to follow their masters, and have spiritual liberty to follow the Lord Jesus Christ. They have even been rejected from meeting with the church, because they would not join the church of their masters. But what did they do in that instance? Why, they suffered, prayed and waited until God opened the way for them. But obey God they would, must and did under all circumstances do, and so it has always been, and even more so must it continue to be, for obedience has been the pride of Baptists of all ages. The negro Baptists have preferred to be in fellowship with God rather than man.

It is strange how Baptists, even in their ignorance, have withstood all of the eloquence of learning and strength of science and of logic and stuck to the plain Bible and its doctrines.

While they have had all of the polished scholars and preachers to contend with, they, in their ignorance, have stood alone with the Bible in their hands and whipped the world thus far. They had even the Church of England and the Church of Rome to withstand, and in defiance of all the pomp and splendor of these powers they have stood the test of time and to-day their colors are lifted to the breeze, and heaven hears the sound, and angels lend influence and glory to this occasion as we stand under this hallowed roof, made so by the grace of God and sanctified and made most holy to us by the prayers, tears, sweat and blood of Bryan, Marshall, Campbell and Gibbons, and now being honored by his reverence, the worthy Emanuel K. Love. D. D.

You ask me, how was it that though slavery raged in all of its horrors, destroying and debauching the moral character of every being that came within its reach, why, you ask. did they allow these negroes to have a church, make rules, and discipline members, etc., and from whence came all of these glorious things seen among negroes who came out of that cursed and damnable institution, slavery? My answer is that, first of all, their foundation was laid deep in the doctrine of God's book. Like Peter, they had learned obedience to their Lord and Master, who said, when faith had been tried and found sincere, "Upon this rock I will build my church, and the gates of hell shall not prevail against it." Who said again, "Ye are my friends, if ye do whatsoever I have commanded you."

Their legal privilege was granted them by the Constitution of the United States as the result of an application made to Congress to grant religious liberty to all men to worship God after the dictates of their own conscience, and not be molested or made afraid.

Baptists believe that the Bible is the only rule of faith, and should be practiced by all men. That it is the right of every man to interpret that book for himself, and in doing so he should be allowed to worship his God in his own quiet way. The supreme legislature of the country, nor the lowest officer in the community, nor any one else, should do the least thing to disturb him in doing this.

Baptists believe in a separation of church and state. They also believe in a democratic form of government. or a government by the people, for the people, and with the people—that is, a congregational government, or a majority rule. governed by the Bible.

The Baptists in all things hold that obedience to the law and testimony is supreme in conscience.

Therefore we appear here to-day, having rested upon this immovable foundation, which is stronger than the hills of old, and will abide when the rocks of Gibraltar shall fail, which have been standing the raging billows for centuries in the past, and yet they are the same.

Had it not been for the all-abiding principles of Baptists we would have been driven to climes unknown. Every denomination has its peculiar pride or religious forte. The Catholics have stood because they had the power over man and coerced them into their pale; hence all that they have done. The Church of England had the money; hence all men gladly bowed to her footstool. It is said of the Presbyterians that because of their education and high doctrine that none could comprehend but the learned. Of the Methodists it is said that they have sung their way around the world. But Baptists have gone into many parts of the world, and all the places where they have not gone they will go upon the word of God. Baptists have come through fire and water and sailed through blood by faith and obedience. When tried, their faith would not yield. On being asked concerning the things of God, even if they believed something that they did not fully understand, they have taken great pleasure in replying: Great is the mystery of godliness. God manifested in the flesh the secret things belonging to God, but those things which are revealed belong to us and our children.

Baptists believe that repentance toward God and faith in the Lord Jesus Christ is the first duty of man. The second is like unto that. Baptism is the second duty of every man. He who believes in the name of the only begotten Son of God believes and knows that immersion in water, when performed upon a proper subject and by a proper administrator, is the only thing that constitutes christian baptism. These few but sublime doctrines constitute the great foundation of the Baptist church. Upon these principles all of the apostles, martyrs and ancient worthies lived, fought, died and went to heaven. There their happy souls wait and rest until their fellow-servants, slain as they were, shall come.

Our church has come through trials and persecution in all ages, from the days of Christ till now. For there never was a time since our blessed Lord said to Peter, "Upon this rock I will build my church, and the gates of hell shall not prevail against it," but that there were men and women practicing and believing just what Baptists are practicing and believing to-day. Though it cost them their lives, yet they have in all ages contended for the faith once delivered to the saints.

Our fathers believed in the Baptist form of government and they stuck to it, though their masters were members of another church. When they would feel a change of heart and wish to unite with the church they would have to get a pass from their masters. When asked to what church they wished to connect themselves, and the Baptist church was named as the church of their choice, they were then asked, "Why can't you join Mr. A.'s or Mr. B.'s church." When better reasons and privileges were given to join the church named by their masters, they could only say, "I want Mr. D. or E. to baptize me." After being denied for no good reason at all, and made to suffer the awful consequences of laying off from the church for months, and sometimes for years, they nevertheless, like the impassionate widow, continued to seek until, for some reason, they were granted the privilege of joining the church of their choice by undergoing some hard treatment. They chose to take punishment rather than join any other than the church of their faith, the Baptist church. The suffering of God's children has often brought others to be His disciples, for God has often seen fit to cast us in the furnace of affliction.

Baptists believe in giving to God that obedience that takes in all his word. Faith and obedience are inseparably connected. The Baptists also believe that he who truly believes God's word will obey Him. And he that believes is made a new man in Christ Jesus, born again, or made after the new man created in righteousness. So he that is created in righteousness will yield implicit obedience to God. Our blessed Lord and Master said: "To whom ye yield yourselves to obey, to him ye are servants." Jesus said: "If ye do whatsoever I have commanded, ye are my friends." So friendship with God depends upon our obedience to Him. When Abraham obeyed, it was accounted to him for righteousness. Hence he was called the friend of God. "If ye believe in me, ye shall know of the doctrine." Christ says, belief and obedience make, first, children of God; secondly, and as children of God we are Baptists, or those who side with Baptist doctrine.

I have been puzzled to know how any man can claim to be a child of God, and live in actual disregard of God's law, and worse still, set up a system of doctrines or opinions contrary to those set up by the God of the church, or to adopt those set up by men. I ask, can such men plead ignorance? Can a man who takes the opposite side of a question, ever get to the place where he can plead his ignorance? Can any man who is wise enough to build up doctrines contrary to those established of God, ever plead his ignorance and thereby be pardoned? I trow not. The name, "Baptist," originated not with them, but with their opponents. The main difference between Baptists and other denominations centers in the ordinance of baptism. Not that Baptists are erroneous in their views, but that others are not willing to follow the divine rule on this fundamental doctrine. In this they are willing to substitute this ordinance for the tradition of men. Yet they profess to be the children of God. They delight to live in open rebellion to the government of God. Let us obey God, that good may come to us. Then we can say, as another:

> "Now liberty is all the plan,
> The chief pursuit of every man whose heart is right.
> One word into your ears I'll drop,
> No longer spend your needless pains
> To mend and polish o'er your chains,
> But break them off before you rise,
> Nor disappoint your watchful eyes.
> What says great Washington and Lee?
> Our country is and must be free.
> What says great Henry Pendleton
> And Liberty's minutest son?
> 'Tis all one voice—they all agree,
> God made us and we must be free.
> Freedom we crave, neither envy's breath,
> An equal freedom or a death,
> If needs there be—yea, tax the knight,
> But let our brave, heroic minds
> Move freely as celestial winds;
> Make vice and folly feel your rod,
> But leave our conscience free to God.
> Leave each man free to choose
> His form of piety, nor at him storm;
> And he who minds the civil law,
> And keeps it whole without a flaw,
> Let him just as he pleases pray,
> And seek for heaven in his own way.
> And if he miss, we all must own,
> No man is wrong but him alone."

HISTORY OF THE COLORED BAPTISTS OF GEORGIA.

BY REV. G. H. DWELLE, AUGUSTA, GA.

Dear Chairman and Brethren of the Centennial:

I have been appointed by your committee to deliver an address before this christian body, which has assembled here to celebrate the one hundredth year of our existence in this State. Who is able, who is adequate, who can know the history of the colored Baptists of Georgia? Where are their records kept? Who has been their recorder, writing the true history of the pioneer fathers who have passed on before? No one, and a full and true history can never be known on earth! Some parts may be gathered, but the full and complete history has passed away with those faithful heralds for Jesus into the spirit world. Here and there we have caught a faint glimmering of the greatness of those faithful pioneers of our denomination in Georgia, and of their labors.

We will say a word touching our history, which begins with Rev. Andrew Bryan, who organized the First African Baptist Church in this city one hundred years ago, and was its first pastor. In the early morn, before it was yet light, he came to this field with seeds from the granary of heaven, given him from the Master's own hands, to sow. "They were sown in weakness; they were raised in power." They took root downward and sprung upward and brought forth fruit, some thirty, some sixty, and some an hundred fold, to the honor and glory of God.

Soon after the Lord sent another into the field, Rev. Andrew Marshall, a strong man for God and his cause, who worked faithfully in this part of Georgia.

The work began spreading toward the interior, borne along by Revs. Robert McGee, Cæsar McGrady, Jesse Peter, (sometimes called Golplin), Kennard, Ghan, Jacob Walker, Henry Johnson, Joseph Walker, Henry Watts, Ephriam Rucker, Frank Quarles, Frank F. Beal, William J. Campbell, Tellinghast, Pope, Romulus Moore, John A. James, Henry Williams, Allen Clark, David Hill, Prince Williams, Thomas Hardwick, Joe McGrady, George Gibbons, Abraham Burk, Louis Barber, Jerry M. Jones, P. B. Borders, Jerry Freeman, George Jones, George Bull, and hundreds of others that I cannot now remember. They all labored faithfully in their Master's cause, and to-day are rejoicing in heaven with their Master, whom they served on earth even till called away by their Lord. Who can tell the sufferings, privations and hardships which these men of God endured during the early days of our church.

In those dark days when the servants of God had been laboring hard and speaking for Jesus, they would sometimes receive, some fifty and others an hundred lashes or more for speaking for God. To say *all* were whipped for preaching would be untrue; but to say that none were whipped for preaching would be a lie. It is said that some white Baptists have been whipped for preaching; then think you the negro could escape? Nay, he had his share doubled; but our God saved them all. Those were hard times in Georgia; but the seed were good, right from the Master's hands, handed down to his faithful servants to be sown on the seacoast, swamps, mountains and valleys broadcast—scattered all over the land. It must have been good seed to yield 166,429 living souls, to say nothing of those already gathered from the field, and that through the storms of adversity, the floods of affliction and the draughts of persecution. Surely God was with the sower and in the seed. Yes, the faithful men toiled on at great disadvantage, illiterate, fettered, deprived at times of food and clothing. Still, through the darkness and gloom they toiled on, singing:

> "Through floods and flames, if Jesus leads,
> I'll follow where he goes;
> Hinder me not, shall be my cry,
> Though earth and hell oppose."

They went on, but not alone; one was with them who said: "I will never leave thee nor forsake thee: lo, I am with thee to the end of the world. Amen." And to-day in every valley and plain, on every hill and mountain you may traverse in Georgia, lo, the Baptists are there. Thus the kind hand of God has led us along and here are we to-day, with gratitude giving praise to our God, "from whom all blessings flow," and we would shout and say,

> "Praise Him, all creatures here below;
> Praise Him above, ye heavenly host;
> Praise Father, Son and Holy Ghost."

We now stand at the cradle of the Baptists of Georgia. We have come from all parts of the land to lift high and throw to the breeze the Baptist banner that was borne aloft so faithfully in the darker days by those veterans, and has never been allowed to trail in the dust for one hundred years in this grand old Empire State of the South. That banner will ever stand, all stained with hallowed blood, marked, "Salvation's free to all the world through the blessed Son of God." We would not forget our brothers of the white race, who kindly assisted us and cheered us on to greater efforts of success, helping us to organize and set up churches, and in prosecuting the work. They rendered much valuable help in the establishing and building of the 1500 churches, with 500 ordained ministers and 2,000 licensed preachers, presiding over the 166,429 members, all springing up from the little seed planted one hundred years ago.

As to culture and refinement, these can be found in large numbers in our ranks. For thrift and wealth, there are many with us. We have towering churches and fine seminaries, and school buildings as good as are found in the land. As to intellect, morals and spirituality, we have some second to none in this country, especially our young men and women coming out of our schools and seminaries. Of them we are truly proud, and will ever thank God for them. Our press is making rapid progress, and now ranks with the best in all the South. Able men are the editors, and they are a power for good to the denomination and our people. Yes, dear brethren, for nearly seventy-six years the colored Baptists of this State toiled and labored under many disadvantages; but when it pleased the "Supreme Ruler" of heaven and earth to blot out human slavery, the curse of this American land, the negro Baptists of Georgia came at once together as one man to prepare for the new order of things pertaining to our denomination. They had the interest of the race and the cause of Christ at heart. The education and moral training of the young men and old ones —the spiritual good of all was before them. These were thoroughly and minutely considered and discreetly prepared for by our leading brethren. A number of them met at Hilton Head, S. C., and organized the Zion Baptist Association, and then there was a move all along the line. The brethren met at Augusta, at the Springfield Baptist Church, to consult about forming the Ebenezer Baptist Association, which was formed after this meeting. Then followed the Shiloh Association, Mount Olive, and in all, to-day we have some fifty or sixty more associations, all prospering and doing much good. They are dotting every nook and corner of our State, and our work is advancing.

In 1870 there was a call made by the brethren of Atlanta and Augusta for brethren of the State to meet at Augusta, with the Central Baptist Church, for the purpose of organizing a State Baptist convention. Accordingly, a large number of brethren met, and on May 17, 1870, organized the Missionary Baptist Convention of Georgia. Its object was to establish a normal and theological school, and to support missionaries in the State. At the meeting we enrolled eighty-four delegates, and their names are recorded as the founders of our State convention. Before this, however, our associations were sending out missionaries in the field. Especially do I remember Rev. J. C. Bryan, Henry Morgan and A. De Lamotta, who were sent by the Ebenezer Association to the upper part of the State, while I believe brethren in this part of the State were equally as active.

In 1874 the convention sent out Rev. W. H. Tilman. Soon we could hear of missionaries all over our State. As time rolled on, the American Baptist Home Mission Board, the Georgia Baptist Convention (white), the American Baptist Publication Society, all took hold to help us, and there was much good done by these faithful missionaries in our State.

Early we began to invite help in our educational work, and the American Baptist Home Mission Society heard our petition, learning through Rev. W. J. White our needs, and came to our relief. They gave us the Augusta Institute, which was moved to the city of Atlanta about 1879, and is now the Atlanta Baptist Seminary for young men.

This did well for our young men, but where, oh where, were our young women? To what place were they to be gathered for training? The brethren decided there must be provision made for them, and in answer to prayer to God from those christian hearts help came. While Rev. Quarles was on his knees praying, God, through the Home Mission Society, sent Misses S. B. Packard and H. E. Giles to our aid. They opened school in the basement of Friendship Baptist Church, in the city of Atlanta, and began work April 11, 1881. They began gathering our old and young women for training, and little by little they grew till what was a school of fifty, or a little more, can now call a roll of 600. Thus beginning lowly, God has raised our Spellman Seminary and made it a school second to none in all the South. Our different associations are building high schools in their bounds which can and will become good feeders to our two seminaries, meeting the needs of our people, and thus God is with us in our work.

Passing through the last twenty-four years we come to our centennial. Not that we entered this work one hundred years ago as our fathers (then the slaves of the State), but as free, twice made free, free from sin and death and American slavery. If the Son makes you free, ye shall be free indeed. What negro Baptist here to-day is not proud of the little record that can be gathered of our fathers, who, with heavenly weapons, fought so bravely the battle of our Lord, finished their course, kept the faith and now have the sure reward. I know, dear brethren, you do rejoice in your hearts. If this little history which we have be so grand, what must their true history have been. Where is there a people afflicted under like circumstances who can produce a record more rich with fruit for Jesus? Ah! the full and complete history is kept by the Judge who will do right, and to-day we should move with new impulse to achieve greater victories, and move on the Baptist chariot, conquering and to conquer, until we shall plant the Baptist church upon every mountain, hill-top and valley, from shore to shore, from pole to pole, until we can truly say Satan's power and his kingdom on earth are demolished, and all the world shall belong to Jesus. And when our next centennial comes, and the colored Baptists of Georgia are assembled, we that are here to-day to speak of those who sleep the long sleep of death, with no towering monuments, no shaft lifting its head to the skies, to mark the place or to speak of their deeds. Some of their graves are

African Baptist Church. 231

not known. But God, their Redeemer, lives and ever from the skies looks down and watches all their dust till He shall bid it rise. We who attend the meeting to-day, if our eyes were not holden, I imagine might see bending over the battlements of glory our beloved fathers, who, we imagine, are saying with their heavenly voices, be faithful unto death and come, we await your coming. We who meet here to-day in friendship and brotherly kindness shall be able to read without error our true history at home in our Father's house above, where there shall be no more parting, where the wicked cease from troubling and the weary are at rest. They sowed the seed on earth, and the harvest has been great. Surely

"God moves in a mysterious way,
His wonders to perform;
He plants his footsteps in the sea
And rides upon the storm.

Ye fearful saints, fresh courage take,
The clouds ye so much dread
Are big with mercies and will break
In blessings on your head."

BAPTIST CHURCH HISTORY.

An Address Delivered by Rev. W. H. Tilman, Sr., of Atlanta, Ga., Before the Negro Baptist Centennial.

Dear Brethren:

My object in this discourse shall be to locate the church of Christ. Whatever church we shall find founded by the great head of the church is the church of Christ. These questions are often asked by persons not acquainted with Baptist history: Where did the Baptists originate? How old are they? These might be considered as secondary questions, and of no importance at all to a Baptist. Their history is not more peculiar than the practice of that which they believe. Their faith is important, "For whatsoever is born of God overcometh the world: and this is the victory that overcometh the world. Even our faith."—I. John, v, 4.

God is the author and head of the church. He is the head of every family in heaven or on earth. What skeptic will deny God named the Baptist? Neither Zachariah nor Elizabeth named John; but God sent his name as John from heaven by an angel, and the Spirit has been pleased to leave on record

John the Baptist. What skeptic will deny that Christ, the great head of the church, was baptized by John? Who will deny that this was John's special and only mission? Before Christ was baptized, John baptized multitudes, and many afterwards. John diminished, but Christ increased. His preaching was to awake the world from its sleep. Christ's baptism was to set the example of practice and give the world the needed light of his church and to quicken the elected stones for the Master's use.

2d. As to the Baptist Church History. It may be said, as God said to Abraham, "Can you count the stars of heaven or number the sands on the sea shore?" This is admitted to be an impossibility. So with the history of the Baptist church, the church of God, I ask you can you read the dust of the earth, the smoke of the past century? Or can you analyze the sands of the ocean's depths, or call from the graves, the mountains and deserts and caves, the millions of charred and bleached bones that have gathered from the days of the elect Able down to the last martyr's?

Do you say this account reaches back too far? Not as far as we are authorized to go. Hear the word of Jesus: Matt., xxv, 34: "Then shall the King say unto them on his right hand, Come, ye blessed of my Father, inherit the kingdom prepared for you from the foundation of the world." Here is the demonstration of the truth that God's first designs are lastly carried into execution. He made a world, then made man to occupy it. He prepared a kingdom, a church for his own glory, then elected man to occupy it until he comes again. John, xvii., 5: "And now, oh, Father, glorify Thou me with Thine Own Self with the glory which I had with Thee before the world was."

At what time and on what occasion was this prayer made?

After he had brought that needed light and the world had seen and owned it to be a light from God. Yea, devils had tested it and trembled, because it was that light which shone in darkness and the darkness comprehended it not. Note the occasion when the broken link was mended and the capital of the broken column, which had so long lain moulding beneath the debris and rubbish of ages, was found, raised and stood upon its foundation, the rock of faith, and pointed heavenward. A watcher was placed on the pediment and ordered to turn his face to the four parts of the heaven and the earth and cry, saying, "God was in Christ from all eternity reconciling the world unto Himself." In looking down the unknown ages the crier spied the church of Christ in its primitive glory. Filled with amazement and holy awe, he said, "Who is she that looketh forth as the morning, fair as the moon, clear as the sun, and terrible as an army with banners?"—Song of Sol., 6–10.

3d. Christ says to His church, "Ye are in the world, but ye are not of the world, for there are three that bear record in heaven, the Father, the Word and the Holy Ghost; and these three are one. And there are three that bear witness in earth, the Spirit, the water and the blood; and these three are one."— I. John, v., 7–8. Was not Christ our witness in the world? Though the world was made by Him, did the world know Him? No, no. Has the world any better knowledge of Him to-day than it had then? No. The world has a better conception of His will and purposes as it grows wiser, but not of Him. The world's wisdom is foolishness. Christ's church and Himself are one. If the world does not know Him, it cannot know His church, for what He saith of Himself is synonymous of His church.

4th. The Baptist church history, we claim, is written in blood. During all the world's dark ages they were preserved among all the nations and called by all manner of names—heretics in the first two centuries. They mingled with the Messalians, Euchites, Montanists; in the third, fourth and fifth centuries with the Novatians, and Donatists; in the seventh with the Paulicians; in the tenth, the Paterines; in the eleventh century, the Waldenses, Albigensis, Henicians and Christians. They have ever been in principle and spirit really the same people. These sects grew and flourished, though they suffered great persecutions.

The story of the slaughtering is enough to curdle the blood in the veins of a demon, yet they faltered not. They contended for the faith, and that faith was that the church founded by the great Baptist leader had not for its foundation, "gold, silver, precious stones, wood, hay, stubble (I. Cor., iii. 12), but that Christ might dwell in your hearts by faith; to make all men see what is the fellowship of the mystery which, from the beginning of the world hath been hid in God, Who created all things by Jesus Christ. To this intent that now unto principalities and powers in heavenly places might be known by the church the manifold wisdom of God. The church, then, is that source of light to the world, and the hope and joy of its members. The world is dependent upon the church for this light, each member of this mystic body being a small principality in himself. Each is accountable for his portion to be done. Do we know what we should do, and when we have done enough? The good book tells us, "What your hands find to do, do it with all thy might." Much is yet to be done. One hundred years have passed since this Southland, this State of Georgia, learned to their astonishment that the negro had knowledge of his election, by God's grace, unto salvation through Christ, and courage to tell it.

Andrew Bryan lifted the light, unfolded the Baptist banner, with a handful of ignorant slaves to hear his words. No doubt, many times he knew not what he should say to the few. But 100 years have told a wonderful story. The ignorant hearers have passed away; their places are filled with bright, intelligent listeners. And while Father Bryan, the pioneer, patriot and hero of a hundred years ago, compelled by death to vacate his pulpit, what has been the result? Of what have we to boast to-day? A grand army, a full corps of students, well equipped, holding in their hands the gavel of the church and the sword of knowledge, they are clothed in beautiful regalia, 166,429 strong.

From the mountain to the seaboard the line is unbroken. No discord in our song, no uncertain sound in the written edict, one Lord, one faith and one baptism. Again, old and young have learned to chant the song that Father Bryan sang in his day:

"Shall Wisdom cry aloud,
And not a speech be heard?
The voice of God's eternal word,
Deserves it no regard?

"I was His chief delight,
His everlasting son,
Before the first of all His work,
Creation, was begun.

"Before the flying clouds,
Before the solid land,
Before the fields, before the floods,
I dwelt at his right hand.

"When he adorned the skies,
And built them I was there,
To order when the sun should rise,
And marshal every star.

"When he poured out the sea,
And spread the flowing deep,
I gave the flood a firm decree,
In its own bound to keep.

"Upon the empty air
The earth was balanced well;
With joy I saw the mansion where
The sons of men should dwell.

"My busy thought at first
On their salvation ran,
Ere sin was born or Adam's dust
Was fashioned to man.

"Then come, receive my grace,
Ye children, and be wise;
Happy the man that keeps my ways,
The man that shuns them dies."

The first thought of Christ from creation was to save, then to prepare a plan of salvation, then to prepare a kingdom, both in heaven and on earth, to keep securely the saved. Then created he the subject, man, from whom he would make his selection. Lastly, he elected them for his own glory.

Who are they that are elected to grace?

Hear the answer: All things work together for good to them that love God, to them who are called.

How called?

According to God's purpose. For whom He did foreknow He also predestined and foreordained. Christ did foreknow His people; not simply knowing them, but His foreknowledge of them as His people included the gracious purpose of bringing them into a state of salvation, not for His church, but through His church. All who are saved shall be saved through His well-ordered plan, His church. Moreover, whom He did predestine, them He also called; and whom He called he also justified; and whom He justified He also glorified. And to such, tribulations, nor distress, nor persecutions, nor famine, nor nakedness, peril nor sword—not if all the human powers of earth and demons of the infernal regions, nor death itself—if every angel of the paradisaical world should come down and stand in the pathway of Christ's church, the Baptist church, they would fail to separate us from Him. He has called us, and to Him we must go.

8th. Our peculiarities—The Baptist church practices.

It may be said those sects heretofore mentioned did not claim the name Baptist. We will admit that. While minus the name, see their practice:

1. No man could join the band until he could give the necessary proof of a regenerate heart.

2. He could in no wise be received into fellowship until he had passed into the door baptized by immersion.

3. They had no desire for amalgamation with any others.

Like some rivulet which pursues its way from the mountains to the sea, parallel to, but never mingling with the broad and turbulent stream, they have come down from the first ages of christianity preserving and transmitting to posterity the finest form of practical godliness and gospel faith known to history during those long succeeding centuries of darkness and corruption. Are not these the same peculiarities of the Baptist church to-day? We have no objection to exterior, yet we are more than jealously concerned about the interior. All who favor the band and join it must give good satisfaction of being born again. There are 80,165,000 christians in the world who speak the English language. The Baptists number among them 8.06 per cent. of the whole number. After more than eighteen hundred years of fire, sword and starvation, after drenching hills and valleys of every land, America not excepted, with the blood of untold millions, yet the Baptists live and are not a barren waste. The life and spirit of her captain are infused into every fibre. They rose like the green bay tree planted by living waters; her leaves will not wither. Like the poplar tree her beauty. Like the cedar of Lebanon her strength. She lives because Christ lives. She is beautiful because she is dressed in her bridal robes. She is pregnant with strength because she is held by the law and gospel. So she has a wall and a cannon loaded with sixty-six deadly missles—the whole Bible. The Baptists have eaten the whole book. Part of it may be bitter, yet there is sweetness enough in the twenty-nine new books to assure the Baptist there is no danger.

> "One army of the living God,
> To His command we bow,
> Part of the host have crossed the flood,
> And part are crossing now."

THE HISTORY OF THE BAPTISTS.

BY REV. LEVI THORNTON.

Dear Brethren of the Baptist Family of Georgia:

In appearing before you on this auspicious occasion I feel deeply grateful for the honor conferred upon me in being invited to speak on this occasion.

1st. We will speak of the faithfulness of our fathers, who, being called of God to enter into their fields of labor, did it faithfully, believing that they built on the foundation which was laid by Jesus Christ. They were faithful in preaching the gospel of Christ as they understood it. They lived in the dark age of the world, yet they held fast and struggled for liberty. They, faithful to their principles as Baptists, did not let the banner of the Lord Jesus trail in the dust.

2d. Their Christian zeal. They were zealous in the cause of the Divine Master. Though their enemies were strong and active, they remembered the words of the Apostle Paul, "Be ye steadfast, unmovable, always abounding in the work of the Lord, forasmuch as ye know that your labor is not in vain in the Lord."

African Baptist Church.

3d. Their trials and long suffering. In 1630 Roger Williams established a Baptist church in this country, but not without great suffering. He contended for soul liberty. The Baptists have furnished quite their share of martyrs and fully their quota of able men fighting for the divorce of church and state, and contending that man should worship God according as he understood the dictates of the gospel. All through the winding ages the Baptists have been called to endure keen sacrifice and terrible suffering. Their suffering has tended to develop their strength, and made them search the scriptures, which they have used to the discomfort of their opponents. Let us rejoice that there has been no disposition upon the part of Baptists in any age to shun the hallowed road of suffering, which is the King's highway. For 100 years our denomination has been contending with wickedness in high places. At times it seemed that the hallowed old ship would go down, but it was upheld by a hand divine, and for an hundred years she has been contending with the mad billows of life's tempestuous sea. Our fathers planted the banner of the Lord here, and we are determined that it shall not trail in the dust. A century has demonstrated the fact that their labors were not vain in the Lord; neither shall ours be

Father Andrew Bryan, in much trouble and sheer suffering, planted the first negro Baptist church in this State an hundred years ago. He was whipped until he bled profusely, but his blood was but an heaven-born fertilizer, to enrich and make grow the heavenly plant. His tears were bottled by a covenant-keeping God, and his groans a loving Jesus heard. From four, the church soon numbered hundreds, and later on, thousands. "So mightily grew the word of God and prevailed."

Father Andrew Marshall followed him only to suffer as he did for the same cause. He was a great man, and the people, white and black, felt him. He swayed an influence second to none over men. The people would obey him at will. Soon after this Father Cæsar McGrady, of Augusta, came forth bearing the olive branch of peace, and the Springfield Baptist Church, of Augusta, Ga., came forth fair as the morning. Rev. Jacob Walker, Rev. Kelly Low, Rev. Cyrus Thornton, of Augusta, and Rev. W. J. Campbell, Henry Cunningham, of Savannah, are also among those who did valiant service in the cause of Christ among our people. To this list of worthies may be added Revs. Frank F. Bealle, Peter Johnson, Henry Johnson, Henry Watts, of Augusta, Frank Quarles, of Atlanta, Rev. Jacob Wade, of Thomasville, Rev. Owen George, of Atlanta, E. Rucker, of Columbus, and a host of others who have been long since gathered in peace to the saints' rest. "These all died in the faith, not having received the promises, but having seen them afar off, and were persuaded of them and embraced them, and confessed that they were strangers and pilgrims on the earth."

The church edifices an hundred years ago were very common. They could not have been otherwise. They were built by poor slaves who could not control a moment of their own time. It is a wonder that they built any at all. It is wonderful how God blessed and led along our fathers in those dark, bloody days. They preached with a burning eloquence that did as much to astonish the slaveholders in those days as did the ignorant Galilean fishermen in the early days of christianity. The fathers have a very few of their representatives now living. Deal tenderly with them, young men. Do not run over them because you are educated, young and strong. Nothwithstanding their superstition, the people are living in them. Take time, the field will be cleared quite soon enough, and waiting for you before you are ready for the work. These fathers will soon join the flock above, and you will have all the room you want.

Just twenty-three years ago God tore loose the iron bars of slavery and set us free. Many of the fathers prayed for this but did not live to see it. They look down from the upper world upon 166,429 negro Baptists in Georgia. From four they have come. George Leile, Andrew Bryan, Jesse Peter, Andrew Marshall, Henry Cunningham, Jacob Walker, Cæsar McGrady, and all of our fathers must be looking down from the balconies of the New Jerusalem rejoicing with us at the glorious success that has attended the army of the Lord for these one hundred years. A little while, dear fathers, and we will be there with you. A few more battles and the captain will call us off of the field of battle to join the flock above and the church of the first-born that is written in heaven.

"O when, thou city of my God,
Shall I Thy courts ascend.
Where congregations ne'er break up,
And Sabbaths have no end."

THE WANTS OF THE COLORED MINISTRY.

By Rev. W. H. McIntosh, D. D., Theological Instructor of the Negro Baptists of Georgia under the State Mission Board (White), Macon, Ga.

By this I understand what is necessary to an effective ministry among the colored people, and to this I reply, Just what is requisite to an effective ministry among any other people. The gospel is intended for all men; there is no respect of persons with God (Rom., ii, 11). All men are sinners; all men need salvation; all men are saved in the same way, by repentance towards God and faith in the Lord Jesus Christ. The qualifications of a minister are given in the Scriptures, and so clearly that there need be no misunderstanding: "No man taketh this honor unto himself but he that is called of God as was Aaron." —Ex., 28; I. Heb., v, 4.

I believe that God calls men to preach, and when he calls them he makes it apparent to them and to their brethren. What, then, are the qualifications of a minister of the gospel? A regenerated heart, a heart that has experienced the power of God's spirit in the renewal of his nature. As the new birth is the condition of entrance into the kingdom of God, so is it pre-eminently essential to him who is to lead others into that kingdom. This is so plain that I need not dwell upon it further than to say it is now so easy to get into the church that it becomes us to be doubly guarded, in setting apart men to preach, that they give good evidence that they themselves "have passed from death unto life," who are to be the guides and instructors of others. But all regenerate men are not called to preach. The desire of a good man to preach is not the only thing to be considered. David desired to build a house for God. It was a good desire. God accepted the desire, but not the work. That was reserved for Solomon, David's son. "If a man desire the office of a bishop, he desireth a good work."—I. Timothy, iii., 1. Then follows the qualifications. Of the existence of the desire the candidate himself is the exclusive judge, but of his fitness for the office, the church and those who are called to lay hands upon him and set him apart to the work, are the judges.. Let us look at these qualifications. "A bishop must be blameless," of irreproachable character for truth, honesty, chastity—in a word, an upright, godly, godlike man; "the husband of one wife," vigilant, circumspect, watchful over himself as well as others; "of good behavior, given to hospitality, apt to teach," having the ability to impart instruction to others. He is a teacher and must have something to teach. This implies a knowledge of the scriptures and a disposition to acquire it. "Study to show thyself approved unto God. A workman that needeth not to be ashamed, rightly dividing the word of truth."—II. Tim., ii, 15. "Give attendance to reading, to exhortation, to doctrine. Neglect not the gift that is in thee, which was given by prophecy, with the laying on of the hands of the presbytery. Meditate upon these things; give thyself wholly to them; that thy profiting may appear to all. Take heed to thyself, and unto the doctrine; continue in them; for in doing this thou shall both save thyself and them that hear thee."—I. Tim., iv, 13–16. Now what does all this teach? Why, that the man of God must have a knowledge of the things God has revealed in His word; for "All scripture is given by inspiration of God, and is profitable for doctrine, for reproof, for correction, for instruction in righteousness: that the man of God may be perfect, thoroughly furnished unto all good works."—II. Tim., iii, 16. Here is the foundation of spiritual knowledge open to all, and he is wise who drinks of the pure water of life.

There is no prescribed amount of learning of the schools which qualifies a man for the ministry, but he must have a knowledge of the scriptures—a knowledge of the things he is to teach others. There is a thought with some that if a man wishes to preach the church should ordain or license him; that his desire constitutes a call. I do not find it so in the word of God. There must be a desire on the part of the candidate, and the apostles say it is a good desire, but he lays down other qualifications quite as important. Now when the candidate has a desire, of which, I'll repeat, he is the judge, and the church finds him qualified by moral character, and other requirements, among them ability to teach, where the church can approve him as a good man and capable of instructing men in the way of salvation, and the judgment of the church and his convictions of duty coincide, I think that may be regarded as a call to the ministry. In substance, these are the views of that good and wise man Andrew Fuller. I commend these thoughts to your consideration. Not my suggestions, but the thoughts of the holy spirit; the rules which he has given in setting apart men to preach the gospel, by the observance of which you may have an effective ministry. Do not ordain a man to the ministry simply because he wants to be ordained. Do not ordain a man whose character is not above reproach. Do not ordain a man who is not "apt to teach." Yet if he had all the learning that all the schools and colleges in the land could afford, if he had the wisdom of Solomon, but did not give evidence of a regenerated heart and a consecrated spirit, no consideration could induce me to lay these hands on him and set him apart to the work of the ministry.

Sanctified learning is a blessing to its possessors, and to those who are brought under its influence, whether he be a preacher or a private member of the church. I do not know that ignorance is a blessing to any one, and yet there are some who seem to set a premium upon it. They have the idea that the apostles of our Lord were unlearned and ignorant men, and therefore that ignorance is not only no bar to the ministry but a recommendation to it. It is true the apostles had not what we would call a liberal education. They had not like Saul of Tarsus (after his conversion known as Paul) been brought up under the teachings of the wise men of that day, but they could read and write. Two of them—Matthew and John—wrote the gospels bearing their names. Peter wrote two epistles, and shows by his preaching that he was a man of remarkable ability. John wrote in addition to the gospel bearing his name three epistles and the Book of Revelations. James wrote one epistle, and Paul wrote and preached with power that made kings tremble. These men were inspired, but they were men of good common sense, and were for three years (except Paul) under the "Great Teacher," the wisest teacher the world ever saw, who "spake as never man spake." They witnessed His works, they heard His words and were His daily companions.

Who ever had in the world's history such a teacher? And then on the day of Pentecost, by the miraculous gift of tongues, the ability to speak languages of which hitherto they were ignorant, they preached the gospel to Parthians and Medes and Elimites, and the dwellers in Mesopotamia, and in India, and Cappadocia, and Pontus, and Asia, Phrygia, and Pamphylia, in Egypt, and in the parts of Lybia, about Cyrene, strangers of Rome, Jews and Proselytes, Cretes and Arabians, who heard in their own tongues the wonderful works of God. I tell you they were the most learned ministers in everything pertaining to the subject of salvation and in human learning necessary to convey to others the knowledge of God and Christ, and heaven and eternal life, that the world ever saw or ever will see again.

God does not work miracles now in the bestowment of such gifts upon men, but he does require them to study His word, acquaint themselves with His will therein revealed, that they may be wise to win souls. "The entrance of the word giveth light; it giveth understanding to the simple."—Ps. cxix, 130.

The men who preached the gospel in the early history of Georgia were not men of great learning, but like Apollus they were "mighty in the scriptures." They had few books, but they had *the* book, the word of God, and they drank in its divine lessons as a thirsty man drinks water. They studied the Bible on their knees and when they went before the people they carried a message of divine truth to be enforced by the power of the holy ghost. I point to these men as illustrations of what may be accomplished when men are consecrated to God and do the best they can with their opportunities. Many of our early preachers preached all day, and by the light of pine-knot fires studied such books as they could get, but chiefly the Bible. I hold in reverence the men who in heat or cold, in poverty and persecution, with apostolic zeal preached the gospel and laid the foundation of denominational prosperity in which we rejoice to-day. The progress of Baptist principles in Georgia, expressed by figures, counts up: White Baptists connected with the conventions, 103,232; friendly to, but not connected with it, 27,286; anti-missionaries, 12,000; total, 142,518; total colored Baptists, 166,429; grand total, 308,947.

"So mightily grew the word of God and prevailed."—Acts, xix, 20. Among those of the colored preachers who deserve special mention, and who have done good service in the cause of Christ in this part of the State and in this city, were Andrew Bryan, the first pastor of this church, Andrew Marshall, Henry Cunningham, and, in later days, Cox, Campbell and many others occupying less prominent positions who were godly men, laboring in word and doctrine, were true to God and man. I mention these because they were identified with the origin and growth of the denomination before and during the times of the old Sunbury Association. There are others as prominent in parts of Georgia, but I have not the record of their labors.

This church enjoyed for many years the labors of Andrew Bryan and Andrew Marshall. The latter I knew personally. He was a remarkable man and wielded a large influence, as did also Henry Cunningham. They were good men, useful in their day, "and their works follow them."

The opportunities of colored preachers of to-day are far greater than theirs. You have schools and books and a seminary especially for young men looking to the ministry. If to obtain an education you have to practice self-denial, let me say to you, an education will be worth all the sacrifices you may make to secure it. To the young men I would say, do not be impatient to enter upon the work of the ministry before you have made the best preparation that you can make. If you have not the means to pay your way at school for a year, work half the year and go to school the other half. Better live hard and dress in plain clothes, like John the Baptist, than to rush into the ministry without any preparation for it. A man who resolves to have an education, I mean a young man unincumbered with a family and has the pluck in him to endure hardness, will accomplish his purpose. And do not be in a hurry to marry. "Marriage is honorable," but an education is indispensable to him who would "make full proof of his ministry." But there is a number who are not able to take advantage of the schools. They have families dependent upon them, and some are advanced in life. What can they do? I am glad to testify to the self-improvement of many of this class who are studying the Bible and getting books as best they can, and who are anxious to receive instructions by means of institutes and in every way in which it is accessible. You want help. Your white brethren are deeply concerned about you and earnestly desire to extend the helping hand in every practical way.

SOUTHERN BAPTIST CONVENTION.

"The report of the Committee on Colored Population was submitted by Dr. Sydnor, of Virginia. The report expressed conviction of the importance of fraternal relation between the two races, and the duty of the whites to extend a helping hand to the colored people. In some respects the condition of the negroes is better, and in some respects worse. The negroes prefer their own people to minister to them, and our effort should be to help them with counsel and money. The committee approve of the work the Home Board is doing in this direction.

"Rev. Miller, of Arkansas, approves the report, and speaks words of commendation of the work the negroes are doing. He urges that we help them.

"Rev. Booker, colored, of Arkansas, speaks to the convention. He is not here to speak on social or political questions, nor an exodus movement. He is here to present the claims of the colored Baptists. We are one denominationally and sectionally. You are ahead of us, and we need your help. Especially I speak on education. In Arkansas we have established a colored Baptist college. The past year we had forty-five preachers at our school. What we need is your help. We need light among our people in Arkansas. It is your interest to help us."

REPORT OF THEOLOGICAL INSTRUCTOR APPOINTED BY THE GEORGIA BAPTIST CONVENTION.

"The interest of the preachers is unabated, and they express gratitude for the service rendered. Many of them exhibit a commendable desire for improvement, and receive gladly such aid as I can give them in procuring books. This I have been enabled to do to a limited extent by recommendations to the American Baptist Publication Society for Ministers' Libraries, which are furnished gratuitously by the society. The colored Baptists of Georgia are preparing to celebrate by appropriate services the hundredth anniversary of the organization of the First African Baptist Church in Savannah. It is worthy of record that this church, with others subsequently organized, was recognized by their white brethren as a regular Baptist church. As such it united with the Sunbury Association, and in its ministry and work in the cause of true religion has an honorable history. Upon the whole there are hopeful signs of progress in the ministry of the colored Baptists of Georgia."

It will be seen from the extracts which I have read that you have the sympathy of your white brethren; that they are ready to help by counsel and with money as far as they are able. The Georgia Baptist convention and the Home Mission Board of the Southern Baptist Convention have shown their willingness to aid you, not only by coöperation in the work of missionaries but by the appointment of a theological instructor, whose exclusive business it is to hold institutes for the benefit of your preachers and deacons and all others who choose to attend. Our Northern brethren have established a seminary in Atlanta, to which I advise every man, young and old, who can attend it to do so. Take every opportunity to get knowledge that will enable you to understand God's word under the enlightening power of the Holy Spirit. If you cannot go to Atlanta, do the best you can at home.

A minister is said to be a workman. Paul says, "According to the grace of God which is given unto me, as a wise masterbuilder, I have laid the foundation, and another buildeth thereon. But let every man take heed how he buildeth thereupon."—I. Cor., iii, 10. These words should ring in the ears and fill with trembling the heart of every man who stands before the people as a messenger from God. As a workman you cannot be too careful of the doctrines you preach and the materials you bring into the house of God. An intelligent consecrated ministry is the most important factor in the elevation, physically, intellectually and morally, of any people. You have opportunities never before opened to your race. Great opportunities bring grave responsibilities. With you preachers rests largely the future destiny of your race. You are their chosen leaders;

you mould their opinions, and give tone to society. You need to be "wise as serpents and harmless as doves." It is a tremendous responsibility that you bear; not only their well-being in the present life, but you are dealing with souls that shall live in heaven or hell forever.

> "'Tis not a cause of small import
> The pastor's care demands,
> But what might fill an angel's heart,
> And filled the Saviour's hands."

I pity the man who preaches for the praise of men, who fails to declare the whole counsel of God lest he offend his hearers. He will get his reward, but it will not be the "Well done, good and faithful servant," from the lips of the Master and the final Judge. The man who preaches for filthy lucre's sake, "supposing that gain is godliness," will receive his wages, but it will not be the "crown of life" that Paul expected. "To this man will I look, saith the Lord, even to him that is poor and of a contrite spirit, and trembleth at My word."—Is., lxvi, 2. "Not by might, nor by power, but by My spirit, saith the Lord of Hosts."—Zech., iv, 6. I have confined myself to this particular view of the subject because I regard it the very foundation of an effective ministry, and an effective ministry as an absolute necessity to the progress of your people, socially, morally, and in their material prosperity.

We view with heartfelt gratification the evidences of progress and prosperity manifest on this occasion. This is but the beginning of your career. What its future history shall be must depend chiefly upon yourselves. As the years roll on may they find you "forgetting those things that are behind, and reaching forth to those things that are before pressing towards the mark for the prize of the high calling of God in Christ Jesus." And when the warfare of life is over may each of you, preachers and people, be found in Christ and receive "the crown of life."

THE WANTS OF THE COLORED MINISTRY.

An Address Delivered by Rev. Alexander Ellis at the Centennial Celebration, June 7th, 1888.

This is rather a comprehensive subject, and to some extent it is fraught with vagueness. Our wants are many and varied. Some are reasonable while others are unreasonable. One minister may want a house and lot; another a horse and buggy.

One a new suit of clothes; another a few books. One may want popularity; another only a little rent-money, etc. Indeed it would be a difficult task to find any two men who want precisely the same thing.

But as our subject is a comprehensive one, and as our time is limited, we will confine ourselves to one aspect of it, and so endeavor to suggest a few thoughts relative unto and deducible from it.

In order fully to appreciate and discuss this subject, therefore, let us consider a few things pertaining to the Present Age and the Christian ministry suitable for it.

We are living in an age which is unquestionably the ripest in the history of the world. It is an age laden with all the forms of good—civilization, freedom, religion, virtue and happiness, all of which have been growing and accumulating from the beginning. This is an age richer in knowledge, experience and all the means of enjoyment than all the former ages taken together. It is richer in hope and expectation, because it is nearer the millennial day than any other age. It abounds in schemes and agencies for realizing this epoch more than any other. Moreover, it is the age in which we live, which has made us what we are, on which we reflect the influence of our character and doings, whether for good or evil, and which we are bound to render mightily efficient in ameliorating and blessing the ages which are to come.

Many are the hearts at this moment beating and panting, and many are the minds which are eagerly contriving and resolutely determined to do something which shall not only benefit and adorn the present age but create for it a perpetual claim on the warmest gratitude and sublimest admiration of coming generations. Legislators and politicians, philosophers and men of science, moralists and religionists, are all intent on a new and better order of things and the best method of achieving it.

The elevation of the country and the world in intelligence, in justice, in liberty, in moral improvement, and in all the means of private and social happiness is a subject which is occupying a greater number of ardent and generous spirits to-day more so than at any former period. As a matter of course our sympathies are chiefly with the religionists, those who profess to have no hope of the true advancement of either the present or any future generation save on the basis of a genuine christianity.

In common with other Protestant denominations, as Baptists we believe, and do insist, that the true enlightenment, renovation and happiness of this or any future age is absolutely dependent upon the deep and wide diffusion of the religion of

Jesus Christ, which calls for a ministry "worthy and well qualified" to preach its doctrines and precepts and administer its sacred ordinances. But to do this we must have a ministry much better reinforced in mental strength and vigor, as well as in more varied attainments and in more liberal temporal provision. Churches and communities are to-day calling for a ministry better able to meet all the requirements of the present age, and ministers are looking for churches better able to compensate them for their devotion and service, their capacities and gifts, so that they may live above penury and want. A hungry minister cannot preach. An untidy preacher cannot fitly represent the gospel of Jesus Christ, which is the quintessence of purity.

A preacher may not necessarily be profoundly versed in all sciences and literature; he may not be a master of all languages, not even those which are called sacred; he may not have threaded all the labyrinths and mazes of history; he may not be able to discuss the principles and deductions of philosophy; he may not have slaked his thirst at all the fountains of poetry, whose pellucid streams flow from the verdant land of imagination, emptying themselves into the ocean of the soul, where the tranquil breeze of love regales its recipient into the ecstacies of devotion; he may not have thoroughly studied and mastered the dogmas and tenets of all religions, and he may not be equipped for encountering and successfully repelling every conceivable objection against christianity; but he wants, and should have, the grand prerequisites of natural capacity, good common sense, and, above all, genuine piety. He should know the word of God, and be respectably read in general literature. In a word, he should have a mind to understand, a heart to feel, a tongue to speak and a message meet to be delivered. This last is a stern necessity.

In one respect, therefore, and that a deeply vital one, there is a demand on the present ministry of all denominations to see to it that its mental and spiritual life be of the strength and energy commensurate with the progress and calls of this present age. There are certain characteristics of the period which can be successfully dealt with by no ministry of ordinary mental vigor and attainment. Spiritual life, in its proper and normal degree, consists of love to God for his adorable perfections and benignant acts, of grateful devotedness to Christ for his matchless condescension and self-sacrifice in the work of our salvation, of an insatiable hungering and thirsting after righteousness in all its forms for Christ's sake, of warmest benevolence, in imitation of Him, for all our brethren of the human race, and of readiness to do or suffer whatever may savingly befriend them. It starts at the touch and thought of sin, is smitten and captivated by the beauty of holiness, and longs to be pervaded and clothed with it. It is familiar with the glories of the invisible world, is not seduced into a false estimate of the specious shadows of terrene things, sees with instant and piercing glance the priceless worth of souls, and is persuaded that in heaven, as well as upon earth, there is no work so angelic or God-like as to labor for the salvation of mankind.

Now it may be doubted whether the piety of the ministry in any section of the christian church is at present of this divine order. Otherwise, how is it that their labors, so extended and multiplied, not only from week to week, but from day to day, and seconded by all the manifold auxiliaries and agencies which they have created, gain so little on the irreligion and worldliness of the multitudes whom they are endeavoring to quicken in the life of godliness? Is it not the universal feeling with themselves and all who are interested in their success that there is a mournful disproportion between the efforts made and the results obtained? that for one who is rejoicing because his labors are richly blessed, there are twenty discouraged and perplexed by the fact that, while they have prophesied to "the valley of dry bones," there has been no divine breath to revive and animate them? And nothing would be more hopeful, whether for present or future progress, than for the whole ministry—of whatever rank, or race, or religion—to lay this matter to heart and to ask God, in deep humiliation and earnest prayer, that He would be pleased to shed light on their counsels and doings, and so replenish them and their labors with the grace of His holy spirit that in ardor of zeal and strength of faith, in personal sanctity and unsparing devotedness, and in quenchless sympathy with the utmost claims of their momentous vocation, they might resume their labors and find in them an unwonted refreshment, recompense and gratification. This would put them into harmony with the wants of the age, and give them power over whatever may have thus far resisted them, more so than the largest endowment of learning, knowledge and eloquence, by an increase and quickening of their spiritual life. They would have an instinctive perception of the truths most proper to be taught and enjoined; would deliver them with the divine and captivating unction which surpasses all the arts of rhetoric, and with the conscious presence of the Holy One granted only to lowly self-distrust and prayerful reliance on His aid. Nor would they have to lament that but few of superior capacity and gifts aspired to share the responsibility of their sacred office. Their improved and enlightened ministrations would infuse fresh life into their flocks, and thus yield a far greater number of pious young men, who, abandoning the mediæval rant and cant, would show themselves "worthy and well qualified" for their high christian service by the intelligence of their utterances and the gravity of their demeanor, while their own commanding example, now attracting so much veneration and love, and adorned with the fruits of holy usefulness would fire those youthful aspirants with a hallowed and noble emulation to be admitted to their priestly ranks without any other lure or compensation than the smile of their Saviour and the opportunity of serving his divine cause of salvation and benevolence.

And such a ministry whose spiritual life had been raised to that vigor and energy worthy of the faithful service of Christ, and our obligations to him would be unquestionably equal to the necessities of this day and generation. Shall we not, therefore, arise and watch and pray? Mourning over our deficiencies, humbled on account of our past failures, surveying the urgent claims of the multitude around us, and knowing wherein our chief strength for answering them lies, shall we not betake ourselves to the throne of grace and plead mightily for such a baptism of the holy spirit as shall conquer self and make us instrumental in effecting the salvation of others? So shall we best serve our age and realize in its sublimest sense the double benediction of being "blest and made a blessing."

THE WANTS OF THE COLORED MINISTRY.

BY REV. W. G. JOHNSON, AUGUSTA, GA.

The first thing necessary to prepare a man to preach the gospel of Christ is to receive the gospel himself. The apostle says, "First take heed to thyself, then to the doctrines." The preaching of the gospel is the proclaiming the news of salvation through Christ. No man can recommend Christ well except he knows Him. It is the religion of Christ that gives to the minister that burning eloquence that no training can give. Religion makes the flash of the eyes, the enthusiastic gestures, which are great auxiliaries in producing the desired effect. True religion alone makes a man a true representative of Christ on the earth.

A distinguished divine tells of a missionary who preached in a desolate country the glorious gospel of the kingdom, where the people could not understand the many doctrinal truths related, but the fiery zeal with which he spoke moved thousands to believe.

The next very important need is good morals. Even a christian with corrupt morals will fail to accomplish much good. Of the minister it ought to be said, "Behold an Israelite, indeed, in whom there is no guile." These prerequisites in ministerial character are not more wanting in the negro's ministerial qualification than that of any other people. But there are two things necessary that are more wanting generally in the colored ministry than in many others.

Education.—The indispensable need of ministerial education can't be too much emphasized. Education, according to Webster, is the cultivation of the mind and the training of the manners. Education is not the learning of a few Greek sentences, or to solve a few mathematical problems, but it is the result of these investigations upon the mind. It causes the mind to expand, and enables it to grapple with thousands of mysteries. Had we continued perfect as God created the first man, perhaps the perfection of our nature could have supplied in itself a sufficient tutor. As sickness and disease have necessitated the use of medicines and physicians to restore nature to its normal state, so the only end of education is to restore our natural nature to its proper state. Education is reason borrowed, which goes as far as possible to supply original perfection. It has been said that as physic may justly be called the art of restoring health, so education should be called the art of recovering to man his rational perfection.

2d. The manners are very essential. To this end, Pythagoras, Socrates, Plato and all of the ancient instructors labored. They endeavored to teach their pupils the nature of man, his true end, the right use of his faculties, the immortality of the soul, the agreeableness of virtue to the divine nature, the necessity of temperance, justice, mercy and truth. Education that does not refine the manners is not worth having. Education cultivates the mind, polishes the manners and opens up an avenue of new discoveries. It gives the possessor a keen-eyed, quick perception and a wonderful power of speech.

If education is so necessary for the lawyer who represents our interest at the bar of legal justice, how much more necessary is it for him who must grapple with the deep mysteries of God and who must be the counselor of our souls to be educated. No class of men appear before the public from two to three times a week as the clergy. No class of men appear before so large a number of persons at one time with original discourses as the preacher. Often the minister is called upon to speak upon the spur of the moment, hence the need of preparation. When disease makes an inroad upon the system and preys upon constitution, prostrating its victims, how we seek the skilled physician. How the physician trembles in dealing out the remedies, seeing it is a dangerous case. Since the physician for the body must thus be prepared, how much more should the prescriber for the soul be. A very distinguished divine once said: "I can meet the arguments of my opponent and look him in the face, but I can't walk up my pulpit stairs without my knees striking together in fear."

Oh, how vast and important the work of saving souls. The scriptures say, "He that win souls is wise." The gospel must be preached sublimely though simply, and simply though sublimely. We live in an age of progress, in an age of mental excitements, and he that doth not heed the mandate, "get knowledge," must take a back seat. The vast number of men and women coming from our schools each year sets forth most strikingly the urgent need of an educated ministry. Water will seek its level. Other denominations are educating their ministry, and if our pulpits remain unfilled by intelligence, our own children will leave us and be caught in other nets. The apostles were not ignorant men; they were in advance of the masses. Besides, the need of education could have been more easily dispensed with, since they walked in the immediate presence of Christ.

The fathers, whose names we revere and whose memory we cherish, have done well. They have accomplished much. We love them for it, and when they are gone and our kindness prompts us to look over the graves where their bodies shall lie, we will moisten their dust with our tears and exclaim, "Thank God the fathers lived." We must recollect that the fathers lived in a time when there were only two successful denominations, Methodist and Baptist, and as the Baptists had the Bible on their side they easily predominated. But things are changing. Silver-tongued orators of other denominations are trespassing on Baptist ground, and stealing the hearts of our young people.

Catholicism is growing into popularity among the negroes. The fathers did not have this to contend with. The Catholic church is building schools, teaching our children, riveting their doctrine in them so strongly that it will not be easily removed. All they ask is to get the young, and they will have the future church. As our people become educated, they will seek the educated pulpit. Atheism, skepticism and Catholicism, all make it more important to have an educated minister.

BOOKS.

The educated mind is always in search of truth. Always thirsting for more knowledge. Always exclaiming, "Give me understanding, for education is the only means of ascertaining that all men are fools." One book read again and again may lose its nutriment and become dry. We need good libraries containing books upon such subjects as we are compelled sometimes to handle. Each minister ought to have such a library. If he alone cannot buy it, those in his community ought to raise a fund and secure it for him. The American Baptist Publication Society has done much to aid the poor colored ministers in securing books. Many hundreds of dollars have been given to Georgia in this way.

MONEY.

The minister is the greatest officer under heaven. His calling is of God. No position should be so respected as his, for it is written, "How beautiful upon the mountains are the feet of him that bringeth tidings of good, that publisheth salvation and saith unto Zion, thy God reigneth."—Is. lii, 7.

Notwithstanding the dignity of the minister, the immensity of his work and the indespensible need of performing this task, he is the most poorly paid officer under heaven. The common idea among men is that the minister must necessarily be poor. The lawyer charges his fee and it is paid. The physician makes out his bill, presents it, and it is paid, but the poor minister, who is the spiritual counselor and soul's physician, must allow some one else to make out his bill, which is paid or neglected.

The colored ministry is suffering for want of means to-day, and especially the Baptists. He is poorly promised and poorly paid. He is not promised much and not paid what he is promised. Many people think that the minister ought to suffer; that his wife ought to go half-dressed; that he ought to be equal or below them in the financial situation in life. The very class who holds so tenaciously to these base ideas, are those when they see the minister in good circumstances, if erecting a dwelling, or accumulating property, however great was the sacrifice made to do this, will deny him their support and will implore others to do likewise. Hence we learn the rule to do well is to suffer, to have money is to lose friends, honor and salary. If the minister is expected to feed his flock with spiritual food then they must furnish means for him to support his family.

It is said in the scripture that he who will not provide for his house is worse than an infidel. Oftentimes the minister can not preach because he is confused about his temporal affairs. This spirit among our people is very damaging to ministerial success. The servant is worthy of his hire.

THE RELATION OF THE WHITE AND COLORED BAPTISTS.

BY REV. T. J. HORNSBY, OF AUGUSTA, GA.

Mr. Chairman, Ladies and Gentlemen of the Great Centennial of the Colored Baptists of Georgia:

Among others I have been appointed to address you at some hour upon the "Relation of the Colored and White Baptists of Georgia, As It Was in the Past, Is Now, and As It Should Be in the Future." According to the assignment of my name, I find it my duty to speak mainly of the relation as it was in the past, or the days that preceded emancipation. The white Baptists embraced, believed and preached the same doctrine that they embrace, believe and preach to-day, contending most sternly for a converted membership and the solemn immersion in water of the professed believer in the name of the Father, Son and Holy Ghost by a properly authorized administrator. The colored Baptists embraced, believed and preached the same, yea, the very same.

One might suppose from the non or faint association of the white and colored Baptists in *ante bellum* days, that there was no relation existing between them, but when we examine the basis of their hope in Christ and ferret out the principle of each, we find them the sons of the same Father, operated upon by the same Spirit, redeemed by the same Saviour, therefore they must have been brethren. The white Baptists believed and preached the very same doctrine that the apostles believed and preached, and the "brother in black" believed the same. Hence, before God they were brethren, and, as the apostle says, there was no difference. If the brother in white was drawn to God by the influence of the gospel, and by accepting Christ as the Redeemer, was adopted into His family, and thereby became sons of God, the brother in black was likewise drawn and adopted, placed in the same category, with the same identical relationship to God.

On account of condition or circumstances one may ignore a brother by actions, and refuse to accord to him a brother's recognition, but it does not destroy the relationship. In the by-gone days the Baptist church was entered by white people by repentance, regeneration and baptism by a properly authorized administrator. The colored people did the same, or entered the church the same way. I assure you, that with your humble servant there is nothing pleasant in recalling the past, fraught with such indifference as may appear in discussing this subject, but history says that we are now 100 years old, and the world presumes that when one has lived so long, when he talks the truth should be told. So, if in this discussion you should get a glimpse of anything dark and unworthy of a Baptist, you will pardon your servant, as this is the first hundred years he has seen.

In most of the white churches there was a colored element attached, who had sought the same Saviour under trying circumstances. They came with fear and trembling and related their experience, and if it met the approbation of their owners, who sometimes were Baptists and sometimes strangers to my God, they were given a pass and allowed to unite with the church, and thank God, sometimes indorsing him or her as a good, obedient "nigger." Before the church they professed Christ; in the sight of the people they were buried in baptism, which made us brethren, and the white Baptists knew it, and they also knew that we as a mass didn't know it. So the time of our ignorance God may have winked at, but it left us brethren still, and sons of the same God.

If I may speak of individual treatment of this fraternity, the negro Baptists were quite as kind and polite as the white brother, for in the week the white Baptists called him Pete, Hamp and Bill, but sometimes on Sunday they would say Peter, Hampton and William, while this negro Baptist, in his presence, would invariably use the same title, "Master," (behind his back something else, of course). Neither was perfect.

Where the colored people existed, their converts were baptized by the pastor in charge, who was (of course) the white Baptist. When he had gotten through dipping the white converts, in walked the colored proselyte and was buried in the same water; yea, sometimes in the same spot.

They worshipped in the same church edifice, occupying the seats in the rear. They sang the same songs the white Baptist sung, listened to the same sermon, joining in the service of song; but, I tell you, in this capacity they were not near so noisy as in these latter days.

After the white Baptist had been served with bread and wine, it was taken to the brother in color. Though a little late, it was the same supper prayed over by the same pastor.

Sometimes in the summer, when the days were long, the pastor would preach especially for them on Sunday afternoon, allowing them to advance nearer the front, and, if time allowed, they were permitted to offer public prayer, and this to our ancestors was a jubilee, to know that sometimes they could call on their God at church.

The pastor would preach to them earnestly and faithfully, and at times growing truly eloquent in his discourse, and, among many other good things, he would not forget to exhort them to obey their masters, to be honest and industrious, for this is your reasonable service. And, I tell you, the doctrine to the brother in color was both appropriate and timely.

When services closed they were quietly dismissed, and they hurried home on foot to take their brother's horse and bring him cool water to drink; but I can't say in the name of Christ. O! yes, the colored brother was ready and willing, when duty came, to brave it like a man. If allowed to pray, he would arouse you with his pleadings; if called upon to preach, he would astonish you in doctrine, and if let loose to sing, he would charm his more favored brother until tears fell from his eyes. In other parts of the rural districts, where the population of the colored people would warrant, they were permitted to have a house of their own. They gladly seized the opportunity, felling the trees and hewing the timbers by night, singing:

> "Must I be carried to the skies
> On flowery beds of ease,
> While others fought to win the prize,
> And sailed through bloody seas?"

They were in these houses of worship preached to mainly by white pastors, but sometimes by a minister of their own color, such as Rev. Joseph Walker (deceased), Revs. Nathan Walker, Stepney Martin, Lewis B. Carter, E. C. Crumby, Father Bealle and some others. When this liberty was used they were overseed by a white man, perhaps a white Baptist.

This intimidated him, but being zealous of good works he prayed on. In this city, Macon, Atlanta and Augusta, they had hours of worship apart from the white Baptists, whose pulpits were ably filled by such pioneers as Andrew Bryan, Andrew Marshall, Campbell, Tillinghast, Frank Quarles, Peter Johnson, Henry Watts and Henry Johnson. These men stood in doctrine shoulder to shoulder with the white brother, holding up the gospel banner, crying, "One Lord, one faith, and one baptism."

Their churches with them contended earnestly for the faith once delivered to the saints. They required a converted membership like their brother; baptized like him, but quicker; sang like him, but louder; prayed like him, but in more haste; preached like him, but under greater embarrassments, for they feared God, their masters and the devil.

There were among the white Baptist family good men who helped the brother in black, such as Rev. J. H. T. Kilpatrick, Sr., deceased, the lamented son of Mercer, Rev. W. H. Davis, Rev. E. R. Carswell, Sr., and Rev. W. L. Kilpatrick. I say they have rendered valuable service in due time.

Our brothers' situation and circumstances were better than ours, as they possessed capital, culture and land, while we had neither. But bless God, the same being was our Father and the same heaven our home. O yes, in the same length of time, with the same means, we can do all that our brother has done, except it be to persecute and ignore a brother and think that we are doing God's service.

See we stand here to-day frank enough to acknowledge our brother's intellectual superiority, humble enough to confess his financial gain over us, yet bold enough to say that we are equals before God and one in His church—one common family of the living God, to His commands let us bow. Part of this host have crossed the flood and we are crossing.

Oh, astonishing oneness, in which I see the Father in His manifold wisdom, Jesus in love that passeth all understanding, the Spirit in grace, which defies all the power of earth and hell to make void the place occupied by the colored Baptists of Georgia, or resist the influence which is being so powerfully exerted by this grand old army.

We are sorry to say that while we have been brethren for the last century, the world hasn't been able to discern that brotherly affection which characterizes brethren. Apart from selfishness, bias, prejudice, animosity, with hatred toward none, but charity for all, let us grasp our brother by the hand and say to him: "You are bone of our bone and flesh of our flesh; you are our brethren. We saw your track an hundred years ago, but you had ascended the hill of intelligence and the ladder of fame. Ever since Andrew Bryan espied you we have been trying on your clothes, and they have fitted many of our rank, and they appear perfectly graceful in them. A hat like that one you sometimes wear has been put on the head of Rev. E. K. Love, and we can justly hail him D. D., so that in earnest, in faith and in love we offer you our hand. Oh, brethren, for 100 years we have been trying to catch you. We really thought sometimes that you were running from us instead of running toward us. However, while we were perplexed, we kept our hope. Though distressed we have not despaired. We swam rivers, ploughed valleys, scaled very high mountains. We sang the songs of the Lord; we prayed, we preached, we cried, we fought the devil, we called for help, we have been bruised soldiers fallen on the field; the enemy tried hard to cut off our communication, but thank God, we are by your side at the age of an hundred years. You were our brethren in *ante bellum* times, you are our brethren now, and you will be our brethren to-morrow. Where you live we will live, where you die we will die, and by your graves will we be buried; and when the records of our earthly career shall have utterly perished, our work shall fill heaven with its wonders and eternity in praise to God."

Let the spirit of God shine until the world shall see no difference; shine until this knotty question shall no longer be discussed. Shine, spirit; shine until this Baptist influence shall not only be felt in Georgia, but all over God's universe. Shine, great spirit; shine until the white and colored Baptists of Georgia, locked arm in arm, shall tread all the powers of darkness down and win the well fought day.

Oh, God, let thy spirit shine until this great united army shall be saved in heaven with Thee, and be permitted to lift the glowing strains :

> "Praise God from Whom all blessings flow,
> Praise him, ye creatures from below;
> Praise Him with us, angelic host,
> Praise Father, Son and Holy Ghost."

THE RELATION OF THE WHITE AND COLORED BAPTISTS IN THE PAST, NOW, AND AS IT SHOULD BE IN THE FUTURE.

BY REV. G. S. JOHNSON, THOMSON, GA.

To this General Baptist Family:

DEAR BRETHREN.—What does all this mean? From whence cometh this people that compose this choir, which renders the sweet music which fills our hearts with praises and gratitude to God? Is it possible that this despised race has come to this? Is the oppressed just freed, and have made this wonderful progress? My thoughts have taken a retrospective view of the past, and have traversed Bethlehem's plain, where God's Son was born, and when that angelic choir sang in the air the sweetest music earth ever heard—"Glory to God in the highest, and on earth peace and good will toward men." We are but out upon the plains; we have just caught the ball that our fathers started to rolling an hundred years ago. Though they were illiterate, they preached the gospel of the Son of God as best they could. They understood clearly this truth: "One Lord, one faith, and one baptism;" and, bless God, in one hundred years we have caught the sweet old story.

All nationalities have days to celebrate in honor of some historical event. The negro Baptists of Georgia were organized into a church in this grand old Forest City one hundred years ago, and we have come from the mountains and from the valleys to celebrate it with thanksgiving.to God for keeping an oppressed people, and enabling them to "contend so earnestly for the faith that was once delivered to the saints." I feel highly honored to be thought worthy to take part in such a grand affair, though I feel my inability to perform the task that was assigned me. While I attempt to discuss this topic— the relationship that now exists between the white and negro Baptists—I am here with prejudice toward none, but brotherly love for all.

Israel of old was persecuted and ostracized, but the God who has always fought the battles of His chosen, and caused them to be victorious over all their oppositions. was with them. Our God fought our battles through the darkest days of slavery. We are not the only people who have undergone religious persecution. As far back as 1535, when the Roman church attempted to persecute the Huguenots, the priests obtained the "royal edict" from the King to totally suppress the printing of the Bible. Their effort to turn the world back failed then, and will fail now. Furthermore, I would not attempt to discuss the subject of social equality. No, not I. I am only here to speak for an oppressed people, and of our religious affiliation. We are brethren of the same family.

There is one thing you'll not find among the negro Baptists that is found among the white Baptists. Among the negroes there are very few Free Will Baptists and open communionists. They believe that the Lord Jesus instituted the supper for none but converted and legally baptized disciples, that is, by immersion, and this baptism must be performed by the proper administrator—one who has been legally baptized according to the faith of the gospel. Have you not seen, in all of your life, in a family, two brothers, one blessed with this world's goods, and the other seemed as if fate was against him? And on account of popular sentiment that brother who was blessed with this world's goods scorned the brother who was not blessed with the same, but through whose veins ran the same blood, for he was the son of the same father and mother. Yet he could not resist popular sentiment, and had to treat him as though he were not. And when he had company, instead of his unfortunate brother feeling welcome to come in at the front gate was forced to go in at the back gate. Instead of being permitted to enter the house to engage with the guests upon the subjects under consideration, was debarred from these privileges.

Our white Baptist brethren do not deny our relation through the blood of our Lord Jesus Christ, but popular sentiment is so much against social equality that our brethren are afraid to allow us religious affiliation for fear that it might be termed social equality. Yet they do recognize us as brethren, for we are one in doctrine and church ordinances. Not that I don't believe that our white Baptist brethren are interested in us; far be that from me; for they have shown their interest by the appointment of Rev. Dr. McIntosh to labor among the ministers and deacons of our churches, and his work has redounded to the glory of God and to the uplifting of our people, for which I say, "Bless God."

In their coöperation with our Conventional Board at the last session of the Southern Baptist Convention held in Baltimore, Md., a resolution was passed looking to the establishment of a better feeling between the white and negro Baptists of the South, for which we are grateful. But take us in our religious assemblies, such as our conventions and associations, where fraternal delegates or corresponding messengers are sent. When they send them to our bodies we receive them gladly and accord them brotherly affiliation; but when we visit their bodies in like capacity, instead of being treated as brethren our names are received and we are given back seats as usual. Dear brethren, I say this not in a harsh mood, but my authority for entertaining this as a breach of our relation as the great Baptist family of this grand old Empire State of the South is from the great head of this family.

St. John, xv., 12-17: "This is my commandment, that ye love one another, as I have loved you. Greater love hath no man than this, that a man lay down his life for his friends. Ye are my friends, if ye do whatsoever I command you. Henceforth I call you not servants; for the servant knoweth not what his lord doeth: but I have called you friends; for all things that I have heard of my Father I have made known unto you. Ye have not chosen me, but I have chosen you, and ordained you, that ye should go and bring forth fruit, and that your fruit should remain: and whatsoever ye shall ask of the Father in my name, He may give it you. These things I command you, that ye love one another."

This is my authority. I am sure that the Lord Jesus Christ hath given this world into the hands of his recognized church. I believe He hath divided it off geographically, and commissioned his church, irrespective of color, to take the part allotted them—the north her part, the east her part, the south her part and the west her part; and this Baptist banner must wave over this world, as the star-spangled banner waveth over these United States. But we cannot conquer, and carry this world to the Lord Jesus Christ, while we allow these little petty differences to separate us. "In union there is strength." In armies the generals should be in union, and should meet and consult with each other as to the best way of attacking their enemies. The Lord Jesus has committed His church into the hands of the ministry, and they must watch for souls, as to the Master they must give account.

Now as to the white and colored pastors: Do we meet in council, and advise one another relative to the work of the Master, or do we stand aloof from each other? Do we grasp each other by the hands as servants of the Lord Jesus Christ, or do we pass each other as mere strangers? In large cities, to some extent they meet their brethren in council, when called on, and if not in company, on the streets they will speak; but in most of the smaller towns, where prejudice runs higher, they pass you by as a mere stranger. I have lived in towns in this State where a white pastor who had negro members in his church passed them by as mere strangers. But I must speak of a model pastor, Rev. J. H. Kilpatrick, D. D., pastor of White Plains Baptist Church, who would not pass his brethren by without a word of advice and brotherly greeting. Rev. Mr. Eden and a few others have the same christian spirit.

The success of our cause depends largely upon the generals; therefore there should be perfect love in our ranks, as we are commanders-in-chief, for love among the generals will create love among the soldiers. I now close by reading you the following poem, composed by Mr. P. R. Butler, of Augusta, Ga.:

UNION.

"Let us, brethren, live together
In the vineyard of the Lord;
Let there be no strife among us;
Let us rest upon His word.

"Let us battle for Christ's kingdom,
Battle 'gainst the powers of hell;
Let us follow in His footsteps;
Let us fight the Infidel.

"Let us not stand idly waiting,
　Grasping ostracism's hand;
Let us clasp our hands in union;
　On the solid rock let's stand.

"Christ has no respect of color,
　Therefore, let us stand for God;
Let us follow in the footsteps
　That our Master's feet have trod.

"Let us fight for lovely Zion;
　Christ, our Lord, is looking down.
Let us stand, and fight, and conquer,
　For the world in sin is drown'd.

"Enemies attempt to bribe us,
　Let us fight until we die;
Let affection dwell among us;
　Angels watch us from the sky.

"We are one in Christ, our Master,
　Then united let us stand;
We're the people of His pasture;
　Holy angels 'round us stand.

"Friendship, love and truth let's cherish,
　Till the evening shadows fall;
If we are His true disciples,
　Let us hearken to His call.

"Let us, on this field of battle,
　Stand for God till time shall end;
Let's tear down the thrones of darkness
　For our King, our dying friend.

"Let us rally for the Bible;
　Let the Church of God hold sway;
Let us stand for Christ and Jordan,
　Till that awful Judgment Day.

THE AMERICAN BAPTIST PUBLICATION SOCIETY AND ITS WORK FOR THE COLORED PEOPLE.

BY REV. E. K. LOVE, D. D.

There have arisen in the North many societies looking to the amelioration of the condition of the negroes in the South, the abolitionists and other kindred associations. They have done a good work, for which we are profoundly grateful; but that society which endeavored to give us the word of God and thereby educate our morals, sweeten our character, and lift up our people to heaven and God must be greater than them all.

Among the institutions that have done most for us in this line is the American Baptist Publication Society. He who protects my manhood commands my respect and admiration; he who ameliorates my condition should have my support; he who refines my manners and trains my thinking faculties makes me a better citizen; he who educates me arms me for future usefulness to mankind, adds new charms to civilization, and lends science a welcome student and advocate; he who gives me money adds to my comforts; he who gives me water slakes my thirst; he who gives me a home shelters my body; he who gives me raiment protects my body, but he who gives me the Bible puts eternal life in my reach. He brings God nearer to me, he draws me nearer to God. He protects and defends my soul. He gives me the bread of life, of which if a man eats he shall never hunger. He gives me the water of life, which shall be in me a well of water springing up unto everlasting life. He gives me that which shall build me up and which forms the basis of true character and manhood. Any structure which is not built upon the word of God will crumble and fall and be forgotten.

The American Baptist Publication Society has been for many years scattering broadcast over this land the word of God. Just what we would have done but for the American Baptist Publication Society we do not know, except that God would have in some way provided Himself a way of communicating His truth to fallen mankind. But since He has seen fit to use the American Baptist Publication Society as a mighty instrument in flooding the country with a knowledge of Jesus in many tracts and the Bible, pure and simple, let us support the society by patronizing it in the purchase of all of our religious literature and bless God for its existence. It is our society. We have never been ashamed to beg it, and the society has never been above helping us.

Many of our preachers have received libraries from this society, and hence the society has preached the gospel very effectually in Georgia through them. The more we support this society the stronger it will grow, and therefore be the better prepared to preach the gospel in Georgia, and doubtless will preach more effectually the glorious gospel of the Son of God in Georgia. The society has been scattering seeds of kindness for many years, and we must leave the grand story for eternity to tell of its pleasing, munificent and glorious harvest. Thank God, that this society did not forget the negroes while it was scattering blessings all around. The work of the society has been of incalculable good to the negroes, and should, as it does, form a very important part in our history.

I look forward with pleasing anticipation to the day when, in our Southland, the Publication Society will have a branch house in all of the large Southern cities, managed by competent, honest and faithful negroes. This state of things will not come in the natural order of things. It is too pure a gem to be found lying promiscuously around on the ground. It must be dug up, for it is deep down, locked in the womb of the future. I confess that we have not deserved this recognition yet, but as we are the children of the future, it is not, in my opinion, raising the standard too high to aim at it. I oppose unmerited recognition in church or state. I think it is injurious to the recipients and unwise in the bestower. We can merit it, and whatever we merit we can demand. We need a wiser organization and concentration of our forces. We need more system in giving. We must urge a constant giving. The work of the Lord is a life-time business, and however much a person may do to-day there is something for him to do to-morrow, except he dies. We must cure our people of a spasmodic giving. The christian's work is no more spasmodic than his life is. No people have gone to success in a day. No person can enjoy what is given as he can that which is earned.

We ought to set apart a day, at least once a year, to take a collection in all of our churches for the Publication Society. When our patronage to the society and our wisdom to manage affairs shall be fully attested, I doubt not the inevitable conclusion that the recognition about which I have spoken will follow, as the irresistible fruit of well-doing. The churches should be very careful about the character of literature that is used in their Sunday schools. The society is endeavoring to put the gospel in reach of the children, to do which it has employed missionaries in almost every State to do Sunday school work. The work done among children in the Sunday school promises to yield the richest harvest. Those who reach the children with the gospel reach and bless the nation at home. The society is doing this, and hence is reaching the children at home early in the morning before they go out to play, and to prepare them for bruises, temptations and duties of the day. This is almost saving the nation in the cradle. The man who is leading this great society is the Rev. Dr. Griffith, whom I now, with unfeigned pleasure, present you as the speaker of this hour. May God bless you, my brother, and the great society he has called you to lead. May your fruit abound unto holiness, and the end an everlasting life, and when on earth our work is done, may we be gathered home to the saints' rest, where the sower and the reaper shall rejoice together. Then shall you and the faithful host you have and are leading never regret your labors in the vineyard of the Lord. "For I reckon that the sufferings of this present time are not worthy to be compared with the glory which shall be revealed in us. For the earnest expectation of the creature waiteth for the manifestation of the sons of God." God bless your labor, for Jesus' sake.

THE AMERICAN BAPTIST PUBLICATION SOCIETY AND ITS WORK FOR THE COLORED PEOPLE.

BY REV. N. W. WATERMAN, OF THOMASVILLE.

Brother Chairman and Brethren of the State Baptist Centennial Committee of Georgia and Friends:

It becomes my duty this morning to address you upon the subject, "The American Baptist Publication Society and its Work for the Colored People." This institution is the offspring, or grew out of the Tract Society, established in 1824, as the result of the mature consideration of earnest and faithful-hearted men and women, of what was then regarded as the great need of the Baptists. For the establishment of the Tract Society a meeting was called. Only eighteen men and seven women responded; and there, in that meeting, after prayerful deliberation, the Baptist General Tract Society, now the American Baptist Publication Society, was formed. Perhaps those noble-hearted pioneers had no greater object in view than the issuing of tracts for the special benefit of the unsaved, and to unify the Baptist family the land over. But God, in whose name the work was begun, granted His benediction upon the feeble undertaking, so that this and still other objects have been successfully prosecuted by it. That the formation of this institution is the work of God through human agencies we cannot have the least hesitation, if its history is to be considered. Its existence, seemingly, is proof of its continuance, though in the beginning it had very severe trials. At times its dissolution seemed sure and sudden, because of financial embarrassments. While those christian brethren, then in front of the institution, saw the almost inevitable catastrophe that hung just over this well-begun work, they were about to abandon hope. Doubtless they prayed to God for help, and in answer to their prayers, from some unexpected and perhaps unknown sources money was sent them for the prosecution of their work. Then there began to beam a ray of hope, that nerved them to more determined efforts. The work was God's, and He raised up friends everywhere to come to its rescue, till, in 1840, when was felt the need of increasing its labors, the name of the "Baptist General Tract Society" was dropped, and the society began to exist under the name of the "American Baptist Publication Society," assuming, at the same time, the great work of caring for the Sunday schools and the publication of books. Under that name it still exists, being under the skillful management of wise and faithful men, led, as was Israel of old, by a pillar of cloud by day and by a pillar of fire by night, until it has become the pride of the Baptist denomination in America.

The organization of the society was as the seed sown in good ground: it sprung up; though surrounded by thorns and thistles, it grew; the winds blew upon it and shook it, but its roots clung downwards firmer and firmer to the ground, taking hold on rocks, and its branches reared toward heaven. The thorns, thistles and tempest served to strengthen it, till at last we have an institution—in respect of its growth, its success in furthering its object, and the good accomplished by it—that stands peer to any institution of its kind anywhere. It unmistakably meets the great exigencies of the Baptist denomination. Its books, tracts, periodicals and papers ought to be found in every home, Sunday school and church of the Baptist family.

Books are to man as company. How many characters trained in the right direction have been switched off the track by associating with bad company? And how many weak Baptist parents and children have been led away from the faith of the Baptists by studying at their homes and Sunday schools literature other than Baptist? To check this tide of floating annoyance we must place into the hands and homes of our great denomination' literature that breathes the very doctrines and sentiments of the Baptists. This emergency the American Baptist Publication Society meets. Its publications are strictly Baptistic, and tend to unify the Baptist family in doctrine and sentiment. Its accomplishment in this direction cannot be reckoned. Who can realize the good that results from the distribution of religious tracts and the thousands of Bibles given away by this institution to poor individuals and schools annually. By these means thousands of souls have been converted, and have become faithful and conscientious members of the Baptist church. An exceeding great multitude of immortal souls snatched from eternal ruin, stands to evince the incalculable worth to the denomination. Ministers of the gospel and Sabbath school workers have received from the society gratuitously many very valuable books, which have been of great worth to them in the prosecution of their work. The Sunday school literature published by the society, such as the international series, have been and are of inestimable worth to the denomination, not only in leading the young to Christ, but in establishing them in the doctrines of the Bible and instructing the old, so that they are not to be moved by every wind of doctrine.

The society has not manifested prejudice in its methods of work. Its labors are not confined to the American soil, nor to white Baptists, nor to negro Baptists. Its motto has been "Onward to Conquest." It has pushed its work across the ocean into Sweden, France, Italy, Turkey, Switzerland, Africa and other countries, so that on every hand they are constantly cheered with the news of the glorious results of their labors. The society's work among the negro Baptists of these United States, according to their ability, has been cheering. They have given our Sunday schools thousands of dollars' worth of Bibles and other reading matter. They have now in nearly every State and Territory missionaries and colporteurs traveling in every direction, and everywhere preaching the gospel and organizing Sunday schools and churches, giving to those not able to buy the Bible the Word of God. Who can estimate the good done by this institution for our people? Only God. Here we were when emancipated with but a small percentage of general culture. Though we were Baptists, we were unintelligent. A compromising, a sort of anything-will-do-Baptists. With such to contend with, there is no telling where we would have landed. Perhaps we would have lost our substance, having nothing left us but the mere hull or name Baptist. Doubtless we would have been a little of every denomination. We can but thank God for the successful work of the society among us as negro Baptists in assisting us to do our work intelligently. It has done for us what we could not do for ourselves. When we laid by the wayside, torn, bleeding and powerless, gripped in the poisonous talons of ignorance and superstition, the society, Good Samaritanlike, took us up, and is still strengthening us in our weakness to go forward in the great work assigned us. It is everywhere dispensing its liberalities, leading a host to Christ and the doctrines which he has taught.

Never should we allow ourselves to think that this noble institution belongs to the white Baptists of America alone, but to us as well, though managed by white brethren. Its books, periodicals and other literature are as accessible to us at the same charges as to them. Its charities are as freely extended to us as to them. It can and has already done more for us than it can ever hope to be remunerated, and is still making greater efforts to build up our people.

Its object being to promote evangelical religion by means of the Bible, printing press, colportage and the Sunday school makes it an institution unfounded upon financial consideration to benefit a few. It is not to enrich a few but to bless the people. Every negro Baptist in America should feel proud of the society. Every Baptist Sunday school and church should be encouraged to use their Sunday school supplies and books. Not only that but they should be called upon to give donations to the society, and thus assist them to further prosecute their grand and glorious work. Whatever we might now be able to do for the society would be but a scanty return. Let us hold up its arms, give our patronage and donations, our sympathy and prayers, that it may live till the end of time a mighty agent in the hand of God for the promotion of evangelical religion and bringing back all sects and creeds to the doctrine of one Lord, one faith and one baptism.

THE BIBLE AS BELIEVED BY BAPTISTS.

BY REV. J. C. BRYAN.

This presumes that Baptists believe the Bible in a peculiar manner, or in an altogether emphatic sense, and this is true. This is the very matter of my contention.

All christians profess to believe the Bible, especially the Protestant christians.

Chillingworth's immortal words have been accepted as the motto of nearly all denominations—"The Bible! The Bible!" the religion of Protestants, and yet the motto belongs to Baptists with a propriety which other bodies of christians can not claim justly.

Baptists found their pretensions on the Bible, derive from the Bible their tenets, and appeal to the Bible as the justification of their practices.

To go into particulars, Baptists believe

1. That the Bible is truly inspired, that it is God's own book—God breathed. They believe that holy men of old wrote it as they were moved by the Holy Spirit. They do not hold it simply the best of books, the greatest of books, but as a divine book. They maintain not simply that it contains a revelation of God's will, but that it is such a revelation. I do not mean to enter upon theories of inspiration, whether oral or dynamic, whether sacred writers were simply the penmen and amanuenses of the Holy Spirit, or wrote freely under a

simple divine illumination and impulse. All that I insist on now is that the Bible is truly the Word of God, and as such, is distinguished from all other books.

No work of human genius approaches it or is like it. Some parts of the Bible no doubt are more valuable than other parts, but this is no disparagement of it as being inspired throughout.

The Baptists believe that the Bible is a finished book—that the sacred canon is completed. They do not believe in a progressive revelation or a progressive orthodoxy. They grant, indeed that the Bible may be more truly interpreted, but they deny that additions have been made or will be made to the substance of its teachings.

Not a few so-called christians in our day hold that the Bible is inspired only as all works of high genius are inspired, such as those of Shakspeare and Milton. Far away from this opinion is the Baptist estimate of the Bible.

2. Baptists believe that the Bible is the sole and sufficient directory in religious faith and practice.

Roman Catholics believe in the Bible, but they put the church and Pope above it. Many exalt what they call the "Christian consciousness" above the Bible, or to a level with it, and practically say that we are to believe the Bible only so far as it harmonizes with our own judgment and feelings. We cannot help thinking and saying that it is through an imperfect faith in the Bible with some denominations that sprinkling has taken the place of immersion in the act of baptism, and that infants' baptism has been introduced into the church, and that aristocratic forms of church government has been allowed to supplant the simple democracy of the New Testament.

Baptists reject all human authority on the formation, creeds and rules and conduct, and claim that the Bible is the first and last appeal in religious matters.

3d. Baptists believe that the Bible is a simple book, easily understood by persons of the right spirit. The Bible is its own interpreter. Hence, Baptists believe in the right of private judgment, the sacred and inviolable rights which they have been the defenders of unto death.

Let us beware of making the Bible an idol or of thinking that its mere presence in the house is enough. Baptists believe, as to the Bible, that it will be of no avail unless it pass into practice, etc. We thank God for the Bible and for salvation through Jesus Christ our Lord, and for the gift of the holy spirit to enlighten our minds. May our centennial celebration be one of success and great joy, and redound to the glory of God, and to the advancement of our Redeemer's kingdom on earth.

THE BIBLE AS BELIEVED BY BAPTISTS.

BY REV. G. M. SPRATLING, BRUNSWICK, GA.

Having been invited by your committee to speak on this important subject, I cheerfully comply. Baptists are often asked for information respecting their faith and distinctive practices. We must give the Bible for our answer. The Bible "was written by men divinely inspired, and is a perfect treasure of heavenly instruction. It has God for its author, salvation for its end, truth without mixture of error for its matter. It reveals the principle by which God will judge us, and therefore shall remain to the end of the world the true center of christian union and the supreme standard by which all human conduct, creed and opinions shall be tried."

Let us begin with the New Testament before us. Who can read that blessed book with serious attention without coming to the conclusion that the religion upon which it treats is that which Baptists believe and practice? It is personal and voluntary. None are worthy to be called christians but those who worship God in the spirit, rejoicing in Christ Jesus, and have no confidence in the flesh.—Phil., iii, 4.

When Moses addressed the Israelites and exhorted them to obedience, he included their children in his exhortation, because the children were in the covenant. Judaism, with all of its privileges and responsibilities, was hereditary. The rights and duties of the parents became the rights and duties of their offspring as such. It is not so now; I mean under the new dispensation. We are not born christians nowadays, and neither can there be born such; but they become christians when they repent and believe the gospel. The Apostle John makes known that fact (chap. i, 12-13): "But as many as received Him, to them gave He power to become the sons of God, even to them that believe on his name: which were born, not of blood, nor of the will of the flesh, nor of the will of man, but of God."

Judaism was a national institution, but christianity is an individual blessing. The Jews were a nation—dealt with as such, and separated from all other people by their peculiar rites and ceremonies; but christians are believers, and made fellow-citizens of the household of faith. By reading the New Testament, we find that "There is neither Greek nor Jew, circumcision nor uncircumcision, barbarian, Scythian, bond nor free: but Christ is all, and in all."—Col., iii., 11.

Hence when the apostles wrote to christian churches their mode of addressing was altogether different from that adopted by Moses. They did not say you and your children, or represent the children as in covenant with God, and therefore entitled to certain rights and bound to the performance of certain duties. The churches to which they wrote their epistles were spiritual societies, that is, associations of individuals professing repentance toward God and faith in our Lord Jesus Christ, to whom they had surrendered themselves. If those individuals were parents they were taught to bring up their children in the nurture and admonition of God; but mark you, their children were nowhere classed with them in the New Testament as the children of the Jews were in the Old Testament. Nor could they be till they themselves repented and believed the gospel. It is easily seen that no modern society deserves to be called a christian church which is not founded upon such principles as these. If you were to place a New Testament in the hands of an intelligent, impartial person who had never heard of our divisions and denominations, what idea would he be likely to form of the spirit and design of christianity and the christian church? Would he not see in every part of this book appeals to men's understanding and emotions, and such requisitions as could only be addressed to those who were capable of thinking and acting for themselves? Would he not conclude that christianity has to do with the mind and a christian must be a person of faith, and that a church is a voluntary society formed and made up of such persons?

We now come to the question of baptism. What is baptism? "It is the answer of a good conscience toward God."—I. Peter, iii, 21. "It is putting on Christ."—Gal., iii, 27. It is the voluntary act of a believer; an act of obedience, of self-dedication, for such is the uniform meaning of the term. "And there went out unto Him all the land of Judea, and they of Jerusalem, and were all baptized of Him in the river of Jordan, confessing their sins."—Mark, i, 5. So the Samaritans, "But when they believed Phillip preaching the things concerning the kingdom of God, and the name of Jesus Christ, they were baptized, both men and women."—Acts, viii, 12.

Mark well, men and women. No infants believe in Christ. The profession of faith was held to be essential to baptism and to church fellowship. None could profess faith who were incapable of exercising it. The act of profession doubtless implied understanding, approbation and choice. This, then, is the test point. Here is the beginning of the history of the Baptists, with the New Testament only before us. We find baptism connected with profession of faith. It is a voluntary act, and such acts only are illustrative of christianity of the nineteenth century. There is a service of another kind. That is sprinkling, and not immersing; and the subjects in many cases are infants, and not believers, which service is in opposition to the teaching of the New Testament; not in opposition to the Baptists' doctrines and practices only, but to Christ, our wonderful Teacher. We find, by attentive researches of the New Testament, no such thing as baptizing and receiving infants into the church before they have sense enough to think and act for themselves. As Christ only gave those whom He sent permission to baptize such as had sense enough to believe the gospel; so we read in Mark, Preach the gospel, and he that believeth and is baptized shall be saved. I believe it is treason against heaven and an insult to God to so daringly oppose His command. It is also an imposition upon the pure, helpless babe to pour water on it and receive it into a certain society without allowing it to grow large, old or wise enough to think for itself. It is, in substance, but a gag law upon humanity, and a death blow aimed at true christianity. There are a few historians who wrote of infant baptism. But there are a great many others who deny and denounce infant baptism. Thus you may see that a large majority of historians oppose it. Therefore, Justin Martyn and Ireanus are assuredly standing in the side-track, for their assertion is not in accord with the New Testament, and when history does not accord with the Bible, it is bogus, so far, at least, as christianity is concerned. All lexicographers, all encyclopedias, and almost all historians, Baptist and pedo-Baptist, and a large majority of the best commentaries are in sympathy with Baptist doctrine, or Bible doctrine; not because of its weakness, but of its strength; not because of the church recruit or organization, but because of its primeval existence. The Bible and history, according to that, bears out the Baptists.

We read in the Song of Solomon, vi, 9, these words: "My dove, my undefiled is but one; she is the only one of her mother, she is the choice one." Although the church underwent severe changes through the severest dispersions, that of patriarchal and Mosaic, but not enough to destroy it. Christ was watching His church, for she was His choice, and He brought her through the darkness until He saw fit to identify Himself with His church. Isaiah saw Him "coming from Edom with dyed garments from Bozrah." He was then on His way to meet His church. He identified Himself with the Baptist church in baptism. He was also identified in that of close communion and in repentance, for He preached it.

The identification of the Saviour is in our favor. The Bible is full of such doctrine as the true God, the fall of man, the way of salvation, justification, the freeness of salvation, repentance and faith, God's purpose of grace, of sanctification, the gospel church, baptism and the Lord's Supper, the Lord's Day, righteousness and wickedness and the world to come.

If I am to name the church it is the Baptist church, for she has one Lord, which is her great head, law-giver and judge. One faith, which is her escort into the kingdom of heaven, and one baptism, which is her divine ordinance, introduced by authority of heaven and by the Father loudly thundering through the Holy Ghost in the River Jordan, when John baptized His Son, "Thou art my beloved Son in whom I am well pleased."

The Baptists believe that the Bible teaches a democratic form of church government. Popes, bishops and elders, as practiced by other denominations, are entirely unwarranted by the New Testament. Baptists believe that the Bible forbids prayer or homage to departed saints or angels. Rev., xix, 10: "And I fell at His feet to worship Him. And He said unto me, See thou do it not: I am thy fellow-servant, and of thy brethren that have the testimony of Jesus: Worship God: for the testimony of Jesus is the spirit of prophecy."

The Baptists believe simply this: What the Bible forbids, Baptists reject, and what it teaches they accept as the word of God. Would that the world reverenced the Bible as the Baptists. Amen.

THE QUALIFICATION AND DIGNITY OF THE MINISTRY.

BY REV. CHARLES H. BRIGHTHARP.

I feel myself somewhat flattered in having been called on to speak on so grand and momentous a subject as the gospel ministry.

Permit me to say the called minister of God stands paramount to all men in Christendom.

The Governor of State, the President of States, Kings of their domains, and the Queen, with her crown, must adhere to the humble minister of Christ. For it is by him that the word of God must be preached. This being a fact, he ought to be a man of character. When I use the word character, I mean as referred to men. Character is what the man is, and stands far above reputation, which men will give and seek to take away. Character is a God-given property, and every person once in life has it. In speaking of character, I mean all the adjuncts that go to form it—virtue, sobriety and integrity. These must need be in every preacher who would succeed.

1. I now call your attention to an example found in the Bible. Barnabas, who is worthy of emulation, is called the son of consolation. During the terrible persecutions in the days of the Martyrs, Stephen and the brethren were scattered abroad. The church at Jerusalem sent their son of consolation, for he was a good man, and full of the Holy Ghost, and of faith, and much people was added to the Lord.

If the standard of the ministry was lifted higher, by having good men, full of the Holy Ghost and faith, thus with the Father, Son and Holy Ghost on our side, we cannot but succeed to wage war against sin and the devil.

2. I mean to say that he was not only a christian, but good in the common sense of the word. He was eminently good. This epithet is often given as a sneer. But not so with Barnabas. He was good in principle. He, like the Apostle Paul, did not value himself upon those things wherein he differed from other men, but gloried in those principles which he possessed that were common to every good man. The inspired apostle says that he gloried in those things which he had that were common, to all men—charity, (that is, love), as used in the new version. "Wherever there is love, goodness is her eldest daughter." Barnabas loved God; hence he was willing to do good for the cause of Christ. The people heard him, because he was a good man, working for a good cause. Let us, like Barnabas, be ready for every good work, and then churches will look for us, and save us the embarrassing trouble of looking for them.

Brother ministers, the chief thing we should value is character. All men should keep a circumspect eye over it. We live in a busy age, in which the snare of the great arch fiend of hell may take us unawares. A nail driven through a plank knocks out nature's grain, and all the putty and paint the most skilled chemist may make cannot put nature's mark back. Nor can a fallen minister fully reach the place from whence he has fallen. One ounce of prevention is worth a pound of cure. Stay up, and you will not have to get up.

Character must be valued at home in your own family circle. If you walk not close with God there you will not be able to work for him elsewhere. It is at home and around your own fireside that true judgment is set.

I. Goodness is one of the strongest attributes that goes to make character, and beyond a doubt every minister ought to have this epithet attached to his name. Shakspeare says there is nothing in a name, but Solomon says a good name is rather to be chosen than great riches.

II. Barnabas was full of the Holy Spirit, and so must he be who heralds this glorious gospel of the Most High God. The Holy Spirit sometimes denote His extraordinary gifts, as in Acts, xix, where the Apostle Paul puts the question to some believers in Christ whether they had received the Holy Ghost. But here it signifies His indwelling and ordinary operation, or what is elsewhere called an unction from the Holy One. It is very needful, my brethren, that he who preaches the word of God should be filled with the Holy Ghost from on high. God is a spirit and seeketh such to worship Him in spirit and in truth. Unless the man of God is spiritually minded he can not communicate with God, Who is all spirit. He who metes out the word of life must live nearer to God, that he may be well qualified to teach his fellow-man the deep things of God, which are only discerned by spiritually minded men. This is a fact that can not be eradicated. The man who bears this heavenly news to lost sinners must be richly imbued with the vital spirit from heaven. He will guide the subservient minister in the way of truth.

III. The minister of Christ who wills to succeed must be full of faith. The word "faith" is difficult to understand, though it has been used ever since the fall of man. It is hard to ascertain with precision the real meaning and extent of this term. We have it "trust," "confide," and, in Hebrew, "to lean on." Therefore he who teaches the gospel of the Son of God must lean on Him for succor, for He is a present help in the time of need. We must pray to God and read the Bible with faith that we may be well-gospeled ourselves.

IV. The ministers of to-day must be educated, or they will be forced from their pulpits by the rising pews. The negro ministers of this period fill a peculiar office. One part of their congregation is not educated. The other wants to hold to old custom. The third part has some education, or are educated. They all must be reached. The old fathers and mothers who have gone before us have laid well the foundation for us to build upon; therefore they must be kept alive. The young must be trained, for they are our future hope of the negro race. The old saying, "Open your mouth and God will fill it," will not do for this progressive age. He who preaches the gospel must know how by ardent study. The inspired apostle, moved upon by the divine inspiration, said to Timothy in his last writing: "Study to show thyself a workman that needeth not be ashamed, rightly dividing the word of truth."

The minister should be well informed before he enters the pastorate. The word of God must be a living power in the minister, that he may be elected, and thereby elect his fallen brothers, who are sailing over life's ocean amid the breakers that may cause an eternal wreck. Long-winded tales, false zeal and stamping of feet will not preach the gospel, my brethren. Thus saith the word of holy writ: "If a man, therefore, purge himself from these, he is a vessel unto honor, sanctified, meet for the Master's use, and purified unto every good work."

> "So let our lips and lives express
> The holy gospel we profess;
> So let our works and virtues shine,
> To prove the doctrine all divine."

V. Dignity.—This means "above," and as the ministry is a high calling, it behooves the minister to be dignified. God has called him out of darkness into light; therefore, He Who is Light, has called the minister to walk in the effulgence of the Son of God. Dignity is not fine apparel nor flippant speech, but it means a rounded man, filled with all the principles that constitute a minister. The servant of God should do right at all times. "Be sure you are right, and then go ahead," ever holding to your integrity. Christ has committed to his preachers his church. They stand next their Master, Who is pure and holy, and calls upon us to be holy, as He is holy. God has opened the way for his preachers. They tell the people how to come, that they may receive them.

> "Come as a teacher sent from God,
> Charged His whole counsel to declare,
> Lift o'er our ranks the prophet's rod,
> While we uphold their hands with prayer.
>
> "Come as a messenger of peace,
> Filled with the spirit, fired with love,
> Live to behold our large increase,
> And die to meet us all above."

THE DUTY OF BAPTISTS TO HOME MISSIONS.

BY REV. E. J. FISHER, LAGRANGE, GA.

Mr. President and Brethren Composing the One Hundredth Anniversary of the Negro Baptists of Georgia:

It affords me no small degree of happiness to have the pleasure of even appearing before this intelligent, heaven-bound denomination, for the purpose of speaking a word. There have been many important subjects under discussion, which were handled with ability, and others to be discussed, among which there is one appearing on the programme with vital import, viz.: "The Duty of Baptists to Home Missions," and among the other names, I find E. J. Fisher, of LaGrange, and that happens to be my name.

Therefore, allow me to quote you a passage of scripture, which can be found in Joshua, xiii, 1, where the Lord said unto him: "Thou art old and stricken in years, and there remaineth yet very much land to be possessed." He was a man of obedience. God sustained and blessed his efforts. He was also about one hundred years old. Nothwithstanding he had taken many cities and lands, still there were many more to conquer, viz.: the southland, governed by five lords, and westward, as far as Sardonia. It was his duty to go, because God sent him. In like manner, Jesus, after he had arisen from the dead, and was about to make His ascension back to heaven, told His disciples to "Go ye therefore and disciple all nations."

Looking this commission in the face, seeing it comes to us as to them, since we claim that we are keeping pace with His teaching and the practice of His disciples, it becomes more imperatively the duty of the Baptists to do mission work than any other denomination, for our message is of God and of His Christ. Therefore, the saving of the world is upon us. And, as the disciples were to begin at Jerusalem, ours is to begin in Georgia, and continue throughout these United States. For no other can stand as do the Missionary Baptist, and cry, "One Lord, one faith, and one baptism." And, as we are the sent of God, the duty is not a small one. Hence, this army is to go on crying until Georgia is saved totally, and then reach out to save the world.

Since the Baptists believe the whole counsel of God, and that counsel is truth, and as the world is to be saved by the same, it follows that the Missionary Baptist is to do this home mission work; for they are better prepared to do it than any other, because they have what is necessary for its accomplishment, save the money which we are making great efforts to get. May the Lord assist us in getting the needed amount of money to carry it out. Since we have the men and the food we only need the train. Let each of us see that it is supplied. Now, I appeal to every Baptist, since it becomes our duty to do the mission work. As we are called of the Lord to do this work, I ask, Shall we have the train for conveyance, which is money, since we can not do without it?

Listen. Before the birth of Christ, at the call, when the prophet said he saw an angel with six wings flying from the altar with a live coal in a pair of tongs, which he took therefrom, and came and touched his tongue, then there was a voice heard saying, "Who will go for us, or whom shall we send?" Isaiah answered and said, "Here am I, send me." In like manner when God called about one hundred years ago this army under the leadership of Revs. Leile and Bryan answered the same, and to-day we are still declaring one Lord, one faith and one baptism.

THE EVILS OF INTEMPERANCE.

BY REV. S. D. ROSIER.

Mr. Chairman, Ladies and Gentlemen:

Among the many things which call forward the men of this generation upon the stage there is nothing more important than the temperance movement. And as the sacred duty of speaking to you upon so important a subject is imposed upon me, I purpose to speak to you of the evils of intemperance.

Intemperance is one of the most formidable agents the devil has ever commissioned; the principal outcome of the pandemonium council of hell.

In 1865 the proclamation of peace and freedom was published throughout the land. The tolling bells pealed forth the glad news in almost human tones. Nor scarcely has the foot of man trodden upon the battle grounds of that eventful crisis that he has not thought of the precious blood that was shed for the purchase of peace and the stability of the Union. It was a hot struggle, and all but exhausted the fount of American tears. All this, remember, was but for the adjustment of the government of the nation.

But even when this was done, there still remained a rotten beam in the fabric of the nation's fame—Intemperance; for the untamed flames of this infernal fiend still burns in our famous cities, humble hamlets, and prosperous communities, and by which judges, lawyers, doctors, statesmen and clergymen are being consumed.

We may boast of our halls of science, art, and literature, and of the ten thousand temples which rise and point to heaven, silently proclaiming man's fellowship with angels in the skies. We may boast of civilization, and of such triumphs and trophies as the earth has never seen amid the countless number of thrones and empires of glorious birth. But, sir, until this blighting curse is removed, our social and national greatness is at stake.

Considering the present state of society, where shall we go to find peace and freedom? The tippler and rum-seller may cry, "Here is peace," or "There is peace;" but there is no peace where men live within the "iron grasp" of this diabolical foe. They plead the rights of personal liberty. I am on the side of every man who pleads the rights of personal liberty, provided he agrees to abide the divine law of personal liberty. That law prohibits an infringement either directly or indirectly upon the rights of other men. And, if I could speak of personal liberty as the boundary of the United States, I would say personal liberty is bounded on the north by the rights of others, on the east by the rights of others, on the south by the rights of others, and on the west by the rights of others. Cross this boundary line, and you affect the moral and social progress of humanity. Sir, if this is not the condition of America, I beg leave to be silent.

There need be no display of hygienic knowledge to prove the evils of intemperance. Go where dwell the victims of intemperance, and there you will see "houses without windows, gardens without fences, fields without tillage, children without clothing, schooling, morals or manners; and could the ghosts of many a lost son and daughter come back to earth to-day, they would never rest until they clenched their fiery fingers into the souls of their drunkard fathers and mothers, and drag them down among the damned and doomed. Look at the dynasties it has overthrown, the nations of which it has been the downfall, and by which the church has lost many of her brightest sons and daughters. Dionysius, King of Syracuse, went to the expense of his throne and lived a slave to the disgraceful habit of drinking. Alexander, when he had conquered the world, and prayed for more worlds to conquer, at last, conquered by intemperance, went from the imperial throne down to a drunkard's grave. Shakspeare, Byron, Burns, Lamb, Goldsmith, and many others of like ability, died slaves to the cup. These are a few examples of the past, but let us return to the occurrences of our own time.

The expense of making and selling intoxicating liquors in this country is enormous. In 1880, the expense of manufacturing and selling intoxicating liquors, the cost of time and money lost by the drinker, and the accidents it caused, was estimated at the sum of $1,200,000,000 per year. Do you ask, "Who were they who expended their time and this vast sum?" I answer, that class of people who constitute the staff of this country— the laborers. But who can tell the number of the infinite millions lost? Of "years, fortunes, talents, honors, positions, characters, homes, comforts and lives lost?" Heaven alone knows the awful record.

Intemperance is nine-tenths the cause of murder, criminality and pauperism, the insanity of powerful minds—minds which might have moulded and shaped the opinions of nations—and could we but redeem the financial results of this black demon, and call the slumbering drunkards from their graves, we might repeople an empty world, make states, build kingdoms, erect religious and social institutions, and dedicate them to the honor and glory of God. But alas, they are forever beyond the confines of time.

It was the rum traffic which deprived us of our freedom in our fatherland—the dearest pledge of our existence. It has been the price of the negroes' influence in the government of this great republic, the perversion of legislation, and a bar to the administration of justice. Shall we undervalue these God-given powers and exchange them for the "fool's pence?" Can we afford to sell our "birthrights for a mess of vile, blood-red pottage?" God forbid! The voice of mothers, widows and orphans now pleads for freedom at the bar of civilization; they bend the knee at the feet of statesmen on the very threshold of the Senate chamber. Can we hold our peace? Exterminate this hydra-headed monster, and society will be renovated, public school houses, colleges, universities and churches will rise upon its ruins, more means and men will be raised for the redemption of fallen humanity.

This is the individual, public, national and religious battle of the nineteenth century, and we must stem the current, however rapid, and under the white banner of prohibition lift men and women above the billows of drink, and with dauntless courage of duty make the world ring with our repeated strokes until this worst of foes lies vanquished at our feet. Then may we sing to the Author of Liberty sweet freedom's song from pole to pole.

ARE WE ADVANCING AS A DENOMINATION?

BY PROF. M. P. M'CRARY, VALDOSTA, GA.

Mr. President, Friends and Brethren:

In submission to the request of the "Centennial Committee" I address you.

That we are advancing as a denomination is known and acknowledged in all christian lands. And this fact the world sees, and is fast learning how and why it is that with such rapidity we do move on to a glorious victory. I am on board the ship of this progressive and advancing denomination. The question comes to us to-day, "Are we advancing as a denomination?"—a question of great and vital importance, the answer to which I shall give, backed by truth, in the affirmative, in behalf of not only a few, but millions.

To advance is to move forward, to rise, to increase. Therefore, I would say as a denomination these are some of the characteristics that mark our numerous attainments and very rapid progress. The wonderful increase, numerically and financially, the pleasing moral and intellectual advancement exhibit a noble picture in favor of the denomination's progress. I would declare most emphatically that our advancement as a denomination is plainly marked and indelibly stamped upon the pages of history. But to prove whether or not an organization is advancing, be it a religious body or otherwise, it is very essential, I think, first to prove or know its foundation, the source of its origin, whether it be a rocky or sandy foundation. It is indeed quite requisite to know the legality, or illegality of the organized body.

I said just now that as a denomination we are advancing. Now to avoid any one asking me, now or hereafter, why do I say so, please permit me just here to state my answer:

1st. The Baptist denomination is founded upon the rock Christ Jesus.

2d. Christ is the legal authority of the denomination.

3d. Christ was a member of this denomination because he founded it and submitted to it ordinances.

4th. Christ is the life and success of this denomination.

Lastly, it has lived over eighteen hundred years and made its advent into most all the world. That these are facts indisputable you will all agree.

Now, then, if Christ is the origin, the base and rock upon which this pure and grand old Baptist denomination stands, it is quite evident that it has an infinite, living source.

It has been infallibly established that the Baptists began their denominational life under the ministry of our Saviour, hence its rapid growth, fine health and universal acceptance to-day.

Allow me just here, my friends, to state this fact. It is the true and living beginning received by Christ, our great founder and leader, that promoted our growth and predicts our future triumph.

Another grand evidence of our certain and decided progress is that during the dark, gloomy and critical ages of the past, amidst danger and even death, appearing, as it were, amid the wreck of matter and the crush of crumbling worlds, we flourished and grew but the more. I say, as a denomination we are advancing most assuredly. The past has recorded plain testimonies in proof of this fact, the present confirms and more fully establishes it, and the future awaits, with infinite gravity, to welcome the consummate development and victory of the denomination.

Judging from the past and the present, we can but feel that as a denomination we are destined to spread over all the world, and unfurl the banner of truth and victory over every home and heart of Adam's family, upon which the finger of inspiration has inscribed the words, "One Lord, one faith, one baptism."

Dr. Cathcart, in speaking of the Baptist denomination, has with ability and truth said that the Baptists "are the parents of absolute religious liberty wherever it exists in christian nations." They are the founders of the first great Protestant missionary society of modern times. The British and Foreign Bible Society was formed by the counsels of a Baptist, and in which every Bible society in the world felt an interest. These are plain proofs of our advancement.

Another reason for our so advancing is that we have the Bible, which is the book of God, the book of books, the revealer of God to man, His interpreter as the God of nature. This is the great light by which we travel in this world, and through which we inherit our religious advancement.

As a denomination dating further back than any other can, every month, every season, every year and every century unfolds the rapidity, the grandeur and glory of the advancement of this old and true denomination.

While the denomination's growth and advancement have been astonishing as it has come through the ages, it is well to state that it did not escape persecutions nor fail to meet the most stubborn objection and suffered punishment of the most cruel nature. Yet the height, depth and width of its growth, advancement and achievement are the tokens of preëminence and complete victory.

Thanks to the Father, the giver of every good and perfect gift, that this grand old denomination of which our Saviour was a member has by means of grace broken down and surmounted the greatest of its obstacles, and that the least as well as the greatest must bow to its God-given power and lie vanquished at its feet. Seeing, therefore, as a denomination, that we are advancing we have a right to rejoice and be glad, the right to be here to-day celebrating the one hundredth anniversary of our existence.

Oh! hearer, think for a moment of those dark, gloomy and bitter years of the past, and imagine the denomination as it struggles for religious liberty, and see its bold and wearied travelers almost fainting on the way, its leaders, some of whom fell as martyrs to the enemy, dying, giving their lives for the spreading of the gospel of Christ to every creature, and contending for the faith once delivered to the saints. And then come with me again, not in imagination, but in reality, to this glorious present, and see if you do not see a pleasing, grand and glorious future. It gives us joy to say that we are advancing. We may say, "We are coming, we are coming, we are coming, blessed Saviour; we are coming, we are coming, we hear Thy welcome voice."

The Baptists have more than fifty colleges and theological seminaries, and numerous and splendid academies, all of which show their amazing progress and deep interest in education. These schools, together with our several great societies, such as the American Baptist Publication Society, and Home Mission, Foreign and other societies, with their mighty influence upon the human family, show conclusively the wonderful progress of our denomination.

The numerical standing of our denomination is not silent in evidence of our advancement; for in this country there are 26,060 churches, 16,596 ministers, 2,296,327 members, and in all lands there are 30,699 churches, with 2,769,389 members. It is also estimated that more than 8,000,000 persons belong to the Baptist denomination; and besides these, our principles are extensively held by members of other communities.

The establishing of Sunday schools, and their rapid and continued increase, also go in as prominent factors to demonstrate the appreciable increase and onward march of the denomination. The Baptist Sunday schools of America have grown with such rapidity that they number, so far as reported, more than 13,493, with 116,355 officers and teachers, and 1,000,000 scholars. This, alone, tells for us great success and progress. And who can value its lasting influence upon society in its instilling of christian doctrine, and in training the young in the path of rectitude? That we are advancing as a denomination, and that with inconceivable velocity, is self-evident.

One of the peculiarities of the Baptist denomination is, that whenever and wherever she is planted, she lives. We are advancing, and our source is sufficient for the perpetual progress of the denomination. Illustrative of the advancement of our denomination, consider the small seed planted here in Savannah, January 20th, 1788. Did it die? Was it plucked up and destroyed? No. It lived; it grew and became a mighty tree, yielding abundant fruit every season, some of which have ripened, and are now gathered into the garner of the Lord. This tree having grown exceedingly large, its branches extend now into every conceivable part of this grand old empire State, and are no less fruitful than their parent tree.

While the ripe fruit has been gathered into the Master's garner, this mother tree represents to-day, in the State of Georgia, 1,500 branches, or churches, with 166,429 members. Behold, what a number! Baptists, we are advancing; we are marching on to greater achievement; yes, to victory. The grand conclusive evidences that we are advancing, through Christ, our great leader, our 30,699 churches, with 20,000 ministers and 2,769,389 members; our 13,493 Sunday schools, with 116,355 officers and teachers, and 1,000,000 scholars, and our fifty colleges and theological seminaries, and numerous academies, are living proofs. With these we have all that is needed. And we may, advancing as we are, safely hope for a victorious future, as signal and pleasing as it will be glorious.

Feeling assured that as a denomination we are truly advancing, I conclude by saying:

"Onward christian soldiers,
  Onward to the fight,
 Hold the banner firmly,
  Battle for the right.

"Hold the cross of Jesus,
  As your banner, high,
 Never must you falter,
  Never must you fly.

"Jesus is our captain,
  And we'll surely win,
 If we do His bidding,
  We may conquer sin,

"Clad in heavenly armor
We'll o'ercome the foe,
Triumph o'er the tempter,
Jesus tells us so.

"Then when warfares over,
When the fight is done,
When the foes are vanquished,
When the victory's won.

"Laying down your armor,
Clad in snowy white,
You shall reign with Jesus,
In eternal light."

THE DUTY OF THE PASTOR TO THE CHURCH.

BY REV. J. W. DUNJEE, AUGUSTA, GA.

Mr. President and Fellow-Christian Workers of the Centennial Celebration of the Baptist Church of Georgia:

I am, by the appointment of your committee, to address you at this hour on "The Duty of the Pastor to The Church," but in order to define that duty, we must define the true relation between the pastor and the church. This can be done only by first clearly understanding the terms of the contract between the church and the pastor.

Therefore, if the church has the right to make a contract with the pastor, that right must depend upon the legal and lawful existence of the church itself as God's agent. This position must be defined in accordance with God's word. Dr. J. N. Brown says: "A gospel church is a congregation of baptized believers, associated by covenant in the faith and fellowship of the gospel, observing the ordinances of Christ, governed by His laws, and exercising the gifts, rights and privileges invested in them by His word."

It is clear that the only scriptural head or leader of the church is a trained bishop, elder or pastor, whose qualifications, claims and duties, are defined in the epistle of Timothy and Titus, (I. Tim., iii, 1–8); "This is a true saying, If a man desire the office of bishop, he desireth a good work. A bishop then must be blameless, the husband of one wife, vigilant, sober, of good behavior, given to hospitality, apt to teach; Not given to wine, no striker, not greedy of filthy lucre; but patient, not a brawler, not covetous; One that ruleth well his own house, having his children in subjection with all gravity; (For if a man know not how to rule his own house, how shall he take care of the church of God?) Not a novice, less being lifted up with pride he fall into the condemnation of the devil. Moreover he must have a good report of them which are without; lest he fall into reproach and the snare of the devil."

Titus, i, 5–8: "For this cause left I thee in Crete, that thou shouldst set in order the things that are wanting, and ordain elders in every city, as I had appointed thee: If any be blameless, the husband of one wife, having faithful children not accused of riot or unruly. For a bishop must be blameless, as the steward of God; not self-willed, not soon angry, not given to wine, no striker, not given to filthy lucre."

These two passages, with many others that might be quoted, are conclusive evidence that the office of the ministry is of divine appointment; the great duty of the pastor is to pasture or feed the flock of God—the church.

Having shown that the office of pastor is one of divine appointment, we will now endeavor to define the word "Church," employing the language of some of the best writers.

The Greek word for "church" signifies generally an assembly, either common or religious, and it is sometimes so translated, as in Acts, xix, 32, 39. In the New Testament it means a congregation of baptized believers in Christ, as in Matthew, xvi, 18: "And I say also unto thee, that thou art Peter, and upon this rock I will build my church; and the gates of hell shall not prevail against it." This reference must be to the christian church of baptized believers, regularly and orderly constituted after the divine pattern. Heb., xxii, 23: "To the general assembly and church of the first born, which are written in heaven, and to God the judge of all."

It seems to me useless to quote other passages to prove that the church and ministry are of divine appointment. This fact is accepted by the christian world.

The christian minister, with his divine commission in his hand, and the church, as God's only instrumentality in the conversion of the world, are to be married to each other in divine and christian wedlock, in accordance with the divine plan, which was ordained of God from the foundation of the world, as the best and only way of converting the world from sin unto salvation. The divine order, then, is church and pastor.

This relation should always be formed in the most prayerful and deliberate manner. Out of the union thus entered into arise the responsibilities and duties of the pastor to the church. He in no sense holds the relation of a mere hireling, who is to perform a certain amount of work for so many dollars and cents, and if he happens not to please the deacons in everything is to be discharged at their will. While the pastor should always be well paid, the relation goes beyond dollars and cents. It is a moral and spiritual relation of the deepest and most sacred character, which is sanctioned and approved by the great Head of the Church.

The minister is the under-shepherd, overseer, leader and bishop of the flock of God. Acts, xx., 28: "Take heed therefore unto yourselves, and to all the flock of God, over which the Holy Ghost has made you overseers, to feed the church of God, which He has purchased with His own blood." Now, out of this most beautiful and tender relation above stated, grows the duty and responsibility of the pastor to the church.

1. It is the pastor's first duty to the church to feed the flock with spiritual food, by the constant and faithful administration of the word of Christ, without regard to favors or frowns.

2. He is bound to discharge his duty as pastor to every family in the church, rich or poor, by keeping a zealous watch over their spiritual welfare, in their homes and also in the church, and assisting in the settlement of all difficulties in the spirit of Christ, as far as it is possible for him to do.

3. The pastor has a special duty to the poor and sick, whom he should never overlook in his most tender spiritual administration.

4. It is the duty of the pastor to overlook all of the affairs of the church, and keep himself informed as to the condition of every department of church work, and, from time to time, make such recommendation as will, in his judgment, improve the condition of the church, either spiritually or financially.

5. It is the duty of the pastor, under the authority of the word of God, to take the entire leadership and oversight of the church, and, if by any rule of the church, he is deprived of his gospel rights, he is not in the truest sense pastor, but merely a "supply."

6. It is the duty of the pastor to give to the church, on each Lord's day, carefully prepared sermons; he should never go before his people without thorough preparation.

7. It is the duty of the pastor to cultivate a spirit of love and kindness toward all the members of his church, with a view of making his administration as pastor a blessing to the cause of Christ.

8. It is the duty of the pastor to so conduct himself in all of his dealings with the church as to hold the confidence and respect of the whole church, if it be possible; but it is not his duty to relinquish the high responsibility of his office to please a few church "cranks" and constitutional grumblers, which may be found in all churches.

9. The true pastor of the church, divinely called, and placed over the church by God's authority, who is head of the church, never should be removed from that position, except Divine Providence indicates that such separation is for the good of the cause of Christ; and this separation should be brought about by the same christian deliberation which was used in forming the union when he became pastor of the church.

THE DUTY OF THE CHURCH TO THE PASTOR.

BY PROF. ISAIAH BLOCKER, AUGUSTA, GA.

Without argument to prove it, were that argument necessary, let us agree that the church is a divine organization; that it is a body of organized christian believers; that it is more than a mere society, more than a simple lodge, or order of whatever character. It is not only after the divine pattern, but it is that pattern. Regenerate believers in Christ, "those that gladly received His word," compose the church. It is not complete in its organization without a pastor. No body of christians, calling themselves a church, has the right to dispense with the services of a minister. Not any more could a church do so than it could dispense with religious worship, or the other officers of a church.

In life, men sustain relationships. We all are debtors, one to another. Men are mutually dependent. Man is only partially an independent being; for most of his life he is dependent on his fellow-men. But there is no relationship more important and sacred than that which exists between a church and its pastor. A true pastor is a friend, and a true friend is a rare possession. The relationship between friends is essentially close.

> "There is no friend like the old friend,
> Who has shared our mourning days!
> No greeting like his, no homage like his praise!"

The relationship of husband and wife is sacred. They are one, and yet they are two. Both the same, and yet both different. But these relationships between friend and friend, husband and wife, suffer somewhat in comparison with that relation subsisting between the pastor and the church. The marriage estate is for this life alone. The relationship between pastor and church is spiritual; hence it has to do with the future state—eternity—and in this is superior.

Every church has the right to elect its own officers. So also ought every church have the right to choose its own pastor. It is not true, however, that all churches have this prerogative. Among Baptists this right is inviolable. Possessing the freedom of choice, and having made selection of its pastor, a church owes him duties and obligations far-reaching in their character. The church is the first party to the contract, as the man is to the marriage contract, it having made the proposition for the agreement, which makes them one in interests, and mutually obligated. And, as a man or woman should look well and rationally and prayerfully before marriage, to ascertain the similarity of age, oneness of tastes, equality of position, harmony of mental calibre, and that physical prerequisites are found in his or her life's companion, so ought also a church, before making choice of a pastor, to look well into the character of the man who would be their shepherd, trusting to Divine guidance.

That which a person is bound by moral obligations to do or not to do, is a sufficient definition of duty. A pastor is an elder, a shepherd, a commissioned officer of the Lord Jesus Christ. He is a servant and an embassador for Christ. His office and duty may be briefly defined in this passage from I. Peter, v, 1-4: "The elders which were among you I exhort, who are also an elder, and a witness of the sufferings of Christ, and also a partaker of the glory that shall be revealed: Feed the flock of God which is among you, taking the oversight thereof, not by constraint, but willingly: not for filthy lucre, but of a ready mind; Neither as being lords over God's heritage, but being ensamples to the flock. And when the chief shepherd shall appear, ye shall receive a crown of glory that fadeth not away."

To "feed the flock of God," and "taking the oversight thereof," are the duties of the shepherds. "Ensamples to the flock" they are to be. "Lords over God's heritage," they are not to be. Feeders and overseers are their offices. "Whosoever will be chief among you, let him be your servant." Apparently, the world does not understand what is meant by being a servant. Could church members, and people in society generally, be brought to understand that those among them who work, who serve, will be chief, will be most respected, and most beloved, and most honored, there would be fewer drones in church and in state.

What, now, is the duty of the church to him who feeds her, and who overlooks her affairs spiritually? The first duty I shall mention as being due a pastor, is the reverence and christian love of his flock. He should enjoy their entire confidence. The reward, and the chiefest reward, he might hope for in this life is the love and reverence of his people. The constant companionship and friendship of the church officers and the Sabbath school superintendent would be an inspiration to him. Among the numerous duties which are due him by his congregation, I ought not to fail, in passing, to mention the apparently insignificant duty of visiting him and his family.

We can not help him unless we feel an interest in his work. It is not the duty of the church to expect him to do everything. It is not just nor right that the officers and members should leave the financial burden of the church to the pastor. To themselves, to their pastor and to God, church members owe the everywhere-neglected duty of becoming intelligent Bible christians. Among those who can read, just the same as among those who are unlettered; with the white people, as with the colored; in churches for white people, as in churches for colored people; so far as I have been able to observe, there is a woeful neglect of Bible reading, and in cases, too often, there is the absence of the Bible itself from the church members' homes. If we knew more about the "Thus saith the Lord," our pastors' sermons would be more helpful, and we would praise where we now frequently censure. We would note and appreciate God's providences, where now we trample His mercies under our feet. If we wish to aid our pastor, we should study our Bibles. He knows a Bible student within his fold, and rightly values his industry and the earnestness with which he listens to his sermons.

Whether close communion is right, or whether open communion is wrong; whether theater-going, dancing, or card-playing be wrong or right; whether being temperate or a total abstainer is right, or whatever question, you will have no trouble to determine, should you study your Bible, nor would you give the pastor or the church any trouble. Let us know our doctrine. "The word of God is the only rule of faith and practice," "Be not forgetful to strangers," and "Use hospitality one to another, without grudging," are passages which must suggest to the thoughtful virtues, the value of which always will be properly estimated by a true minister.

I wish I could dwell longer on this point, but I cannot. Indeed, the cultivation of any christian grace is a help to the pastor. And could christians be brought to the fullest point of development in the exercise of every talent and liberality, no trouble would be experienced with regard to the pastor's support, the last point on which I shall speak.

Let us all understand that surprise parties cannot support a pastor; that a minister should live of the gospel the scriptures most clearly and conclusively teach. And his support should be ample. His entire time should also be devoted to the "ministry of the word."

But the grasping, digging spirit in any minister will hardly be gratified.

Every church should have a pastor who should preach to that church every Sunday. It is a most serious mistake to have preaching only once a month, and it is a worse mistake for one minister to have often as many churches to serve as there are Sundays in each month. There is little or no growth in such churches. As a rule, the people are running astray, and I doubt if there is a more serious error in the management of our churches (country churches, as well as city churches, if you please) than that of having preaching once a month, thus making it possible for one minister to serve two or three bodies. Look into this a little, and we shall not be long in discovering that the laborers are not quite so scarce as to require this practice, and that there are many worthy christian men who would show themselves qualified to preach to these churches, if given a chance. The trouble lies, I believe, in the fact that they do not wish and will not support a pastor. They prefer that three churches undertake the work of supporting one minister to having one church do that same work. Liberality is what is needed.

The apostle said: "But we will give ourselves continually to prayer, and to the ministry of the word."

Paul said: "Even so hath the Lord ordained that they which preach the gospel should live of the gospel." Or, "I only and Barnabas, have not we power to forbear working? Who goeth a warfare any time at his own charges? Who planteth a vineyard, and eateth not of the fruit thereof? Or who feedeth a flock, and eateth not of the milk of the flock? Say I these things as a man? Or saith not the law the same, also? For it is written in the law of Moses, Thou shalt not muzzle the mouth of the ox that treadeth out the corn. Doth God take care for oxen? Or saith He it altogether for our sakes? For our sakes, no doubt, this is written: that he that ploweth should plow in hope; and he that thresheth in hope should be partaker of His hope."—I. Cor., ix, 6–10. "Have I committed an offense in abasing myself that you might be exalted, because I have preached to you the gospel of God freely? I robbed other churches, taking wages of them, to do you service. But I rejoice in the Lord greatly, that now at the last your care of me hath flourished again: wherein ye were also careful, but ye lacked opportunity. Not that I speak in respect of want: for I have learned in whatever state I am, therewith to be content. Notwithstanding ye have well done, that ye did communicate with my affliction. Now ye Phillipians know also, that in the beginning of the gospel, when I departed from Macedonia, no church communicated with me as concerning giving and receiving, but ye only. For even in Thessalonica ye sent once and again unto my necessity. Not because I desire a gift: but I desire fruit that may abound to your account as a sacrifice acceptable, well pleasing to God."

You will observe that these scriptures fully demonstrate that a pastor must be supported—supported by the church to which he preaches. No member of a Baptist church who wishes to do his full duty, can read these scriptures and not feel that he violates the commands of God, if he does not, to the extent of his ability, aid in the support of the pastor of the church to which he belongs. It is the experience of every church, that a few liberal members bear all the burden in the support of the church. The young members, somehow, think they might spend their earnings in every other way, and for every other conceivable purpose, than that of helping to sustain the church.

But the pastor must visit all the sick and distressed, bury all the dead, and pray for all the children and all the sinners in a community, the young folks and old folks, and receive little or no salary. It is a common practice, also, to give the minister or the church that which we, ourselves, do not want. When the month expires, the pastor wants his salary, as every man does. It takes as much to maintain his family as any other family. He should practice economy, and lay by some money, as other men. Why not? But that humble, and faithful, and self-sacrificing minister, who does his duty and gets little pay, and whose family is in sore need, is to be prayed for and to be beloved.

Many people have mistaken views with regard to God's word in its teachings on this subject. People give in proportion as they love. Love lies at the base of all christian giving; and it would be a safe rule to measure a christian's love by the willingness with which he gives, and the amount which he gives. Have first the willingness, and secondly the industry and frugality, which will afford us the means to contribute.

In Luke, xxi, 1-4, we find this passage: "And He (Jesus) looked up, and saw the rich men casting their gifts into the treasury. And He saw also a certain poor widow casting in thither two mites. And he said, Of a truth I say unto you, that this poor widow hath cast in more than they all: for all these have of their abundance cast in unto the offerings of God: but she of her penury hath cast in all the living that she had."

"The first of the fruits of thy land thou shalt bring into the house of the Lord thy God."—Ex., xxiii. 19.

"All the best of the oil, and all the best of the wine, and of the wheat, the first fruits of them which they shall offer unto the Lord."—Num., xviii, 12.

"And to bring the first fruit of our ground, and the first fruits of all fruit of all trees, year by year, unto the house of the Lord."—Neh., x, 35.

"But the liberal deviseth liberal things; and by liberal things shall he stand."—Isa., xxxii, 8.

These passages are from the Old Testament.

In I. Cor., xvi. 2: "Upon the first day of the week let every one of you lay by him in store, as God hath prospered him."

II. Cor., viii, 12: "For if there be first a willing mind, it is accepted according to that a man hath, and not according to that he hath not."

II. Cor., ix, 7: "Every man as he purposeth in his heart, so let him give: not grudgingly, or of necessity: for God loveth a cheerful giver."

Just one word more.

"Take heed, and beware of covetousness: for a man's life consisteth not in the abundance of the things which he possesseth."

From these passages we ought to see our duty to the pastor, to the church and to Christ. If these do not teach us our duty, no further words from me will.

DUTY OF THE CHURCH TO THE PASTOR.

BY DEACON R. H. THOMAS, OF SAVANNAH, GA.

What is the duty of the church to the pastor?

First, let us see the relation between the church and pastor.

It is said that the pastor's duty to the church is parallel to that of the shepherd in the eastern country, whose duty it is to feed the sheep, lift up the fainting, care for the sick and infirm, take up the tender lambs and fold them in his arms. It is the duty of the pastor to care for the sick and bereaved, and, best of all, should bring them a fresh supply for every day's want.

Therefore, the church being the recipient of his labors of love, it is her duty to reciprocate the same.

Therefore, the church is under many obligations to her pastor, because he is a messenger sent from God, and ought to be so regarded by the church and the community at large. It is the duty of the church to seek of its pastor spiritual instruction. The church should regard him as her spiritual director, and show her appreciation of the instructions given, by putting them into practice. It is also her duty to seek spiritual guidance of him, not only for herself, but also for others.

It is not the duty of the church to attempt to teach him, but to be taught of him. He is supposed to be God's representative, acting and pleading for God. Hence, it is her duty to obey and be governed, and not to govern.

It seems to be prevalent to-day that nine-tenths of the churches attempt to dictate, to lead and teach their pastors, and not to be led. Two-thirds of the church troubles of to-day arise from just such causes. It is also the indispensable duty of the church to watch carefully against caucusing parties against the pastor. Sometimes the truth becomes too strong to be tolerated by some of the members. I am sorry to say so, but it is found to be true. Sometimes he is too strict for the committee on finance; sometimes the trustees will not work, because they can not do as they please, and too often the deacons, like Peter, want to fight, because they cannot invite their friends to preach at their will in the pastor's pulpit.

Sometimes when the pastor is from home laboring for the church in some way or other there comes along a preacher, if you please, and you get him to preach once or twice, and he wants the pastorate right away. He has gained a few friends and now he wants the church.

There is another class of preachers in the church who are too lazy to work up for themselves a congregation. Watching the pastor, hoping that he may soon get sick and die, so as to take his place. It is the duty of the church to guard her pastor in all of these points, and to see to it that all of the implements necessary for the discharge of his duty be put within his reach, that the best men be selected out of its number to serve as deacons, as trustees, and good, honest men for the committee on finance—men that do not have tar on their fingers nor leaks in their hands, if so, the pastor will starve and the church go down. She should select as deacons men that will fill the office as the original calling would indicate, giving active service to both church and pastor. When they fail to do so, whether it is by inability or duty neglected, they ought to at once be removed and their places filled by others. Let me urge this point, that it is one of the highest duties of the church to its pastor that the best qualified men be chosen to labor with the pastor, both for the good of the pastor and the good of the church, and for the advancement of the Redeemer's kingdom on earth—men who are full of the Holy Ghost and blessed with the happy grace of self-denial for the cause of Christ.

It is also her duty to see that the pastor has sufficient light; that is, books, and a good choir that will give music for his help. The church should pay her pastor promptly. No church ought to pay off its pastor in promises, but rather pay him his salary as contracted; for the Bible tells us, "He that laboreth at the altar shall also partake of the things of the altar;" "the laborer is worthy of his meat;" don't muzzle the ox that treadeth over the corn.

It is also found in the covenant of the church, "That we will strive together for the support of a faithful, evangelical ministry among us." These are the teachings of the Bible, the "book of books," which has God for its author, salvation for its end, and truth, unmixed with error, for its matter.

I believe that most of you are familiar with the science of agriculture, and hence will agree with me that in order to reap a liberal harvest, three things are necessary:

1. Good ground.
2. Good seed.
3. Faithful work.

Let us say that the church is the good ground, the work the good seed, and the pastor the worker, while we all join him. We are to hold up the pastor's hands while he wrestles with God and we contend with the enemy. Hence, the church can not and must not become inactive, because of its good name. The pastor cannot live on the church's good name. He must be cared for as other men. It is true love to see his faults. The church that loves her pastor truly sees his faults, and ought to make them known to him in a loving, christian way. I believe that it is also the duty of the church to watch her pastor with the eye of christian love; not only to guard, but also pray for him, that he be able to better discharge his duties. The Bible tells us that while Peter was in prison, the church met and prayed for him, and that while they were yet praying he was delivered unto them.

It is also the church's indispensable duty to watch her pastor with a spiritual eye, both for her own good and the good of the community at large, and to see that he does not divert from the path of virtue, love and truth. So soon as he desecrates his high calling, it is the duty of the church to leave him to himself until he repents.

One of the great evils of our day, that has destroyed so many of our churches, is that the church puts sympathy in the place of justice in some of the blackest crimes. Sympathy has predominated in the face of right, and it is more frequently practiced in the little country churches, where the people depend upon a few leaders for light. Once the pastor gets himself into the sympathies of the church, he feels himself safe to carry her to honor or down to shame, at his will. It is the duty of the church to guard against this evil.

There is a man who meets his friend while on his way to church, and asks him to go with him to church. "No," says his friend, "I do not wish to go." "Why not?" "Well, because every time I go to church, since I and the preacher fell out, he takes his text on me, and when he ends, he ends on me. When I go to church I want to hear the gospel preached to me, and that will make us better, if anything will, and not be picking at me, because I cannot answer him back.

Let it be known that it is the duty of the church to have a pastor who knows the gospel, and not only knows it but will preach it at all times and under all circumstances.

Our blessed Lord said: "When I am lifted up I will draw all men unto me." St. Paul also said: "I desire to know nothing among you save Christ and Him crucified."

The churches of this age want men to know the Bible, and that will teach the Bible, and not only teach but also let the Bible be the rule of their lives. This age of progress demands money and an enlightened ministry, and the ministry is demanding better pay and better treatment.

WHAT IS OUR DUTY TO THE INSTITUTIONS OF THE COUNTRY?

BY PROF. H. L. WALKER, AUGUSTA, GA.

Mr. Chairman and Honored Sirs:

The question which your committee has assigned me for treatment at this hour is one which so impresses me with its profundity that all of my powers are invoked to impress you with its importance. In the midst of this nineteenth century, an age of religious tolerance and denominational activity; an age when christendom is at rest, and not convulsed by the throes and horrors of a French revolution, or the ascendency of Catholicism over Protestantism; an age when all denominations are energetic, and seeking by conquest to make proselytes of the Gentiles by planting every corner of the globe with their emissaries; an age when a desire to open up commercial intercourse with the unexplored heathen lands is screened behind the efforts of the various denominations to plant missionaries; yea, at a time when pious, well informed christian young men and women are in demand—it is in the midst of such circumstances and under such influences that I find it impossible to suppress the interrogation, "What is our duty toward the Baptist institutions of our country?" In this centennial year of the colored Baptists of Georgia, and at this very moment, I hail this occasion as one for veneration and congratulation, to stand in the presence of these old fathers and time-honored Baptist veterans, to whom the solution of this question is an issue of most vital concern.

The first duty we owe, therefore, to our Baptist institutions is to see that they are officered by a faculty of christian men and women thoroughly indoctrinated in Baptist principles and possessing a high order of intellectual ability, and that general fitness for the profession of which allows no embarrassment when they are thrown into competition with the other denominational and educational institutions of our country. Such an institution, so officered, and so planted upon the hill top of Georgia, will be like the handful of corn upon the top of the mountain, yea, it will serve as a sentinel at the doors of ignorance, and the matured fruits thereof shall shake like Lebanon dispensing their heavenly benedictions throughout the land.

All institutions must grow or they will retrograde into obsolete insignificance. A grain of corn must be brought in contact with the elements of the fertile soil, receive the farmer's cultivation and care, receive the fruitful seasons and the early dews from heaven before we are permitted to behold the appearance of the shoot, the stalk, the blade and the full fruitage of golden corn. The benefactions accruing from our Baptist institutions are not unlike the grain of corn in the needs and dependence for parental care as they move from the stage of incipiency into that of efficient manhood.

That we may be the better instructed as to our duty toward our Baptist institutions, let us ask ourselves the questions, "How stand our schools, and what influence are they exercising throughout the United States?"

According to the educational report of Dr. Henry L. Moorhouse, we have denominational schools planted at Washington, D. C.; at Richmond, Va.; at Raleigh, N. C.; Columbia, S. C.; Atlanta, in Georgia; at Live Oak, in Florida; Selma, in Alabama; at Nashville, in Tennesse; at Louisville, in Kentucky;

Natchez, in Mississippi; New Orleans, in Louisiana; Marshall, in Texas, and at Tahlequah, in the Indian Territory. All of these schools are doing much to materialize that portion of the Master's vineyard in which they are most fortunately planted. But noticeable among them in efficiency and utility, we can point with pride to the Wayland Seminary, at Washington, the Shaw University, at Raleigh; the Roger Williams University; the Spellman and Atlanta Baptist Seminaries, both of which are situated at Atlanta. These institutions are sending hundreds of trained young men and women into all the avenues of life, and, as teachers, ministers, mechanics and master-hands in the different professions, they take very enviable rank, and the presence of this august, venerable and grave assemblage of Baptists, with the men and women trained at our schools prominent among its leaders, claim this to be ample attestation of the fact that our schools are doing a work that shall yet tell in ages—tell for God.

Again, we must congratulate ourselves upon the fact that all these institutions are located in the South, where colored Baptists propagate, promulgate and multiply in a ten-fold ratio. They are placed, as it were, at our doors in easy access to all of our Baptist families. Such is the advantage of the present age over the past. But with all of these advantages, we must yet ask the question, have these institutions done all they could, and if not, what is still our duty toward the Baptist institutions of our country?

One of the primal duties of the Baptists of Georgia is to supply our well-equipped institutions with a larger amount of raw material, in the shape of untutored boys and girls hailing from Baptist families.

The newest statistical reports give to our State above 166,000 Baptists. Let us suppose one-tenth of this mighty army is composed of Baptist children, and we shall have above 16,000 Baptist children to fill our universities and seminaries.

Again, according to this census, the school population of the State of Georgia alone was 520,416. It is reasonable and fair to suppose that the children from Baptist families constitute at least one-tenth of the school population, and we should have for our institutions above 52,000 Baptist children. Suffer me to advance still another supposition. Suppose circumstances rendered it possible and practicable for but half of this 16,000 children to attend our seminaries, we should then have 8,000 children growing up at the feet of Baptist Gamaliels, learning wisdom.

But the facts show in regard to the education of our boys and girls that at the Baptist Seminary this scholastic year, about

150 pupils were enrolled. At the Spellman the enrollment reached 600 girls; in all about 750 pupils at our two schools. Not 1,000 boys and girls in our Georgia institutions. Where are the Baptist children of our State? Is it not possible that more can be done to fill our seminaries? Fathers, mothers, and lovers of this glorious cause, we are in a large measure responsible for the attendance at our schools.

In the United States there are 18,000,000 children of school age. As Baptists, let us see to it that a fair and substantial number of this throng is captured by our denominational schools. But, venerable sirs, our institutions will not stand alone. if they are not fostered by the maternal care of that people by whom and for whom they were created. And in order that their years may be crowned with goodness, and that their paths may flourish and drop fatness, so that they may be potentialities, energizing the communities in which they are planted, the chief articles of sustenance which they need to strengthen their vitality are dollars and prayers. Dollars, in order that the temporal prerequisites and the wants of the physical may be fully met; prayers, in order that divine unction from heaven may be distilled, like early dews, to bless the efforts which our schools and seminaries are putting forth, to garner in a large harvest for the Baptist church and for God. And may we not conjecture that when the great day of reckoning shall come, when the quick and the dead shall stand before the Great Judge, to have their records reviewed, may we not indulge the conjecture that denominations, as well as individuals, shall be held accountable for the work they have done?

Let it not be said of us: "You wicked and slothful Baptists, depart from me." Many of our churches are calling for trained ministers, deeply steeped in all scriptural knowledge, and with an appointment from above. For such a class of workers the demand is far greater than the supply. As Baptists, let us train up a greater supply of ministerial timber. The hour is at hand when many of our churches are calling for a better-informed ministry. Yea, the things and empty customs of the past have passed away. And the present, with all its modern demands, is upon us. These recruits to our ministerial ranks must file in from our schools. Each Sunday school, each church, each benevolent society should be interested in some worthy and promising member, or members, of their organization, and shoulder the responsibility of sending them to our seminaries, and furnishing them with a liberal supply of dollars and prayers. It is only in this way that the latent elements are to be drawn out.

A larger number of our girls and young women must be entered at our schools, so that from there shall spring up larger numbers of well-ordered, well-regulated christian families, that shall render very substantial aid in making the civilization of this nineteenth century the grandest that the pages of history have yet beheld; for woman, in her sphere, is like a diamond in the jeweled crown of a King, and a civilization without her work is woefully, grossly incomplete. Our Sunday school and our secular need the work of our trained young women, and these must come from our seminaries. Hence, arises the imperative duty of sending our girls to our schools, and supplying them with a full quota of dollars and prayers. Our institutions of learning are our "lambs," which, in Holy Writ, we are enjoined to feed.

Prominent among the reasons which make it imperatively necessary for us to guard with a zealous care the education of our children, is the fact that all the other denominations are energetic in christianizing the world in the tenets of their individual dogmas, and their missionaries are finding their way from pole to pole and from sea to sea. It is this denominational competition which must energize all and give vivacity to our trade. Shall we lie supinely by and refuse to send laborers into the Master's vineyard to possess the land? Let us not be deluded, sirs, with the siren songs of such culpable inactivity. We can not afford it. In the evening of this nineteenth century the Congregationalists, Presbyterians, Methodists and Catholics have their denominational schools planted all over this Union and thronging with numbers as they vie with each other in legitimate warfare for the mastery of the world. The footholds that the Catholics are gaining in this country draws the most serious apprehension and the profoundest concern, and these demonstrations are not only energetic but they are surprisingly sagacious and diplomatic. The Catholics of to-day have much to do with the body politic and the shaping of American politics. The President of the United States has just sent to the Pope of Rome a present in the shape of the constitution. This act of recognition of the Pope has no small significance.

In this literary convention among the leading denominations of the world let not the great Baptist family of this country seem remiss in planting her schools upon every hill top and in every vale, so that they may tower toward heaven with goodness and may herald the dawn of the millennium on earth among men when God's kingdom shall be fully come and His will performed in their hearts.

Finally, using our schools as a powerful instrument, our denominational family is to wage an uncompromising war with superstition, beat back the forces of Paganism and make religious conquests in China, in Japan, in Asia, in Africa, and even in Rome, the very heart of Catholicism. When we remember that of the one thousand and four hundred millions of souls belonging to the human family only one-fourth of them profess the christian religion, and when it is remembered Mohammedanism, with its sword and its Koran as the ensign of its power, holds powerful sway in the southwestern part of Asia and a large part of Africa; yea, when our missionaries in foreign fields must admit the fact that the followers of Buddism and Brahminism comprise more than one-fourth of the inhabitants of the globe, and that the Roman Catholics, with their order of Jesuits overrunning every portion of Africa to which they can gain access, then you will not fail to be impressed with the magnitude of the obligation which lies at the doors of christianity, and how herculean must be the efforts on the part of the Baptists of this country to subdue and supersede the various forms of pagan religion as they flourish in heathen lands.

Christianity alone is responsible for the subjugation and the checking of the spread of these empty relics of heathen worship, and reclaiming the world for Christ. And, my honored Baptist fathers and veterans, may this centennial celebration be to us as the great day of Pentecost, the tarrying at Jerusalem, as our Mecca, until we shall be endowed with wisdom from on high, and then, from this point as a century, let us radiate, with a view to making conquests at home and abroad, and with this motto "The World Must Be Ours."

> "From Greenland's icy mountains,
> From India's coral strand,
> Where Afric's sunny fountains
> Roll down the golden sand;
> From many an ancient river,
> From many a palmy plain,
> They call us to deliver
> Their land from errors' chain."

THE IMPORTANCE OF PURE BAPTIST LITERATURE.

BY REV. E. P. JOHNSON, PASTOR CALVARY BAPTIST CHURCH, MADISON, GA.

Says a noted writer: "Literature is, excluding the recorded knowledge of positive science, the entire result of knowledge and fancy preserved in writing. Literature proper is addressed to man as man, and is catholic, universal, not exclusive.

The importance of literature is very apparent to all thinking minds. What the mighty rivers and water courses of a country are to its fertility, productiveness and prosperity, that literature is to the inhabitants thereof. Indeed, we might liken the great thinkers and writers of any age, country or clime to high hills and lofty mountains from whose bases flow the clear, sparkling, limpid, crystal streams of literature to elevate, enlighten and instruct the minds of the people, to make glad their hearts and to better their condition financially, mentally and spiritually.

What the silver, twinkling stars are to the natural world, that literature is to the mental and spiritual world. The student of the world's history looks back to the time when the world as to literature was as dark, gloomy and foreboding as the heavens at night would be without a single star. Each religious denomination, each political party and each section of all enlightened countries show their appreciation of what they call pure literature by establishing and supporting papers, journals and periodicals proclaiming and advocating their respective views.

We must now hasten to the discussion of the subject under consideration. By pure Baptist literature is meant the writings of eminent Baptist scholars in prose and poetry touching Baptist faith and Baptist views.

1. It is very important to have pure Baptist literature, to show and demonstrate that we are the only New Testament church on the face of the globe, and thereby proving our identity with the apostolic church, and our right, therefore, to exist as a separate and distinct denomination, and "contend earnestly for the faith once delivered unto the saints."

2. By New Testament church is meant a church ruled and governed according to Christ's teaching and that of His immediate followers, and whose offices are such as accord therewith. In order to show this great fact, it is very important to have pure Baptist literature, to present to the world our distinct tenets and doctrines in clear and unmistakable terms, and yet

in so simple language that the most illiterate may understand them. In the second place, it is very important to have pure Baptist literature, to prove the unbiblical stand taken by other denominations, and to show the errors in their tenets and doctrines, and the great evils resulting therefrom; to show the rise of popes and bishops, the sprinkling and pouring of adults and infants, and their attendant train of evils. These innovations create new positions, these positions give new authority, unwarranted by the Holy Scriptures: the suppression of personal liberty, because man was not allowed to reason or think for himself; finally there was a union of state and church, and at last came the dark ages, that hung for many centuries like the appalling darkness of Egypt.

3. We need to have Baptist literature to help conquer the world for our blessed Master. We need it to help herald the glad tidings of the rich, free and glorious gospel of Jesus, the Christ. The walls of China have fallen; the interior of Africa is being explored; the heathen gods are tottering on their thrones. Mexico, handicapped for centuries by priesthood, is crying for help to break the chains. Cuba and the Isle of the Sea are trying to rise and throw off their galling and oppressive yoke. The whole European continent is like the great tempest-tossed sea, that cannot rest. All of these circumstances and events are calling in thunder tones for pure Baptist literature to help solve the problems of the world.

4. In the fourth place, the Baptist being the only aggressive denomination that has no taint, no savor of Roman Catholicism about her garment, like some lofty mountain detached from all others, she stands alone, towering up through the centuries, and at the same time, like some lighthouse by the deep, dark seas of human woes and human depravity, sending forth the clear electric light of God's word, saying to poor lost man: "This is the way the King of glory went; follow Him."

5. We need pure Baptist literature to help mold and shape public opinion, and thereby help to give to the world laws and governments for the betterment of man.

Be it ever remembered that these United States, the greatest, the grandest and freest country on the face of the globe, owes its greatness to the Baptist idea of civil and religious liberty. The Puritans, with all their purity, with all their love of God and man, with all their longings and struggles for freedom to worship God according to the dictates of their own consciences, were not willing to accord the same privileges to others. This was because they were laboring under the smoke and cloud of the Church of England. The Baptist church may be considered the church of the people, for the people. and by the people, under the direction of Christ, their head.

6. The fact that we are living in an age of progress, in an age of scientific investigation, in an age of schools, colleges and universities, in a thinking and reading age, bespeak the grave importance of pure Baptist literature.

The day is coming, and I think I see its dawning in the near future, when the great mass of common people will read and think for themselves, unbiased by the commands of bishops or the edicts of popes. Give this vast host pure Baptist literature, and they will throw off all forms and come to the New Testament idea of church and worship.

Come, blessed Jesus, help us hasten forward the ushering in of that glorious day, when there shall be but one flock and one shepherd.

THE WORK AND PURITY OF THE CHURCH.*

BY REV. HENRY JACKSON, OF AUGUSTA, GA.

Dear Brethren of the Baptist Family of Georgia:

In discussing the subject that has been assigned me by your committee on programme, I ask your attention to James, ii, 22: "Seest thou how faith wrought with His works, and by works was faith made perfect."

Here the purity of the church and its works are indicated. The church must first be pure in its faith. If the faith of the church is not pure its works can not be, since faith actuates to works. If the church would be pure in its faith its doctrines around which faith must twine must be pure. The center of the doctrines of the church must be Christ crucified. If the church would be pure in its faith it must cling eternally to this. The church can not be pure in its faith if it countenances affinities. The church should not tolerate members who believe in and work for societies.

The great subject of the gospel is the history of the Lord Jesus Christ. In this wonderful personage we have a character which stands alone in all history the most spotless, the sublimest, the brightest and best. The life which He led was the most wonderful and blameless. The morality which He taught was the purest and most elevated. The death which crowned

---

*The majority of the hearers being members of some societies, this address was not enthusiastically received, and Rev. Jackson could not finish his speech as prepared. This is greatly revised.—ED.

His wonderfully useful life was the most shameful, agonizing, and yet most sublime the world has ever witnessed. So He laid the pattern for all the faithful who would in all ages follow Him. He has not led the way into affinities, and how dare His followers to go into them and covenant with unbelievers without His example. By the power of the example of Christ, the triumph of His death, He has laid the foundation of a kingdom the working and purity of which embraces the strength and commands the homage of every civilized nation upon the globe, and against which the powers of hell can never prevail.

All the acts and purity of Jesus are wonderful, indeed, and hardly less wonderful are the purity and works of the true gospel church. Anti-Christs may rise to annoy and destroy the church, but it shall stand upon its pure foundation, upon Christ, the solid rock. The Baptist Church is the best prepared to give the world the pure gospel, as it is in Jesus. The church is to fight against impurity, and, therefore, should itself be pure. The church cannot be pure and have fellowship with the lodge. The ministers of the Lord Jesus Christ should not be members of the lodge, if they want a pure church. That the lodges are sapping the very life of the church, is a stubborn fact, and that ministers are taking part in them cannot be denied. What can be the object of these societies? Are they intended to glorify God? Are they of divine origin? Are they auxiliaries to the church? If so, who made them thus? Is not the church adapted to the wants of mankind, and is all that God wanted it to be? Has He required help at our hands by organizing secret societies? These societies and the church conflict, which is the surest proof that the societies are not divine, for there is no conflict in divine institutions. Government, both civil and ecclesiastic, are of divine origin, and these work together and accomplish different ends, but all to the good of man and the glory of God.

To claim that the lodge is of divine origin is simply preposterous, and wholly without foundation, as all authentic history will attest. Since the lodge is of human origin, it may go beyond the aims and purposes of its originators, and be productive of great evil; for man is a creature of mistakes. God alone makes no mistakes. Is the lodge the handmaid to the church? Is it the friend of the church, or is it antagonistic to the church? Does the lodge promote the morals of the people? Does it advance the spiritual interests of men? Does it work in line with the church in promoting man's truest and highest interest, or does it antagonize it? I assume, as is universally admitted, that the purposes of the church are right. I do not design to arraign the Almighty by so much as a question of its right and adaptation to an end worthy of its infinite Author. To antagonize the church is war upon the throne of God, and rebellion against His most righteous government.

Masonry claims to be a religious institution. It even claims universal adaptation to the wants of man—not as the christian religion and the church, suited to all classes, climes and countries—but adapted to all religions—open to receive Jew, Gentile, Greek, barbarian and Turk, and mass them in one conglomeration, without leavening them with the leaven of righteousness. It makes no claim to christianize. It rejects the cornerstone, elect and precious, upon which the church of God rests. It claims to be religious; that is all. As the play of Hamlet, with Hamlet left out, so is the lodge christian, with Christ left out. Rejecting the only foundation of the church, the antagonism is appallingly serious. The oaths required for persons to take in the lodges upon being initiated into the different degrees in Masonry is contrary to the spirit and genius of christianity. While I have referred to Masonry particularly as the great parent of all secret associations, my remarks are applicable to all such secret, oath-bound associations. They all impose an oath of secresy to obey a code of unknown laws.

Let us consider the object which the church is seeking to accomplish. What does God mean by gathering His people and organizing the church? Manifestly to bring man back to his pristine allegiance to Him, that His throne might be established in the earth, and the rebellious subjects made to bow to His loving scepter. He would have prominently among these the elevation of men, the refining of their minds, giving them very exalted views. To magnify the Lord, and to worship Him in the beauty of holiness is the work of the church. The church is to exalt the glorious name of God in the world, by teaching the people of God to reverence His name, obey His word and observe the ordinances of His house.

But what says Masonry? (See Mackey's Manual of the lodge, page 57). "Speculative Masonry, now known as Free Masonry, is therefore, the scientific application, and the religious consecration of the rules and principles, the technical language and the implements and materials of operative masonry to the worship of God as the grand architect of the universe."

Israel in the plains before Mt. Sinai's rugged, cloud-capped summit did no more idolatrous and rebellious work in making the golden calf than is this deed of Masonry. It exalts its rules above the Word of God and appoints its implements, its square and compass, as symbols in the worship of God, or, in other words, it sets at naught the teaching of God for the commandment of men. This is high-handed wickedness and unwarranted by God or the want of man. Masonry claims that it is an institution of God whose duty it is to transmit the miraculous works of God, that is, practically to assume the place of the Old Testament church, and yet with such arrogant claim it rejects the name of Jesus Christ and exalts nature to a supreme place.

The end sought by the pure church is more than the mere literary or scientific or moral elevation of man. It seeks to change his heart and make him a new creature in Christ Jesus. The church teaches perfect obedience to God. This requires more than an intellectual or formal politeness. The church aims to give back to man that he lost in the fall by pointing him to the Lamb of God which taketh away the sin of the world. This the lodge can not do or help to do. It is not befitting for members of the church to declare in the church that salvation is in none other but Jesus and then go into the lodge in the presence of Jews and pagans and dare not open their mouths of Jesus or breathe His holy name.

The work of the church comprehends much nowadays. It consists of bazars, grab-bags, neck-tie festivals, church suppers, fairs, cake-walks, broom drills, ice cream festivals, and I don't know how many other things. The more attention that is given to the purity of the church the less use we will have for these things, and money for church work will be raised from a principle. Then shall the church become the glory of all the earth. Let us guard the purity of the church, and the Lord grant us understanding in all things.

MONEY AS A FACTOR IN CHRISTIANIZING THE WORLD.

BY REV. W. R. PETTIFORD, BIRMINGHAM, ALA.

Looking from the preëminence of christianity, which it has attained in eighteen hundred years, our eyes naturally turn, with marked eagerness, in search of those things which have contributed to so noted a growth. But a few centuries ago the world looked upon christianity in its infancy. The little group of twelve disciples, almost penniless, were faithful adherents to their Lord and Master, who had not where to lay His head.

Notwithstanding the great motive which led the Lord to leave heaven and come to the earth to execute the plan by which man might be saved, and notwithstanding He had called men from among their followers, He inaugurated a system that seemed as a vehicle to disseminate the power of the gospel to all the world. The opposition which was met was then, as now, disguised and deeply seated. Judaism, which had given birth to christianity, positively refused to give place to the latter. The high priests and rulers found pleasure in asking sharp questions to entrap our Lord. The Sanhedrim sought not only to paralyze the cause, but to blot out the name and influence of Christ. Their orders were to Peter and John not to preach or teach in His name. The lawyers appeared in garbs of deception, and loaned the aid of their will to the existing opposition, which threatened the overthrow of the blessed cause. The immorality of the age served as a great fort of defense for the cause of the enemy. But Christ, with His everlasting love for fallen humanity, and His powerful way of demonstrating it, as in His humiliation at Bethlehem, His zeal and energy as a Missionary, His agony in Gethsemane and His death on the cross, soon began to draw men to him by a powerful and silent influence that the world knew not of.

From these humble fishermen and the despised Nazarene, who gave their lives for the cause they loved, has gone out to every nation the good tidings of the way of salvation. And it is truly said:

> "The morning light is breaking,
> The darkness disappears,
> The sons of earth are waking
> To penitential tears.
> Each breeze that sweeps the ocean
> Brings tidings from afar,
> Of nations in commotion,
> Prepared for Zion's war."

Money, the great commercial medium of the world, has contributed more to the growth of this cause than any other known article of civilization.

1. Money as a convenience.—Those who obeyed the great command, "Go ye, therefore, and teach all nations," were dependent upon the commodities of civilization for the comforts of the body, as upon the Lord Jesus for the comforts of the soul. As money is a medium in the commercial world, it also serves in a similar capacity for the cause of the religion which we love. Remove the monetary system, and that itself brings into existence the barbaric system which has had its day. In building the tabernacle in the wilderness, the people were required to bring gold, silver and brass, not as money, but as material,

along with the ram skins dyed red, and badger skins, and blue, purple, scarlet and fine linen. Instead of our taking up lumber, brick and mortar, when we go to build a house for God, we use money, with which we may more conveniently do our part. This valuable agent is one of the greatest blessings God has given to man through the hand of civilization.

In Old Testament times money both coined and uncoined found its place in the furtherance of salvation. By its use we may help the missionary, on both the home and foreign fields, bringing souls to Christ. It brings to these faithful laborers of the Lord the sympathy of their brethren in a tangible form— for there is no earthly sympathy like this for a poor, hungry and naked missionary. We may sing, "From Greenland's icy mountains," or, "Over the ocean wave," and pour out long and elaborate prayers for the servants on the field, but nothing helps him so materially as to send him money. Hence you see money is the scale upon which we weigh our sympathy for the toilers of God. It is the rule by which we can measure our devotion to the cause. It is the medium through which we can express our gratitude to God and love for His cause, and no man should hesitate to lay down his money for that which his Master laid down His life.

2. That money is an important factor in christianizing the world—the request of our Lord that we should give it, not spasmodically, but systematically—The scripture gives us a complete system of raising money. God says to us in Mal., iii, 10: "Bring ye all the tithes into the storehouse, that there may be meat in mine house, and prove me now herewith, saith the Lord of Hosts, if I will not open you the windows of heaven, and pour you out a blessing, that there shall not be room enough to receive it." Observe, that God asks for the tenth part of all that comes into our possession, with a promise of a blessing that shall overflow our capacity to hold it, and the threat of a curse if we rob him.

The New Testament also calls for systematic giving. I. Cor., xvi, 1, 2: "Now, concerning the collection for the saints, as I have given orders to the churches of Galatia, even so do ye. Upon the first day of the week let every one of you lay by him in store, as God hath prospered him, that there be no gatherings when I come." These scriptures show that we are not only to give the tenth of what we make but that we are to give it weekly—the first day of the week.

The rich and poor were to give according to what they had received. Let every one of you lay by in store. You are not only to give the tenth weekly but you are to delight in giving.

II. Cor., ix, 7: "Every man according as he purposeth in his heart, so let him give; not grudgingly, or of necessity: for the Lord loveth a cheerful giver." We are to give the tenth of what we make; we are to give it weekly. We are to give it cheerfully, not because the church needs money, nor that the pastor is to have his salary, but for greater reasons still, we are to give because God commanded us to give, and that giving is worship. No amount of money in the treasury, or the wealth of the pastor, will excuse us from giving.

The tax collector calls upon us for our taxes if there is money in the county treasury, and when they collect our tax we make no complaint that there is money in the State and county treasury, but we pay it cheerfully. How much more so should we pay our money into God's treasury for the support of His earthly kingdom.

3. God blesses the giver.—First He lays down a proposition that is full of encouragement to those who desire to do their duty in giving. Christ said, as quoted by Paul in Acts, xx, 35: "It is more blessed to give than to receive." In proof of this you will notice that there is a great deal said in the Bible about the giver but a very little is said about the receiver. In Luke, vi, 38, we are informed that giving has a tenfold blessing, also, as a reward: "Give, and it shall be given unto you; good measure, pressed down, and shaken together, and running over, shall men give unto your bosom." It is said that Abraham presented the tenth of all his property and even the the tenth of the spoils from his victory to Melchisidec. Jacob, after his vision at Luz, devoted a tenth of all his property to God in case he should return home in safety, Who were blessed more than they, both spiritually and temporally? In this God has put himself on record that he will keep faithfully his promise, and that if any man will accept the proposition in good faith he cannot but be blessed.

4. Again, God has wonderfully blessed the use of money in the christian world, in erecting houses of worship all over the land. Money has played a conspicuous part, upon which rests the eternal blessing of God. It has fed the hungry family of the preacher, and relieved the burdened pastor of his obligations. It has made glad the hearts of the sexton and organist, and turned the church creditor home with light steps. Money has taken the missionary to the homes of pagans in foreign fields, clothed and fed him while he broke the bread of life to the perishing multitudes. It has directed the stream of the waters of life upon the scorching and sandy deserts of sin. By its use, God has overthrown idolatry, and established instead

thereof the worship of the living God. By its use God has caused empires and kingdoms to tremble, fall and give place to the kingdom of our God and His Christ. Money has been the forerunner of christianity, to make the hilly way level, and the rough way smooth. It has been the wings upon which the good cause has reached every nation under heaven, and made known the Messiah's name. It is the great driving wheel of the old ship that shall take us all home.

Now, since there is no wickedness on the part of man more paralyzing to the cause of Christ than his refusing to properly give of his earnings, let us see to it that there is a reformation in this part of our worship. Let us first, as ministers, take up the system which I have tried to show, and teach it to our people, and it will not be long before every church will be out of debt, every pastor will receive regularly his salary, the places of worship will be beautified, and the missionaries' support will be all that is desired, and we will be multiplied an hundred times. Then the kingdom of Satan shall be overthrown, and christianity shall sweep the land as the mighty floods. Who of us will not be contributors to the coming of the millenium, when Christ alone shall reign?

No one thing would retard the progress of the christian work more than for men to lock their hearts and pocket-books to the call for means. And no people should be prouder than should we to rise up as one man, and bless God for the money that has been given for the education and christianization of our race. Let us swell the stream of liberality until every nation under heaven shall know Jesus, our Lord and Master, whom, to know aright, is life eternal. "The wise men presented to the new-born King of the Jews, the Lord from heaven, gifts, gold, frankincense and myrrh."—Matt., ii, 11.

BAPTIST CHURCH GOVERNMENT.

BY REV. J. L. DART, CHARLESTON, S. C.

If a Romanist, Episcopalian, Methodist, or a member of any other prelatical church, were asked to give a brief statement of the rule and government of his church, he would at once refer to the decisions of the several general councils and conferences, as well as to the rulings of the various ecclesiastical dignitaries of his respective church.

Likewise, if a Lutheran or Presbyterian be asked for a statement of the principles governing his church he would at once turn to the laws and regulations established by the several assemblies and synods of his church. But when a member of a Baptist or Independent church has to unfold the principles and laws which govern his church he must immediately turn to that sure word of prophecy, for the New Testament is the rule both of the faith and practice of his church.

The mark that distinguishes the Baptist denomination from any and all other evangelical churches is its tenacious hold of the plain and simple teachings of the New Testament touching all matters of faith and practice. The Baptists regard the scriptures as being preëminently their chart and compass, and they profess to be strictly a Bible-obeying denomination. Their churches are governed by no popes, cardinals or bishops; their churches are regulated by no ecclesiastical councils, assemblies, presbyteries or human traditions; but the creed and constitution of their churches are found in the New Testament. With the Baptists the question always is: "What saith the scriptures?" "How readest thou?"

In speaking of this complete dependence of the Baptist denomination on the teachings of the New Testament in matters of faith and practice, Dr. Francis Wayland says: "The fundamental principle on which our difference from other evangelical denominations depend is this: We profess to take for our guide, in all matters of religious belief and practice, the New Testament, the whole New Testament, and nothing but the New Testament. Whatever we find there we esteem binding upon the conscience. What is not there commanded is not binding. No matter by what reverence for antiquity, by what tradition, by what councils, by what consent of any branches of the church, or of the whole church, at any particular period, an opinion or practice may be sustained; if it be not sustained by the command or the example of Christ, or of His apostles, we value it only as an opinion or precept of man, and we treat it accordingly. We disavow the authority of man to add to or take from the teachings of inspiration as they are found in the New Testament. Hence, to a Baptist, all appeals to the fathers, or to antiquity, or general practice in the early centuries, or in later times, are irrelevant and frivolous. He asks for divine authority as his guide in all matters of religion, and if this be not produced, his answer is, 'In vain do ye worship me, teaching for doctrines the commandments of men.'"—Principles and Practices, p. 85.

It is the aim of this paper to show that the independent form of church government, as held by the Baptist denomination, is more in accordance with scriptural teaching, and comes nearer to the practice of the early christian churches than any other form of church polity.

In considering the subject of Baptist church government, we shall be greatly aided in the discussion by deciding first the question, what is the pattern of a church, as laid down in the New Testament? How was an apostolic church constituted and governed? For, according to this divine and inspired pattern, all christian churches should be remodeled. The examination of the Greek word, *ekklesia*, which is translated "church" in the New Testament, throws much light on this matter of New Testament church polity. This word is derived from a Greek verb, meaning "to call out or forth," and the gathering of those called out from their places of abode may be either for a political or religious purpose. A careful study of this word will lead one to the following conclusions:

First, that this word is used to denote an assembly of the people, convened at their public place of council. In Acts, xix, 39, we are told that the Greeks were accustomed to determine an important matter of state in a lawful assembly *(ekklesia)*.

Second, that in all the uses of this word, excepting two, made by New Testament writers, and where it is rendered in the English version by the word "church," it signifies a company of christians, or, as Grimm says, "An assembly of christians gathered for worship, observing their own religous rites, holding their own religious meetings, and managing their own affairs according to regulations prescribed for the body for order's sake." As the final step in dealing with an incorrigible brother, Christ says, "Tell it to the assembly." When Paul and Barnabas had ordained elders in every assembly *(ekklesia)*, they commended them to the Lord, on whom they had believed.

Third, that in two passages (Acts xix, 37, and I. Cor., xi, 22), the word refers to the house in which the worshippers assembled.

Fourth, that the word in the singular is never employed in the New Testament to denote several churches or assemblies in a large city or district, but, on the contrary, when the number of christians in a community is so large as to render their assembling in one place impossible, the word is used in the plural, indicating separate local assemblies. We read of "the churches throughout Judea," "the churches of Galatia," "the churches of Macedonia."

Fifth, that, as a consequence of what we have said respecting the New Testament use of this word, the use of the English word "church" in such forms, "The church of England," "The church of Rome." "The Presbyterian church," "The Methodist church," is altogether foreign to the signification of the original

Greek word, *ekklesia*; since these organizations, having their members widely dispersed over large extent of territories, can never literally, but only representatively, assemble in one place.

It is evident, from our investigation of this important word (*ekklesia*) and from a consideration of several passages of scripture, some of which have already been referred to, that an apostolic and primitive church was an independent body of believers in Christ, maintaining his doctrines, administering the ordinances of baptism by immersion and the Lord's Supper, governing itself, having two orders of officers (elders and deacons), and full and final powers of discipline.

But some one may object to this doctrine of the independence of the apostolic and early churches by referring to the meeting of the apostles and elders at Jerusalem, mentioned in the fifteenth chapter of Acts. The three main things taught in this passage are: (1) That the Gentile christians in Antioch were perplexed and divided by the teaching of Judaizing parties from Jerusalem. (2) That Paul and Barnabas were sent by the church at Antioch, and by divine command, to confer with the apostles and the elders and brethren of the church at Jerusalem. (3) That the decision of the assembly was arrived at first by James, the same having been proposed merely as his opinion, and not as any authoritative dictation on his part, and moreover, this opinion was concurred in by the apostles, and elders and "the whole church at Jerusalem."* Since there were only two churches represented on this occasion, this assembly was simply an advisory and informal council, such as are held in these days by our churches. It was not the first christian and ecclesiastical council as it is sometimes called. We do not find that the apostolic and early christian churches were accustomed to hold general ecclesiastical councils, nor that these churches were organically united in one ecclesiastical body, superintended by several orders of officers subject to one supreme human head. Church history clearly shows that the prelatical form of church government, which gave rise to many corruptions, was introduced by men into the church in later years. Dr. Dagg makes the following quotation from Giesclcr's Ecclesiastical History to show the gradual progress of infringement on the original church order, with respect to the independence of the early churches, the equality of the bishops, and the right of the people

---

*Says Dr. Samson, in this connection: "The purely moral or advisory character of the decree is manifest throughout the letter, declaring their decision in such expressions as these: 'It seemed good unto us, being assembled with one accord;' 'It seemed good to the Holy Ghost and to us to lay upon you no greater burthen than these necessary things;' and in conclusion, 'from which, if ye keep yourselves, ye shall do well.'"

to elect their church officers. The historian considers it a progress and improvement rendering the churches "better organized and united," but we think it a progress toward popery:

"The influence of the bishops increased naturally with the increasing frequency of synods at which they represented their churches. Country churches, which had grown up around some city, seem, with their bishops to have been usually, in a certain degree, under the authority of the mother church. With this exception, all the churches were alike independent, though some were especially held in honor, on such grounds as their apostolic origin, or the importance of the city in which they were situated. We have seen that the sphere of individual influence amongst the bishops was gradually enlarging, many churches in the city and its vicinity being united under one bishop, a presbyter, or a country bishop presiding over them. But we have now to speak of a new institution, at first found chiefly in the East, which had the effect of uniting the bishops more intimately amongst themselves. This was the provincial synod, which had been growing more frequent ever since the end of the second century, and in some provinces was held once or twice a year. By these associations of large ecclesiastical bodies, the whole church became better organized and united."

Rome was made the center of this ecclesiastical organization, because of the political and commercial advantages of that city, and of Peter's supposed labors there.

Both scripture and early church history teach us that a warm, fraternal and christian fellowship existed among the separate local churches, manifesting itself in the frequent exchange of epistles, borne by friendly messengers, and enabling one church to receive into its fellowship a duly accredited member of another.

But if it be objected to what we have said concerning the independence of the early apostolic churches, that since in other cases God unfolded His plans of operation gradually it is highly probable that in planting the church the principles of church polity were incorporated in the organization to be developed and applied afterwards in the progress of christianity, we reply that while it is conceded that the New Testament contains very little in the form of direct teaching respecting the government of churches, it must be borne in mind that some important instruction in duty was given to the churches by the inspired example and conduct of the apostles no less than by direct command. Christ and the apostles gave us much valuable instruction by their examples and actions on the subject of church government, the formation of churches, the election of officers, the equality and privilege of members, the manner of dealing with the erring.

All writers on this subject of church polity readily admit that a scriptural church practice cannot be arrived at without a careful study of the inspired examples found in the New Testament, which were designed by the Great Head of the church to be in all succeeding ages for the guidance and instruction of the churches.

"If, instead of leaving dry precepts to serve for our guidance," says Dr. Dagg. "the apostles have taught us, by example, how to organize and govern churches, we have no right to reject their instruction, and captiously insist that positive commands shall bind us. The apostles designed that their modes of procedure should be adopted and continued. We arrive, therefore, at the conclusion that, whatever the apostles taught, whether by precept or example, had the authority not only of the Holy Spirit, by which they were guided into all truth, but also of their Lord, Who had commissioned them."

When the apostle commended the church at Corinth for having kept the ordinances (or the traditions, as the revised version has it), as he had delivered them; when we see Timothy left in Crete to ordain elders in every city, and to set in order the things that were wanting—when we hear Timothy exhorted, "The things which thou hast heard of me, the same commit to faithful men, who shall be able to teach others also," —we understand that the apostle intended that his faithful disciples and their successors should follow his teachings and example in the essential particulars, and not the minor features, in governing the churches. The development in church order, which is claimed by some, has not been a natural and logical thing; it has been rather retrogression than progress, rather a marring than a mending of the divine plan and work; for what development is there in calling a man master, and bowing to a pope as father, when Christ said, "Call no man master" or father, and "Ye are all brethren?" What development is there in appealing to ecclesiastical tribunals, when our Divine Master said to the local church, "Let him be unto thee as an heathen man and a publican?" What development is there in having two classes of church members, a converted and an unconverted, when our Lord ordered a regenerated church membership by saying, "Ye must be born again?" Surely, if this is progress, it is in the wrong direction.

This independent and democratic form of church government, which is derived from the scriptures and practiced by the Baptist denomination, has some important advantages, chief among them its being a check put upon the ungodly ambition of the clergy, which, in the early days of christianity, gave rise to the Roman hierarchy.

This independence of the churches leaves no provision for combinations of churches, except as in an associative and voluntary capacity, and which are had mainly to sustain the unhallowed ambition of the clergy, and in which, at times, have been practiced and witnessed the most shameful political methods to secure power and position, such as "wire pulling," "ballot-box stuffing" and the "most bare-faced proceedings," as the New York *Herald* said in reporting the proceedings and the election of bishops at the Northern Methodist Church Conference in New York, in May last. This principle of the independence of christian churches establishes equality among the ministers of Christ; it fixes the equality and emphasizes the individual responsibility of the members of the churches, and therefore it tends greatly to promote holiness in their lives.

If it be said that this principle of independence has its disadvantages and works some evil as well as good, we would say in reply that this doctrine is not adapted to a self-seeking, ambitious and hireling ministry nor to an unregenerate church membership. Most of us can testify that independence and popular suffrage given to churches whose members and officers are wanting in intelligence, brotherly love, and are without the spirit of Christ, have been abused and made to work the most shameful and fearful results in those bodies. Why are there so many disagreements and clashes between pastors and deacons in our Baptist churches? Why are so many selfish and disgraceful splits so often witnessed in our ranks? These evils are all due to a misconception and perversion of this grand scriptural doctrine of the independence and self-government of the individual church. We take it that it is the solemn duty of every true Baptist to discourage and oppose all crooked proceedings wrought in the name of liberty, especially when these things lead up to church splits. "Brethren, ye have been called unto liberty; only use not liberty for an occasion to the flesh, but by love serve one another." This doctrine, which we regard as forming the very foundation of Baptist church government and being the key to the superstructure built thereon, grows out of such plain and well established Bible principles as these:

1. Religion is a personal matter between the individual soul and God.

2. Every man is free to worship God according to the dictates of his own conscience.

3. God has furnished to us in the New Testament a perfect rule of faith and practice.

4. The scriptures being a revelation to the individual, every man should be free to interpret and understand them for himself.

5. Individuals who have examined the scriptures and arrived at the same conclusions as to their teachings and requirements form themselves into a church for the cultivation of christian graces and the advancement of the cause of Christ. In this church none are superior; but as to their spiritual privileges all stand on the same level, nor has it any human head, for "God hath given Christ to be the head over all things to the church."

It was for holding to these and like principles, upon which is based the independence of the church, that our Baptist forefathers on the old continent and in America, during all ages, were persecuted, imprisoned and scourged. About two hundred years ago Roger Williams was banished from the State of Massachusetts among the heathen of Rhode Island; at the same time Crandal and Clark were fined and Obadiah Holmes was "well whipt," as his sentence read, and all these things were suffered for maintaining Baptist principles.

We come now to inquire as to the officers in the apostolic church. There were two orders, elders or overseers, and deacons. The first class also bore the title of presbyter or bishop. That these terms are the Jewish and Gentile designations of the same office is proven by the fact that they are often used interchangeably in the scriptures. In Acts, xx, 28, the elders of the church at Ephesus are styled overseers or bishops. In I. Peter, v, 2, elders are addressed as having the oversight of the flock, which implies their authority as overseers or bishops. In Titus, i, 5, after the ordination of elders is mentioned, the apostle immediately begins to enumerate the qualifications of a bishop; and the connection plainly shows that these terms were titles of the same office. Several of the christian fathers bear testimony to the same fact. Ignatius exclaims: "What, indeed, is the eldership but a sacred constituted body, fellow-counsellors and judges with the presiding pastor!" Irenæus, living about a century after the apostles, and writing as "episcopos," or presiding pastor, speaks of this identity; and Jerome argues at length what his predecessors had occasion to allude to, saying: "The elder is the same as the bishop or presiding pastor. Should any one think it is not the sentiment of the scriptures, but our opinion, that the bishop and presbyter are one, (this was the name of the office in that age), let him read again the words of the apostle to the Philippians, 'Paul and Timothy, servants of

Jesus Christ, to all the sanctified in Christ who are at Philippi, with the bishops and deacons, grace to you and peace.' Philippi was a single city of Macedonia, and certainly in a single city there could not be several such as are now regarded bishops. But since at that time the same men were bishops as were called elders, therefore he spoke indiscriminately of bishops as elders."

It appears that each church had one or more elders, whose duty it was to "labor in word and doctrine," "to rule well." not as a civil, but a moral officer, exercising no coercive powers, but exacting voluntary obedience. They were under-shepherds, to "feed the flock," and as such they were required to be "apt to teach," from which we infer that teaching was a prominent part of their work.

In order that the pastors might devote their energies to the spiritual service of the church, the office of deacon was originated. whose duty it was to serve tables and to minister in secular affairs. The qualifications of the diaconate, as of the eldership, are of a high moral order, but, as aptness to teach is not among them, they are, therefore, not appointed as public teachers of the Word; but it is evident from the manner in which the deacons are spoken of in the scriptures. that the strongest obligations rest upon them to be forward in promoting the spiritual interests of the church. When a deacon feels that he is called to preach the Word, he ought to resign his office of deacon, saying, "This one thing I do." In this connection, it should be remarked that Baptist churches should exercise very great care in licensing and ordaining candidates for the ministry, as well as in the selection of deacons. Not only moral and theological, but intellectual attainments should be insisted upon in those who apply for ordination.

In many of our churches ignorance holds sway in the pulpit, and it is a sad fact that in some instances grossly immoral men stand before the altar of God, to minister in holy things for the people. The standard of the Baptist ministry should be elevated and kept high. Let no man be set apart for the Baptist ministry unless he is sure that he is called of God; unless he is unquestionably a regenerated man; unless he has an intelligent knowledge of the great truths of the Bible; unless he has a pure personal character; unless he has some knowledge of men and books; unless he truly loves Christ and the souls of men, and, therefore, unless he has "an enthusiasm of humanity," to use a phrase from Ecce Homo, and a burning desire to preach the everlasting gospel of the Son of God. Then the future Baptist minister will be a higher type of a man, and a more useful and acceptable preacher to the people. He will reach the standard mentioned by an eminent divine, in addressing the students of the Boston Divinity School a few weeks since, when he said:

"The future minister will be, in the first place, a man called by God. His call will be known by the fact that he will not be able to choose any other calling. In the second place, he must be a man who appreciates the work of the ministry of the past, yet one living in his own time. He will recognize the spirit of the age, and allow it to help him in his work. He will use art and science in adorning and adding lustre and interest to truth. Thirdly, he will be a preacher of the Book. The most monstrous sham of all shams is a Christless, crossless sermon. Lastly, the future minister will be a man of burning faith and pure character."

Upon the selection and ordination of deacons the same careful and prayerful attention should be bestowed. "Should a church ordain a man for a deacon when he has not reached the required qualifications of the Bible?" is a question for discussion found in the *Georgia Baptist* a few weeks since. We reply, No. By no means let him be ordained. A good plan has been found to be to try the candidate for a few months, and if he fail to come up to the Bible requirements of faithfulness, gravity, truthfulness, unselfishness, temperance and purity—if in these and other qualifications he is not found blameless, let him be rejected.

The officers in the apostolic churches were elected by popular suffrage. In illustration of this truth numerous scriptural precedents and precepts of significant import are to be traced. We read that when an apostle was to be selected to fill Judas' place, the whole company of disciples was appealed to in common in reference to the election; that when seven men were to be selected to superintend the secular administration of the church, the whole church coöperated in their election; that when Paul and Barnabas were to be separated and set apart as the first foreign missionaries the whole church took part in their election, while the "prophets and teachers" ordained them.

It is disputed whether Paul and Barnabas appointed the presbyters in the case of Acts, xiv. 23, by their own act solely, or whether they ratified a previous election of the church made at their suggestion. This passage (in Titus, i, 5,) decides nothing definite as to the mode of choice, and therefore the free action of the churches is not necessarily excluded. It is reasonable to suppose that Paul, and Barnabas and Titus appointed and ratified men as elders who had been previously elected by the communities. It might be well to state Neander's conclusion on this subject: "As regards the election to church offices, we are in want of sufficient information to enable us to decide how it was managed in the early apostolic times. Indeed, it is quite possible that the method of procedure differed under different circumstances. As in the institution of deacons the apostles left the choice to the communities themselves, and as the same was the case in the choice of deputies to attend the apostles in the name of the communities (II. Cor., viii, 19), we might argue that a similar course would be pursued in filling other offices of the church. When Paul empowers Titus to set presiding officers over the communities who possessed the requisite qualifications, this circumstance decides nothing as to the mode of choice, nor is a choice by the community itself thereby necessarily excluded. The regular course seems to have been this: The church offices were intrusted to the first converts in preference to others, provided that in other respects they possessed the requisite qualifications. It may have been the general practice for the presbyters themselves, in case of a vacancy, to propose another to the community in place of the person deceased, and leave it to the whole body either to approve or decline their selection for reasons assigned. When asking for the assent of the community had not yet become a mere formality, this mode of filling church offices had the salutary effect of causing the votes of the majority to be guided by those capable of judging and of suppressing divisions; while, at the same time, no one was obtruded on the community who would not be welcome to their hearts.—Ch. Hist., vol. i, p. 189.*

Lastly, the independence of the church puts all discipline into the hands of the local church. Among Baptists there is no higher body or authority to which appeals can be made. Christ says, "If he will not hear the church." Paul says, "Put away from among yourselves that wicked person;" "Withdraw yourselves from every brother that walketh disorderly, and not after the traditions which ye received of us;" "If any man obey not our word by this epistle, note that man and have no company with him, that he may be ashamed."

---

*All these testimonies lead us to the same conclusion as that of Dr. G. W. Sampson, when he says "that the official heads in the christian church are the selection of its membership, having only advisory authority as agents of the church; while the church has no other province than that of watchcare over the spiritual life of its members, and the securing of co-operation and christian effort for others. It seems apparent that associations of churches are made up of representatives selected by individual churches; that their authority is simply advisory, and that it relates only to such subjects as belong to the christian advancement of those already believers, and union for the extending of the gospel to those that either have not heard or have not believed the Word."—Essay on Church Polity.

Each church, as a distinct and independent christian society, possessed the right to admit or refuse to admit members. In such a voluntary community, exclusion was the ultimate penalty.

These grand principles of independence and self-government, and all that are implied in them, have always been held dear, and sacredly guarded by Baptist churches. Their influence has been and is felt in the civil life of this and other countries; for Thomas Jefferson incorporated them into the very foundations of this government. The great German Krummacher was evidently thinking of the practices no less than the doctrines of the Baptists when, some years ago, he said to the lamented Dr. Sears, "You Baptists have a future." In all our principles and practices let us continue to do and make all things according to the pattern showed us in the Mount.

LETTER FROM REV. H. H. TUCKER, D. D.

To the Negro Baptists of Georgia Holding a Centennial Celebration in Savannah, June 6-18, 1888:

DEAR BRETHREN—I have had the honor of being invited by your committee of arrangements to attend your meeting and to deliver an address before you. To my great regret, circumstances have prevented my acceptance of your invitation; but I beg to submit these lines as an acknowledgment of your courtesy, and also as an expression of my fraternal regard and sympathy.

Some months ago I had the pleasure of furnishing to one of your number, the Rev. E. K. Love, some information of interest in regard to the early history of the Negro Baptists of Savannah. This information was embodied in some historic documents written by my grandfather, the Rev. Dr. Henry Holcombe, who in the latter part of the last century and in the beginning of the present, and while pastor in Savannah, gave much of his attention to the religious interests of his negro brethren, who I doubt not were the ancestors of many of those whom I now address. I am glad I had it in my power, even in this small way, to contribute to the interest of your meeting.

While thus addressing you, I beg that you will pardon me for expressing a few thoughts in regard to the relation sustained to each other by the two great races of men who compose our Baptist Zion in the United States.

As one of the results of the late war between the States, our civil relation to each other has been wholly changed. We are no longer masters and slaves; we are all free alike, and are all fellow-citizens of the great American Republic, whose constitution guarantees to us all, without distinction, equal rights and equal privileges forever. I rejoice in this fact, and I believe it is heartily acquiesced in by all right minded men.

Your ancestors of a few generations ago were either caught or bought on the coast of Africa and brought as slaves to this country. This atrocious crime was perpetrated by Northern men, not by Southern men. Not a solitary Southern vessel was engaged in that traffic, nor yet a solitary Southern man; nor was there a single dollar of Southern capital engaged in the enterprise. The business was carried on either by foreigners or by men of New England. The slaves found ready purchasers in Boston, and elsewhere in the Northern States no less than in some of the Southern States. Experience soon made it plain that the climate of the higher latitudes was not adapted to the negro constitution, and that hence it was not profitable in that climate to hold them as slaves. Their owners were shrewd enough to sell them to those who could own them to better advantage; and thus from no benevolent or philanthropic motive, but merely from self-interest, they relieved themselves from the burden of slavery, and thus the slaves drifted southward. The introduction of slavery was protested against by the authorities of the State of Georgia. Nevertheless, by the avarice of those who imported the slaves, and of those Northern slaveholders who found that in purchasing them they had made a bad bargain, and by the unwise action of our people here who purchased them, many slaves were brought into the State; and in time slavery became a recognized institution, not by law, but by usage established in disregard of law.

There were many who never liked it, but who, nevertheless, after it was introduced and became thoroughly interwoven with the social fabric, defended the position of the slaveholders. I was one of these. I was never in sympathy with those Northern pirates who foisted slavery upon us. On the contrary, I always regarded them and their deeds with abhorrence. But I was born in a State where one-half of the population was held in legal bondage by the other half, and neither half was responsible for the relation in which the two found themselves. I always believed that the slaveholder, who inherited this condition, was as innocent of wrong as the slave, who also inherited it. I am still of that opinion; and, though a slaveholder from birth until the happy demise of the institution, I am wholly unrepentant of the share I had in it, and feel that I have nothing to repent of. If anybody has anything to repent of it is the descendants of those who originated the system of slavery and inherited the money, with its enormous increase, for which the imported slave was sold. In a moral sense, the price of the slave is the slave, and the price of him is all over New England and old England to-day. But I acquit all the living of wrong, whether they inherited the slave or the price of him. Our highly esteemed brother, the pastor of the Baptist church in Beaufort, S. C., (the Rev. Arthur Waddell), was once my property. I think he was as much to blame for being born my slave as I was for being born his master. The truth is that neither of us had anything to do with it. One generation sinned and another bore the penalty. The sour grapes of the fathers set the children's teeth on edge.

Now, that slavery is gone, I know not which to congratulate the more, the slaveholder or the slave; for while it is true that the slave was bound to his master, it is also true that his master was bound to him; and in my opinion freedom from each other was a boon to both, and I think we do well to shake hands in mutual congratulation and cement anew the friendships formed under other conditions, and bless God that he has struck from us all the fetters fastened on us by the slave dealers of two hundred years ago.

But it is well to contemplate the fact that our civil relations are the only relations that are changed. In every other respect we are just what we always were. We are two separate and distinct races. We learn from the scriptures (Acts. xvii. 26), that originally we were all of one blood, and that all the nations on the face of the earth descended from a common ancestry. But this was a long time ago, and since then vast changes have taken place. The origin of the diversity of races is lost in the depths of antiquity; but our inability to account for this diversity is no reason why we should not accept the fact. It is true that the creation of God made us one, but it is also true that the providence of God has made us two; and what God has put asunder let not man join together. As God has made two races of us, there ought to be two; he would not have made two if one had sufficed. If infinite wisdom has thus decided on plurality, it is our highest wisdom to acquiesce in it. If God himself has drawn the color line, it is vain as well as wicked for us to try to efface it. The real well-being of each race, and of the human family at large, is best promoted only when each race preserves its integrity, and keeps itself free from admixture with any other. God's plan is the best plan, and His assorting of the races is the wisest, and any attempt to interfere with His purposes must be as disastrous in its results as it was wicked in its inception. Unfortunately, all this has, in many cases, been lost sight of, and an unnatural hybridism is the result. But the sooner the Caucasian blood which has intermingled with yours is so absorbed as to be lost sight of, the better it will be for your welfare, no less than for your honor. It is evidently the Divine intention that like should consort with like; hence, as we find ourselves providentially divided into two races, let us so remain, keeping separate in all our social relations, living peaceably side by side, and each maintaining its self-respect by maintaining its own individuality.

A blessed thing it is that the war has made no change in our relation to each other as friends, while yet it has intensified our friendship. Until the frightful emergencies of war were upon us, we never knew how affectionate and how faithful you were. It took war itself to bring your virtues into adequate notice; nor could anything less than this have ever convinced the world of the genuineness of the friendship between the master and the slave, and of a fidelity on the part of the latter which has never been surpassed. And your unwavering adherence to your masters in those dreadful days is an unanswerable refutation of the charges of cruelty and tyranny so often brought against them. It took the war to bring to the front the good in both races, and the amiable relation which they sustained to each other, and to show to the world how greatly slavery was mitigated by christianity. The spectacle presented to the world was a sublime one, when one race, held in bondage by another, was true in time of peril to the friendships formed during that very bondage, refusing to throw off its bonds when it could easily have done so, and loyal still to the dominant race, gave it, in the hour of its extremity, an unfailing and hearty support. You were in chains, it is true, but they were chains of love. Christian masters and christian servants were never enemies. Never can we of the white race forget who it was that during those awful years took care of our wives and children, and of all our aged and infirm, when they might all have been slaughtered or left to starve to death. Never can we forget whose toil and whose sweat it was that sustained our armies in the field for four years against the most stupendous military power the world ever saw. Remembering all this, we shall never cease to wish you well, and to do what we can to promote your interests.

On the other hand it is well for you to remember, that as God brought good out of evil when Joseph was sold by his brethren into Egypt, so blessing has come to you, by your having been brought from the land of your fathers to this country. Civil slavery was the germ out of which gospel freedom sprang. Here you are civilized, and speaking the English language instead of the gibberish of savages; and christianized, while your cousins across the water, descended from the same ancestors, are to this day idolaters, barbarians, and some of them cannibals. In this case, God, instead of sending preachers to the heathen, has brought heathen to the preachers, and has made the wicked act of man-stealers and pirates the means whereby salvation is brought to thousands and millions of his elect. Thus gloriously has God caused the wrath of man to praise Him. So it has been, at any rate, that the two races have mutually benefited each other in times past, and happily the relations of the two, notwithstanding the persistent efforts of outsiders to alienate them, are still friendly, as they have always been, and our prayer should be that this harmony and kindliness of feeling should be maintained forever.

I regard with great delight the fact that your ecclesiastical relations are just what they always were. A Baptist church is a Baptist church, whether those composing it are white, or black, or brown, or yellow, or red, or in any way intermingled, for, says an apostle "By one Spirit are we all baptized into one body, whether we be Jews or Gentiles, whether we be bond or free: and have all been made to drink into one Spirit."—I. Cor., xii, 13.

The original Savannah Association was composed of five churches, two white and three black; and churches once composed almost wholly of slaves, retain their individuality absolutely undisturbed, now that all those once slaves have now become free. No change in our civil relations can change or in the least degree affect our ecclesiastical relations, rights or privileges. "For," says our brother Paul, "He that is called in the Lord being a servant, is the Lord's freeman; likewise also he that is called, being free, is Christ's servant."—I. Cor., vii, 22. And again, says the same apostle, "There is neither Jew nor Greek, there is neither bond nor free, there is neither male nor female: for ye are all one in Christ Jesus."—Gal., iii, 28.

If you think best to have ecclesiastical organizations of your own, separate and apart from those of the whites, there can be no harm in so doing. But this is only a matter of expediency, and not a matter of principle. Experience shows that those of a kind do best together, and that, as a general rule to which there may be exceptions, the greatest efficiency is attained when the organizations are homogeneous. Still, while thus divided into families, kind and affectionate correspondence should always be maintained.

Above all, brethren, let us remember with rejoicing that our fraternal relations are exactly what they always were. We were brethren in Christ in the days of slavery, and we are brethren in Christ now. One God is the Father of us all, one Saviour died for us all, one covenant—the everlasting covenant between the Father and the Son includes us all; and one heaven, one holy, happy, blessed heaven, is in reserve for us all, where distinctions of race will be forgotten, and where we shall all dwell together forever in the presence of God and of the holy angels.

I dwell with deep gratification on the facts that hundreds, perhaps thousands, of your race have sat under my ministry; that many of them have been baptized by me; that many of your preachers have passed under my instructions, and that I have ordained a number of them to the work of the gospel ministry. Above all am I happy in the belief that some of your people have been brought into the Kingdom as the result of my labors in the Lord.

And now, dear brethren, with heart-felt salutation to your Centennial Convention. I subscribe myself, ever fraternally yours in the faith and hope and love of the gospel of Christ,

HENRY HOLCOMBE TUCKER.[*]

ATLANTA, GA., June 12. 1888.

---

[*]The above communication from Dr. Tucker is able and timely. In the main it meets the most hearty endorsement of the editor of this book. The point touched on concerning social equality meets our fullest approval. We have never urged social equality as a prerequisite to negro greatness. We think it rather damaging than helpful to the race. The slave trade is treated of very largely by our venerable brother, the blame of which is largely laid at the door of our Northern brethren. Without questioning what he says, we remark that the South appears to be equal heir to the great wrong done Africa, and suffered in common for this sin, atoning for it with the blood of her noblest and purest and general devastation of property. The Southern white boy, it is true, found himself in possession of negro property, which was not his fault, but so soon as he learned that it was wrong to hold human beings as slaves then it was his fault. The sins of the fathers were visited upon the children, and hence the children were wrong. Dr. Tucker has a record of never having entered fully into sympathy with the inhuman and ungodly system of slavery; but he was a Southern white man, and it required more nerve than nature has favored any one man with, as a rule, to oppose what everybody (in the South, and many in the North) then believed to be a God-given legacy. Such men as Dr. Dagg believed and taught that slavery was the express will of God. We can fully sympathize with our white brethren who grew up under such influences and such teachings. We thank God for the revolution and reaction which He, himself, has brought about.

THE ACT OF BAPTISM.

BY REV. J. H. KILPATRICK, D. D., WHITE PLAINS, GA.

Baptism is a New Testament ordinance. Jesus himself was baptized, and He commanded His followers to be baptized. But what is baptism? If we know not what baptism is, how can we know whether we have ever been baptized, and so have obeyed the Saviour's command? All Baptists, and many who are not, believe that immersion, and that only, is the baptism of the Bible. As a general thing, doubtless, this conviction has come from reading the English scriptures and understanding them in their plain and natural meaning. Moreover, this conviction thus obtained is strong enough to satisfy perfectly the conscience of all who have been immersed, and it may be added, strong enough, also, largely to unsettle the consciences of many who have not been immersed. Since, however, there are various opinions professedly as to what baptism is, and some have alleged that the scriptures properly interpreted do not teach immersion, it is natural that every intelligent and honest seeker after truth, though not a scholar, should yet desire to examine the subject for himself, and for himself see just what the truth is. To assist in meeting this desire is the special object of the present discourse. It has not been prepared for the witless and slothful who blindly follow the say-so of others, but rather for all persons of good common sense who love the truth and desire personally to inspect the foundations of their faith.

And now for our question, What is baptism? As baptism is a New Testament ordinance, of course to the New Testament we must go in order to answer it. But the New Testament was written in Greek, and the most of us have no knowledge whatever of that language. Never mind; if you have common sense, and will exercise it, that will do just as well or better.

Now, remember, our word "baptize" has come from the Greek *baptizo*, and the real question first is, What does this word mean? that is, in what sense did the old Greeks use it? How can we find out? Just simply by finding out the circumstances under which they used it. That is the way our children learn the meaning of words when they begin to talk. Does a child go to a dictionary before he knows a letter in the book? And yet he learns the meaning of words from noticing how they are used. A little child just learning to talk sees and feels a certain action called "whipping," and it does not take him long to learn what the word means. Now, I want to read to you some instances where the Greeks used this word *baptizo*, and I will only give those where I, myself, have seen the original Greek.

1. Polybius, a historian, describing the passage of an army through a swollen stream, says: "They crossed over with difficulty, the foot soldiers being baptized (*baptizo omenoi*) up to the breast."

2. Hippocrates, illustrating the folly of blaming others for what we bring on ourselves, says: "Shall I not laugh at the man who, having baptized (*baptisanta*) his ship by the abundance of freight, finds fault with the sea for engulfing it?"

3. In Æsop's fables we have this: "A mule laden with salt, having gone into a river, accidentally slipped down; and the salt dissolving, he rose up lightened. He perceived the cause and remembered it, so that, always while crossing the river, he cunningly lowered down and baptized (*baptizein*) the sacks or panniers," which held the salt. Adopting the same expedient for lightening his load when laden with sponge and wool, the poor fellow found the result disastrously different.

4. Strabo, speaking of the march of a certain army between a mountain and the sea, along a narrow beach which was sometimes flooded, says: "It happened that they walked for a whole day in the water, being baptized (*baptizomenoon*) up to the waist."

5. The same writer, in the same work, speaking of a certain lake, whose waters were probably impregnated with salt or asphaltum, says: "It happens that those who cannot swim are not baptized (*baptizesthai*), but float like wood."

6. Diodoras, speaking of the annual overflow of the Nile, says: "Most of the land animals being surrounded by the river, perish, being baptized (*baptizomena*), but some, escaping to higher places, are saved."

7. Strabo, writing about a salt lake in Phrygia, says: "So readily does the water crystallize around everything that is baptized (*baptisthenti*) into it, that whenever they let down a circle of rushes they drew up crowns of salt."

These examples from classic Greek (and their number might be greatly multiplied), show unmistakably the sense in which the old Greeks understood the word in dispute. But some one may say, these writers were heathens, and unacquainted with the rites and ceremonies of the Jews; might not the apostles, therefore, who were native Jews, have understood the word differently? Fortunately, and I believe providentially, we have a Greek history, written about the same time with the New Testament, and by a native Jew, and in the very sort of Greek in which the New Testament was written—Josephus' History. In this work the word *baptizo* frequently occurs, and not once in a sense different from that in the examples already given from classic Greek. We give a few instances:

1. Describing the murder of the boy Aristobolus, he says: "Continually pressing down and baptizing (*baptizantes*) him while swimming, as if in sport, they did not stop until they had completely drowned him."

2. Narrating the case of Jonah, he says: "The ship being just about to be baptized (*baptizesthai*), the sailors, the captain and the pilot began to pray," etc.

3. Describing a battle between the Romans and the Jews on the sea of Galilee, he says: "When they (the Jews) ventured to come near (to the Romans), they suffered harm before they could inflict any, and were baptized (*ebaptizonto*) along with their ships; and those of the baptized (*baptisthentoon*) who lifted their heads above the water were either killed by the darts or caught by the ships" [of the Romans.]

4. Again he says, narrating a personal adventure: "Our ship having been baptized (*baptisthentos*) in the midst of the Adriatic Sea * * * we swam during the entire night."

But why multiply these instances? I will give but one more from Josephus:

5. Describing the manner of purifying the people during the thirty days' mourning for Miriam, he says: "Casting a little of the ashes [of the red heifer] into a fountain, and baptizing (*baptizantes*) a hyssop branch, they sprinkled" (*errainon*), etc.

6. And now, just one more to conclude, and this from the Greek translation of the Old Testament: "And Naaman went down and baptized himself (*baptizeto*) in the Jordan seven times," or as it is rendered in your family Bibles, "Dipped himself seven times in the Jordan."

Now, friends, you have examples of Greek usage of this much controverted word *baptizo*, and you can judge for yourselves the meaning of it. You need not go any more to lexicons, or commentaries, or to learned men. Your own eyes have seen, as in a picture, just what the Greeks meant when they said a person or thing was baptized. And you are now prepared to try the rights of proprietorship in this word. There has been a number of claimants. The most common are sprinkle, pour and immerse. In the light of the preceding examples, is it possible to doubt for a moment which claimant has a right? And not a single witness has yet been found in the whole range of classic or Hellenistic Greek literature that utters a discordant voice. Here are the witnesses. You have heard their testimony. Nay, by their graphic witness, they have carried you in person to the lakes, the seas, the rivers, and given you the evidence of your own eyes, enabling you to see, as in a panorama, things animate and inanimate, ships, men, animals, etc., sinking beneath the waters.

If this testimony does not establish the right, title and claim of the word immerse as the legitimate heir and successor of *baptizo*, then it is useless to try to prove anything; and if this testimony will not convince, neither would people be persuaded though one rose from the dead. To make the case stronger, though, if such be possible, we need only bring sprinkle and pour to the test of these examples. Try them as translations of the word *baptizo*, and if there had been a lingering doubt before, this practical test will drive it away as chaff before the wind. (Here make the test of a few—say Nos. 1, 2, 3 in classic Greek, and 1, 2 and 4 in Josephus).

But enough; if the Greek word *baptizo* does not mean immerse neither does immerse itself mean immerse. And if the Greek *baptizo* can be made to mean sprinkle or pour, or pour upon, so also, and just as easily, can the English word immerse—no more, no less. Now this word *baptizo*, an acknowledged member of the Greek language, and proved by incontrovertible evidence to mean immerse, and nothing else, (for if it bear any other meaning in the whole range of the Greek literature extant when the New Testament was written, the instance is yet to be found), this is the very word adopted by the holy spirit to designate and describe the act of christian baptism. The command, therefore, to be baptized is a command to be immersed, and nothing else will fulfill it. If Jesus intended for us to be sprinkled, what possible reason for not using a word having that meaning? If Jesus intended for us to have water poured upon us, what conceivable reason for not using a word that said so? If He did not intend for us to be immersed, why did He use a word that means immerse? These questions are simply unanswerable.

Right here this discussion might legitimately stop. The question, "What is the act of baptism?" has been answered. Since Jesus in commanding us to be baptized has used a word signifying immerse, this should settle the whole matter—both the question of fact and also of duty. Nothing remains but to accept the fact—immersion the baptism of the Bible, and fulfill the duty—receive this baptism, if not already baptized.

"But," says some one, "don't words change their meaning?" So they do, but there is not one particle of proof that *baptizo* changed its meaning when introduced into the New Testament.

And says another, "I don't see how immersion could have been performed in every case of baptism mentioned in the New Testament." And must your inability to see how a thing could be done 1800 years ago outweigh and set aside the explicit command of your Lord and Master? Grant that there were a thousand difficulties, there still stands the command in letters of living light, "Repent and be baptized," and there is still the inspired testimony "Then they that gladly received His word were immersed, and the same day there were added unto them about 3,000 souls." But I do not grant that there are any difficulties at all in the way of understanding immersion to have been the one and exclusive baptism of the Bible. The difficulties (and they are many and insuperable) are all the other way—sprinkling and pouring, as christian baptism, are not only without the shadow of a foundation in the original, but they are utterly inconsistent, both with scripture language and scripture facts. But let us go to the New Testament and take a search for these wonderful difficulties: and just remember they must be proved:

1. "Such vast multitudes could not have been immersed by John." Answer—(1.) John may not have baptized personally one hundreth of them. (2.) It cannot be proved that such "vast multitudes" were ever baptized. The Jews as a nation rejected both John and Jesus.

2. The 3,000.—"Their baptism was impossible. (1.) The apostles could not. (2.) Not enough water. (3.) The Jews would not let them use it, even if it were there." Answer—(1.) No proof that all were baptized in one day. (2.) No proof that the apostles were the only administrators; (3.) Even if they had been they could have done it, and in three hours. (4.) History records two cases of three thousand in one day by immersion, and within the last few years the Baptist missionaries to the Karens baptized in one day largely over two thousand. (5.) The objectors must prove not enough water; but modern researches have proved that there was scarcely a city in the world better supplied. (6.) As to the Jews not letting them use the water—no proof of it, but the contrary.

3. The jailer.—"The jailer could not have been immersed at midnight, and that, too, in the jail." Answer—No proof that it was done in the jail, but the contrary. As to facilities, no proof that they were not ample. You must prove the difficulties real—imaginary ones are worthless.

4. The beds and tables.—"Impossible," one says. But you must prove it impossible, and that is impossible. But reliable Jewish writers say the Jews did do these very things.

5. "The Red Sea baptism, was that immersion?" Yes, an immersion. They went down into the sea; the waters were a wall on right and left, and the cloud was overhead—they were hidden from sight. A beautiful figure of believers' baptism!

6. "The Spirit's baptism."—Just remember that when the writer said "pour" he used a word that meant it. The pouring took place and then the baptism.

Here, again, this discussion might stop. We find nothing in the New Testament necessarily inconsistent with immersion, and so must accept it. *Baptizo* in the New Testament, as well as out of it, means immerse, and immerse only; and so immersion, and immersion only, is the baptism of Christ's appointment. If there were no further evidence on the subject, what has been already adduced should be sufficient for all who desire to know and to do the will of their Lord and Master. As if, however, to put the matter beyond even the shadow of a doubt, the Holy Spirit has introduced into the sacred volume facts and circumstances which unmistakably point to immersion and to nothing else.

1. Going to the water, and not bringing the water. "But what of Cornelius' baptism? Did not Peter say, 'can any man forbid water?' *i. e.*, to be brought." And if it had been the way some people baptize (so called), the water would have been brought. The subsequent command proves that baptism could not be conveniently attended to just then, and so could not have been sprinkling or pouring.

2. Going to a place of "much water," (1) Enon; (2) the Jordan.

3. Baptizing in the Jordan—the Greek *en* and *eis*.

4. Going down into the water, and coming up out of the water.

5. Baptizing in water; the element water opposed to the element Holy Spirit.

6. The natural meaning to all the words gives immersion—*baptizo*, *eis*, *ek* and *en*. Now, while we adopt the natural meaning of all these words, affusionists, on the other hand, have to adopt rare and far-fetched meanings, if they be meanings at all, and even these they have to vary from time to time, sometimes making the same word have different meanings, and sometimes different words the same meaning. In the case of *baptizo*, while agreed in forsaking the natural meaning, they can by no means agree among themselves what unnatural meaning

they shall adopt. The prepositions *eis*, *ek* and *en* suffer like violence at their hands. In order to keep Philip and the eunuch out of the water they plead for *to* as the meaning of *eis*. When, however, they come to the baptism of Jesus, as narrated by Mark, to say "baptized *to (eis)* the Jordan" would make nonsense, and so they have to adopt *at*. So also with *en*. John did baptize in *(en)* the wilderness. Here they admit the natural meaning. In the next verse, however, this natural meaning would give us "baptized in *(en)* the river Jordan." But this points too plainly to immersion, and therefore the unnatural meaning *at* is brought into requisition. In verse 8, this same troublesome preposition *en* comes up again, but here *at* will not serve the affusionists. "Baptized you *at* water," "baptized you *at* the Holy Ghost"—this would be too incongruous, and so *with* is resorted to—"baptized you with water"—"with the Holy Ghost." Now, what do we see here in the space of a few verses? In verse 4, *en* is admitted to mean *in*; in verse 5, it is said to mean *at*; in verse 8, *with* is claimed as the meaning, while in verse 9, the meaning *at*, which had just been given to *en*, is ascribed to *eis*, which latter preposition, mind you, in the case of Philip and the eunuch, is alleged to mean *to*.

Alas! what hopping and skipping we have here. What shifting and veering and dodging! And can it be that the truth requires the assistance of such tactics? Take a single one of these little prepositions in its natural and common sense meaning, and the spell is broken, and we have immersion as the baptism of the Bible. Take them all in their natural sense, and the proof of immersion becomes cumulative and overwhelming. That even one of the words in dispute, *baptizo* included, should be used unnaturally in a plain narrative of important gospel history, would be strange, but that they should all be thus used, surpasses belief. And yet this wonderful thing, for which there is not one particle of evidence, must be received as true, before the claims of immersion can be set aside. Verily, it is not saying too much when I solemnly declare that the system of interpretation which has been used in this baptismal controversy by the opponents of immersion, if applied elsewhere, would destroy every doctrine and change every command of God's word.

7. The testimony of Rom., vi, 4, and Col., ii, 12.—The testimony of these two noted passages is so plain and so generally admitted that I need not dwell on them. The learned and the unlearned of every age and country have found immersion taught here. "Buried by baptism," "Buried in baptism," this seems to be the very thing itself. To see immersion here, one only needs to look. Not to see it requires tedious and tortuous pro-

cesses of reasoning, a continual struggle against the testimony of one's own eyes. But let us stop a little while.

1. In Romans we have these words: "Therefore we are buried with Him by baptism into death," and in Colossians "Buried with Him in baptism, wherein ye also are risen with Him through faith of the operation of God." Combining these, they declare that we are buried with Christ by baptism and in baptism, and in it raised up again. Being a declaration of scripture, this must be true. But how? It can not be true *literally*, for in a literal sense the Saviour was alone in His death, His burial, and His resurrection. To suppose that baptism puts our bodies in Christ's literal grave and raises them up again, is too absurd to think of. Neither can it be true *spiritually*, except indeed we should adopt the dogma of baptismal regeneration and say that the new birth takes place in and by baptism. For, mark, it is distinctly stated that this burial and rising again take place in baptism and by baptism. And if this be true in the spiritual sense, then we have baptismal regeneration full and complete, there can be no escape from it. If we reject the literal theory as self-evidently false, and the spiritual one as plainly subversive of vital scripture truth, the only alternative is to understand the apostle to be speaking figuratively—just as Jesus did when he said, "This is my body." He did not mean that the bread was actually His body, but that it represented or symbolized His body. So Paul did not mean that we are actually buried with Christ by baptism and with Him raised again, either in a spiritual or literal sense, since baptism, however important in its place, does neither one; but that the ordinance of baptism, including as it does our immersion in water and our subsequent emersion from it, represents our spiritual union with Christ in His burial and resurrection, thereby proclaiming to the world our own death to sin and resurrection to newness of life, both of which really come through "faith of the operation of God."

2. We reach identically the same conclusion by a different and independent line of argument, thus: In combating the licentious principle that we may live in (sin) in order to make more conspicuous the forgiving grace of God, Paul refers to the fact that all believers are dead to sin, and in proof that they to whom he was writing, themselves, recognized this fact, he alleges the testimony of their own baptism. Still further explaining and emphasizing this point, he continues: "Therefore," because of this death to sin, "we are buried with him by baptism into death, that like as Christ was raised from the dead by the glory of the Father, even so we also should walk in newness of

life." Now, to make Paul reason logically, our baptism must testify that we have died to sin with Christ, with Him to have been buried, and with Him risen again.

But how can baptism give this testimony? Baptism has no voice, but it has a form, and its form must speak, and this it does most expressively and impressively when we are buried beneath the waters "in the likeness of His death" and raised up again "in the likeness of His resurrection."

Understand baptism to be immersion, and Paul's reasoning here is clear and forcible. Reject immersion, and the whole becomes hopelessly involved and confused. Hence the justly celebrated work of Conybeare & Howson says, (and mark, they were not Baptists, but Episcopalians): "This passage cannot be understood, unless it be borne in mind that the primitive baptism was by immersion."

And this closes our reference to the New Testament proofs of immersion. More might have been said, but let this suffice. Really, the demonstration was complete without any of this corroboratory testimony. The Greek word *baptizo* having been shown to mean immerse, when it was adopted by the Holy Spirit to teach the ordinance, of course it must be understood in this sense, without some clear and unmistakable proof for another meaning. Examining the inspired volume, however, we find not only nothing against this meaning, but abundant and decisive evidence for it. Immersion, then, and immersion only, must stand as that "one baptism" of the Bible.

THE TESTIMONY OF FACTS.

The argument for immersion is complete—it needs no supplementing. Like a demonstration in Euclid, it proves itself—as soon as it is seen, it is seen to be true. Some, however, will not look at it. To arrest the attention of such, and show them that the truth certainly does lie on the side of immersion, the following facts are presented. Now mark: These facts form no part of the argument for immersion. That would remain just as complete and conclusive if not a single one of these facts were in existence. But be it also marked, that while these facts form no part of the argument for immersion, they do testify in trumpet, nay, in thunder tones, to its validity. If the argument for immersion were not so overwhelming, these facts would not exist. But now listen to the facts, and judge of the worth of their testimony:

1. It is a fact that while immersionists have not a particle of doubt or difference as to the meaning of *baptizo* in the gospel

ordinance, anti-immersionists seem utterly at sea. Some make it "sprinkle," some "pour," some "pour upon," some "purify," some "wash," and so on; and some claim that while meaning none of these, it may yet include them all! Now, why all this? Why are learned affusionists so bewildered as to the meaning of a simple Greek verb? Why are some clinging to this meaning, and some to that, and some to no meaning at all? Just because they are on the wrong side, that is all.

2. It is a fact that while immersionists generally, and Baptists in particular, are fond of talking about following the Saviour in the ordinance of baptism, "being baptized just as he was," "imitating the example He set us at the Jordan," etc., our affusion brethren don't do it. At least, I never heard it. On the contrary, they quite generally oppose the idea that we are to look upon Christ's baptism as a model for ours. Why this difference? Suppose we grant that Jesus was not baptized just to set us an example. He commands us to be baptized, nevertheless, and his own baptism furnishes a decisive illustration of what baptism is; and is it not sweet to feel that we are walking in his footsteps, and receiving the very same rite which he hallowed by submitting to it himself? Why, then, should affusionists so generally endeavor to turn away the eyes of the people from the Saviour's baptism? I can think of no reason but a consciousness, more or less distinct, of contending for something as baptism which they do not believe their Lord received.

3. It is a fact that while Baptists universally press the duty of strict compliance with scripture command and scripture example in the matter of baptism, affusionists are notoriously given to pleading for christian liberty—"that it doesn't matter about the quantity of water, so the heart be right." Why such talk, if they do not feel that they are not following the sacred scriptures?

4. It is a fact that Baptists are perfectly satisfied that they have been scripturally baptized. Multitudes who have been sprinkled or poured upon are to this day dissatisfied. Why this?

5. It is a fact that many are coming to us every year from the Methodists, the Presbyterians and other affusion denominations, because of dissatisfaction with their baptism. It has not come to light that a single one has left our ranks because dissatisfied with his immersion. I do not say that none leave us, but they do not leave us because dissatisfied with their immersion. Why this great difference, if it be not that there is an overwhelming evidence for immersion as the baptism of the Bible?

6. It is a fact that many who fail to seek immersion nevertheless have a notion that it is the primitive baptism, and they only fail to seek it because they think it is not essential to salvation. How often do we find the last resort of the hard-pressed affusionist to be, "O well, I think I can get to heaven without being immersed." But who ever heard of a Baptist solacing himself with the thought that he could get to heaven without being sprinkled or poured upon? They don't talk that way. Well, why not? Most undoubtedly this pleading that immersion is not essential to salvation is proof that those who make the plea nevertheless believe that it is the baptism of God's word. It also proves that if the reception of the identical baptism of the New Testament were essential to admission into heaven, many more would be found seeking a place of "much water." Yes; suppose an angel should be sent from heaven, and that all knew of a truth that he was so sent, and this angel, by God's authority, should make a proclamation that all who did not receive the identical baptism of the scriptures within a week's time, should infallibly be lost. not giving us any further light than we now have, well, I don't know what would happen; but is there any harm in telling what one believes? I'll do it, then. While I do not believe that a single Baptist in all the earth would seek to be sprinkled or poured upon, I do verily believe that the affusion brethren would quite generally betake themselves to the water; yes, and among those thronging multitudes would be found the most, if not all, of those venerable divines who have written and preached so learnedly against exclusive immersion. I think they would reason thus: "Affusion may do, yes, may be so, but if I have got only one chance for my life, let me be on the safe side and take immersion."

7. It is a fact that while witnessing the ceremony of aspersion or of affusion has never been known to convert any one to that way of thinking, the witnessing of the ordinance of immersion has oftentimes so disturbed people's minds that they could not be satisfied until they themselves went down into the water.

8. It is a fact that many pious and ardent affusionists who have undertaken the investigation of the baptismal question for the special purpose of disproving the Baptist view, so far from converting others from that faith have converted themselves to it. I am not referring to the many who have studied the subject because of their own private dissatisfaction and their honest desire to know and obey the truth, and as a consequence have espoused our views, but I refer especially to those who were put forth by their people, or came forth of themselves, as lead-

ers of their hosts and champions of their faith. Such men, for example, as Milo P. Jewett, a learned author and educator, who being requested by his church to preach on the subject of baptism "to silence the immersionists" and settle the disturbed minds of some of their own members, determined to go into an original and thorough investigation of the whole matter, and in consequence, contrary to his expectation, his interests, his desires and his predilections, became a convert to the very views he set out to disprove. Or Alexander Carson, the world-renowned critic and philologist, who thought before he tried it, to use his own words, that he "could demolish the arguments of the Baptists as easily as one could crush a fly." After investigating and writing for a whole month, he threw all his work in the fire, and to the amazement of his people announced himself a Baptist.

Take just one more case: Burmah's great missionary, Adoniram Judson. Young, pious, gifted, zealous for the custom of his Puritan fathers, went forth to the heathen, bearing a commission from the most ancient, and probably, at that time, the most honored affusion denomination in America. In a little time, much to his own surprise and the surprise of the world, we find him, like his celebrated prototype, joined to the sect everywhere spoken against, and "preaching the faith which once he destroyed." How did this marvelous change come about? It is substantially the same story that has been told in a multitude of other cases. Mr. Judson, expecting to meet the Baptist missionaries at Serampore, "felt it important, for the honor of his denomination, to be able to defend its sentiments." He had been taught from childhood to believe his system correct, now he essays to prove it so. But alas for the cherished faith of his childhood! and alas for his own peace of mind! The more he examined the subject, the more he became conscious that both as to mode and subjects of baptism he was in error. A painful conflict at once began between principle and preference. He did not want to be a Baptist. His whole soul shrank back from it, but the truth was his object, and the truth made him a Baptist. I earnestly commend the case of Judson to every pious and intelligent opposer of immersion. His conversion to the Baptist faith, under the circumstances, is truly wonderful. Just see: Judson's piety and indomitable energy had given birth, under God, to the foreign mission enterprise in America. To sustain him and his associates, the first American foreign mission society had just been organized; and he was the chief spirit, the very soul of that first missionary company which had ever left the shores of the New World. To him all eyes were directed. and in him all hearts confided. Surely, in his case, self-interest, reputation, family, social and denominational attachments, the memories of the past and the glowing hopes of the future—nay, every conceivable earthly motive—all combined to keep him where he was. Judson, then, must have believed that truth lay on the side of the Baptists, else he had not joined them.

But now (and here comes the test question), how could he have thus believed, under all the circumstances surrounding him, unless compelled by the irresistible force of the truth? Every possible influence tending to prevent an impartial judgment of the issues involved was against the Baptist side, and in favor of his own. And be it particularly observed, that he began the investigation with all the burning zeal of a youthful partisan, anxious to establish and defend the faith of his fathers. That such a one, under such circumstances, with such antecedents and such surroundings, should have come to the conclusion that the "immersion of a professing believer in Christ is the only christian baptism," seems little short of a voice from the skies, saying, "This is the way; walk ye in it."

But some one may say, "What about conversions from the Baptist view? What do they prove?" I cannot tell; for I have never heard or read of any such as I have described, and many others that I might give. There may be, and doubtless will continue to be, many departures from the Baptist ranks, and for various reasons. Unfortunately, many people do not make denominational connection a matter of principle, but simply of pleasure or of policy. But if there has ever been a case where a zealous Baptist, of undoubted piety and intelligence, after a thorough and prayerful examination of the subject, and with no conceivable motive but love of the truth and loyalty to Jesus, came to the deliberate conclusion that he had never been baptized, and therefore went over to the affusionists, asking for scriptural baptism—why, let it be produced. But no such case has ever occurred, or will ever occur, and nobody expects any such to occur.

Well, why this great difference? No one can naturally prefer immersion, but the contrary; for it is decidedly more inconvenient, to say nothing else. And so, if there were no preponderance of evidence for immersion, every one would eschew it and adopt affusion; and particularly those whose interests and prejudices were already on the side of affusion would be sure never to give it up. How comes it, then, that so many of every age and sex and rank, learned and unlearned, rich and poor, teachers and the taught, in spite of the inconvenience of immersion, in spite of their early training and consequent prejudice against it and in favor of affusion, in spite of the natural shame of confessing one's self wrong, in spite of the powerful influence of family, social and religious ties, and the frequent jeopardizing of important temporal interests, how comes it that so many in the face of all this array of opposing motives give up affusion and adopt immersion as the only christian baptism? There is no possible explanation but that on the side of immersion is found the truth. And now, christian friends, you who have repented, and yet up to this hour have suffered yourselves to put up with something which your conscience told you was not the baptism the Saviour received, what are you going to do about it? "Well," some of you may say, "good and great men have believed in and practiced affusion, is it not safe to follow them?"

The question is not what have good men believed, but what does the Bible teach? Not what good men have done, but what has your Lord commanded? Will you follow men or Christ? Whose example is the more precious to you? "But baptism is nothing but a ceremony, it doesn't matter much whether we submit to it or not." Baptism is a ceremony, but not a mere ceremony. It is a ceremony, it is true, but it is one of God's selection and appointment—to neglect or despise it, is to treat with contempt the One who ordained it. "But you Baptists do not believe that immersion is essential to salvation, we can be saved even if we do not go under the water." Ah! here is your final refuge; when routed from every other place you hide here. Here you think you can rest in peace. But what a resting place for a christian! You have a strong conviction that immersion is the baptism taught in the Bible, that Christ was immersed, and that the apostles practiced immersion, but because you think you can be saved without it, you let it alone! To save your souls you would be willing to submit to immersion, but to be immersed in order to obey Christ and to follow His example, you are unwilling. And yet you claim to love Jesus! Jesus says: "He that hath my commandments and keepeth them, he it is that loveth me."

Obedience is the final and best test of love. Whatever we do or don't do, let us be sure to "Fear God and keep His commandments, for this is the whole duty of man: for God will bring every work into judgment, with every secret thing whether it be good, or whether it be evil." Amen.

NOTE.—Much of this is but an abtract of Dr. Kilpatrick's able discourse. Much of it was delivered extemporaneously.

BY REV. J. H. KILPATRICK, D. D., WHITE PLAINS, GA.

NO ROYAL ROAD* TO CHURCH PROSPERITY:

Or, The Necessity for Patient Continuance in the Scripture Plan of Promoting the Prosperity of Our Churches.—Ps., xxxvii, 34.

Every lover of Christ must desire the prosperity of His churches. All pious hearts are one here. Moreover, when the question is asked, "How is this prosperity to be secured? what is the best plan?" doubtless all will readily agree that the best plan is the scriptural plan, whatever that may be. The object of the present endeavor is to ascertain this scripture plan, and to urge upon all its adoption and a patient continuance in it.

* As to the expression, "No Royal Road," to give its reputed origin will best explain its meaning. It is related that Euclid was once asked by a certain king, Ptolemy Lagus, I believe, whether there was not a shorter and easier way to a knowledge of geometry than that which he had laid down in his Elements; whereupon the great mathematician replied, in words which have been stereotyped for all coming time, "No; there is no royal road to geometry," meaning that there was no short and easy method for him, a king, any more than for others; that the same need of toilsome, patient effort pressed upon all alike. What was then and is now true of a knowledge of geometry, is also true of church prosperity.

Church prosperity may be viewed in two aspects—the internal and the external. Churches are composed of individuals, and these individuals should be new creatures; and these new creatures should, day by day, be growing up into Him who is the head, in all things, and ever walking as becometh His gospel. Now, in proportion as churches are actually composed of such new creatures, thus growing and thus walking, in like proportion may they be said to be in a prosperous condition. This is

INTERNAL CHURCH PROSPERITY;

and it is to be sought (1) by making our churches accord with New Testament antecedents in members, officers, operations, doctrines and ordinances; (2) by cultivating, as individuals, a high degree of personal piety, striving to bring every thought and feeling and affection and principle into complete and loving subjection to Jesus, and manifesting this subjection of our hearts by the blamelessness and consecration of our lives; and (3) as promotive of the foregoing, by maintaining a godly discipline. This is internal church prosperity; and this is the scriptural plan for attaining it. If we desire the prosperity, let us adopt the plan.

But it is mainly of the external church prosperity that I wish to speak. Of course, our churches should earnestly seek after internal growth and prosperity; but this is not enough, and it should not and can not satisfy them. The internal is really but a base, upon which and out of which is to rise a higher and nobler prosperity—the external. Botanists divide plants into two classes—those which grow within, and those which grow without. The churches of Christ embody both in one. The Saviour's kingdom is to be advanced not only in individual christian hearts, but also in the world; and it can only make progress in the world by conversions from the world. This growth of the churches by accessions from the ranks of the ungodly is

EXTERNAL CHURCH PROSPERITY.

And here let us dwell at greater length.

Jesus came to seek and to save the lost. And those who are found and saved forthwith desire to be instrumental in finding and saving others. This is the law of the new creation. He who is saved by Christ is at once brought into fellowship with Christ, and so into a cordial sympathy with the object which brought Him into the world. The saved soul not only desires an increase of the Saviour's dominion in himself, but that it should extend over others. Now the churches of Christ, normally and properly, are but communities of these saved souls—not only themselves saved, but ardently desiring the salvation of others. And churches were originated not only for the development and growth in truth and holiness of their individual members, but that thus these might labor more efficiently in bringing the outside world to Jesus. In this latter purpose of a church's organization is found its highest and last subordinate end; and thus only, according to the divine plan, can the kingdom of Christ, in its present state, be perpetuated from generation to generation, and all the number of the redeemed be finally brought in. Hence it is that the Lord's people are said to be the light of the world; but if none are guided by them into the way of life, is not their light virtual darkness? And so they are said to be the salt of the earth; but if none feel their salvatory influence, wherein is the fleshly mass of humanity the better for their existence? While, therefore, churches should assuredly seek after the largest inward development—the completest conformity, in heart and in life, in faith and in practice, to the divine requirement, they must not, and surely they can not, be satisfied with this: the culmination of all church progress, the final results of all healthy and matured church life, must be looked for in a spiritual posterity rising up around them to take their places and perpetuate their name.

And as it is natural and right that churches should desire to see souls converted, so they ought to expect it; and when these desires and expectations are not realized, as they so far fail to accomplish the end of their being, they should distrust the healthfulness of their condition. Surely there must be a cause for this abnormal state of things. And we should not too soon fly to God's sovereignty to find a solution. May there not be some cause personal to ourselves? Some derangement, organic or functional? Some obstruction? Some lurking disease, which demands attention? Brethren in Christ, churches of the saints, if souls be not converted in connection with our labors, we should suspect the presence of evil somewhere, and should earnestly search for it, and finding it, should earnestly set about effecting its removal.

But let us suppose that we are measurably prepared for the great work of leading sinners to Christ. And we must work in this way, whether fully prepared or not. Laboring to rescue others will help to rescue ourselves from the dominion of sin, and increase our efficiency for further labor. The great law of the Kingdom of Grace is, "He that watereth shall be watered also himself." While striving to save those without, reflex benefits will flow in upon our own souls.

But how shall the churches best fulfill this their great mission? In other words, what is the

NEW TESTAMENT PLAN OF SEEKING THE SALVATION OF SINNERS?

An attentive consideration of the teachings, the lives and the labors of the Saviour and His apostles, shows that this plan involves two, and only two, essential points: First, the earnest, faithful presentation of the truth, especially the truth concerning Christ and Him crucified. Secondly, sincere prayer for the Spirit's power to accompany the truth so presented, preparing the way for its reception, and making it effectual to the salvation of the soul.

Under the first of these two may be mentioned, especially, the public preaching of the Word—this justly occupying the foremost and highest place. Nearly allied to it is the presentation of gospel truth and gospel motives to sinners under any circumstances, and by anybody—whether parents, Sunday school teachers, or any other lover of Jesus and of souls. Here, also, must be included the circulation of the scriptures, religious books, tracts, and all publications which unfold and enforce the truth as it is in Jesus. In short, the sinner and the gospel must be brought together. If he will not come to it, we must carry it to him; and if he will not hear it from living lips, we must try to get him to read it from the printed page.

The second part, prayer, of course implies an antecedent—faith in God, and a firm reliance upon Him, and Him alone, for success, and includes all earnest, believing prayer, whether going up in breathings and ejaculations from amid the pressure of daily business, or in more deliberate and formal manner, from the closet, the family altar, the social prayer meeting, or the public congregation.

THE SCRIPTURAL PLAN OF PROMOTING CHURCH PROSPERITY.

The preaching of the gospel, therefore, or the presentation of the truth as it is in Jesus, and prayer to God, may be called the New Testament plan of laboring for the salvation of sinners; and this completes the scriptural plan of promoting the prosperity of our churches. Let all workers for Christ adopt it.

But before going any further, let us mark this: To adopt and truly carry out this plan requires self-denial, self-sacrifice, self-consecration—a high sense of individual responsibility, followed and thus verified by earnest individual effort, and the expenditure of time, and talent, and strength, and fortune, in the service of the Master, and that according to the measure of the ability and the opportunity. And very especially (and here is revealed the grand instrumental power for the conversion of the world, but alas, greatly wanting in these latter days), it requires not only that the gospel be presented to the ungodly, but that it be lived before the ungodly. In a word, it requires on the part of both preachers and people, a close walk with God—earnest, faithful living and working for God—abiding trust in God, and constant, importunate prayer to God.

Now we are ready to consider the

NECESSITY OF PATIENT CONTINUANCE IN THIS SCRIPTURAL PLAN OF PROMOTING CHURCH PROSPERITY.

A number of scriptures clearly present and enforce the thought here suggested. "For ye have need of patience, that, after ye have done the will of God, ye might receive the promise."—Heb., x, 36. "That ye be not slothful, but followers of them who through faith and patience inherit the promises."—Heb., vi, 12. "And let us not be weary in well doing: for in due season we shall reap, if we faint not."—Gal., vi, 9. "Rest in the Lord, and wait patiently for him: fret not thyself because of him who prospereth in his way, because of the man who bringeth wicked devices to pass."—Ps., xxxvii. 7. And especially our text, "Wait on the Lord, and keep His way, and He shall exalt thee to inherit the land."

The tenor of these scriptures, taken as a whole, is about this: Adopt God's way; continue in God's way patiently; a patient continuance in God's way will lead to success. The plan which we have just been considering is God's way to church prosperity—no so-called "royal road," widened and smoothed down and paved to suit the demands of princely ease, and indolence, and self-indulgence, and worldly lusts, but the true royal road, the King's highway of holiness, along which the ransomed of the Lord shall be led upward and onward to prosperity and usefulness here, and to glory and happiness hereafter.

1. Let us adopt it. It is God's plan. Every deviation from it springs from a sinful deference to fleshly pleasure or fleshly wisdom. It is simple: involving no complex machinery, the youngest child of grace can understand it. It is practicable: its requirements fall within the capacity of the weakest and obscurest saint, while yet they give full scope to the learning and zeal of a Paul or the eloquence of an Apollos.

2. Let us not only adopt it, but hold on to it, and hold on to it patiently. A patient holding on implies an actual and earnest desire to see the end attained—souls saved, Zion prospered, God glorified. And it implies a desire to bear a part ourselves in securing this end. Some seem quite anxious to see the cause prosper, but they are more anxious to see others do the working and spending and sacrificing. A patient holding on to God's way implies not only a willingness to be personally employed, but much employed—to work and to work hard—to toil and toil on—to make sacrifices, and to make many and great sacrifices. We may desire the end, and even desire to do something to secure it, but our desires may not be strong enough to overcome our natural love of ease, or other selfish propensities. Especially, a patient holding on implies and requires a controlling sense of obligation to obey God, and an unfaltering trust in God, let the immediate issue be what it may. Any of us can work pretty well when we see the fruits of our labor quickly following. To work and wait, to toil and not faint—this requires not only an ardent desire for the end, but a strong faith and a heroic obedience. He who patiently keeps God's way will often be compelled to walk by faith, for sight will fail him. Like Moses, he will have to endure "as seeing Him who is invisible."

3. A patient continuance in this plan will be sure to have a happy issue, and nothing else will. "My soul, wait thou only upon God." "Wait on the Lord and keep His way, and He shall exalt thee to inherit the land."

And right here my discourse is complete, so far as the line of thought is concerned. But in the times now upon us there seems to be special reason for emphasizing this patiently-holding-on idea, and that is just what I desire especially to do.

A RESTLESS AGE.

Our lots have fallen in a restless, impatient, greedy, and yet ease-loving age. Railroads, telegraphs and the like have been begotten by, and in turn have begotten, a general demand for short routes and quick results. Air lines, lightning expresses and close connections are the order of the day. The old paths are being forsaken and new ones opened up. Rivers are bridged, mountains tunneled, continents cleft in sunder. And it is not only nigh cuts and short routes that are called for, but easier routes and cheaper routes. Time, and money, and labor, all must be economized; and time-saving, and money-saving, and labor-saving machines and devices are in the ascendant.

Now, why should the children of this world ever be wiser in their generation than the children of light? Modern christianity seems determined to wipe off this old reproach. It means to keep abreast with the times. While everything else is moving, must it still be hampered and retarded by the cumbrous and flesh-mortifying methods of eighteen centuries? Shall commerce, and manufactures, and agriculture, and education, and even the art of human butchery, be emancipated from the moss-grown systems of the past, and religion have no part in the general jubilee? Not so; the religion (?) of this progressive era claims equal rights and concurrent immunities —yes, the churches (many of them) have manifestly caught the spirit of the age, and disdaining the slow and plodding processes of prayer, and work, and self-denial, and self-sacrifice, and patient waiting. have struck out for quicker methods and easier routes to the salvation of souls and the prosperity of Zion.

THE ECCLESIASTICAL SHORT LINE.

Some seem to have had wonderful success in running the short-line schedule. Others have looked on. They are unwilling to be distanced in the race. They covet the glowing results, and yet they are not disposed to toil and pray and wait, do their duty, and leave the event with God. The pressure is heavy upon them. Their own restless hearts cry out for results, and an impatient world demands results; but the results don't come. What shall they do? The only alternative is to forsake the old path, and take a nigh-cut.

How is it with our churches—aye, Baptist churches? Have they escaped the infection? Is it not largely true that where not shamefully indifferent to the prosperity of Zion, as many of them are, they are seeking out methods which will necessitate the smallest possible outlay of faithful, self-denying labor? We want prosperity; we want to see souls converted and the cause advanced. So far, so good. God's plan is to accomplish these ends through the prayers, and efforts, and sacrifices of his people. But this doesn't suit the carnal nature. It requires too much self-denial; too much closet religion; too much every day religion. Besides, it takes too long. Can we not think of some shorter and easier way? Here then come in various nigh-cuts and short roads—by-ways to avoid the "hill of difficulty."

PROTRACTED MEETINGS.

1. Is the protracted meeting. Now hear before you strike. I do not object to protracted meetings as such. There may be occasions when they would be eminently appropriate, and, if properly managed, eminently useful. And I am not now objecting to their customary management, which in the main is exceedingly unwise, and generally quite disastrous in ultimate results. What I am objecting to is the foundation principle upon which they are usually based—the immediate, underlying motive which too often induces us to desire them, and to hold them.

Just see: A church is in a cold—it may be, a declining condition. No new recruits are coming in; things drag heavily; other churches and other denominations are outstripping. What is to be done? Instead of purifying their ranks and purifying their hearts—cutting off evil doers from their fellowship and forsaking their own covetousness and worldliness, and numberless inconsistencies—rooting up the thorns and noxious weeds, and breaking up the fallow ground, and casting in the pure seed, and watering it with their prayers and tears, they conclude to have a protracted meeting and do the work of a year, or ten years, in a week or two. And it will be well if, even during the meeting, a tithe of the members can be induced to lay hold and work. They want to see the cause prosper, oh yes, and they want the protracted meeting, but they don't want to work in it. They favored it under the idea that it was a labor-saving device; and now that it is started, they expect the preacher or preachers, and a few singing and praying brethren and sisters, to do the work. They look on; discuss the propriety or impropriety of what others do; it may be, enjoy the season somewhat, and at the close are perfectly free to disparage and condemn the whole, if unsuccessful, but if successful, quite ready to talk of what a glorious meeting we have had.

Mark: I am not arguing the protracted meeting question; much might be said on either side. I have simply instanced this case to show the false and ruinous principle upon which protracted meetings largely proceed. They are often, though perhaps not intended so to be, really and actually substitutes for duty—substitutes for duties slighted, for duties neglected —substitutes for the slower and more laborious and flesh-mortifying methods which God has marked out, and to which our carnal nature is averse—nigh-cuts to church prosperity —labor-saving machines in the Kingdom of Jesus. In no other way can we reconcile the vast number of protracted meetings and so-called revivals with the general low state of practical piety in the land. Whatever protracted meetings might be made—whatever they may be intended to be made—in most cases they are made substitutes for that life of labor, and prayer, and self-denial, and godliness, which the Bible requires. And hence, we find churches whose members are notoriously loose in their lives, many of them paying their debts neither to God nor to man—spending their money as free as water, it may be, for worldly lusts and pleasures, while doling out but a bare pittance for the support of the gospel at home and its extension abroad; and yet, they are able to get up a rousing revival (so-called) every twelve months. Let protracted meetings be, as they should always be, simply times of special prayer and effort for that zeal and love which are ever seeking after and improving opportunities of service—chosen seasons for extra toil in seed-sowing and in reaping on the part of those, who, day by day, sow beside all waters—and some who now favor them most will be the last to hold them.

"But even as now commonly originated, don't they do some good?" So they may. But so often as they are made the occasion of fostering the false and corrupt principle just pointed out, they are sure, in the end, to do more harm than good. Pastors and churches have quite largely come to rely on these meetings to do that which consistent and consecrated piety, patient toil, and importunate prayer alone, under God, can accomplish, and the consequence is the churches generally have sunk into a state of chronic coldness and barrenness, relieved only by these annual, or biennial, or triennial arousements, whose apparent success largely tend to produce and perpetuate the very evils under which we are already groaning.

It must be borne in mind that when anything, however good in itself, comes to be the occasion of neglecting something vital and indispensable, it thereby and therein becomes a positive evil. Commercial fertilizers are, doubtless, a good thing; but when they are relied upon to the neglect of a thorough preparation and cultivation of the soil, and a diligent gathering and application of home fertilizers, they prove a curse. Cotton is a good crop, but when it is relied upon to the neglect of all other branches of husbandry, it surely leads to poverty and final bankruptcy. It is well for the farmer to especially bestir himself at certain seasons—to put forth extra and protracted efforts when the interests of his business require, and a favorable opportunity presents, and sometimes even to call in his neighbors to help him; but he who sits idly down the most of the year, and expects to make up for his idleness by these occasional efforts, will certainly come to want. Let the children of light learn wisdom. Whenever and wherever protracted meetings are relied upon, as they now largely are, to supply the place of daily prayer, and labor, and self-denial, and faith, and patience, and holy living, in all such cases will they be curses to the churches.

THE EVANGELIST SHORT ROAD.

2. Next is the resort to evangelists or revivalists. A church wants to make headway in the world—may be really desires a revival, and doubtless does need one. The scripture plan, however, requires sins confessed and sins forsaken, and time and talent consecrated to the Master. Work is required, and much work, and patient work; prayer is required, and earnest and constant prayer. The demand is too great. Even a respectable protracted meeting requires more than they feel willing to undertake. What is to be done? Why, send off and get some noted revivalist or evangelist, prepare the way for his coming by a series of meetings, but expect nothing, really pray for nothing, until this mortal man shall come and take matters in charge, and "deliver them out of their distresses."

Now, let no one misapprehend me. There can be no kind of objection to proper persons traveling through the country, stirring up the churches and preaching the gospel to the masses; it is scriptural. But the special need now is for some one, or rather a good many, to go up and down in the land, calling upon the people of God to return to the "old paths," and to do their own work, yes, and their own praying, too. There is too much reliance upon other people's labors and other people's prayers—too much looking to man, and not enough looking to God. At the present time, in many places, there are more earnest desires and prayers for the coming of some of the great evangelists of the day than for the descent of the Holy Spirit; and manifestly the expectations of success center in their coming rather than in the attendant presence and power of the Spirit. Am I mistaken? Wherefore, then, such elation when their speedy coming is announced? Wherefore such despondency when their coming is delayed? Verily, this looking to men, and running after men, and crying unto men, is not only dishonoring to God, but even to our own christian manhood. What! is not Jehovah our God as well as theirs? Have we not the privilege of access to Him as well as they? Is it possible God will not hear us as readily as them? And will He not bless our labors as well as theirs? And will He not own His Word when spoken by us, though we be unknown to fame, as well as when spoken by these whose praise fills the land? I do not say that God will thus do; but if not, the reason is to be found in our and our church's unfaithfulness, and indolence, and worldliness, and unbelief; and it is vain to think to escape the legitimate consequences of our sins and failures by flying to others, however good or great, or even successful they may be. Yes, these evangelists may all be godly men, and, for aught I know, may be very successful in leading sinners to Christ, as doubtless some of them have been; but those pastors and churches who sinfully neglect their own work, and then expect to evade the just consequences of their shortcoming by calling in the aid of men, thus virtually hoping to circumvent the Almighty, sooner or later will find out their mistake.

THE NEW PREACHER SHORT ROAD.

3. The same general desire to abridge labor and self-denial has opened up the new preacher short road. The affairs of a church are unsatisfactory, and perhaps they ought to be; but, instead of rallying around the pastor they have, and going to work themselves, they set longing eyes upon some new man, whose past reputation for building up churches excites the hope of similar results with them. Some way or other, no matter how, the old preacher is gotten rid of, and the new one called. For a little while everything moves on swimmingly; their hopes

are bright; at last they have got the man they were so long wanting—i. e., the man to do his work and theirs too. In another little while, and a change comes over the spirit of their dream. They find their condition essentially the same—it may be, worse—it is reasonable that it should go from bad to worse. They soon conclude it is the preacher's fault—they mistook the man, or he has run his course. And soon again they are without a pastor, and still again are they in search of the man who shall be able to do what God never meant to be done, and still are destined to disappointment.

SHORT PASTORATES.

But there is another view to take of short pastorates, which, though not exactly in the line of the present thought, yet merits a passing notice. It often happens that the pastor himself, anxious for quick returns, or impatient of hard work, is unwilling to stay where he is. Permanent church prosperity is largely dependent upon permanent pastorates. As a general thing, however, long pastorates require of a minister much patient and self-denying toil—brain work, heart work, life work. Many are not disposed to honor the draft, and so they look out for other fields, more fertile, it may be, or more easily cultivated: at any rate, fields where the well-worn plow-shares of many furrows may still do creditable service; yes, and where the same system of superficial tillage will in turn be followed by the same results. The condition of many of our churches is remarkably like that of many of our farms, and the same desire for easy methods and quick returns is largely responsible in both cases.

Now I do not say that ministers should not sometimes change their fields of labor—doubtless they ought; but I will say, they should never do so simply because they want to escape hard work or patient waiting. And I do not say that churches should not sometimes seek a change of pastors, but certainly they should not do so under the vain hope of finding a man whose piety, or zeal, or eloquence, or other qualification shall absolve them from the duty or the necessity of earnest consecration to the Master's service.

And here is a good place to call attention to a wide-spread evil. Our churches, whether they retain the same pastor from year to year, or frequently change pastors, still, all alike, are depending too much on their pastors to do whatever is necessary to bring prosperity to Zion. It is not exaggeration to say, that as the "eyes of servants look to the hand of their masters, and as the eyes of a maiden to the hand of her mistress," so quite generally the eyes of churches are directed to their pastors. They are largely looking to these pastors not only to do their (the churches') work, but even that of the Holy Spirit. There is a great and calamitous mistake just here. The churches know better. They know that Paul may plant and Apollos may water, but that God alone can give the increase. And yet, practically and actually, they are looking to their pastors for the increase. My brother in Christ, esteem your pastor; esteem him highly; esteem him very highly in love for his work's sake, this is the divine command; but when you place such reliance upon him—when you look to him to do your work, and even that of the Spirit too, you lay on him a load of responsibility that may well crush him to the earth. And it is not, perhaps, too much to say that the consciousness that the churches are thus looking to their pastors, and leaning upon their pastors, and expecting success at their hands, is even now pressing the very life out of many a devoted pastor in the land. He feels his utter inability to meet the demand upon him and is sinking beneath the burden. O brethren, look to God—trust in Him.

THE WIDE DOOR OR LOW GAP DEVICE.

4. It only remains to notice the wide door or low gap short-road. This is the final nigh-cut towards which all the others incline, and falling short of which they largely fall short of fatal injury. The others, when not pursued as nigh-cuts, may not be in all respects evil; but this is evil in itself—it is evil, and only evil, and that continually. A church longs for the prestige of numbers—the *eclat* of large and frequent additions. Great is the pressure upon the pastor for this proof of his success, and his heart, quite likely, beats in unison with the hearts of his people; and it is right to want to see "much people added to Lord." O that we all were ten-fold more anxious for this! But God may not see fit to give immediate success in the way of additions. More generally, perhaps, pastor and people have not been willing to live, and labor, and pray, and trust, and so come within the pale of the divine promises. But still they want success, and that means numbers. They conclude to make special effort, and that means a protracted meeting. They send for some noted revivalist, or perhaps, the pastor gets to help him some warm revival preachers from around. The meeting begins, and the meeting goes on, and a goodly number profess a hope and knock for admission into the church. Now mind you, the desire for members is still strong.

Numbers are still the adjudged proof and measure of success. The pressure upon the pastor is still unabated, and his heart still yearns to gratify the longings of his people. Besides all hearts are now warm and generous—love is glowing, and feelings generally have reached melting heat. Is it strange, then, that under the circumstances, the procrustean rigidity of the old standard of admission should be relaxed, and a lower gap, or a wider door offer easy ingress to the thronging applicants? "What! give up a converted church-membership!" "O no; hold on to that. But, you inveterate old fossil, don't let us put up the fence so high as to keep out Christ's lambs. Besides, you need not expect everybody to be converted. Was not Judas one of the twelve? Did not unbelievers creep in, even in the apostles' day? Does not the gospel net gather of every kind? Don't be so very particular. Don't pry so closely into the experiences of the professed converts. Don't expect babes in Christ to be old theologians.* Do not count an applicant not converted until he gives some proof that he is; but rather count that he is converted until he proves that he is not. And then, do not require an intelligent and spontaneous profession of faith in the atoning sacrifice of Christ, as evidence of a changed heart; but reverse the order, and accept the profession of a change of heart as proof of the possession of faith. Finally, remember that people are timid, and if they can not tell a consistent and satisfactory experience help them out a little, or may be, tell all for them by asking questions which suggest the proper answer.† The immediate results of all this are seen in the vast and rapidly increasing array of formal professors, whose influence rests as a fearful incubus upon the life and power of the churches. The final results eternity alone can reveal.

Now all these devices, and others which might be mentioned, proceed from the same evil root, namely, an eagerness for success which centers more in self than in God, and a consequent dissatisfaction with God's plan and God's time, and the success which God sees fit to give. Success is wanted, and success we feel we must have; but we are not willing to work for it, we are not willing to wait for it.

Such unworthy feelings and motives are referred to in the preceding discussion, that careless thinkers may be disposed to

---

*This is no fancy sketch. These very things have been said to me by pleaders for more laxity, and in most cases, *in these very words*.

†If pastors would require applicants to tell their own experiences, and then require, in these experiences, reasonable proof of an intelligent apprehension of faith in Christ crucified or as the way of life and trust in Him, improper persons would seldom come in.

question their existence in the hearts of God's people. Well, God's people ought to be free from such, but, unfortunately, many of them are not. Besides, none are without sin; and sin is essentially selfish and deceitful, even though found in the heart of a christian. A cursory examination will not always reveal to one's own consciousness the motives which determine conduct. Let the best man among us actually explore the recesses of his heart, and he will there find principles and motives just as reprehensible as those here condemned. And a part of our business in this life is to drag out into the light these hidden abominations, whether found in ourselves or in others, and hew them in pieces before the Lord. So have I endeavored to do.

CONCLUSION.

1. How vain the hope of finding an easy way to church prosperity! The ingenuity of man has done much, but it can not override a divine law. Man's wisdom is displayed in discovering God's laws, and in adapting himself to them. This is the secret of the success and usefulness of all the great discoveries and inventions of these latter days. But there has not yet been discovered, nor will ever be, an easy road to heaven, or an easy road to church prosperity. The reason is found in the fact that the carnal mind is enmity against God; and so, that which accords with it must, for that very reason, be opposed to Him. Accordingly, when we seek for flesh-pleasing methods in serving God, we seek for an impossibility. Deny thyself, and take thy cross, are the inexorable terms of discipleship. And so long as self-denial, cross-bearing, the crucifixion of the flesh with its affections and lusts enter into christian life and christian duty, just so long will it be vain to expect to achieve purely spiritual successes and yet listen to the demands of the flesh. These things are antipodal, and the endeavor to bring them together is worse than futile. It is but the old, oft-repeated, century-stricken, but hopeless and ruinous, attempt to combine the service of Mammon with the service of God.

2. How vain the hope of finding a *shorter way* to church prosperity than that which God has marked out! It is a true proverb, that the longest way round is often the shortest way through. Even in this day of steam and lightning, we still sometimes see that "slow and sure" go hand in hand. Quick results are quite often as worthless as quick. God seems to have intended to teach us this truth in nature. The insect comes to maturity in a few days, while man, the noblest work

of the Creator, requires long years. The mushroom springs up in a night, while the lordly and valuable oak grows for centuries. But let nature's lessons be what they may, God's plan for bringing prosperity to His churches is fixed, and we might as well undertake to heave the sun from its place in the sky, as to reach real church prosperity in any other way.

3. Why can we not be content to work for God *in His own way?* Is not His way the *best* way? Are we ashamed of the Gospel of Christ? Is the simple, unmethod-trammeled preaching of the cross no longer the power of God unto salvation? Has this fast, progressive age, outrun the divine wisdom? "Where is the wise? where is the scribe? where is the disputer of this world? Hath not God made foolish the wisdom of this world?" Yes, verily; and quite signally do the failures of latter-day wisdom attest the fact. Rest assured, my brethren, it still pleases God "by the foolishness of preaching to save them that believe."*

4. And why can we not be content to abide God's time to reap the fruit of our labors? Why this restless, feverish impatience for results? Can we not trust God to fulfill His own promises? Is the prosperity of the cause dearer to us than to him? Are we more jealous of His honor and more concerned for His glory than Himself? Let us not deceive ourselves. This demand for quick results is not all zeal for God. It is rather a selfish impatience of the very toil, and sacrifice, and self-denial which he requires, and which we want to escape. Zeal for God? Nay, nay, but for ourselves. A single eye to His glory would make us choose His way and abide His time.

5. How dare we not be content to work for God in His own way, and then leave the issue with Him? Do we not belong to Him? Has He not the right to command our obedience? If He should see fit to require us to toil all our days, and still see no fruit, is that our business? We are His—the kingdom is His—the power is His—the glory is His—all is His. Who are we that we should dare to be dissatisfied with what pleases Him?

6. These nigh-cuts do generally give apparent success. But when we contentedly go on in them, neglecting the heaven-appointed highway, it would seem that in realizing apparent

---

*Not long before his death, Dr. R. Fuller, of Baltimore, wrote thus: * * * "Some evangelist is called in to arouse the slumbering energies of the church; and then 'many are added.' But alas! how few of these are truly converted, the melancholy history of six succeeding months most sadly testifies. Moreover, evangelists would soon forsake their calling if they were required, like the apostles, to rely upon their sermons. We rejoice in the good they accomplish, but the measures they adopt are an acknowledgment that the 'foolishness of preaching' can no longer avail for the conversion of souls to God."

success we attain that which we are really seeking after, and like the hypocrites of old, have our reward. But apparent success is only apparent after all. It may deceive us and flatter our vanity—it may deceive the world and give us their applause, but sooner or later its real character will be developed. It contains the elements of its own overthrow. The higher and grander the tower, the more certain its fall, if it be not well founded and well built. And the more a church has of merely apparent success, only the more certain, the more signal, and the more disastrous its final shame and ruin.

7. If we can not have real success let us have none. The semblance of success attained, often so deceives and satisfies as to prevent our seeking after that which is real. But real success comes from God, and from Him alone, and must therefore be sought in His way.

My brother, my christian brother, whoever you be, do you want success? Do you want real success? Do you want real and permanent success—a success that will abide the winds and floods of time, and the fires of the great day? Wait on the Lord and keep His way, and He shall exalt thee to inherit the land. Amen.

THE DUTY OF PARENTS TO SUNDAY SCHOOLS.

BY PROF. JAMES ROSS, PRINCIPAL OF EAST BROAD STREET SCHOOL, SAVANNAH, GA.

Mr. President, Ladies and Gentlemen:

On such an occasion as this, where so many parents are present, I should not judge it out of place to speak to you something concerning your relation to the Sunday school. There is no greater institution in modern times than the Sunday school, and more hearts are being educated within its consecrated walls than anywhere else. It is the most God-like institution we have and is the very embodiment of law, having a profound respect for morality and religion without which freedom would have no lasting foundation and no certain protection.

The Sabbath should be a day of rest from worldly cares and pleasures; a day for the study of God's Word; for the discussion of the highest themes that concern immortal souls. On every side we observe disaster, discomfort, sorrow and death, in many cases properly attributable to the botching of life by not having sufficient truth instilled into the tender ones' minds to guide them along the path of rectitude.

We were placed here, just a little lower than the angels, to live a life useful to God and to man. How much of that life we live depends largely upon how much we know about life and how much of it we execute. "He most lives who acts best, feels noblest, and that life is the longest which answers life's purposes best."

More interest in your children's welfare will make less candidates for the prisons. Teach your children more studious habits, in attending Sunday school, by more deeds than words, and they will honor you in old age and heartily indorse your judicious management. Urge upon them the imperative necessity of punctuality, diligence in pursuit of the great riches found in God's Word, and they will reflect much credit upon you, congratulating you for building lasting monuments for future generations as criterions by which to test the abstract excellence of all pure christianity.

Your interest in the Sunday school will encourage the teacher as a gospel herald, tendering good tidings of great joy to all who will receive the grand blessings embodied in their message. I shall not presume it out of place, just here, to say that too many grown persons think they are too old to improve, so they draw themselves within their encrusted shells and presume their work is done. Many excuses can be found or framed for negligence, but remember this is an age of sentimentality, and there are people who would attempt to render an excuse even for Judas, whose name has been a synonym of infamy. Have you thought how cheerful and happy is old age to him who has kept life green and realized the importance of his mission of usefulness until God called him beyond this veil of tears?

Let us be not careless about our duty any more, let us breathe not the malarial air from the surrounding fields, let not the deadly sewerage gas come into our homes by modern conveniences, let our children no longer be dragged about the streets on Sundays by some one they call friend, but let us manage our own affairs while on earth we stay. Some one has said, "If the effects of carelessness came upon us like a deadly serpent we could avoid it, if, like the north wind, we could shelter ourselves from it, but its footsteps unheard creep silently and cautiously upon us, and, ere we are aware of the danger, our whole system has been poisoned," making us unfit to live in this world or the world to come—a sight only to make hell laugh and heaven weep.

The church has now largely over 5,000 members. This makes it the largest negro church in the United States, and in all probability, in the world. It is an interesting, orderly, intelligent church. It is perfectly devoted to its pastor. The church never denies him a request. Whatever he intimates that he wants he can get it, regardless of the cost. His influence over the members is simply amazing. The church, however, is not more devoted to him than he is to them. They will make mutual sacrifices for each other. This is just as it should be. There never was more unanimity of opinion and concert of action in any church than that which characterized this church in its endeavors to extend its house of worship. In revivals the church comes together in such a christian-like manner that the influence upon sinners is wonderful. The church is very polite to strangers and everybody visiting the church is made to feel at home. The choir is good, and visitors are generally charmed by their singing. The Sunday school is without a single exception the largest and best in the State. Most of the most substantial members of the church grew up in the Sunday school. The church is justly proud of her Sunday school and her noble corps of humble christian teachers.

This church, notwithstanding her great troubles, has been as a city that is set on a hill, which cannot be hid. Her good works have been witnessed far and wide and many thousands have been led to a saving acquaintance with the gospel of the Son of God. For one hundred years she has been battling with sin and Satan, winning glorious victories all the way. Notwithstanding all the bitterness she has been called to taste, she has scattered seeds of kindness for the reaping by and by. She has always conquered her enemies and heaped coals of fire upon their heads. God has caused her to pass under the rod because He loved her. He has made her go through the fire to purify her and to refine her as gold is refined. She has put her trust in Jesus and He has never allowed her to be confounded. That church which has leaned on Christ for repose He will never desert to her foes. That church, though all hell should endeavor to shake, He will never forsake. Happy is that people whose God is the Lord.

This church has organized many branches. In fact, all of the churches in this part of Georgia must trace their origin back to this church. She is their legitimate mother. Her children, many of them, have done noble work, but they have not equalled the old lady. Her strength and influence have increased with her age. She has constantly contended "for the faith once delivered to the saints." She has walked alone when she felt that she was not in company with the right. When others would walk with her in the same happy road she has rejoiced.

This church has buried four as noble men as pastors as ever graced the pulpit; some as noble men as deacons as have ever honored the christian church, and some as grand men and women as ever lived. The writer has not the power to do justice to the history of this grand old church. No church has been more prosperous than this church. Like a mighty army she has gone forth, locking the powers of darkness to her chariot wheels and conquering in the name and strength of Christ her Lord.

It would require volumes to do justice to the history of this church for the last one hundred years. Most of these years were spent in the dark days of slavery when the right to worship God after the dictates of the gospel was denied them. They preached a gospel of freedom on Sunday which they dared not attempt to practice on Monday. Yet the church was signally blessed of God. The members of the church were man's slaves but God's freemen. It does appear that the services which were held under fear were much sweeter then than now. The sermons were much more earnest and tender, the prayers were clothed in simpler language, and were uttered with more zeal, and fervor, and pathos, and the singing was less artificial and was more of the character of humble praise in which the soul soared in unspeakable gratitude in search of its God. Those who enjoyed the services of those days might crave a return of service but for the horrors of slavery which characterized those days.

The church, however, is more cultured, and there is more intellectuality in the church now than then, but, perhaps less spirituality. The people of the long ago knew no better than to serve God with all their hearts. That ignorance is bliss which knows no hypocrisy. That weakness is strength which can not do wrong nor mistreat a brother, but simply lean upon God. The church is wonderfully successful. When her toils on earth are over and she shall have landed upon the glittering shores of the heavenly Canaan, then sweet and glorious will the harvest be.

She shall not regret her sufferings here when she shall be invited to lay her burdens down and at Jesus' side sit down to receive palms of victory and crowns of glory. Then shall she sit forever around the throne of God, and basking in the sunlight of eternal peace smile over the troubles through which she has come, and count them as nothing compared with infinite rest in heaven. There is a grand future for the church here, and a more pleasing, holy, charming and glorious inheritance on the ever green shores, "where no storms ever beat on the glittering strand while the years of eternity roll."

The glorious time is swiftly rolling on when the church of the Lord Jesus Christ shall be the glory of all the earth; when from the least to the greatest shall hear of Jesus the mighty to save. This must be accomplished through the church as his instrumentality. God grant the church grace and strength to do His will in the world in such a manner as to honor His holy name, for Jesus' sake. Amen.

www.ingramcontent.com/pod-product-compliance
Lightning Source LLC
Chambersburg PA
CBHW020259240426
43673CB00039B/644